# DAS ARKANSAS ECHO

# Das Arkansas Echo

## A YEAR IN THE LIFE OF GERMANS IN THE NINETEENTH-CENTURY SOUTH

*Kathleen Condray*

The University of Arkansas Press
Fayetteville
2020

ISBN: 978-1-68226-145-3
eISBN: 978-1-61075-729-4

Manufactured in the United States of America

24 23 22 21 20 5 4 3 2 1

Designed by Liz Lester

⊗ The paper used in this publication meets the minimum requirements of the American National Standard for Permanence of Paper for Printed Library Materials Z39.48-1984.

Library of Congress Cataloging-in-Publication Data
Names: Condray, Kathleen M., author.
Title: Das Arkansas Echo: a year in the life of Germans in the nineteenth-century South / Kathleen Condray.
Description: Fayetteville: The University of Arkansas Press, 2020. | Includes bibliographical references and index. | Summary: "In examining Das Arkansas Echo, one of three German-language weeklies published in Arkansas at the end of the nineteenth century, this volume explores how German immigrants navigated life in the American South at the turn of the century"—Provided by publisher.
Identifiers: LCCN 2020010000 (print) | LCCN 2020010001 (ebook) | ISBN 9781682261453 (cloth) | ISBN 9781610757294 (ebook)
Subjects: LCSH: Arkansas Echo—History. | German American newspapers—Arkansas—History—19th century. | Immigrants' writings, German—Arkansas—History—19th century. | Germans—Arkansas—History—19th century. | Germans—Southern States—History—19th century.
Classification: LCC PN4885.G3 A75 2020 (print) | LCC PN4885.G3 (ebook) | DDC 071/.67—dc23
LC record available at https://lccn.loc.gov/2020010000
LC ebook record available at https://lccn.loc.gov/2020010001

*For my grandfather, Lorenz Schneider, a first-generation American;*
*and my children, Sophia, Liam, and Alexander Condray,*
*the newest generation of Americans in our family*

# CONTENTS

# PREFACE

On a hill in the small rural community of Paris, Arkansas, one can imagine oneself in Switzerland. The Subiaco Benedictine Abbey, founded in 1878, is housed in a structure with a beautiful courtyard that would be at home in any canton of the mother country. It was established by Swiss monks sent to Arkansas as missionaries. The largest portion of their flock was provided by the Little Rock and Fort Smith Railroad, which made a bargain with the Catholic bishop of the state to offer German Catholic immigrants affordable farmland next to the rails and to build churches and schools to provide for their spiritual well-being. In return, the bishop assisted the railroads in securing a local population for the newly established lines. Other German speakers, Protestants, came to Arkansas to farm in the Delta, a few Austrians were attracted to coal mining in the west of the state, and German and Austrian Jewish immigrants settled primarily in the political and commercial capital, Little Rock, with others scattered around the state. While most Arkansans were struggling to adjust to a new reality following Reconstruction, this group of immigrants was striving to adjust to the South more generally. Many aspects of their new lives were exciting, such as religious freedom and the prospect of owning land, while others were frightening and bewildering, such as negotiating race relations or southern attitudes toward alcohol. This book follows the German speakers of Arkansas for one year to examine all aspects of one German experience in the South. It does so by reading the immigrants' own words, as published in the German language newspaper *Das Arkansas Echo*[1] (The Arkansas Echo) during its inaugural year of 1892.[2]

Much has been written regarding German-speaking immigrants in the Northeast and Midwest, yet those in the South have left less of an impression on the collective history of the United States. Carl Wittke, in his investigation of the German language press in America, expresses surprise at the number of German papers published in the South.[3] This is in part because fewer German speakers migrated to the South, including Arkansas. The German-language community constituted less than 1 percent of the state's population, but it was influential in shaping the areas in which it was concentrated.[4] The community was diverse in terms of national origin, occupation, and religious practice, and it was not self-evident that

German speakers would coalesce into a united community; conceivably, the provincial rivalries and differences anchored in Europe could simply have continued in Arkansas.

To be sure, the crucible of a shared experience as outsiders formed bonds among the German speakers. But even in 1892, the publishers of the German-language weekly *Das Arkansas Echo* expressly sought to establish greater unity among the German speakers. Published out of Little Rock from 1891 to 1932, the *Echo* created a linguistic virtual community in and of itself among its readers. This bond overcame nationality, religious doctrinal differences, and distance in rural nineteenth-century Arkansas. This was possible partly because of the strong reading culture that has existed historically and continues to exist today among German speakers. The editors regarded this linguistic community as a resource to be proud of and to be protected, since they believed that only German culture, imparted through language, could provide the immigrants' children with the necessary religious, educational, and moral upbringing they desired. They were determined to continue to speak German, to preserve the language in the community, schools, and houses of worship, and to raise the next generation in the rich traditions of the European Enlightenment. By drawing on a shared cultural tradition that it viewed as inherent to Germanness, the *Echo* used this ethnic identity to attempt to rally German speakers to work in concert for shared economic and physical well-being.[5]

The *Echo* itself has become an echo in the truest sense of the word; it is a faint recording of the voice of a thriving German-language community in Arkansas that has almost entirely vanished today. Despite the best efforts of the editor and community leaders, the language disappeared in the second and third generations, owing partly to political pressure in the aftermath of world wars and to a great extent to a gradual demographic dissolution, as German-speaking immigrants married other Arkansans. The newspaper records an important voice of this cohesive, if transient, immigrant group. It reveals much about daily life in Arkansas and the South. As outsiders, the newspaper's editor and readers were uniquely positioned to observe and comment on the culture they lived both in and apart from.

Simone Schede, in previous scholarship regarding the German speakers of Arkansas, concludes, "The history of German immigration to the state of Arkansas represents a much-neglected aspect within the field of German-American Studies."[6] This neglect has a long history. Albert Faust's foundational two-volume work *The German Element in the United States with Special Reference to its Political, Moral, Social, and Educational Influence* is a comprehensive examination of all Germans in the United States. It was published in 1909, a time when the German-speaking community in the state was still very active. Yet Faust mentions Arkansas only twice in over eight hundred pages. His first comment is on the works of Friedrich Gerstäcker. Gerstäcker explored Arkansas in the antebellum period, when the state was a largely lawless territory and when few Germans were to be found; he himself spent only about eighteen months total in the state. Faust's second reference comprises a list of the total number of Germans living in Arkansas according to 1900 census data. While neglecting Arkansas, Faust examined the history and culture of Germans in the southern states of Virginia, North Carolina, South Carolina, Georgia, Kentucky, Tennessee, Mississippi, Missouri, Alabama, and Texas.[7] In reading Faust's work, one could easily conclude that the German-speaking community in Arkansas had ceased to exist as an enclave separate from the native English-speaking population. But historian Jonathan Wolfe observes, "Despite the fact that a number of states in the South had larger German populations than did Arkansas, none of them except Texas gained any more German-speaking immigrants between 1870 and 1890 than did Arkansas."[8]

Historians of Arkansas have long known about the *Echo*'s existence. The entirety of its run has been preserved by the Swiss monks of Subiaco Abbey, who for decades spoke only German. However, scholars have at most devoted a paragraph or two to the German immigrant newspaper and have not examined it at length critically. Frederick Allsopp mentions the *Echo* in his 1922 monograph on the history of Arkansas journalism. He gives brief publication information and notes, "It is the representative paper of the German people, and enjoys a liberal patronage."[9] James Woods, in a study of the history of Catholic Arkansas, discusses the newspaper in a short paragraph emphasizing its publication data. Father Hugh Assenmacher, focusing on a narrower part of the history of Catholicism in Arkansas with a discussion of the Subiaco Benedictine Abbey, examines the role of Father Bonaventure Binzegger in the creation of the paper. A fellow Benedictine, Sister Herbert Huber, undertook a study in 1989 entitled *Arkansas Echo 1892–1906: An Arkansas German Language Newspaper*, largely a catalog of some of the titles of articles (in English translation) published in these years.[10] Michael Dougan has offered to date the most detailed treatment of the paper; he devotes about two pages to the *Echo* in a study of the state's newspapers. Dougan gives basic facts about the newspaper's run, provides an overview of the general content, and examines editor Carl Meurer's feud with Philip Dietzgen, the editor of the rival German newspaper in the capital city. Shirley Schuette, in a master's thesis, mentions the *Echo* and focuses on a few stories of immigrant experiences from 1930. Simone Schede offers a paragraph on the *Echo* in her study of Germans in Arkansas. She also argues that, even though German speakers were not a significant cultural presence in Arkansas's overall population, they represented a sizeable portion of immigrants who resided in the eleven counties that border the Arkansas River. In his lengthy and detailed 1957 study *The German Language Press in America*, Carl Wittke only mentions the *Arkansas Freie Presse* (Arkansas Free Press), and not the *Echo* or the other German newspapers in the state, and notes in a one-line aside that "the number of German newspapers published in the southern states in the closing decades of the nineteenth century was surprisingly large."[11]

There has been much excellent work about Germans in Arkansas, most notably by Jonathan Wolfe and Kenneth Barnes. Their research lays an important framework in discussing how German speakers came to reside in Arkansas and how the realities of the state differed from what they were promised by recruiting material and testimonials. But the emotional and economic challenges these newcomers faced—specifically those aspects of southern life that would have been unfamiliar to them, such as the region's race relations, politics, and commerce—have not yet been discussed from the German speakers' own perspectives. This book represents the first comprehensive look at Arkansas through the eyes of its German immigrants; its goals are to provide specific information regarding the community of German readers served by the *Echo* and to explore larger issues of Germans' interactions with their neighbors in the postbellum South. It is intended to be of use to researchers of Arkansas history, but it is my hope that it will also be of interest to Arkansans of German heritage. Parts of the book will make readers feel as though they themselves are reading the *Echo*; this is by design. I would like to give the many German descendants who have not had the opportunity to learn the language a sense of the world of German immigrants to Arkansas, and the inclusion of extended quotes in translation provides a more immersive experience.

I generally use the term "German" interchangeably with "German speaker" for the sake of ease of reading. I am well aware that German speakers in the state of Arkansas hailed from many locations in Europe, including what would become Germany, Austria, Liechtenstein, and Switzerland. An exception to this practice is the section regarding German national identity in the second chapter, in which the discussion of "Germans" refers directly to those who immigrated from the area that would become part of the Second German Empire, founded in 1871.

Finally, I would like to acknowledge that not all of what appeared in *Das Arkansas Echo* during its inaugural year flatters the editors or the German community, especially material regarding race relations, and this might be upsetting to descendants of German settlers. But this book gives an accurate accounting of the immigrants in their own words, and it is important to make this information accessible to English speakers who can no longer read the original paper. Issues of race relations are briefly mentioned in chapters 1 through 4, when they are relevant to those chapters' discussions, but the topic will be treated extensively in chapter 5.

# ACKNOWLEDGMENTS

I am most indebted to my colleagues Tom Dillard and Timothy Nutt, who alerted me to the existence of *Das Arkansas Echo* and who offered advice regarding important resources. Timothy Nutt also read and provided feedback on an early version of this manuscript. They, along with Patrick Williams, Jeannie Whayne, and Michael Pierce, helped me connect with the extremely knowledgeable historians of the state and, with Linda Jones, provided feedback regarding my research. While I was reading the primary sources on loan at the University of Arkansas's Special Collections, the staff provided support and encouragement, especially Cat Wallack, Joshua Youngblood, Valerie Robertson, Geoffrey Stark, and Megan Massanelli. My thanks to Lori Birrell, the current Head of Special Collections; Timothy Nutt, former Head of Special Collections; and Randy Thompson, Director of the Young Law Library, who allowed the copies of the paper to be housed safely throughout the writing process.

Father Jerome Kodell and Father Hugh Assenmacher of the Order of St. Benedict generously loaned me Subiaco Abbey's copies of the *Echo* for several years, as my institution's microfilm copies of the paper have become seriously degraded in parts. Both have provided encouragement and shared their enthusiasm for the topic of German-speaking immigrants to Arkansas. Father Assenmacher has regrettably since passed away, but his scholarship on Germans in the state lives on, and I will always appreciate his assistance.

My colleagues in the Department of World Languages, Dr. Jennifer Hoyer and Dr. Brett Sterling, make all aspects of my work, be it teaching, research, or service, both possible and enjoyable. My former colleague Sarah Jäkel provided feedback on a completed version of the chapter on race relations, for which I am grateful.

The research for this book was made financially feasible by a sabbatical during which I was supported by the Fulbright College of Arts and Sciences of the University of Arkansas as well as the US Fulbright Commission, which awarded me a Senior Lecturer Award in 2014 at the Albert-Ludwigs-Universität in Freiburg im Breisgau.

I became interested in this project as a native Arkansan from a German Catholic family. I would like to thank them for their support, especially my husband, Collin Condray; my children, Sophia, Liam, and Alexander

Condray; and my parents and sister, Martin and Virginia Roy and Beth Horton; and Beth's family, Peter, Jack, and Ginny Horton. My aunt, Josephine Schneider, a legendary English teacher at Catholic High School for Boys in Little Rock, played a large role in teaching me how to write; and my uncle, Albert Schneider, was always willing to practice German when I was a student in preparation for going abroad and meeting our family members in Germany.

# DAS ARKANSAS ECHO

CHAPTER 1

# The Founding of a Paper

## *Establishing a German Community*

THE HISTORY OF German-language newspapers in the United States is a long one, dating back to 1739 and the *Hochdeutsch-Pennsylvanische Geschicht-Schreiber* (High German Pennsylvania Story Writer), founded by renowned printer Christoph Sauer.[1] The history of German-language newspapers in Arkansas began more than a hundred years later, when there were enough local German speakers to support publication. There was the *Arkansas Staatszeitung* (State Newspaper), first published briefly in 1866, then revived in 1869 as a weekly that managed to remain solvent for a year and a half. Revived yet again in 1877, this final incarnation lasted until 1917.[2] As "the only German newspaper in the states of Arkansas, Alabama, and Mississippi until the 1890s," it was a rarity in the South.[3] Unfortunately, there are few extant copies of these early German-language papers published in Arkansas.

Two historical trends contributed to the thriving German-language newspaper market in Arkansas in the late nineteenth century. First, there was a remarkable influx of German-speaking immigrants at the time (which I will discuss later in the chapter). As the historian Jonathan Wolfe, examining Arkansas in the larger regional context, observed:

> Despite the fact that a number of states in the South had larger German populations than did Arkansas, none of them except Texas gained any more German-speaking immigrants between 1870 and 1890 than did Arkansas. . . . In fact, the increases in German population of the two next highest states in German immigration in the region, Kentucky and Tennessee, fell short of the amount received by Arkansas by nearly one thousand people.[4]

Second, as many scholars have noted, this period represented the highpoint in the establishment of new German-language newspapers, some dating the top of the curve to *Das Arkansas Echo*'s very founding year of 1892. This national trend resulted from the large influx of new immigrants seeking an escape from political and economic circumstances in Europe, and the fact that the first generation of German speakers preferred periodicals in their native tongue.[5]

Arkansas, boasting three German newspapers in 1892, led many southern states in the number of foreign-language newspapers printed. At the time, no foreign-language papers were produced in Alabama, Georgia, Mississippi, or North Carolina. Virginia and Tennessee each had three (all German), and Kentucky had four (all German), although all three states each had approximately a half million more residents than Arkansas at the time. South Carolina, with roughly the same number of residents as Arkansas, had only one foreign-language (German) newspaper, which was comparable to the *Echo*, with a circulation of 550 at an annual subscription price of $2.50.

The outliers in the South were Louisiana and Texas. Louisiana's population was almost identical to Arkansas's, but as a major point of entry for international travel, the state boasted eighteen foreign-language publications, three of which were in German. Texas was twice the size of Arkansas and had twenty-four foreign-language newspapers, seventeen of which were printed in German. Another trend seen in both Louisiana and Texas was hybrid papers, published half in English and half in French or Spanish. Despite the exceptional diversity of Louisiana's papers, the vast majority of foreign-language publications in the South appeared in German during the period when *Das Arkansas Echo* was established.[6]

While other southern states had some German weeklies with much higher circulations (such as Louisville's *Der Anzeiger*, with 9,700 for the Sunday edition), the *Echo*'s readership figures and price were essentially comparable to other German newspapers of the time, with most German weeklies in the South charging between $2.00 and $2.50 for a subscription. The *Echo*'s Democratic affiliation was also not unusual, compared to both the South in general and its fellow German-language newspapers. In the presidential election that had preceded the *Echo*'s establishment, every southern state had registered a Democratic plurality. On the other hand, of the thirty-three German papers produced in the South, eight had no affiliation, eleven were independent, nine were Democratic, and three had other affiliations (Catholic, literary, family-oriented). There were only two Republican German papers, both in the state of Texas.[7]

*Das Arkansas Echo* was in some ways the rebirth of an earlier newspaper, *Der Logan County Anzeiger* (The Logan County Gazette). Little is known about this paper, and there is no newspaper directory entry regarding it. However, Phillip Dietzgen, an editor of a rival newspaper, alluded to it in a letter to the *Arkansas Gazette* in 1891.[8] The *Arkansas Gazette* also gave notice that a German newspaper, which it referred to as the "Paris Anzeiger," intended to begin publishing in 1891. This is probably a reference to *Der Logan County Anzeiger*, as the city of Paris is located in Logan County.[9] A letter to the editor of the *Echo* from 1892 claimed the *Anzeiger* had four hundred subscribers, which seems unlikely given its local reach and short existence.[10]

*Der Logan County Anzeiger* was conceived of at a meeting of the Arkansas Staatsverband (Arkansas State Organization) of the Catholic Central Verein (Catholic Central Union) and was published in Paris irregularly from May until December of 1891.[11] The paper was moved to Little Rock and rechristened *Das Arkansas Echo* under the direction of Fr. Bonaventure Binzegger, who was the parish priest at St. Edward's in Little Rock.[12] The founders apparently chose Little Rock for its proximity to journalistic news sources and its status as a seat of power.[13] In the first few issues of 1892, the editors of the *Echo* announced that subscriptions to the *Anzeiger* would be carried over to the *Echo*, further evidence that the *Echo* could be regarded as the *Anzeiger*'s reincarnation.

The Arkansas Echo Publishing Company was officially established on January 12, 1892, not only for the purpose of creating a German newspaper, but also for undertaking job printing, which was a way to create additional revenue using the existing equipment and to ensure solvency. The incorporators were P. B. Binzegger (with sixteen shares), Herman Lensing (fourteen), John Kaufman (thirteen), Adolph Arnold (eleven), Andrew Rust (ten), Fred [Friedrich] Hohenschutz (eight), Charles [Carl] Meurer (five), J. P. Moser (two), and Nic Weny (one). The eighty shares were valued at $25 each. The board of directors was composed of Kaufman (president), Arnold (secretary), Rust (vice president), Binzegger (treasurer), Hohenschutz, and Lensing. Rust was initially under consideration for the post of editor, but Carl Meurer held this position for the paper's entire forty-year run.[14] After his death, the company was reincorporated by his son, Carl J. Meurer, and August Probst, on February 29, 1932. But the younger Meurer was not able to continue publishing in his father's stead, and the company was dissolved only seven months later, on October 5, 1932. Adolph Arnold was the only founding member who still served on the board of directors at the time of the paper's demise.[15]

While many German Arkansans contributed to the establishment of *Das Arkansas Echo*, it came to be associated so completely with editor Carl Meurer that he was known to other German immigrants around the state as the "*Echo* Man."[16] Like many German speakers in Arkansas, Meurer was born in Germany, in the town of Wipperfürth in 1849. He immigrated to Arkansas in 1881, after hearing one of the Holy Ghost Fathers lecture on the benefits of the state, and he intended to join other German Catholics in establishing a settlement a few miles west of Little Rock.[17] In his three decades in Germany, Meurer gained experience in a variety of work settings: a factory, a mill, and the home of a local prince, where he served as a private tutor for the children of the family. He tried his hand at manual labor, since he wanted to better understand the factors that shaped the lives of working men. Upon arriving in Arkansas, he took up yet another line of work, as a farmer. But his stint in agriculture did not last long, and he moved to Little Rock, where he became the editor of the *Echo*.[18] Meurer's myriad experiences and interests were reflected in the diversity of topics that the newspaper covered.

It remains unclear to what extent the other founders of the newspaper contributed to the creation of each edition, and it is entirely likely that Meurer was the main creative force behind the content each week. Two other groups of men were responsible for the *Echo*'s continued existence: the setters and the agents. Without the conflict with the paper's largest rival, *Die Staatszeitung*, the setters' names might have been lost to posterity. The *Echo*'s first edition was much truncated after vandals broke into the office and destroyed the forms that had already been prepared for publication. The setters wrote an affidavit in which they refuted the charge that they committed the sabotage and pointed out that the culprit cut himself on the frames; moreover, while they had no cuts on their hands, drops of blood led to the offices of the *Staatszeitung*, which shared a building with the *Echo*. It was signed Johann Eller and Ludwig Peterek.[19]

After the setters gave form to the content, the agents went about selling the paper. Conrad Elsken represented the paper in Paris, Arkansas, and Georg Dörner sold the paper at 802 Main Street in Little Rock (the editorial offices were located at 214 East Markham). By March, three additional agents had been added: Josef Lienhart in Conway, Paul Reis in Atkins, and Adolf (Ad) Elser in Altus. In August, Josef (Jos) Hummel was engaged to sell to the Fort Smith area. In late October, Franz Brocher began to work for the paper as an agent.[20] Elsken was a prominent member of the German community and a devout Catholic who moved to Arkansas in 1883 and had remarkable success in a variety of business endeavors over his lifetime. In the *Echo*'s inaugural year, he ran for and won the position of Logan County Treasurer.[21]

A programmatic announcement in the January 7, 1892, edition expressly stated the intentions of the publishers. They argued that Germans in the United States had much in common and that many in the state of Arkansas, of a variety of religious creeds, had long expressed the wish to have a good German newspaper. This opening intimated that the editor of the existing rival newspaper was less interested in the common German good and more interested in causing trouble within the community.[22] The *Echo* pledged to pursue the interests of German citizens of the state in regard to natural law, which the publishers considered the foundation of democracy, and above all to advocate for German freedom, language, and customs. Ending on a festive note and setting a high bar for the publication, the editorial staff wrote: "May it echo in a thousand hearts, say something good, instructive, and entertaining to all, and contribute to the intellectual fight of solving the great problems of humanity."[23] It should be noted that German settlers were not excluded from English-language journalism. Valentine Dell was a German immigrant who served as editor of the *Fort Smith New Era* in 1863. Jacob Frolich Jr. was elected secretary at the first Arkansas Press Association meeting in 1873, and he worked for both the *White County Record* and the *Arkansas Gazette* in his career.[24] Nevertheless, the *Echo* editors were interested in a broader mission than news reporting; they regarded their endeavor as an opportunity to forge unity and contribute to the intellectual capital of the immigrant community.

At the time of its founding, the *Echo* became the third German paper in Arkansas. The *Arkansas Volksblatt*, registered as independent and published in Fort Smith by Ernest Pope, was similar to the *Echo* in several regards: both were weeklies of eight pages, charged an annual subscription fee of $2, and had similar self-reported circulations in 1892 (750 for the *Volksblatt*, and 650 for the *Echo*).[25] The larger rival to both papers was situated in the state's capital city, Little Rock. *Die Arkansas Staatszeitung*[26] boasted a circulation of 1,775 and sold for $2.50 per year.[27] The editor, Phillip Dietzgen, took umbrage with the establishment of another paper on his home turf. In the resulting feud, the competing journalists resorted to breaking and entering, vandalism, and assault. In spite of Dietzgen's rather substantial efforts to rid himself of the competitor, the *Echo* managed to survive its first year.[28]

The inaugural issue of December 31, 1891, was a brief affair, due to the aforementioned sabotage, and comprised only a half sheet divided into three columns. The masthead announced the paper's slogan: "*Das Arkansas Echo*: Allgemeine Zeitung für Wahrheit und Klarheit auf politischem und socialem [*sic*] Gebiete" (The Arkansas Echo: general newspaper for truth and clarity in the political and social realm).[29] The issue featured an article from the local English-language paper, the *Arkansas Democrat*, that detailed the vandalism in the *Echo*'s offices, and noted that both the *Arkansas Gazette* and the *Memphis Journal* ran similar stories. The article reported that intruders destroyed the forms and scattered the type throughout the office; indeed, the newspaper's type would eventually be found throughout various Little Rock neighborhoods. The destruction amounted to $400 in damages and made it impossible to publish the full length of eight pages, as the publishers had originally intended. The editor called the resulting rump edition a *wahres Schmerzenskind* (true child of pain) and claimed that the rival *Staatszeitung* was to blame for the vandalism—an accusation that immediately launched the feud between the two papers.[30] It would take Meurer and his staff several editions to bring the paper back to its full publishing strength.[31] The setters complained in an amusing note that it was impossible to lay out the type for a story when the individual letters were still jumbled in a heap; they printed roughly four inches of random letters and explained that this was not *Volapük* (a contemporary artificial language similar to Esperanto) but what they could "read" from the floor of their office.[32]

The *Echo* utilized a mixture of roman and Fraktur (German style) typefaces and divided each of its eight pages into seven columns. Some exemplars of the German American press focused exclusively on one area of reporting, such as local news, a specific trade or field, or literary fiction.[33] Likely in an effort to appeal to the widest number of subscribers, the *Echo* staff attempted to include broadly diverse content. The first page frequently offered a *Wochenrundschau* (review of the week) that allowed readers to survey the most important happenings quickly, from the international to the local stages. Specific international and national news items were gleaned from telegrams and cable dispatches and appeared on the first two pages, sorted by location. Reports from local correspondents rounded out page two or were carried to page three. Articles from other newspapers including the *Arkansas Democrat*, the *Arkansas Gazette*, *Amerika* (a German-language paper), and the *Arizona Kicker* (a satirical paper from the "Wild West") were reprinted on page three.[34] Train schedules and market reports on commodity prices usually appeared on page three. Page four carried publication information as well as editorials. During election season, the *Echo* ran a slate of endorsed candidates in each issue on page five. Articles on a variety of subjects, such as science, technology, history, literature, and philosophy, ran on the middle and back pages, and jokes and humorous anecdotes appeared at the end of columns as filler material. Pages six and seven usually featured a serialized novel or short fiction, and local news about Arkansas most often appeared on page eight.[35] The paper attempted to include late-breaking news by publishing it on pages usually devoted to other subjects with the note "Nach Schluß der Formen" (after the close of the forms).[36] Mistakes regarding formatting or typos were very rare, and when they occurred, the newspaper apologized for them.

In addition to reprinting pieces from the *Arkansas Gazette* and *Arkansas Democrat*, the paper published news items in German translation from the *Fort Smith Times*, especially after this paper published the opinion that *Das Arkansas Echo* was the best German-language paper in the state.[37] A correspondent from Conway mentioned a story he read in *The Wheel*.[38] At least one story was republished from and attributed to *Das Arkansas Volksblatt* out of Fort Smith. This was presumably with permission, as one of the *Echo*'s own stories carried the admonition "Vor Nachdruck wird gewarnt" (warning against reprinting). Items from the national German American press were drawn from *Amerika* and *Die St. Louis Republik*. In a later interview, Meurer's daughter, Mary, mentioned that he also subscribed to a newspaper from Aachen.[39] There is one noticeable absence in source material, however. The *Echo* never drew articles from the politically activist and socialist-oriented German-language outlets based primarily in large cities, such as New York's *Volkszeitung* (People's newspaper) or Chicago's *Arbeiter Zeitung* (Worker's newspaper), even if some of the *Echo*'s coverage reflected a similar affection for and protectionist attitude toward the working man, as will be discussed later.[40] This is probably due to the *Echo*'s unswerving loyalty to the Democratic Party.

Readers of the *Echo* who were not fluent in English would to some extent have missed out on significant news stories and a deeper understanding of the society they had joined by moving to Arkansas, since the paper offered a curated version of local events, apparently republishing only what the editorial staff thought would be of interest to German readers. In 1892 there were still numerous stories in the *Arkansas Gazette* on the Civil War and its aftermath: on Reconstruction governor Powell Clayton; ex-Confederates; veterans; and the Grand Army of the Republic and a GAR reunion. The *Echo* was largely silent on all of these matters. It also did not include items about the active judicial career of Isaac Parker, as the contemporary *Gazette* did. With Parker's reputation for upholding frontier justice and the German immigrants' interest in maintaining the rule of law in civilized society, his absence from the *Echo* is notable. The *Gazette* carried extensive coverage of sports, including horse racing, boxing matches, baseball games, and football. (Since the last sport was apparently something of a new sensation in Arkansas at the time, the author of one *Gazette* article felt it necessary to explain the rules.) Social events and society news were also covered heavily in the *Gazette* but not in the *Echo*. In some cases, the *Echo* excluded stories from the English-language press that would have likely interested its German readers. For example, the *Echo* editors chose not to pick up stories on telephone systems in Prairie Grove, Russellville, and Potts Station. Given the paper's other stories on technology and science, *Echo* readers presumably would have liked to have read about the partial solar eclipse seen in Little Rock in 1892. The *Gazette* also featured many stories on colleges and universities around the state; similar stories are curiously absent from the *Echo*, as German families were interested in all levels of education. The *Echo* additionally omitted news of numerous theater and opera performances covered by the *Gazette*.

Full-form advertisements in the *Echo* were usually relegated to the last four pages, although some small ads occasionally appeared on the first page. One-line print endorsements of various establishments were sprinkled into the rest of the text on virtually every page, which was also the practice in the English press. There were some elements of nationally circulated German American newspapers that the *Echo* did not include: the aforementioned sports coverage and society pages, puzzles, children's pages, and a section for women, though it did regularly include housekeeping features that were presumably as useful for bachelors as for women.[41]

While the newspaper certainly depended heavily on advertising in its early years, it did not defer to advertisers' feelings regarding content, as was the case with other Arkansas newspapers of the nineteenth century.[42] One editorial lamented the surplus of lawyers and politicians in society and urged readers not to neglect other career paths, even though five lawyers were among the paper's regular advertisers.[43] In December, the *Echo* published a note about a young man who used to work at the firm of Levinson and Friedheim—another frequent advertiser—but who had moved on to a new career with the railroads, which enabled him to earn much more.[44] Nevertheless, the paper did not hesitate to blur the line between content and advertisement. A poem intended to be humorous regarding the 1892 flu epidemic ended on a serious note and recommended that everyone be prepared and make a will, and the editors helpfully starred this line and noted that they could recommend the lawyers who advertised in the *Echo* for this purpose.[45]

At other times, one-line or one-paragraph print advertisements were camouflaged within the lines of regular copy, and some companies utilized these in-text placements in addition to the regular format advertisements. Some advertisers were in direct competition with one another. For example, the law firms of Anton Hall and Fontaine & White both practiced in Paris. In Little Rock, the midwives Elisabeth Müller and Friederike Schmand competed for business. All advertised their services in the *Echo*. Some businesses run by German speakers are noticeably absent among the advertisements, such as Roßner's Conditorei (pastry shop) and Papa Geyer's Halle (Geyer's event hall), both located in Little Rock.

Advertisements provide some of the best clues to the initial readership of the newspaper, or at least to the German-speaking residents whom businesses and professionals were attempting to reach with their marketing. One could find seemingly all needed trades among the advertisers, which included businesses selling directly to consumers as well as those appealing to other businesses. Presumably, the *Echo*'s founders had existing business connections in the immigrant community, which enabled them to sign up a wide range of advertisers early on. While many listings advertised goods and services useful to farmers, some ads also provide evidence of a diversified workforce, and thriving middle and smaller professional classes.

The overwhelming majority of advertisers were from Little Rock, with another, smaller concentration of businesses centered in Paris. A handful of advertisers hailed from each of the following towns: Collegeville, Conway, Fort Smith, Mount Nebo, Morrilton, and Prairie View. While companies in Little Rock tended to specialize in a specific good or trade, some stores in smaller communities relied less on specialization and would offer, for example, groceries, dry goods, and hardware under one roof. Ten businesses ran out-of-state ads. Located variously in Illinois, Maryland, Missouri, Tennessee, and Wisconsin, they provided goods that would appeal to German immigrants and likely provided the *Echo* with the same stock advertisements that they sent to other German papers for books, patent medicine, German-style tobacco, seeds, and plant sprays.

Advertisements in the *Echo* suggest a largely established immigrant community. There was only one ad for a company providing transatlantic passage, as the main surge of immigrants to the area had passed by 1892. There are no ads, as seen in other German American newspapers, from individuals who had become separated from their party during the journey to America and were attempting to reconnect.[46] A great majority of the advertisers were businesses offering consumer goods: apparel and shoes; books; furniture; groceries; items offered by stand-alone specialty shops such as bakers, butchers, and confectioners; ice; general merchandise and dry goods; alcohol sold by saloons and stores, as well as farmers offering homemade wine; saddles; carriages; saws; coal; and weapons. Other businesses advertised goods for farmers or other trades: a hardware store, a locksmith, iron and tin works, blacksmiths, pipe fitters, a rubber-stamp works, a tent and awning company, a lumberyard, purveyors of seed, farming implements, livestock, feed and stables, a veterinarian, a mill, and a cotton gin. Some advertised services rather than goods: an architect, banks, a barber, boarding houses and hotels, insurance firms, lawyers, railroads, restaurants, and schools. Members of the medical field advertised both goods and services, as the paper featured ads for doctors, midwives, pharmacies and drugstores, and patent medicine. In the event that no remedy for the ill was to be found, the *Echo* contained advertisements for a funeral director, an artisan who created death masks, and creators of marble and granite monuments. Some of the more unusual advertisements included those for an anatomical museum, Mount Nebo as a summer tourist destination, and a private post connection between Altus and Paris.

Advertisements in the *Echo* represented a wide range of socioeconomic classes. Several ads offered goods and services to readers with disposable income: art, photography, tailoring, millinery, jewelry and watches, private instruction in dance and swimming, pianos, and glass and porcelain.[47] Personal ads sought young Germans willing to serve as domestic labor: a German girl was needed to help with childrearing or housework; a young German man, to help around the house. One young man placed an ad offering to do any kind of work. The Security, Trust, and Savings Company appealed directly to the working class in its copy: "This savings bank guarantees a good and secure site for the savings of train employees and for people from the tradesmen and working classes. We wish for savings deposits from all and promise each customer prompt and polite service."[48]

*Echo* advertisements attempted to attract customers with offers of maximum convenience and promotions. Adolf Arnold both sold and traded new and secondhand goods. J. Kaufmann proposed to sell farm products such as butter, eggs, chickens, corn, and oats on commission for 5 percent below the current market price. B. Briggeler, a butcher, made home deliveries.[49] The December 23 edition of the *Echo* ran a special feature praising advertisers for their unique Christmas merchandise. Notably, the *Echo* wholeheartedly endorsed the celebration of Christmas at a time when some communities in the state, particularly those in Protestant areas, did not accept the practice.[50]

Advertisers also presented unusual schemes to draw customers. Ed Craig offered customers a round-trip train ticket within fifty miles if they did not find the best deal at his store. The Globe, a general merchandise store, used a coupon scheme to attract repeat business: "In addition to the extraordinarily low prices of our wares, we give a Cash Coupon for every dollar's worth of wares that are purchased from us. For twenty of these cash coupons, we pay one dollar in cash." M. M. Cohn, a purveyor of dry goods, regularly had his ad printed sideways, presumably to draw more attention to it (a practice also found in the English-language press). And *The Scientific American* had the distinction of placing the first ad published entirely in English in December of the *Echo*'s inaugural year.[51] The editor also reprinted a recipe from *Scientific American* that farmers could use to safeguard their equipment from rust.[52] Advertisers Dr. N. Weny and Fred Sanders contributed articles on medicine and photography, respectively, to highlight proficiency in their trades.

Aside from advertising, the newspaper had two additional streams of revenue available. First, as mentioned, the parent company, the Arkansas Echo Publishing Company, undertook separate printing jobs. It reminded readers of this in an advertisement and suggested the types of printing one might consider: forms, business cards, pamphlets, and publications for special events such as anniversaries. A customer testimonial from the St. Boniface chapter of the Catholic Knights of America praised the hundred copies of their constitution printed by the company for clear text, quality paper, and a sturdy cover at a low price.[53] Unfortunately, there are no extant records for the company that indicate how much of its annual revenue came from job printing.

The second additional source of income for the paper was subscriptions, which it offered on both annual ($2) and semiannual terms ($1). International readers could also subscribe at a rate of fifty cents above the usual prices. It is impossible to tell if the international subscription category reflected actual readers or was merely aspirational. The editor did publish letters from abroad. These international readers may have been sent copies of the paper by friends or family members who were subscribers in Arkansas; the paper in fact encouraged its readers to send copies to acquaintances abroad in order to promote more immigration from German-speaking countries to Arkansas.[54] A note from January 1892 warned subscribers that they could not cancel their subscriptions simply by sending the paper back.

The *Echo* attempted to impress upon readers the seriousness of the obligation of a subscription by warning that readers were still responsible for the entire amount "nach den Gesetzen der Ver. Staaten" (according to the laws of the United States [set in bold type in original]).[55]

The *Echo* staff tried a variety of measures to increase subscriptions. The *Echo* followed a favorite approach of the German press by printing an installment of a serialized novel in each issue, in the hope that avid readers would purchase copies to follow the story. A notice from the December 16 issue announced that a new serialized novel would begin in two weeks and encouraged readers to renew their subscriptions for the next year in anticipation.[56] Over the course of 1892, six works of long fiction were published, and a seventh was begun in the last issue.[57] The paper promised at its outset only to publish works of fiction by reputable authors, but the titles included would not be familiar to a student of German classics and included well-worn tropes of trivial literature such as forbidden romance, mysterious strangers, and rags-to-riches stories.[58]

Although the serialized story was a regular feature, an editorial stated that the *Echo* drew the line at the crime stories of "dime literature," which were claimed to corrupt the general public and to lead to more, and more brutal, crimes.[59] This high-minded position set the *Echo* apart from earlier German American periodicals, as sensationalized accounts of the deeds of infamous murderers helped to sell German-language broadsides from the earliest days of colonial America.[60] According to Michael Dougan, the inclusion of longer works of literature also was unusual for periodicals in Arkansas, since most editors only printed fiction on slow news days, rather than making it a regular feature.[61]

The *Echo*'s dedication to both short and serialized fiction shows that its readership enjoyed reading and had time to pursue some measure of leisure activity. A less overt tactic to win subscribers and readers via content was to allow correspondents to publish news from their local German communities, which frequently mentioned names of community members in reports of births, weddings, anniversaries, and deaths. The editors may have adopted this practice from contemporary English-language papers in Arkansas, which frequently used rural correspondents in the 1890s.[62] These correspondents occasionally used their reports to encourage readers to subscribe to the *Echo* and to denigrate the rival paper, *Die Staatszeitung*, for what the correspondents claimed were tactics intended to sew discord in the greater German community. The editors regularly printed the names of Germans who had visited the paper's Little Rock office. In July the

*Echo* announced it would move publication from Thursdays to Fridays, in response to subscriber preference.[63]

The *Echo* also resorted to promotions to increase subscriptions. The paper offered an oil painting entitled *A Yard of Pansies* as a bonus gift. Readers were told a subscription to the *Echo* would make a perfect gift for friends and relatives abroad. If readers could not raise the entire $2 all at once, they could purchase a six-month subscription for $1. When the paper featured a vaguely defined contest in which subscribers could win one of three clocks by guessing the number of peas in a jar, a correspondent from Dixie jokingly complained they had no chance of winning since there were no peas in town and they would have to send to Conway for some. The contest apparently generated interest, since a follow-up appeared in late November to clarify the type of jar and peas that were used, and what would happen in the event of more than one correct guess.[64]

The staff roundly mocked the tactic of giving away free trial issues, apparently since it was the regular practice of the *Staatszeitung*. This ridicule of course insinuated that the other paper had to be given away since it could not be sold.[65] Apparently, the *Staatszeitung*'s ploy was to mail free issues to randomly-selected recipients; after three free issues had arrived, the *Staatszeitung* began to bill recipients who did not return the newspapers and ask for their "subscriptions" to be canceled. The *Echo* also published a letter from one Matthias Bauer that accused the *Staatszeitung* of harassing advertisers. Bauer claimed that he inquired with the *Staatszeitung* about running an ad, but decided against it after determining the cost was too high. According to Bauer, the *Staatszeitung* ran the ad without his approval and then demanded payment.[66] The issues themselves do not indicate that the *Echo* had a problem with delinquent payments, either from subscribers or advertisers. If the paper did, it kept this aspect of business out of the pages and handled matters privately.

Who were the readers of the *Echo*? A March editorial addressed this question directly. It began with a discussion of the general nature of work and how the division of labor benefited society. The editors argued that although some men specialized in becoming doctors, everyone still had to know the basics of ensuring good health. Similarly, one could not leave knowledge of the law only to the lawyers; for democracy to function properly, every citizen needed to know the fundamentals of the law. While their fellow citizens went about producing tangible goods or harvesting crops, newspaper professionals culled and disseminated facts: "This duty is comprised of giving to the business people and farmers, who in addition to the activities of their profession can unfortunately dedicate far too little time and leisure to their higher human and civic duties in the general fight for survival, reliable information about all social and political questions in which their interest and their assistance is suitable."[67] The editorial made clear that the *Echo* regarded the bulk of its readers as solidly middle class. They were men who worked for a living, yet still wanted to engage in both civic life and the life of the mind. In a report on Maifest (May festival), the annual gathering to celebrate German language and heritage, the paper also referred to the *bürgerlich* (middle-class) circumstances of those participating in the event, meaning the state's German settlers more broadly, not only to the newspaper's readership.[68]

The readers of the *Echo* apparently enjoyed the middle-class privilege of an education.[69] This would not have been unusual for German immigrants in general, particularly those who emigrated to America after the failed German revolution of 1848. In fact, the term "Latin farmers" is often applied pejoratively to these would-be revolutionaries, who found themselves starting over in America and attempting to farm by somehow applying their knowledge of the classics rather than any practical experience with agriculture.[70] The editor of the *Echo* frequently used Latin phrases without translating them, with the assumption that they would be understood.[71] An editorial on the dangers of laissez-faire capitalism referenced an Aristophanes play, as well as the economic and political circumstances of ancient Greece.[72]

The *Echo*'s readers used Latin in their own correspondence with the paper. A regular correspondent and actual farmer from Pocahontas, writing under the pen name Severus (Latin for "strict" or "serious"), used a Latin phrase to make fun of a local publication called *The Night Owl*: "O si tacuisses, philosophus mansisses" (If you had kept quiet, you would still be regarded as a philosopher [i.e., wise man]).[73] A correspondent from Altus referring to himself as Urian used a quotation from Roman emperor Claudius to indicate that people are the same the world over, and that fools can unfortunately be found everywhere.[74] Another article paid tribute to a former Latin teacher and enthusiastically discussed the virtues of the study of both the language and ancient Rome; long after one had forgotten the particulars of the grammar, he argued, the rigor of the attainment of the language ennobled the mind.[75]

References to the German literary canon, in which graduates of the *Gymnasium* (college-preparatory high school) would have been well versed, abounded. Quotations from Johann Wolfgang von Goethe's *Faust* drove home the point regarding wide-ranging topics, from a warning about counterfeit coffee beans to a diatribe against trusts and tariffs.[76] A history article regarding the naming of America referenced Sebastian Brant's 1494 satire *Das Narrenschiff* (Ship of fools).[77] Readers proved equally adept at using literary quotations themselves to emphasize arguments. A correspondent from Avilla (Saline County) who signed his letter "A." cited a line from poet Friedrich Schiller to chastise those in the German community who were not willing to cooperate with one another regarding Prohibition.[78] Well-read readers would certainly have recognized the *Schildbürger* tradition in a story submitted by frequent correspondent Spottvogel (mockingbird) about the fellow residents of his small town, which he referred to as *Schalksheim* (joker's home).[79] Advertisements in the *Echo* by the firm Benziger Brothers for books in the German language encouraged readers to build their libraries and continue educating themselves.

Other national literatures were of interest as well; the paper published a lengthy two-part series on Shakespeare and a biography of American writer Bret Harte.[80] This interest in ongoing learning appeared throughout the *Echo*'s inaugural year. The paper frequently published articles on historical topics, drawn from all areas of the world. Serious historical treatises included the history of German law at the close of the Middle Ages, early firefighting techniques, a description of Pennsylvania by the German settler Pastorius, eighteenth-century treatments for cholera, and how a fifteenth-century sultan selected his wife.[81] More lighthearted fare was offered in accounts of a historic sea battle between Argentina and Uruguay in which cheese was used as cannon fodder, and a scholarly discussion of whether Hamlet was overweight.[82] It has generally been observed that German immigrants were surprised by the lack of education of fellow citizens in the United States, and so it is perhaps predictable that the *Echo* published a humorous bit poking fun at the *Chicago Tribune* for making Frederick the Great, born in the eighteenth century, responsible for the Thirty Years War of the seventeenth century.[83]

German immigrants were equally fascinated by science, especially its practical application. In its inaugural year, the *Echo* featured stories on new developments in transportation, such as ship construction and electric streetcars (although the editor often ran stories about how dangerous streetcars were for pedestrians). An article on ships gave a theory-laden description of how the "cryptophone" device used sound waves to determine movement, in order to prevent ships from colliding. Stories on inventions featured an industrial dishwashing machine, with the mention of a planned version for home use; a new safe designed by electricians to foil burglars; and a prototype for an incubator for human infants modeled after those used in animal husbandry. Other stories examined materials already in use, such as aluminum and asbestos, praising the latter for its fire-retardant properties.[84]

Another major topic of interest was nature and its exploration. The *Echo* published articles on lesser-known geysers at Yellowstone and the practice of soaping geysers, on developments in forestry, and on the sudden rise of cable cars in the Swiss Alps, which made the mountains more accessible to less fit hikers but irritated nature lovers because of the intrusion of the mechanical into the natural landscape. Admiral Peary's adventures among the Eskimos were the focus of a feature story.[85] While they prominently featured articles on science, the paper's editors were not uncritical. For example, they ran an aggravated note regarding the use of tax-payer dollars for research on how to create rain that had little chance of succeeding. Elsewhere, the paper observed that astronomers had been wrong regarding a comet's arrival. There were also two editorials attacking Darwinism. The first took a religious approach, arguing that the theory could not explain where life and the material for organisms came from in the absence of a creator deity. The second addressed the social implications of the theory, arguing that Darwinism merely encouraged exploitative capitalism; employers could invoke Darwin's theories to construe their abusive labor practices as the promotion of the survival of the fittest.[86]

The paper regularly referenced philosophy, as an intellectual exercise and a means of framing arguments regarding contemporary politics. One editorial examined the Greek philosopher Diogenes in order to discuss the love of money in a society too focused on materialism. Many other editorials appealed to the natural law and the rights of man, including one which outlined historical property rights and drew the conclusion that farmers, rather than property owners, were due the majority of the crops produced. This editorial was especially illustrative of the paper's estimation of reader intelligence, since it quoted two different laws from 1389 and 1438 in the original Middle High German. Another editorial cited Thomas Aquinas's *Summa Theologica* in a discussion of anarchy. Outside the Western tradition, an article rejected the teachings of Confucius and the Buddha, arguing that neither religion had resulted in the ennobling of work or respect for women.[87]

The *Echo*'s correspondents offer further clues about its readership. These letter writers likely provided unpaid content in exchange for the opportunity to share information about their local communities with other German speakers across the state. The editor regularly encouraged readers to send in letters, and the results ranged from a few lines to several columns. The substantial number of correspondents—approximately eighty-eight in total—reflects German speakers who were educated enough to share their thoughts and news in written format, who were proud of their communities, and who had the leisure time to write letters to the newspaper. The editors occasionally responded directly, inserting their replies immediately after the letter. In February, one correspondent addressed another letter writer, creating a sort of virtual discussion via the paper.[88]

Contributors received several specific guidelines for publication. They were to write only on the front side of their paper, presumably to improve legibility. The paper would not publish items that were submitted without signatures (although initials sufficed as a form of signature). This policy might have resulted from an overabundance of caution, given the frequent libel lawsuits of the time. In this way, the editors could prove to a judge if necessary that they had not fabricated the letters out of whole cloth. Occasionally, the newspaper included a note informing those who missed the Tuesday deadline for publication that their letters would appear in the next issue.

Despite the *Echo*'s requirement that correspondents include signatures, the vast majority chose to identify themselves only by their initials. A few utilized generic pen names such as Civis (Latin for "citizen") or Ein Teilnehmer (a participant), if reporting on an event taking place in their town. Others were more creative, with monikers such as Goldfisch (goldfish), Silberfisch (silver fish), and Der hinkende Bote (the limping messenger). The exceptions to the general trend of anonymity included letters discussing the ongoing dispute between *Das Arkansas Echo* and *Die Staatszeitung*, those involving other legal matters, or occasions when correspondents wished their full names to be printed as a matter of public record.[89]

The majority of correspondents were content to submit a single letter, but several were regulars, such as JL in Conway, Pionier (pioneer) in Paris, and Severus in Pocahontas. The most prolific writer, however, came from the fictitious community of Schalksheim (joker's home). Spottvogel (mockingbird) sent twelve letters in a satirical vein to the editors over the course of the paper's inaugural year. The vast majority of these either focused solely on or mentioned the newspaper war. Some of the letters poked fun at other subjects, such as an Illinois law that put a bounty on sparrows' heads, or German farmers who avoided Prohibition restrictions by selling customers grapes, only to accept immediate return of the grapes with the polite request to turn the fruit into wine. Spottvogel was so anti-*Staatszeitung* that the editorial staff may have invented the "author" in order to disguise criticisms of their competitor. Some evidence refutes this theory: Der hinkende Bote, clearly enjoying the witty putdowns from Schalksheim, noticed an absence of the regular letters and inquired about Spottvogel on two occasions. The editor responded immediately after publishing Der hinkende Bote's letter that the residents of Schalksheim were all doing well and that Spottvogel explained that he was tired of messing with the crow (that is, the rival editor). The editor assured readers that Spottvogel's letters were still welcome, and he would be allowed to continue satirizing in whatever manner he thought best. Either Spottvogel was a real correspondent who was growing as weary of the newspaper feud as other German-speaking Arkansans, or the editors realized that their conceit, which could have been used to poke fun at all manner of societal ills, had been too greatly co-opted for attacks against the newspaper's competitor.[90]

Correspondents for the paper came from thirteen counties around Arkansas: Conway (Morrilton, Oppelo, Saint Vincent), Craighead (Jonesboro), Faulkner (Conway), Franklin (Altus, Charleston), Jefferson (Pine Bluff), Johnson (Hartman), Logan (Morrison Bluff, Paris, Prairie View, Shoal Creek, Spielerville, Saint Benedict, and Subiaco), Perry (Dixie), Pope (Atkins), Pulaski (Alexander, Argenta, Little Rock, and Sweet Home), Randolph (Pocahontas), Saline (Avilla, Collegeville), and Sebastian (Fort Smith). Cities with the most published letters included Altus, Atkins, Conway, Fort Smith, Morrison Bluff, Paris, Shoal Creek, and Spielerville. Many of these towns were well known for their German settlements and are relatively close to one another, and not surprisingly, the distribution of most of the communities follows the Arkansas River (the exceptions being Pocahontas and Jonesboro). This pattern aligns with Simone Schede's research on Germans in Arkansas, in which she determined that two-thirds of immigrants living in the Arkansas River valley were German-speaking, and "in Faulkner, Pope, Logan, Conway and Perry Counties, they even accounted for up to 90 percent of the foreign-born population."[91]

The *Echo* received a few letters from other states (notably Kansas and Missouri), from German speakers who had previously lived in Arkansas or who had another connection with the paper. International correspondents wrote from Rapperswyl in Switzerland and both Aachen and Munich in Germany. These letter writers provided another source for foreign news and a fresh perspective on stories relevant to life in Arkansas; for example, a Swiss contributor pointed out that overproduction of cotton in America affected Europe as well, as many Swiss spinning mills suffered financial damage from the fluctuating prices.[92]

It is impossible to tell whether the Germans of Stuttgart, Arkansas, were among the *Echo*'s readers, but they are noticeably absent among the correspondents. In 1893 they started their own German-language newspaper, *Germania*.[93] And while the names of some well-known German-speaking immigrant families, such as the Hubmans of Collegeville, appear in the newspaper, a number of prominent immigrants are not represented. For example, no obituary commemorates Edward Czarnikow, who was born in Prussia, made a name for himself over decades in Fort Smith, and died there in 1892. Another Fort Smith businessman, Rudolph Ney, ran the Boston Store, which was flourishing by 1892, but his name does not appear in the paper.[94] Max Frauenthal and his family made significant contributions to commerce and civic life in Faulkner and Cleburne Counties, but the paper only mentions a presumably unrelated Frauenthal, a young man who was a murder victim.[95] Austrian Peter Hotze was a prominent businessman and partner of John G. Fletcher, who himself served as president of the German National Bank, but Hotze is not represented in the *Echo*'s pages.[96]

A perusal of the *Arkansas Gazette* issues of 1892 reveals many businesses that were likely founded by German immigrants or those of German descent, but who chose not to pursue German-speaking customers through *Echo* advertisements: E. Ellenbogen (shoes), Herman Kahn Company (whiskey purveyors), German-American Building Association (treasurer Nick Kupferle), Palace Park (proprietor A. Gershner), and M. Katzenstein's Millinery. *Die Staatszeitung*, as the older paper, undoubtedly had loyal readers and advertisers among the community. The omissions in the *Echo*'s content could also be due to a lack of geographic coverage, which prompted at least one new subscriber to become a correspondent; Civis from Pocahontas explained he noticed a lack of coverage from north Arkansas and took it upon himself to make sure the region was represented.[97]

Previous scholarship discusses *Das Arkansas Echo* as a Roman Catholic paper, and with good reason. The founders were Catholic; the regular contributors came primarily from Catholic communities; and the paper certainly featured much local news of interest to and regarding Catholics.[98] But these were not the only matters the paper covered, in contrast to the Arkansas diocesan newspaper *The Guardian*, founded after the *Echo*, which focused exclusively on Catholic news. The founders registered the *Echo* as a Democratic paper rather than select a religious affiliation. Further, they clearly did not wish for their paper to be regarded solely as a Catholic paper. In an April editorial, the editors insisted that they intended the paper to act as a unifying force for all German speakers in the state. They noted that these German speakers were members of various religious denominations, specifically stating that Jewish Germans were among their number; they also noted that a significant number of Germans did not identify with any official organized religion, believing that the morality established by natural law was sufficient. They believed this natural law provided an adequate common moral standing on which all German speakers could agree.[99]

In June the editors asked readers to share stories from their German settlements in Arkansas, specifying that they wanted to include Evangelical and Protestant communities as well as Catholic.[100] This request would have been especially applicable to Avilla, a settlement founded by German Lutherans, and Mary Meurer claimed her father's paper was very popular among Lutheran readers.[101] While no evidence exists of Jewish contributors to the *Echo*, editorials frequently appealed to the shared heritage of Judeo-Christian values, and Jewish merchants were among the advertisers. In July, the editors remarked on the passing of Samuel Block and stated that he was one of the most revered men among "unserer jüdischen Mitbürger" (our Jewish fellow citizens).[102]

Judging from the *Echo*'s content, most of its readers were likely not brand-new immigrants but those who had been established in Arkansas or other states for at least a few years. These immigrants wanted to recruit new compatriots to join their ranks, believing Arkansas made a good home for the average German speaker. The history of German immigration to the state has been well documented, but I will provide a general summary here and refer readers to the many excellent sources in the bibliography.[103] The most surprising aspect of German immigration to Arkansas was the hope that a much larger community would exist by 1892. Only a small number of German speakers lived in the state during the antebellum period, and the government made a concerted effort to recruit immigrants to Arkansas during Reconstruction, with Germans being especially sought after due to their reputation for hard work and thriftiness. In 1873, when the legislature devoted $15,000 to print and distribute James P. Henry's pamphlet *The Resources of the State of Arkansas*, a version was translated into German and made up one-fifth of the total copies. In addition, independent agent Joseph Meyer was reimbursed by the state government for his efforts to recruit Germans to Arkansas. Generally, these measures were not as successful as they could have been. Not all Germans who were willing to leave their homeland due to social and political upheaval had the resources to emigrate or the requisite permission of local authorities, and other US states with larger budgets were also attempting to recruit new workers. Northern states with greater resources and existing German-speaking communities proved more attractive than Arkansas.[104]

Nevertheless, some Germans did come to Arkansas, a majority motivated by the ability to purchase affordable land offered by the Little Rock and Fort Smith Railway beginning in 1877–78.[105] A significant portion of the German immigrants bought land; this indicates that they considered Arkansas their new home rather than a temporary residence for seasonal agricultural work, after which they would return to Germany with higher earnings (temporary relocation for seasonal work was a common form of migrant labor practiced by Germans). The greatest immigration by German speakers to Arkansas occurred between 1878 and 1885,[106] which means that there was an established community by the *Echo*'s inaugural year of publication. In one editorial, the paper asserted that most Germans had moved to Arkansas only within the previous twelve years, establishing readers of the paper as those who immigrated since about 1880.[107] Not all German speakers came directly from Europe; some relocated from Indiana, Illinois, and Pennsylvania.[108] Urban immigrants generally congregated in the cities of Little Rock and Fort Smith, although many Germans were engaged in agriculture and lived in the rural areas of counties alongside the Arkansas River valley. Germans celebrated their cultural and linguistic heritage during day-long festivals in Little Rock, which attracted the attention of their English-speaking fellow Arkansans.[109] That Germans were considered successful immigrants is further evidenced by John Lucey's proclamation in 1911: "There are but few counties in the State that do not rejoice in the possession of some German settlers."[110]

Jonathan Wolfe, author of an extensive three-part history of German immigration to the state of Arkansas, considers additional factors that influenced where German speakers chose to locate within the state. He argues that immigrants would have found the existing immigrant communities of cities such as Little Rock or Fort Smith appealing. But most land within city limits was already occupied, and the main draw of the isolated land along the rail lines was its availability and price.[111] There is evidence in the *Echo* that German immigrants considered both of these factors. Advertisers appealed to immigrants' need to find German-speaking merchants within cities, and the newspaper encouraged readers to frequent these establishments and specifically to mention their ads in the *Echo*. A May editorial admonished country dwellers who considered buying farms to investigate who their neighbors would be and encouraged them to acquire lands adjacent to other German speakers.[112] Thus, there was an attempt to extend the community that naturally formed in cities to rural Arkansas as well. Wolfe notes that the existing German community was ever ready to welcome compatriots and help them become established in their new homes.[113] The linguistic effect of this settlement pattern was the continual reestablishment of first-generation German speakers, even as earlier immigrants to the state began to assimilate. Thus, the readers of the *Echo* likely included three separate groups: those who had been established in Arkansas for quite some time; a smaller number who were relative newcomers; and those who were potential immigrants to the state. This trend mirrors a larger pattern of German migration to the United States. The shrinking of a considerable German-language press in America was hastened by the events of World War I, but the process of the loss of linguistic identity had begun long before.[114] Once settled in the United States, Germans proved to be extremely adept at integrating in the second generation; by the third generation, few retained any German-language skills. During its existence, however, the *Echo* faithfully recorded the daily life of these immigrants in Arkansas.

CHAPTER 2

# Shaping the Community and the New Homeland

## *The* Echo*'s Most Important Causes in the Inaugural Year*

THE HISTORICAL RECORD suggests that German-speaking immigrants to Arkansas made a dual impression on their fellow Arkansans. First is the belief that "the German" existed as a kind of monolithic type, with group members sharing identical traits and opinions along with the physical belongings they imported from Europe. But this chapter will show that the collective identity of "German" was not a given; rather, it was in the process of being formed at a global level, in the homeland as Germany became more of a world power, and at a local level, as individuals who previously viewed themselves primarily as inhabitants of regions (Bavarian, Swabian, etc.) came to see themselves as part of a unified group of Germans. Second is the opinion that German speakers were attempting to recreate their homeland by isolating themselves linguistically and culturally. In reality, German immigrants sought to preserve the language and customs of their homeland not because they wished to remain Europeans, but because they believed the values they brought with them could strengthen the United States.

The crusades that the *Echo* engaged in and that are discussed in this chapter created a de facto crucible. The crusades—to encourage further German immigration to Arkansas, to promote German cultural values by preserving the language and educating their children in separate German schools, and to fight against Prohibition— simultaneously allowed German speakers to believe in a joint identity by engaging in common cause and reinforced the bond of unity in the process of attempting to achieve common goals. The outcomes of these crusades were varied in the short and long terms. But the process of the fight was of vital importance to the German-speaking community of Arkansas at the end of the nineteenth century, as they sought to shape their new homeland.

The editorial staff had ample opportunity to reflect on the nature of all things German in October, when German-speaking communities around the state were preparing for "German Day" events. In an editorial that appeared on the front page, the paper first celebrated the unity that Germans sought to create:

> Well met, the unity, the honor, and the influences of Germandom! . . . Unity makes [us] strong! The Germans are quite in the minority in this country—but unity can garner influence and the respect of fellow citizens of other nationalities, which are essential so that Germandom can fill the calling that providence has appointed to it for the benefit of the entirety of the American people.[1]

After the German Days celebrations, the editors reflected further on the common cause that battling injustices in the new land had produced.

> Fifty years ago, such a celebration would have still been unthinkable, since the immigrated Germans did not possess the necessary unified consciousness. Those from Baden and Oldenburg, Pomerania and Bavaria, Mecklenburg and Württemberg wanted nothing to do with one another, because the idea of a united Germany was nearly lost on them. . . . Since the founding of the new German empire, this has changed. The consciousness of belonging to this family of people has come to the fore. And to the extent to which the newly reemerging Know-Nothings attacked German education, German custom, and German sociability, they locked those they threatened ever tighter together.[2]

Why was it so important for German speakers to engage in the campaigns discussed in this chapter? The early German American press did not shy away from expressing strong opinions, largely because the papers were at first financially dependent on the patronage of American political parties. But Carl Wittke, author of a defining work on the German American press, argues that later editors normally did not engage in more zealous campaigns in order to avoid controversy and to keep their papers solvent: "The first responsibility of an editor, whether recently imported or recruited from the local community, was to make his paper financially successful. He was not employed to lead crusades, or for that matter, to develop good relations between the United States and Germany, however desirable that might be."[3] James Bergquist, another scholar of the German American press, discusses a different motivation: editors who left Germany after the failed 1848 revolution because of their political and social convictions believed their task was to educate readers to become better Americans.[4] While Carl Meurer would show himself to be business savvy in keeping the *Echo* afloat for four decades, he belonged to the latter group of editors. To be sure, it was probably a good business decision for the *Echo* as well, since advertisers and subscribers likely shared Meurer's opinions on these matters.

Scholars have long argued that the German American press was fundamentally an American press that happened to be written in German.[5] The topics covered primarily reflected political, economic, and quotidian life in the United States; the *Echo* conformed to this trend, even if it also included news from Europe. Hermann Ridder of the *New Yorker Staats-Zeitung* (*New York State Newspaper*) asserts that because German-language papers explained American politics and traditions to new immigrants, they were actually an important aid in turning German speakers into "good and loyal American citizens."[6] Thus, when Jonathan Wolfe, who so well chronicled German migration to Arkansas, writes, "The *kleines Deutschland* in America sought by the original settlers was not to be," he gives the impression that Germans in Arkansas were seeking to reestablish their homeland on foreign soil.[7] While it may have seemed from the outside that this was the goal of German speakers, given their linguistic insularity, the *Echo* reveals that they were in the process of determining how to be good citizens of their new homeland but doing so in their more emotionally accessible native language. They were very much interested in the surrounding state of Arkansas.

German immigrants to Arkansas were impressed by the state, but they did not hold unrealistic expectations of the benefits that immigration could provide. A common trope in immigration narratives is the shining city on a hill, beckoning to downtrodden newcomers who endure great hardship before arriving in America but who fulfill their every dream through hard work and grit. The *Echo* ran two stories ridiculing this very concept. One recounted a humorous Mark Twain story regarding a German American brewer abroad who met the King of Greece and told him to try his luck in America. Another was a witty tale of two Italian immigrants who moved to America and became rich by cleaning boots. The story closed with the final line with which German fairy tales typically end: "And if they haven't died, they are still alive today"—a realist assertion more suited to the outlook of the German-speaking immigrant than living happily ever after.[8]

German-speaking Europe has a history of pragmatically minded migration to pursue economic opportunity. For the lower-middle classes, migration was a way of life. It was utilized as a bargaining strategy with local employers: either they could improve working conditions and pay higher wages, or the work force would leave and seek better employment elsewhere. Agricultural workers and tradesmen all understood that it was sometimes necessary to relocate.[9] Many nineteenth-century Germans seeking better opportunities pursued shorter-distance migrations, moving to other parts of Germany or Poland. For those who considered relocating abroad, the United States was not the only option; many chose to move south to Latin America.[10]

The *Echo* ran two stories on these sister colonies. One reported that the German colony in Paraguay was experiencing success planting tobacco and corn; the other noted that Brazil's Santa Cruz principality was composed largely of Germans, who were thriving and blending local customs with those brought from their homeland.[11] The German-speaking community of the *Echo* thus had to argue not only that others should join them in emigrating from Europe, but that they also should select the United States and specifically Arkansas as a destination. One article linked this willingness to move, rather than to accept a poor fate, to the virtue of personal industry: "Because as a result of poor harvests and expensive food prices, many hard-working heads of families over there have decided to sell all of their property and move here with the whole kit and caboodle." German immigrants were not seen as victims of poor circumstances that necessitated emigration, but rather as agents who actively controlled their fate.[12]

Before the *Echo*, Arkansas Germans had made a previous attempt to promote further immigration via a German language newspaper. K. L. Bah, Adolph Deutelmoser, and Charles Schaerff published the *Arkansas Staatszeitung* (State Newspaper) in 1869, declaring it to be nonpartisan and for the purposes of "immigration and education."[13] While the *Echo* did not devote itself solely to the promotion of immigration, it did make this matter one of the main focuses of the inaugural year. In March, the paper announced a new series on German immigration to Arkansas; it requested that readers submit inspirational stories, with accompanying photographs, of overcoming hardships in founding communities. Over the next few months, the editors continued to solicit more testimonials from readers. They laid out the arguments for and benefits of such contributions: many

Germans in Arkansas were living in far greater prosperity than they could ever hope to achieve in Europe; the more German speakers who arrived, the easier it would be to maintain their communities; and positive stories about immigration published in the *Echo* could easily be given to family and friends abroad. In September, a reader from Collegeville noted Arkansas's natural beauty and the established status of the German-speaking community, comprised of those who would be willing to aid newcomers, as two additional incentives to relocate: "Isn't it true, it is beautiful here in our mountains. And we are all past the difficult beginning. But there is still room here for many settlers, and our colony is slowly growing. And whoever settles down with us, we would be happy to assist with words and deeds."[14] While the German-speaking community considered it their duty to help countrymen settle in Arkansas, some twenty years earlier—at a time when politicians pined for more of this very kind of immigration—the *Arkansas Gazette* had chastised local authorities for failing to welcome German speakers and help them settle.[15] The pages of the *Echo* indicate that Germans were targeting their countrymen still living in Europe, but German speakers also moved to Arkansas from existing colonies in Indiana, Illinois, Ohio, and Pennsylvania.[16]

Only two readers took up the call to write accounts of the state's immigrants. In June, the editor praised Joseph Glanzman of Altus for describing the history of the families there and asked who would write the next contribution. (Puzzlingly, Glanzman's contribution was never published in the inaugural year, nor was it mentioned again.) The *Echo* further appealed to the various German clubs (*Vereine*) to motivate their members to document their communities in words and photographs. The second reader-contributor was A. Kind, who submitted a four-part series on the history of Randolph County, with a special emphasis on Pocahontas. Kind's narrative was well written and astute, bordering at times on the poetic. He discussed the advantages of the railroad in allowing settlers to carve a home out of the wilderness and enabling the movement of goods to market. But he lamented how this new system disadvantaged river-port cities, a development that affected Pocahontas particularly. Kind praised Randolph County for its numerous rivers and other natural resources, such as timber and minerals. He complained that Arkansas had a bad reputation among German speakers on the coasts, caused by unscrupulous agents who portrayed it as a land flowing with milk and honey.[17] When early German settlers discovered that Arkansas was not a utopia, they claimed the soil was not fertile at all—an accusation Kind considered obviously false. His series instructed foreign readers on the correct pronunciation of English words, under the assumption that the *Echo* was indeed circulating in Europe.[18]

The *Echo* found other positive stories to print about German immigration to the state of Arkansas. In Coal Hill, immigration efforts were alleged to have been so successful that they resulted in a housing shortage that necessitated the construction of one hundred more homes to cover the need. This was regarded as an encouraging development for the farmers in Altus, for whom more residents meant more customers for fresh produce. John Barrow, a candidate for the state legislature, praised immigration in a letter to the editors, which he asked to be translated into German: "The majority of German immigrants are very estimable citizens. They pay their taxes on time and are good examples for the American farmers, and it could be wished that German immigrants would disperse themselves over our entire state, so that all the farmers could profit from the example of their admirable hard work, and their thrift."[19]

Not all politicians were as encouraging of further immigration to the state. A reader letter from Saline County related that a sheriff named Shoppach, himself of German ancestry, proclaimed that no Germans had been selected to serve as jury members because, as he put it, "We dont wont [*sic*] no foreigners." The reader noted that the German voters of the county replied, "We dont wont [*sic*] Shoppach." They would campaign against him in the upcoming election in spite of his heritage: "The German name alone is not enough, we demand German disposition. Renegades are always the worst enemies of their earlier associates."[20]

The paper did not hesitate to publish perspectives that were less than flattering regarding German immigration to Arkansas. Conway correspondent J. L. complained that while all German speakers in the state wished for more settlers in their communities, the constant bickering between the two Arkansas German papers made the area less attractive to potential immigrants. He alluded to *Staatszeitung* pieces that apparently attacked immigrants for, in one occurrence, helping German-speaking newcomers to the area and, in another, daring to run for public office. Unfortunately, the *Echo* provides no other information on these cases. J. L.'s report also mentioned that German farmers were being prosecuted for selling wine, an issue that was taken up in the *Echo*'s crusade against Prohibition (discussed later in this chapter).[21]

There is some scant evidence of out-migration among the German immigrants in Arkansas in the pages of the *Echo*. Although a major project of the paper was to draw more German speakers to the state, it printed a letter from a Benedictine priest in Pierce City, Missouri, who was trying to recruit more farmers for the town of three thousand, making largely the same arguments as the *Echo* regarding good farmland and living among neighbors of the same religion. The priest admitted that the rural surroundings made the town unsuitable for factory workers and tradesmen. Another notice alerted readers to available land in South Dakota as a result of the opening of two Indian reservations.[22] Largely, though, the German settlers in Arkansas gave the impression of being content with their adopted home.

An article regarding a scheme involving railroad magnate Jay Gould provides a curious addendum to the theme of the *Echo*'s coverage of German speakers' migration to Arkansas. Jay Gould passed away during the *Echo*'s inaugural year, and given the paper's utter antipathy toward those it regarded as robber barons, Gould would seem an unlikely subject for a positive story. A few weeks earlier, the paper published a piece declaring Gould the "Warlock of Wall Street," decrying his negative influence on American culture, and noting with a bit of Schadenfreude that his vast wealth could not provide immortality. An article published a week later compared Gould's "deceptive tricks" to those used by gold extortionists in Britain. Nonetheless, a third piece on Gould reported that he had written to J. D. Adams, state commissioner for mining, to declare his wish to help the state develop its natural resources. The article quoted from Gould's letter, which said that everything must be done to assist Arkansas in developing its resources and to encourage immigration. In the September before his death, Gould had apparently promised to pay half of the costs to bring immigrants and capital to Arkansas.[23]

The *Echo* not only promoted the state as a worthy destination for German immigrants, but it also published concrete advice for those undertaking the move. Two separate articles provided warnings regarding traveling. The first admonished travelers to spend the few extra dollars necessary to avoid the mid-deck of the ship, which most immigrants selected because it was the cheapest. The author complained that the mid-deck was a place of extreme lawlessness, including open prostitution. The author claimed that children and women were exposed to all manner of activity in the mid-deck that was illegal on the mainland, and he did not mince words: "In short, the mid-deck is a pig sty, a den of thieves, a pit of murderers, a befouled abyss. Truly, it astonishes me that this swimming hell is not regularly swallowed by the floods." The author suggested that the captain and officers should regularly patrol the mid-deck and put a stop to the illicit behavior, but he doubted the shipping companies would do anything unless compelled by law. This warning undoubtedly resonated among the many religious Germans who made their way to Arkansas.[24]

The second article was essentially an advertisement for St. Raphael's Union and its institution, Leo House in New York, which is unsurprising, since it was written by the organization's director, A. Geyer. The article's main point was to publicize the kinds of assistance the organization could offer immigrants, but it additionally provided valuable information regarding schemes often perpetrated against travelers. It claimed that those who did not demand access to Leo House representatives were kept in rooms and not allowed to leave until their train was departing so that "immigration assistants" could sell them food at five times the going rate. According to Geyer, those wishing to travel beyond New York were handed over to railroad agents who booked passage using winding routes that would cost more. Family and friends ended up divided when different agents selected varying routes to the same final destination. Luggage was booked in a class other than freight, which was three times more expensive. Geyer recommended that immigrants should send the majority of their cash to America by postal order, rather than carrying it. The piece ended with a stern warning that the Leo House could not be responsible for the tragic fate of those who did not use its services.[25]

The *Echo* assumed many potential immigrants to Arkansas would be farmers. As the most important task for a farmer was to choose good land, a number of articles addressed all aspects of this topic. The first step in the process was investigating legal land acquisition. The editors discussed which ways to procure land were still open and warned newcomers that two programs they might have heard of—the Preemption Act of 1841 and the Timber Culture Act of 1873—were no longer options. The editors were happy to report that despite the efforts of the anti-immigration forces, the Homestead Act was still a possibility for German settlers; so was buying land from the railroads or from some individual state governments that were not named, presumably to keep the focus on Arkansas. The paper addressed how to test the fertility of the soil and admonished would-be land buyers to also consider the climate and average rainfall.

The editors regarded solid neighbors as a crucial feature of a good homestead, since agricultural work often required farmers to help one another. The paper warned against "nativistic squatters" and noted that one should be surrounded by neighbors who share one's language and religion, especially considering that one's children would be going to school with neighboring children. This advice masked a deeper anxiety that pervaded stories in the *Echo* throughout its inaugural year: German settlers were fearful of black Arkansans, and they repeatedly warned newcomers to avoid them: "And because man is a sociable creature, it belongs [to consideration] that he is also able to peaceably interact with the neighbors. When he situates himself in the middle of brutal and thieving Negroes, a good harvest or flourishing livestock would do him no good in any case." German speakers in Arkansas were concerned that a race war was a distinct possibility, and they believed surrounding themselves with others from Europe was the best way to insulate themselves against potential conflicts or violence.[26]

In addition to promoting immigration to Arkansas and providing concrete instructions to would-be settlers, the editors kept a watchful eye on national and international developments. A national moratorium would mean no new German speakers in Arkansas, regardless of how much the existing community was ready to receive them. The editorials, news items, and especially the letters to the editor make clear that the US immigration situation was rapidly changing in 1892. Pending legislation restricting immigration, as well as cholera, were the major concerns for *Echo* readers, and there was a real sense of urgency to recruit friends and family members to move to Arkansas before the door closed.

From proposed new laws to court rulings on existing ones, 1892 was an exceptionally busy year for immigration legislation, and the *Echo*'s coverage was comprehensive. A February ruling made it clear why vigilance regarding the legislative process was important. The Supreme Court announced that it no longer believed it had jurisdiction over cases regarding would-be immigrants who had been denied entry into the United States, but rather only over those who were already in the country. This meant that the decisions of the immigration commission and provisions in the existing law were final.[27]

The Congress of 1892 provided plenty of pending legislation to be concerned about. One bill would have required a five-year probationary period, which the *Echo* felt could easily be misused by general opponents of immigration or by locals who might denounce newcomers whom they viewed as competitors for jobs or market share. Another potential law would have held shipping companies responsible for the immigrants they transported. Those operating ocean liners would have had to swear that passengers were neither sponsored immigrants (that is, those without their own resources) nor contract laborers. This policy could have led to departure delays and higher costs for travelers. An additional proposal of this bill allowed one "no" vote among a three-person commission inspecting immigrants to be the deciding factor in returning individuals to their countries of origin.

Another proposal would have required new immigrants to possess a minimum of $100 in cash. One legislator thought he could force wages for existing Americans to rise if all immigration were halted for one year. The editors believed that this was an unlikely outcome, arguing that monopolies that employed low-wage immigrants from Poland or Italy would simply illegally bring in those workers across the Mexican or Canadian borders.[28]

In the last issue of 1892, readers learned of new schemes to limit immigration already planned for the coming year. These included denying entry to immigrants who intended to serve in the US Army, and a possible new requirement that immigrants travel to major cities in their home countries to obtain pre-departure permission, thereby adding to the expense and time necessary to leave one's birth country. Besides disquieting pending legislation and court rulings, the *Echo* reported on concrete cases of immigrants' being denied entry, including Russian Jews who were sent back after a local Jewish group refused to sponsor them, and a number of contract workers from Italy, Poland, and Slovakia who were supposed to be employed in Pennsylvania coal mines.[29] The *Echo* was generally suspicious of contract workers, arguing that they were different from real immigrants who had come to contribute and build up the country; instead, the paper claimed, they were essentially mercenaries with no real stake in the well-being of the nation.

As befits the nature of a crusade, the editors were not content to simply report on the dire news regarding immigration. The paper featured a number of proposed concrete actions to limit or overturn the damage caused by politicians and immigration officials who were opposed to more settlers. The first suggestion was for readers to take their own political action. One editorial reminded readers that not all Americans were glad to have them as fellow residents and that they should remember this when voting in an election year. Arkansas Germans who had not gotten around to obtaining citizenship were admonished do so in order to participate in the political process. The paper proudly quoted Grover Cleveland as being a supporter of immigration: "Generous hospitality, which is one of our most outstanding national characteristics, moves us to welcome the honest and industrious sons of all lands as co-residents and future co-citizens." The editors admitted that there were nativists in both parties but argued repeatedly that Democrats were generally better for immigrants. Since anti-immigrant proposals from both sides were becoming increasingly serious, the paper suggested a second concrete action: urge those considering the move from Europe to America to undertake it immediately. This admonition took on renewed urgency before the elections of 1892. The *Echo* conceded that fall was not the best time to immigrate, but it noted that others had successfully done so in previous years. It urged would-be settlers to take advantage of the brief legislative pause before the elections, after which anti-immigration fanatics in either party could increase their strength, depending on the outcome of the vote. The paper further mentioned that the contemporary immigration commissioner, Colonel (John) Weber, was of German extraction and friendly to Germans.[30]

Additionally, the *Echo* attempted to provide its readers with a wealth of counterarguments to those who opposed immigration. It contended that even if America had ten times the inhabitants it currently did, there would still be enough room for more citizens, which must have been particularly persuasive for German speakers coming from a Europe with a much higher population density. In one sarcastic note, the editors suggested that nativists be given their own sparsely populated state if things were getting too crowded for them. Regarding the argument that immigrants take jobs away from Americans, the *Echo* maintained that the real force depressing the labor market was monopolies. Moreover, immigrants were needed in industry and above all in agriculture, as farmland was being left untilled and because German farmers possessed superior techniques that they were sharing with their American counterparts. While the newspaper routinely celebrated German culture and values, it also used such tributes to argue that America was richer for German immigration. It reprinted a lengthy *Boston Globe* article praising the contributions of German immigrants; another article entitled "The German Influence on the Acceptance of the Declaration of Independence" discussed the contributions of colonial-era German immigrants William Penn and Christoph Sauer. The author of the latter article noted that most German immigrants did not know this history and that American historians did not talk about it, either because they were unaware or were purposely suppressing it. An additional article reprinted from the *Boston Globe* stated that Germans had been making a good impression in America since its founding and noted that George Washington was favorably impressed by the Germans and praised them in letters and documents.[31]

Legislation was, to be sure, a true threat to further German immigration in 1892, but cholera had a far more devastating effect on the cause. In November, the *Echo* cited concrete numbers to demonstrate the impact of the disease: in September 1891, 16,729 people had emigrated from Hamburg; in September 1892, the figure had dwindled to 1,034. The paper took the stand that the English-language press, rather than European immigrants, was most responsible for the spread of cholera—sensationalist accounts of the disease's spread had every American believing himself to have caught it. The editors suggested that a quarantine would easily solve the problem. They then reversed their opinion one week later, arguing that a quarantine was ill-advised for two reasons. First, the proposed twenty-day quarantines would increase immigrant expenditures, since boats would essentially become floating hotels with costs borne by ship companies, which would result in higher prices for passage. Second, a quarantine would cause more immigrants to die: cramped quarters on the ships would provide ideal conditions for transmission of the illness if someone were infected with cholera. The editors advised would-be German settlers to wait until the contagion had passed before making the voyage. The *Echo* lamented that Know-Nothings were using the epidemic to advance their cause. By the end of the year, it was clear that cholera had achieved what the anti-immigration forces could not, namely a complete shutdown of immigration: "Unfortunately, immigration from Germany is as good as cut off. The steamer lines are no longer selling mid-deck tickets. The reawakened cholera in Europe, in concert with the nativistic endeavors which made use of the cholera terror, caused this measure." The editors hoped that, in the new year, the incoming presidential administration could again facilitate German immigration.[32]

The *Echo*'s enthusiasm for further German immigration did not extend to all immigrants, however. One piece of successful anti-immigration law passed in 1892 was the Geary Act, which specifically targeted Chinese immigrants. The *Echo* took a hard editorial line in supporting measures to restrict Chinese immigration for cultural reasons, viewing Chinese immigrants as a corrupting influence on American culture in contrast to the supposed positive effect of German immigrants:

> For we are of the conviction that the Mongolian race should not displace the Caucasian, which has civilized this country since the days of Columbus. The monstrous number of China's inhabitants threatened our union; and even if [only] a part of the four hundred million located there would waltz in here, then indeed there was the danger that their heathen system of religion, their base philosophy and their corrupt morals would cover the germinating civilization of the United States like a ruinous flood.[33]

The editors were not enthusiastic about the new law, though, as they claimed that existing anti-Chinese legislation was already doing enough, and they worried about the increasing trend regarding bills of this sort. For a similar reason, the paper argued that German speakers should be concerned by discussions in Washington to limit Italian and Slavic immigrants, two groups whom the editors regarded as sharing their European values. They believed a limit on these Europeans would eventually lead to a ban on German settlers, and they further expressed the belief that while the Chinese were fundamentally incompatible with Germans, German speakers got along with Italians and Slavs quite well in parts of Austria and Switzerland. The editors drew another distinction between Europeans and Chinese in economic terms. They first argued that Chinese workers were imported by capitalists to bring down overall wages; secondly, the editors believed the Chinese earned money through the dangerous opium trade, which was particularly galling to Germans who saw their production of alcohol as the honest effort of farmers to capture the fruits of their labors: "Their secret society threatens to murder anyone who gets in the way of their immorality and the money-making through dens of vice."[34]

Overall, the Germans aimed to place themselves on equal cultural footing with the prevailing Anglo-Saxon culture of white settlers, and simultaneously to distance themselves from the Chinese, whom they regarded as inferior. Additionally, they were immensely worried that their own communities would be changed by American culture in turn, which is why retaining German culture through language was discussed with such a sense of urgency in the pages of the *Echo*.

In her work on immigrant acculturation, historian Kathleen Conzen discusses how Germans, especially those of the middle and upper-middle classes (as *Echo* readers were), were keen on preserving their culture in order to add it to the proverbial melting pot of American culture.[35] The editors expressed this very attitude early in the inaugural year, when they defended the paper's general stance: "We repeat that we represent the common interests of all German citizens, regardless of religious denomination, to exert through unity [the traits of] Germanness in the share of America's culture to which it is entitled."[36]

Later in the year, an editorial expressly described German culture in contradistinction to the existing culture and praised what Germanness could contribute: diligence, thrift, and a genuine desire to interact with others, in contrast to the coldness of Anglo-Saxon Americans. Above all, the editors believed that Germans' main contribution to American culture would be their willingness to extend personal relationships across class lines.[37] In the same month, the paper reprinted a piece from *New York Magazine* arguing that European immigrants contributed much more to American society than they received and predicting that the culture would be fundamentally changed.[38] Germans believed that the effects of the negative forces contributing to the latent downfall of American culture (such as parental rights being taken away and Prohibition) could be reversed through the influence of Germans: "However, the German influence working together with sensible English[-speaking] fellow citizens may be able to somewhat curb these outrages."[39]

The *Echo* gives no indication that the German community in Arkansas was interested in bringing over a critical mass of countrymen in order to recreate Germany. Rather, they wanted good fellow citizens to populate their new country, and they believed the best citizens would be other German settlers. This belief in cultural superiority would become one of the casualties of World War II. In addition to the heavy guilt of the mass murder of the Holocaust and the deaths of the civilians who perished in the carpet bombing of the allies, Germans had to come to terms with the fact that what they always considered to be a refined and humanistic country, *Das Land der Dichter und Denker* (The Land of Poets and Thinkers) had somehow devolved into *Das Land der Richter und Henker* (The Land of Judges and Executioners).[40]

In order to contribute to American society, Germans first had to establish their own group identity, which in the second half of the nineteenth century was an ongoing project. The *Echo* told its readers, "A people that wants to be good for anything must above all believe in itself."[41] Germans in Arkansas in 1892 likely viewed themselves simultaneously as representatives of their region (as Bavarians, Berliners, etc.) and as sons and daughters of an emerging, unified, and powerful political state. While these Germans would have been navigating a complex historical moment had they remained in Europe, the identities of German speakers in Arkansas were also impacted by their adopted space. Their newly chosen home in the South was experiencing the massive upheaval of Reconstruction, which resulted in an influx of black migrants followed closely by an out-migration, when African Americans realized the disconnect between the promised versus the actual political and economic situation in the state. This out-migration was very much in progress in 1892.[42] A German-speaking Arkansan was thus navigating multiple new identities: a proud representative of regional traditions and dialect; the native born of a rising political power; a resident in a new country; and a white settler in the US South who was competing economically with black Arkansans, some of whom were also new residents. It is not surprising that viewpoints represented in the *Echo* sometimes seem contradictory.

Twenty-first-century citizens of the world may think of Germany as a strong, unified nation, but the present form of Germany was not established as a nation-state until 1871. For much of its history, the area known today as Germany was composed of separate kingdoms and principalities, each with its own rulers, laws, and borders. Citizens regarded themselves as belonging to the particular duchy or principality in which they were born. In the absence of a political entity such as a large-nation state in the nineteenth century, Germans began to regard language as a unifying concept that bound them to a larger group. In 1813 Ernst Moritz Arndt composed an oft-cited poem in which he considers the geographical borders of a potential Germany, imagining the territory to encompass Austria and Switzerland, since his primary requirement is language: "What is the fatherland of the German? / Then name for me the ample land! / As far as the German tongue sounds / And God in heaven sings songs, / That it is supposed to be! / That, brave German, call yours!" Arndt further associates specific virtues with German speakers, such as trustworthiness, loyalty, and love, and defines them in opposition to their historical enemy, the French.[43]

The *Echo* pointedly took up this project of linking virtue with linguistic unity. In the fledgling paper's first month of publication, the editors reminded readers that while German unity back home was a relatively new concept, the country had become one of the strongest in Europe through that unity. The *Echo* urged Germans in America to let go any regional rivalries and present a united front in the new country. Such solidarity would assuredly be needed given the struggles with Know-Nothings, Prohibition, and the state school monopoly. In addition to language, the editorial counted *deutscher Rechtsinn* (a German sense of right and wrong) as an important element of German unity.[44]

How natural was it for German speakers in Arkansas to band together? Historian Jonathan Wolfe presents German unity as a foregone conclusion owing to linguistic difficulties: "Their inability to speak English limited them in society, and so they naturally turned to those around them who spoke German, and who had similar interests. They also became somewhat isolated culturally, which was not at all unusual for immigrants." Following Wolfe's argument, a German newspaper would be a necessity. It should be noted that Wolfe is generalizing about the entire German-speaking population over years. Yet it is clear from the inaugural year of the *Echo* that many readers made a conscious choice to continue using German, as maintaining their native language represented a moral and not linguistic imperative. And this mindset emerged decades earlier, as evidenced by the "German-American Association for the Promotion of Immigration and the

Maintenance of German Habits and Customs," an initiative of Arkansas German settlers in 1872.[45]

But one should examine the idea that Germans in Arkansas did not know the language of their adopted home. Wolfe goes on to state that they were generally poorly educated: "In education these settlers were very much alike. As far as can be known, it seems that most of the German-speaking immigrants were literate in that language, if no other. There were, however, few among them who had any advanced education."[46] As discussed above, the editors and several correspondents knew English, but there are countless indications in the *Echo* of 1892 that the editors expected their readers to be fluent in English as well as German. They frequently offered items from the English-language press with no accompanying translation, as they did in the inaugural issue, which reprinted the *Arkansas Democrat*'s account of the break-in to the *Echo*'s offices. The paper makes direct references to those who had already mastered English, such as when an editorial stated unequivocally that Germans knew and respected English language and literature, and to those who were still acquiring the language, such as a book recommendation for help with English pronunciation, which was deemed utterly illogical. The editors referred to documents produced only in English, such as the program for the bishop's jubilee celebration.[47]

Some items indicate that the *Echo*'s assumption that all Germans had the same facility with English was perhaps aspirational rather than reflective of reality. Germans realized that full political participation in their new country would require fluency in English, yet they always noted which candidates spoke German as well. In referencing an upcoming meeting of the road-construction commission, the paper included the following suggestion to readers: "Also our fellow German citizens who are in enough command of the English language to make themselves understood should attend," given that Germans possessed significant knowledge about how to build roads. English fluency might have depended on the region of the state and most certainly depended on the generation of the immigrant. A correspondent from Pocahontas praised a local candidate for noticing that the Germans were being unjustly excluded from serving on juries because so many, especially the elderly, could not write or speak English—this of course also made it difficult for them to serve as witnesses unless a translator was present.[48]

It is likely, then, that most readers did not subscribe to a German newspaper out of necessity, since those in the second generation had at least some aptitude in English as well. Mary Meurer suggested that many of her father's subscribers appreciated the *Echo* as a sort of "one-stop shopping" news source, realizing that it would provide them with news and commentary from global to local levels. Another reason for acquiring the newspaper was the comfort of utilizing their native language. A correspondent reported on a Mass being said in Fort Smith, observing that the priest announced publicly that he would far prefer to preach the homily in German, but he noted that many English speakers were in the audience and he would therefore proceed in English for their benefit. According to the correspondent, the priest's English was so good that one of the non-Catholics in attendance confided that he usually fell asleep during sermons but this time hung on every word. Apparently, English speakers attended German events occasionally, and while they were sometimes termed "English-speaking fellow citizens," they were most often referred to by nationality as "Americans" in distinction to the "Germans." In one case, there was some grumbling about the presence of Americans: "The Americans were especially numerous, for many Germans too numerous, so that the *Gemüthlichkeit* suffered as a result." *Gemütlichkeit* is a difficult term to translate; most generally, it means a feeling of well-being, but it can also mean sociability. It is quite possible in this context that the Germans were unhappy about the presence of so many English speakers both because they wanted to be with other German speakers and because they did not feel free to imbibe alcohol in mixed company. At a large wedding in Pocahontas, however, local "Americans" were welcomed as guests and were impressed by German hospitality, including alcohol, and reacted with "speechless marvel and amazement," at least according to the German reporting on the event.[49]

Aside from issues of convenience and comfort, the *Echo* made a much grander argument for preserving one's linguistic competence: German was an ennobling language that gave the speaker access to a superior civilization, rich in literature and culture. The paper celebrated concrete examples of this culture's manifestations in Arkansas, such as a performance of a Mozart Mass drawing a large crowd to a Catholic feast-day celebration in Fort Smith, or the importation of stained-glass windows from Germany both by the English-speaking Episcopal church in Little Rock and the German-speaking Lutheran community.[50] A May editorial entitled "On the Nurturing of the German Language and Literature" asserted that educated Americans continued to learn German to gain access to its literature and highly civilized culture. The *Echo*, staunch in its support of everything related to the Democratic Party, even crossed political lines to note proudly that President Harrison's grandson was learning the language of Schiller and Goethe in the White House. It further claimed that those Americans who were *gebildet* (educated) and *edelgesinnt* (noble-minded) joined in the fight against the Know-Nothings trying to stamp out the use of German in the United States. An article reprinted from the *Fort Worth Anzeiger* (Fort Worth Gazette) argued that those who wanted to get rid of German by claiming it would foster more national unity to have a single language in English were ignorant of history: the Austrian empire had many languages but was still united, while the American colonies separated from Britain despite a common language. The *Echo* additionally found inspiration in other German diasporic populations, such as those in Russian-occupied areas who had been able to maintain their language and culture since the early eighteenth century. It argued that, because nativists were so intent on taking their language away, immigrants realized what a treasure it was and therefore strove that much harder to defend it with German-language schools, in newspapers, and at the ballot box.[51]

The *Echo* also made a more intense argument regarding the preservation of language, with multiple articles linking language suppression to the violent past of colonialism and slavery. The editors were convinced that only those on the losing end of expansionist colonial fights were deprived of their language. The paper often compared knowledge of one's native language to an inheritance that could be stolen and admonished German speakers not to be like the blacks and Native Americans who had allowed themselves to be robbed of their culture. If this sentiment were not jarring enough on its own, it was moreover couched in disturbing, racist rhetoric that directly defined German culture as superior:

> Only idiots, who are even beneath the level of Negroes, let themselves have [their native language] taken away. Because what Sambo gave up in slavery here was only a purely barbaric mumbo-jumbo, a literary foothold of disposable Hottentot clicking. A German American however, who imitates the example of that slave bent under the whip, sacrifices the richest treasure of intellectual property that providence has given any people on earth.[52]

This sort of racist terminology illustrates how important the continued use of their native language was to the German speakers in Arkansas. Similarly racist rhetoric appears in the article "Historic Examples," although the argument was extended to provide a model from the past: the paper celebrated the Greeks for their ability to keep their language alive even after being conquered by the Romans and attributed this linguistic survival to the cultural superiority of Greek civilization.[53]

Ironically, in arguing for the preservation of a Teutonic language, the editors again attempted to align the Germans with the prevailing Anglo-Saxon culture and in opposition to cultures from non-white immigrants to the United States. As fellow whites, German speakers felt they should be allowed to keep their language. The *Echo* reminded its readers that this trend was a result of political power and not limited to race, though, and observed that Irish immigrants in the United States were attempting to reclaim Celtic identity in their new homeland, after the invading British had endeavored to rob them of their birthright in Europe.[54] But the *Echo* did not intend German culture to be regarded as equal to Anglo-Saxon culture. The paper portrayed German culture as superior to all other culture in the United States: "Now the free men who emigrated from Germany are by no means to be aligned with the Negro slaves imported from Africa. They are rather the carriers of a culture which is older and more precious than the Puritan culture that prevails here."[55] Regular correspondent Severus, from Pocahontas, used similarly strident language in urging his fellow Germans to only marry others from German settler families, comparing children who result from a mixing of cultures to perishable fruit. He condemned *Landsleute* (countrymen) who "chase after Americans in the insane belief that they stand on a higher plane of civilization."[56]

In a bit of self-promotion, the *Echo* informed its readers that German newspapers had a special and vital role in the battle to keep the German language alive, since, on a daily basis, many more people read newspapers than books. Scholars of the German American press have seen enlightened self-interest in editors' desire to help their fellow immigrants continue their native-language abilities. In an age of dwindling immigration and among a population as willing to assimilate as the Germans, German newspapers stood little chance of maintaining subscriber rolls without appealing to a moral argument to maintain the use of the mother tongue and to impart this "gift" to one's children and grandchildren.[57]

No matter how strongly the editors preached against English, it inevitably made its way onto the pages of the *Echo*. This happened in one of three ways. First, English words were *eingedeutscht* (Germanified): the English word was retained but spelled according to German orthography. For example, a businessman's goal is described as seeing his company "buhmen" (booming), or a citizen was said to have paid "Taxe" (taxes) for his land. In German, these words would have been *florieren* and *Steuer*. Second, German speakers created new half-German, half-English hybrids such as "Weihnachtscandy" (Christmas candy; in German, *Weihnachtssüßigkeiten*),

"Front-Thür" (front door; in German, *Haustür*, or "door to the house"), "Cottonpick-Zeit" (cotton-picking time; in German, *Baumwolleerntezeit*), and "die weiße Race" (white race; in German, *die weiße Rasse*). In one instance, a humorous story about an ill-mannered dog, such a hybrid was even conjugated in the command: "Behäve dich, doch!" (Behave yourself; in German, *benimm dich*, which is also a reflexive verb). Third, some English words were simply taken over wholesale into German, such as: "Ice cream parlor," "Tramps," and "Store," although the German practice of capitalizing all nouns was retained. In each of these methods, the usage applies to events or circumstances encountered in America. It should be noted, though, that the editors imposed little consistency for terms used solely in America. For example, a contemporary American term for jail, calaboose, was Germanified to "Calabuse," whereas a story about a hunting party discussed the killing of a "catamount," with no attempt made at translation.[58] In larger newspaper markets, editors arriving directly from Germany were chagrined by such immigrant efforts to inhabit two linguistic spaces simultaneously, as the strategy resulted in a less-than-pure version of official high German.[59]

There is no evidence that such occasional "Denglisch" (*Deutsch*, or German, plus *Englisch*, or English) particularly troubled either the *Echo*'s readers or staff, who could of course have made editorial changes and eliminated the practice from the paper's pages. It likely strengthened the bond among those living in the German-speaking community in Arkansas, given that they shared specialized knowledge of both the native language and the living circumstances in their adopted home. The contributor A. Kind, keeping in mind the *Echo*'s foreign readers, took the time to give both the pronunciation and meaning of words such as "creek," "county," "bluff," "cotton gin," and "barbeque."[60] This sort of linguistic appropriation was not unique to the *Echo*, as the same trend existed in the German American press since colonial times.[61] German speakers also realized that the language's tendency to form extremely descriptive compound words would have made attempts to Germanize every American expression yield ludicrous results, as this joke shows: "Welches ist die deutsche Bezeichnung für Apotheker? Gesundheitswiederherstellungsmittelzusammenmischungsverhältnißkundiger" (What is the German term for a pharmacist? Expert-for-proportion-of-mixing-together-methods-to-reestablish-health).[62]

A major battleground in the *Echo*'s fight for the German language was the establishment of German schools. The desire to protect an educational space for immigrant children separate from the general (English) public-school system became a heated battle indeed. In this regard, the *Echo* was different from a majority of the German American press. While some German editors across the nation were unhappy with the quality of American public education, they conceded that the public system was important for creating a unified citizenry sharing a common language. But religious-minded Germans, for whom salvation was closely linked to language, advocated for continued and separate instruction in German. The elementary school instruction in German peaked from 1880 to 1910, and the *Echo*'s editors were devout Catholics who belonged to the group of Germans calling for German-language education.[63] One of the paper's advertisers, Benziger Brothers Publishing, was a mail-order German book service located in New York. It made the specific claim that a catechism in German was a necessary product for German homes since many German children no longer spoke the language and therefore could not understand the basic principles of Christian teachings.[64] Historian Jonathan Wolfe notes that German immigrants to Arkansas began building their own schools as soon as possible, with only land-clearing (for farming) and church-building taking higher priority.[65] Given the state of Arkansas schools in 1892, Germans' reluctance to join the public education system is not surprising. The *Arkansas Gazette* noted in 1892 that some fifty thousand children in Arkansas were not enrolled in school at all, which suggests a disparity between Germans' commitment to education and that of their new co-citizens.[66]

To understand why the right to determine schooling for one's children became a crusade for German settlers in Arkansas, one must first examine the state of education in Europe when they left it. The imperative to provide education for all children, not only those of the wealthy, was already well-established in the area governed by Frederick the Great by 1763, when a law was passed making school attendance mandatory for children between ages five and thirteen. This concept had spread to other German-speaking parts of Europe by 1840. While compulsory education was variously enforced in German-speaking realms, the belief that basic education was an important component of civic life led to widespread literacy and respect for learning among the general population.[67]

German settlers' paranoia that the state would interfere in their children's schooling was also rooted in prior experience in the homeland. Prussian Chancellor Otto von Bismarck had, some twenty years earlier in 1872, asserted state control over Catholic schools and removed the Jesuit Order from educational institutions.[68] Convening in 1890, the state meeting of local St. Joseph Societies in Arkansas passed a resolution calling for the prevention of state interference in German Catholic schools.[69] This aversion to government intrusion reflected a larger national trend among German speakers in the United States. Because of their worries about the Prussian state (and because of the existing history of German schooling in the United States dating back to colonial days), US German-language schools never became affiliated with the larger network of *Auslandsschulen* (overseas schools) that shaped German education abroad in other countries with large German diasporic populations.[70]

*Echo* editors made the case often and enthusiastically that parental control of education was important because it was a God-given right, untouched and untouchable by the whims of politicians and civil statutes. Editorial arguments in this matter were anchored in natural law, particularly as described by St. Thomas Aquinas. The *Echo* asserted that parents had three important duties regarding their children, namely securing their "Existenz, Ernährung, Erziehung" (existence, sustenance/feeding, education/instruction). Therefore, parents' desire to educate children in the manner they best saw fit was a simple fulfilling of parental obligation. Editors argued that this duty should not be ceded to the state, as the family existed as a unit of civilization prior to the formal state, and thus it had the older claim to education. To bolster this argument, the paper called on an American education expert, Theodore D. Wholsey, who served as President of Yale from 1846 to 1871. It quoted Wholsey as arguing that the state should not have a monopoly on education and that the freedom to educate was a form of freedom of speech and thought. To expect German Americans to give up the right to continue sending children to their own schools was to treat them as second-class citizens, which was an even greater insult since German-speaking parents shouldered a double financial burden by paying both for private schools and for state schools through taxes. Anarchy, which was regarded as a burgeoning threat at this time, would be the result of a failure to teach proper morals in schools. The *Echo* argued that the state had done a very poor job indeed of educating the youth of America regarding moral education, resulting in poverty, mental illness, rampant crime, and an unhealthy focus on materialism. The *Echo* contended that the ability to discern right from wrong was fundamental to self-knowledge and knowledge about the world, and thus the moral component of education was an essential one. One article, drawing on comments by Bishop Spalding of Illinois, asserted that good education could not remain good if separated from religion. Public schools educated children but did not raise them (the article emphasized the important distinction, in German, between *Unterricht erteilen* and *erziehen*). According to the paper, the connection between religion and education was so fundamental to German thought that German settlers in America often built a school as soon as they had completed a church.[71]

Such strident positions led to criticism from readers, however, making it clear that the German-speaking community in Arkansas was not of one mind regarding the role of Christian morals in education. After publishing a series of opinion pieces that had been sent in anonymously by a correspondent, the *Echo* heard from a number of readers, some of whom in Texarkana apparently even threatened to boycott the paper. In responding to the outcry, the paper argued that, while the state had an obligation to educate children, it absolutely did not have a right to a monopoly on education. It also clarified that religion did not belong in public schools, which is how some readers had interpreted the guest editorial. German speakers, according to the *Echo*, did not want to change the public-school system but did insist on the right to continue to educate their own children separately. In an article reporting on a meeting of Catholic archbishops in New York, the paper conceded that attitudes toward private religious education were changing nationally and that this battle might be lost. The archbishops admitted they would like to see every Catholic child in the United States in a Catholic school, but if that were not possible, then maybe Sunday schools or extra lessons on weekdays could be considered as a substitute. Most of all, the archbishops felt it important to remind parents that it was their duty to provide a moral education if their children were being educated in state schools.[72]

Generally, the editorial stance of the *Echo* was more focused on the national battle for religious German-language schools than on the local battle. This was perhaps because of the lamentable condition of public education in Arkansas at the time, which did not provide much of a viable alternative to the parochial system. In the 1880s and 1890s, only roughly 50 percent of children in rural areas attended classes. One editorial mocked a New York school administrator for claiming that European schools were far inferior to American ones because they were not as strong in math education and because they required one to learn ancient languages such as Latin. The editor added, "Incidentally, whoever is familiar with the circumstances of rural schools here has to admit that they are quite miserable. There is especially a dearth of competent teachers." The only other references to schools in Arkansas published by the *Echo* in 1892 were three articles, two of which were on parochial schools in the state. One discussed how allowing two nuns to teach and dividing the students by ability provided more targeted learning, and another published the curriculum of Little Rock's St. Edward's Catholic School for the upcoming academic year. One additional article referenced the administration of public schools in Arkansas and a petition put forward by the newspaper the *Paris Express*. It called for each county to have a treasurer who would locally administer the money meant for the public schools instead of sending it to Little Rock before getting it back, thereby preventing bureaucratic waste. The editors were perhaps thinking of this problem when they published a report from Louisiana on the luxurious new headquarters that the state school board had built for itself, which cost around $9,000.[73]

The *Echo*'s coverage of the national fight regarding private religious education could be summed up with the adage "politics makes strange bedfellows." The *Echo* argued for a very specific kind of parochial education—that conducted in German—since they believed that one was not possible without the other. As a result, the editors saw allies across religious, ethnic, and party lines. German Lutherans in Illinois were lauded for fighting against a law that would require them to send their children to public schools. German Lutherans in Missouri and Catholic French Canadians in New England, especially Massachusetts, were championed for the solution of agreeing to continue to pay taxes for public schools while funding their own separate religious schools. Another editorial, reprinted from the German-language newspaper *Amerika*, celebrated this interreligious cooperation against secular English-language public-school instruction: "In order to shake off this ignominious yoke, thousands of brave Lutheran heads of families have risen up. Equally as many Catholic heads of families have extended their hands to them. If they stand together, loyal and unflinching, through the wicked agitators, victory will surely not fail to appear." The author went on to say that the goal was never to bring religion into the public schools but rather to secure the right to maintain separate Catholic instruction. Lutherans would not have supported state religious schools anyway, since they knew from "bitter experience" how easily such schools could be corrupted by the state. At the same time, an unnamed Irish Catholic bishop was attacked for being in league with the Know-Nothings against German-speaking parents, as he sold Catholic school buildings to the local school district to be converted into public schools. This stance reflected a larger national trend in which German Catholic immigrants often felt more allied with Protestants who spoke their language than with fellow Catholics who were Irish.[74]

The *Echo* portrayed the Democratic Party as the organized political party that championed German-speakers' right to continue private religious education for their children in America. There was one article, however, appropriately titled "A Strange Admission," in which even Republican president Benjamin Harrison was praised. In a speech to a national assembly of teachers, he celebrated the profession but warned that educating students without morals was pointless. He recommended teaching the Ten Commandments in public schools, although the *Echo* could not resist criticizing the idea that one could teach this moral law without addressing its ultimate provenance. Harrison's statements were seen as another argument for separate schools, since the editor believed the Constitution did not allow for religious teaching in the public schools.[75]

The third major crusade of the inaugural year, against Prohibition, was tied to the support of educational rights in fundamental ways. German speakers similarly regarded Prohibition as a restriction of personal freedom afforded under natural law and the US Constitution, as citizens who had received a morally based education could exercise self-restraint in consuming alcohol. The German American press across the nation had long fought against Prohibition. The fight was driven by the conviction that Germans should be allowed to celebrate Sunday as a day of rest by engaging in music, dance, and drink, often in defiance of local customs and laws.[76] In Arkansas, Germans made arguments that were both practical and philosophical. Prohibition stood in the way of solutions to agricultural problems: specifically, the development of viniculture as a source of tax revenue for the state and as a means of crop diversification. The paper additionally championed alcohol's use in medicine. Nevertheless, the issue of Prohibition remained a major political and legal topic for the German settlers in the paper's inaugural year, and it occasionally caused trouble with their Arkansas-born neighbors.

German speakers in the state faced an uphill battle regarding the use of alcohol, as the opposition began organizing early and in numbers. The Women's Christian Temperance Union was already attempting to bring about Prohibition by 1879, and the Arkansas Prohibition Alliance was created in 1886. The prohibitionists fielded their own gubernatorial candidates from 1892 to 1906. By 1892, the prohibitionists had successfully passed a number of three-mile laws in various communities around Arkansas, forbidding the sale of alcohol within three miles of a church or school. A perhaps satirical letter from a reader in Sweet Home referenced this trend. He reported that German Catholics in the community continued to send their children to Morrison Bluff rather than establishing their own local school because they wanted to be allowed to continue wine production on their farms.[77] A letter from a reader in Conway did not find any humor in the situation and warned against the success of these piecemeal attempts to affect state-wide legislation one county at a time: "Many a German in the state perhaps thinks: 'That has nothing to do with me. Where I live, I can sell as much wine as I want to!' But I ask, 'For how much longer?' Already the next legislative session can make you liable under such a law. If someone here had said four years ago that we would no longer be allowed to sell wine, then everyone would have laughed at him."[78]

Prohibitionists were making a moral argument based in religion, namely that alcohol consumption limited or destroyed the God-given ability to think rationally. This was especially offensive to German settlers in Arkansas. They often referred to the Prohibition-minded Methodists in the state as *Mucker* (grumblers) or *Wasserapostel* (water apostles).[79] German speakers appealed to intellectual gifts provided by God in their counterarguments, noting that God gave man the knowledge of how to create alcohol, which they regarded as harmless when used in moderation. Moderate alcohol use provided a chance to exercise self-restraint, which was compared to a magnet: the more it was used, the stronger it was. Thus, Prohibition was robbing Christians of the opportunity to engage in God-given self-control over their behavior, to practice free will.[80] In a diatribe against a Nebraskan Methodist bishop named Forster, the *Echo* hinted that Prohibition was not only immoral but also un-American. Bishop Forster argued both against using foreign languages in schools and for Prohibition in one lengthy speech, which the *Echo* excerpted in the original English and in translation. The editors noted, "That's a platform that was half overheard from the Turks, and half from the Russians, since the Koran forbids the use of all alcoholic beverages and the Czar attempts to eliminate the 'foreign languages' out of his empire in favor of Russian, which alone can make one happy. Free men and free constitutions, though, are entirely unworthy of such tyrannical meddling."[81]

The *Echo* appealed to other moral arguments as well. The Prohibition movement argued that alcohol had to be forbidden for the good of society, just as a civilized society outlawed behaviors such as violent attacks.[82] German speakers countered that Prohibition was bad for democracy because it encouraged a disregard for the law. Since the discovery of how to make alcohol could not be undone, they argued, it would continue to be produced and consumed. Thus, Prohibition encouraged the average citizen to disobey the state, which in turn undermined governmental authority. They furthermore interpreted the abuse of alcohol as a peculiarly American problem. The editors contended that high taxes on alcohol instituted after the Civil War deterred citizens from imbibing mild alcohol on a daily basis and in moderation. Instead, the tax caused Americans to consume hard liquor in a binge manner as soon as they came into expendable income. Germans rejected alcoholism as a disease and maintained that the only way to combat abuse in American society was with moral education. In a bid to link the moderate use of alcohol with civilized man, they mocked Native Americans as alcoholics: "Perhaps its citizens are exactly as crude and ill-bred as the wild Indians?"[83] The final moral argument made by both the *Echo* and its readers was an appeal to personal liberty. They had been told that America was a free country where one had control over his own fate and property, liberated from the autocratic rule of petty princes. They could not fathom that these rights were now being usurped by fellow citizens who were supposed to have equal, but not greater, political power.

For many German settlers to Arkansas, the right to decide which agricultural product to produce was an explicit part of the bargain. Correspondent Geo. A. from Shoal Creek contrasted the situation in the state with that of viniculture in Texas and California, which were both spending several thousand dollars on promoting fruit-growing for wine production. In Arkansas, wine producers were punished for their efforts with three-mile laws. He concluded, "That's spitting in the soup of the personal freedom that was guaranteed to us."[84] Quite aside from the promises of individual freedom, at least one German-language pamphlet had encouraged settlement by presenting viniculture as a fait accompli. Fr. Joseph Strub, in his Arkansas immigration guide *The Guiding Star to the St. Joseph Colony*, wrote,

> The attempts which have already been undertaken in viniculture have produced the best results, and there can hardly be found another state in the union which could offer the same advantages, since the mild climate, which makes possible a growing season of nine months that is itself followed by a light, mild winter, is assuredly the most favorable to viniculture and will secure a bright future for the same in Arkansas.

The next paragraph described the wide variety of fruits that thrived in Arkansas and would also have been linked to alcohol production in the German farmer's mind, since creating a variety of wines and schnapps was established procedure for utilizing excess produce during the harvest. Being confronted with Prohibition instead of an established and flourishing wine industry was a shock that settlers were not willing to accept without a fight.[85]

German settlers wanted to develop a wine industry in the state not only for their own good, but also to improve agriculture in the state as a whole. The over-reliance on the cotton production meant that every farmer was at the mercy of poor crop yields and that even in good years farmers could not expect much profit, as over-production led to lower prices. It was clear to the German speakers that crop diversification was needed to ameliorate both the land and the financial situation of farmers. They were interested in a variety of crops, but grape-growing for wine production made the most sense to them; they saw bitter irony in their neighbors' wish to prevent them from growing that very crop. In a story on a meeting concerning cotton and possible alternatives, the editors could not resist a bit of sarcasm in reporting the suggestions: "corn, meat, hay, and breadfruits (but by no means wine!—Comment of the editor.)"[86] The editors referred to a *Prohibitionswahn* (Prohibition insanity) that prevented otherwise rational men from seeing that the best crop suited to the Arkansas climate was grapes; religious convictions not shared by the Germans stood in the way of practical business decisions. Another article regarding the Prohibition efforts in Logan County made the ironic suggestion that Germans should hack down their vineyards and plant more cotton to drive down prices even further and teach the natives a lesson.[87]

German farmers believed they had a real chance at developing a marketable product, which added to their frustration. A Collegeville correspondent noted that many Little Rock residents were prejudiced against wine produced in Arkansas simply because they had never tasted it, but he claimed those prejudices disappeared as soon as they had sampled some. He believed they could sell wine at a fair price and have many customers. At least one farmer, perhaps the correspondent himself, followed through with that advice and advertised directly to consumers through the *Echo*: C. Gansley of Collegeville offered one gallon of wine for fifty cents. The German community regularly dreamed bigger in the pages of the *Echo*, however. They believed they could eventually produce enough wine to cover the needs of the state's consumers and have some left over for export.[88]

Aside from the economic argument that viniculture could benefit the state, Germans felt there was a further case to be made for allowing the consumption of alcohol. In fact, "Dr. W.," likely regular advertiser and *Echo* cofounder Dr. Nic Weny of Little Rock, contributed a lengthy article titled "Alkohol als Medizin." The doctor began by acknowledging that consuming too much alcohol could lead to downfall. However, he argued, it was also wrong to regard it as a poison to be completely avoided. He framed the debate in terms of hysterics who viewed alcohol as the devil's work and scientists who had research on their side, as both studies and clinical observation had proven the benefits of alcohol. Dr. W. quoted a number of prominent German physicians and their specific recommendations for treatment with alcohol, and he claimed that nine out of ten eminent doctors promoted the measured consumption of alcohol for health. Included among the ailments treated with alcohol were consumption, diphtheria, respiratory infections, and weakness caused by long fevers or blood loss. The doctor praised beer for its nutritional properties and as being more widely tolerated than wine. (An old German saying is *Bier ist flüssiges Brot*—beer is liquid bread—since they share many of the same ingredients.) Two other articles commented on alcohol's utility as a treatment for indigestion, respiratory ailments, and muscle problems, again acknowledging that the key to its medical use was moderation.[89]

One argument about the necessity of wine production is strangely missing amongst all the others. In this German-language newspaper founded by Catholic businessmen, there is no mention of sacramental wine and its central role in the Mass, neither in articles penned by the editors nor in correspondence. Perhaps the Germans felt it best not to remind their Methodist and Baptist neighbors that their religious beliefs included a central tenet anathema to their Christian brethren in Arkansas, namely that of transubstantiation: that the bread and wine offered in the context of the Mass, while retaining the outward appearance of bread and wine, is converted to Jesus's body and blood to be consumed by the congregants. Protestants in the opposing camp might have turned this doctrinal belief into yet another reason to ban wine production.

German-speaking immigrants to Arkansas saw the ability to engage in viniculture as a matter of freedom, as a good agricultural practice, and as necessary for producing a basic medicine that could heal a number of maladies. They discovered, however, that it was also a divisive political issue. At the local level, candidates for public office apparently promised Germans that they would support the settlers' efforts to overturn Prohibition laws, only to go back on their promises once elected. Correspondents from Paris, Fort Smith, and Pocahontas threatened that they would not accept this betrayal. Many *Echo* readers regarded Prohibition as a central issue of the 1892 fall elections, especially since it was one that affected them directly as both businessmen and consumers. In a discussion of the William M. Fishback gubernatorial campaign, the editors stated, "We want an unambiguous explanation that he acknowledges that the product of work [grapes] belongs to the worker and that no legislation in the world has the right to prohibit him from making use of this product of his work in any way [wine]." Earlier in the same election cycle, the editors proclaimed the national Prohibition Party convention to be "a conference of fanatical cranks" and suggested they simply join the Republican Party, with whom they shared an anti-immigration platform. A cryptic, short entry regarding Arkansas news implied that German-speaking Democrats were also having problems with English-speaking prohibitionists locally, complaining that their tyrannical desire to ban alcohol was making a mockery of the party's high principles.[90]

Given the local-option approach utilized in Arkansas by prohibitionists, German speakers occasionally found themselves in legal trouble when confronted with new laws in their communities. Items published in the *Echo* during 1892 suggest that the immigrants, rather than protesting unjust legislation, simply did not understand the fine points of the new laws. An Atkins correspondent noted that two of the local German citizens (*Bürger*) were brought before the court for selling wine to minors—a foreign concept for German Catholic families, as the father usually decided when a child was mature enough to have a glass of wine. A news item reported that A. Gershner of the Palace Park establishment in Little Rock was accused of violating blue laws both by hosting a Sunday ball on the premises and by selling whiskey during the event.[91] J. L. from Conway complained that one German after another was being brought to court and being made to pay high bail; he argued that the money spent on good lawyers for judicial proceedings would be better spent if Germans would pool their money to hire the same lawyers to argue against the laws in front of the Supreme Court. Apparently, a number of *Echo* readers did not have money to hire lawyers, as the editors made a blanket statement in late November addressing reader questions about hiring agents to sell their alcohol. The paper had contacted several lawyers to ask how the laws were to be interpreted: were farmers supposed to hire only one agent to sell their wine in the entire state, or were they allowed to use different local agents in each region? The lawyers could not agree on a single interpretation, and the editors promised to investigate further and report back. An update published on December 2 apologized that the law regarding agents remained unclear. Even the prosecuting attorney refused to give an answer, since individual judges could disagree with him in their interpretations. The update ended with an admonition to farmers making wine: "Also Vorsicht" (Therefore, be careful).[92]

In addition to legal problems, German settlers' production and consumption of alcohol caused friction with native Arkansans, something long reported by historians and also reflected in the pages of the *Echo*.[93] Jonathan Wolfe uncovered evidence that at least one English-speaking paper attempted early, in 1871, to support the Germans in their assertions that celebrating with alcohol was a part of their culture, when the *Arkansas Gazette* republished a defense of Germans' relaxation on the Sabbath (drinking, singing, etc.) from a Saint Louis German paper.[94] Some twenty years later in 1892, English-speaking Arkansans had still not embraced this argument. Often, reporting on weddings in the *Echo* included a defiant note that wine and beer were consumed *nach deutscher Sitte* (according to German custom). Germans wanted to be able to celebrate in their own social circles as they saw fit, and toasting happy occasions was an integral part of the celebration. Pocahontas correspondent Severus reported that tensions between Germans and Arkansans were high and that the pro-temperance newspaper the *Randolph Herald* was printing ad hominem attacks against Germans, precisely for being German and Catholic. He noted they could "expect unjust and hateful attacks in almost every issue."[95]

Other correspondents did not seem to care when their old-world customs ruffled the feathers of native Arkansans. P. W. S., a letter writer from Morrison Bluff, reported with incredulity that there were plans to open a schnapps factory in Paris and joked, "Our water apostles [prohibitionists] are said to be absolutely going mad and fussing like gutter sparrows about the evil 'Dutchmans.'"[96] Some Germans saw the opposition to alcohol as a case of protesting too much. When a Shoal Creek writer complained that the *Englischen* [*sic*] *Wasser-Vettern und Tanten* (English water-cousins and aunts) were rampaging and demanding a stop to wine sales, the *Echo*'s setter added a line of advice, urging the Shoal Creek residents to tame the prohibitionists by giving them candy and whiskey. An editorial penned in response to the passage of a three-mile law in Logan County argued that only the leaders of the movement were serious about banning alcohol: "Individual fanatical Methodists and Baptists would admittedly exterminate alcohol out of existence, if they could. But most of their supporters are only caterwauling alongside. As soon as they can get ahold of a drop of spirits, they're in." Spottvogel, the paper's satirist, suggested that poisoning the alcohol would be the quickest way to get rid of all the prohibitionists, as a kind of de facto death sentence for their hypocritical behavior.[97]

Over the course of the inaugural year, however, the editors had a change of heart. They cautioned that the German-speaking community would be better served by attempting to win over their English-speaking neighbors than by antagonizing them. A January letter noted that some "liberal-thinking Americans" had joined the German speakers in an attempt to overturn the three-mile laws in Logan County. The paper took a more conciliatory tone after the electoral defeat of the Prohibition ticket: "It is useless to throw abusive language into the face of our fellow citizens, to call them *Mucker* and fanatics. With this [tactic], we cannot make anything better, but very much make it worse." The editorial further argued that older Arkansans all over the state fondly remembered the time before the Civil War, when it was possible for farmers to use excess produce to brew alcohol. In December, the *Echo* expanded this agricultural argument, noting that even English-speaking farmers were looking for a new crop, and vineyards would be a viable alternative to cotton. The *Echo* urged its readers to attempt to win over their fellow citizens and stated that it was not enough in the long term to defeat existing three-mile laws.[98]

This was not empty talk. German settlers believed early on that it was incumbent on them to change the Prohibition climate in Arkansas. Several letter writers noted that German farmers had previously failed to fight for viniculture through the legislature because they had not been united. There was a discussion about local attempts to band together tavern owners, elected officials, and other interested parties, perhaps a reference to the formation of the Arkansas Protective Liquor Association formed in June 1892 by tavern owners and liquor dealers in Little Rock. In 1892 German speakers launched a remarkable campaign to organize against Prohibition in earnest by drafting their own state legislation to fight three-mile laws. The *Echo* recorded the progress of their efforts, as the farmers moved from idea to draft to legal language to understanding the intricacies of the legal process and collecting signatures. It was a case study in American democracy in action for the immigrants.[99]

The idea for statewide legislation came from the *Obst- und Weinzüchterverein* (Fruit Growers and Wine Producers' Association), under the direction of the organization's president, John Hubmann. The petition argued crop diversification and economic growth as reasons for legalizing wine sales, though it also made a more subdued appeal to liberty and freedom. The paper explained that the petition would have to be introduced in both chambers of the legislature, and so Germans should sign both the Senate and House versions. The *Echo* printed an English version of the petition in full, as it was the version to be presented to the lawmakers and to allow German speakers to solicit signatures from their English-speaking allies.[100]

The editors cautioned readers not to believe that ending the three- and five-mile laws in the state would be easily accomplished. They noted that many of the American religious "sects" were fervently opposed and admitted that past alcohol abuse by some state residents posed a legitimate problem. But they felt the agricultural argument was a strong one and were optimistic that at least wine sales would be allowed. The editors felt an obligation to lead efforts both to affect change in the democracy of their new home and to unite the German speakers behind a common cause. They noted that the issue was particularly important to the *Echo* for two reasons:

> The *Echo* is known and respected in the most influential circles of the future Democratic government and legislature for its resolute advocacy of the cause of democracy. And because the editorial staff consists of men who are themselves farmers, who have a keen interest in viniculture, the *Echo* can feel itself called to offer its services for the facilitation and distribution of a wine petition to the organizations of Arkansas.[101]

In the last editorial of the year, the editors promised that they would keep reporting on the *Weinfrage* (the wine issue). In an 1894 pamphlet written to encourage increased German immigration, editor Carl Meurer referred to the battle against local Prohibition laws as ongoing and to the community's hopes for their success in overturning them.[102] The German settlers would ultimately fail in these efforts, however, and statewide Prohibition was enacted in 1916. It is telling that Ben F. Johnson III's *John Barleycorn Must Die: The War Against Drink in Arkansas* includes not even a passing mention of the German efforts at combating early local option laws. They were perhaps considered heroic attempts within the community but went unnoticed in the larger English-speaking culture. But the German immigrants were ultimately triumphant in the matter. A January editorial on Prohibition noted that the alcohol genie could not be put back in the bottle, and today the descendants of German immigrants still produce wine in Arkansas, whether in the successful commercial operation of the Post Familie Winery at Altus or at home for private consumption. In 1892 the struggle against Prohibition provided a unifying cause for German speakers in Arkansas and gave the newspaper a noble cause to advocate for on behalf of its readers.[103]

These crusades were not unique to German-speaking settlers in Arkansas. German immigrants across the United States regularly fought for the opportunity of continued immigration, the ability to teach their children German in school, and the right to produce alcohol; a national lobbying group of German immigrants founded in 1900 made these three topics its cornerstone issues and grew its membership to three million like-minded countrymen by 1916.[104] In Arkansas, these three issues helped to forge a unified ethnic identity among German speakers; immigrants understood the causes as core to their Germanness, and they were under attack. In March, the *Echo* reprinted an editorial on the question of German schools from a Lutheran German paper in Chicago, which alluded to the process of crafting common interests among immigrants: "It is pleasing and encouraging that, in spite of the notorious disunity among us Germans (who generally have three opinions when two counsel one another about a matter), one finds the most beautiful unity everywhere regarding the school issue." Judging by the *Echo*'s efforts, the founders of the newspaper believed they had a crucial role to play in uniting the settlers behind a common cause.[105]

CHAPTER 3

# Strengthening the Bond

## *Connections and Interactions within the German Immigrant Community*

BY THE 1890s, the German community in Arkansas was moving past the early days in which individual families established themselves and survived from year to year. *Das Arkansas Echo* leaves behind a solid record of the Germans' development as a group, of how they interacted with each other, and of the topics that were most important to them as a community. The newspaper provided a virtual space in which the settlers could interact, but it additionally contains much evidence about how the German settlers gathered together physically, in statewide festivities and in smaller groups and clubs dedicated to a specific purpose or interest. The *Echo* addressed the smallest unit of the German community as well, the individual family. In numerous ways, it is evident that the German diasporic community had successfully established a core identity by 1892 and that the settlers relied on one another economically and socially.

Before examining the German community at the state level, it is important to take note of a national trend among German Americans that either did not exist among the settlers in Arkansas or had already resolved itself by the time of the *Echo*'s founding. Within the span of the nineteenth century, German speakers came in several waves to the United States. An 1848 attempt to establish a more democratic form of government in the German-speaking regions of what would eventually become modern Germany failed, and a large number of would-be German democrats fled to America. They tended to be well educated and politically active. Many had careers in the press before emigrating, and they settled in urban areas that allowed them to continue in these jobs or similar work. The countrymen they found in their new homeland, who had arrived in America prior to the failed revolution, tended to come from the lower classes of German-speaking society. Economic reasons had motivated their migration, and they had focused on establishing farms as a first priority, rather than sharing the post-1848 immigrants' view that maintaining German language and culture should be of paramount importance. The two groups became known as *die Grauen* (the Grays) and *die Grünen* (the Greens). The Grays had lived in the United States for decades prior to the arrival of the Greens. The Greens greatly criticized the Grays for being more interested in their own economic well-being than in shaping the future of the country politically. The advent of the Civil War largely put an end to the discord between these two groups, with most Germans throughout the United States supporting an end to slavery. German settlers who arrived after the Civil War were similarly interested in migration for economic rather than political reasons, but they also were generally better educated than the first wave of immigrants.[1]

This diffusion of tension between different waves of immigrants is also seen in the *Echo*. The paper occasionally remarked that some Germans were known in the community for being among the first German speakers to settle in Arkansas, but these mentions always reflected a reverential tone for the elders in the community. The editors did not seem keen to alienate more established immigrants who might be potential subscribers. The 1892 issues of the *Echo* additionally do not bear record of any significant class differences among readers or of class envy within the local German community, no matter how much the editor railed against the larger forces of capitalism at work in the country. Nor is there evidence of tensions between rural and urban populations in a state in which some farmers had begun to become dissatisfied with their lots by the mid-1880s.[2] The sole example of discord within the Arkansas German community in 1892 occurred between the competing German newspapers, *Das Echo* and *Die Staatszeitung*. Over the course of the year, this conflict became a real sore spot in the community, with some readers of each newspaper postulating that the rival editor was causing trouble simply to attack a competing business. The *Echo* certainly reinforced this sentiment in editorial comments: "Divide et impera, divide and conquer, that is the rule through the clever use of which first the Romans and later the French attempted to rule the Germans through their discord. That's how a certain newspaperman, who is ever intent on creating dissension among the Germans, still does it today. . . . In this way he has made it to a pasha."[3] Other historical evidence indicates that the *Echo* and its largely Catholic readership sought to protect this unity because it had to be created in the first place. German Catholics did benefit from a geographic unity in some regions because of religious settlements such as the Holy Ghost Fathers and Benedictines in Subiaco and also because they were living together on railroad lands with neighboring plots. But Jonathan Wolfe notes that German speakers populating these areas had joined their communities through individual immigration, rather than through organized groups, as some Lutheran settlers to Arkansas had done.[4]

This chapter begins its discussion of the ways German settlers relied on each other economically and socially with what might seem an unlikely topic: agriculture, which was a major focus of the paper in its inaugural year. After all, Wolfe argues that economic imperatives compelled the newcomers to integrate with the existing structures of the state: "The immigrants did not exist within the state as a community divorced from the native Arkansans. . . . In business and farming it would have been futile to attempt to hold oneself aloof. . . . The immigrant needed the business community, and it needed his labor."[5] Farming reinforced the group dynamic among the German speakers in a number of ways. First, this occupation allowed some settlers to live in German enclaves on a day-to-day basis, with minimal requirements to interact with English-speaking Arkansans. During an 1881 drought, native Arkansans in fact shunned the German farmers entirely and left the newcomers to solve the problem of a lack of rain on their own.[6] Second, German speakers took their own counsel when it came to farming and considered themselves superior to their American neighbors in agricultural matters. Third, their refusal to accept cotton as the status-quo primary cash crop put them at odds with how things had always been done, and their adamant belief that diversification was necessary resulted in further bonding among the German community. Finally, their common pursuit of viniculture as a viable alternative to cotton production placed them in conflict with religious groups in the state who were working toward Prohibition, resulting in an us-versus-them dynamic. Overall, they viewed their agricultural efforts as successful precisely because they were *German* farmers using *German* techniques, and they understood themselves to be better than their American counterparts. The narrative of farming success that circulated among German settlers during 1892 indicates that they had rebounded from earlier losses. Their perception was that they were doing well and had it in their power to become even more successful due to German ingenuity.

But the German American community's early failures in farming had been significant. In addition to contending with the drought in 1881, settlers still did not know what agricultural products would be suited to the new climate and soil they encountered. Approximately half of the German farmers made the decision to leave the state after this drought. Wolfe claims that the situation was so extreme in immigrant communities that some saw death by illness as a welcome reprieve; others committed suicide.[7] Those who managed to continue to eke out a living in this lean period would find a ready ally in editor Carl Meurer. In his monograph on community newspapers, Michael Dougan describes most small-town editors as "good at book farming."[8] But Meurer had some practical experience in farming, as he had moved with his brother and two sisters to a 120-acre farm outside Little Rock in the drought year of 1881. The family cleared land, built a house and a barn, planted crops, and sold farm products such as eggs, milk, and butter. Yet Meurer also reflects the archetype of the German American "Latin farmer" who had enjoyed a broad classical education but had not farmed as a primary occupation before immigrating. Like most "Latin farmers," the editor quickly decided that he was better suited to urban life and left the farming to his brother.[9] He did refer to other staff members as being farmers, and the *Echo* followed in a long tradition in the German American press, dating back to the colonial era, of giving practical advice on crop cultivation and animal husbandry.[10]

It is not surprising that the *Echo*'s inaugural year conveys German settlers' keen interest in agriculture, as the promise of affordable land available through the railroads is what brought many of them to Arkansas in the first place. Circumstances in Germany would have encouraged prospective farmers to consider settling in America for economic and political reasons. But the occupation of farming carried deep cultural meaning as well for German Americans. Dating back to the American colonial period, German farmers understood their lifestyle to be a fulfillment of God's ultimate plan for them to live in freedom, be masters of their own property, and determine for themselves what crops to grow and livestock to raise. Early German American broadsides espoused "farming as the most important and honorable estate of society; the farmer produced the food that sustained mankind, and without the products of his sweat mankind could not subsist. Thus he, more than any other class of men, fulfilled the command that God had given Adam and Eve: go out and till the soil."[11] Farming in America would enable the German to enjoy the fruits of his labor himself; he would not have to work for a property owner or nobleman.

As indicated above, the *Echo*'s inaugural year provides evidence of German settlers' belief that their agricultural knowledge was superior to that of the native population. A February editorial charged that American farmers did nothing to replenish the soil's nutrients; they merely rotated crops between cotton and corn without considering that this technique would deplete all the nutrients in the soil within thirty years. The writer predicted that a reckoning for this type of irresponsible farming would come when the land became infertile. At that point, he predicted Americans would have to flee back to the *Urwald* (the forest in its natural state), while Germans would be cozily enjoying the fruits of their labors on the homesteads they had created. German farmer's only concern was not to acquire more land than he could cultivate using the proper traditional German methods.[12]

German and American farmers nevertheless did interact in Arkansas. For example, an announcement in German of the yearly meeting of the "Horticultural Society" to be held in January in Little Rock proclaimed that all were welcome. One assumes that Germans would be welcome only as long as they understood English, since the names of the sessions also were reported in the *Gazette* and the titles, such as "Irrigation and Drainage for Small Fruits," were all in English.[13]

Immigration stories are often framed in terms of a push-and-pull narrative, and the American South in the period of Reconstruction provided a strong pull for new settlers who wished to try their farming skills. Southern states needed agricultural workers after the loss of life in the Civil War and the abolition of slavery. Arkansas was no different. In 1872 the Patrons of Husbandry viewed the recruitment of new immigrants as a necessary step to bringing the unsown fields around the state back into production.[14] Arkansas did prove unusual in its draw because of the availability of railroad lands at reasonable terms, a circumstance that Jonathan Wolfe describes as more indicative of the American West than the South.[15] German settlers to Arkansas benefited from the fact that both the Catholic bishop of Arkansas and the Holy Ghost Fathers actively advertised this affordable land widely to the immigrants they hoped to attract. The special attempt to educate immigrants on how to purchase land is reflected in a complaint made by an 1893 black correspondent of *The Freeman* from Crawfordsville that "since 'no one taught [the Negro] to purchase lands, he did not do so.'"[16] German American immigrants were able to benefit from land acquisition in a way that many contemporary black farmers likely were not.[17] A letter to the *Echo* from Atkins additionally indicated that Germans preferred ownership to leasing lands from other large-estate owners, whom they mistrusted: "Lots of bottomland will lie fallow this year. No one wants to lease it, despite the fact that the land barons are offering it at such liberal terms as never before."[18]

By 1892 the majority of German settlers who were to come to Arkansas had already established themselves, but both the *Echo* and the railroads perceived immigration as an ongoing trend, in spite of the growing obstacles to new settlers. A consortium represented by G. A. A. Deane, land commissioner in Little Rock, and comprised of the Saint Louis, Iron Mountain & Southern, and Little Rock & Fort Smith Railroads was a regular advertiser in the *Echo* with this copy: "Railroad lands. Farms and homesteads in Arkansas. Two million acres for farming, meadows and fruit trees, forest and mineral land. Sold in pieces according to the wish of the buyer. Mild climate . . . manifold products. Low prices—moderate interest—easy payment schedule. Cards and circulars free."[19] In a May editorial, the *Echo* attempted to set the record straight regarding ways in which immigrants could obtain land. The paper noted that while calendars and books were still advising newcomers to take advantage of the *Vorkaufsgesetz* (preemption law) of 1830 and 1840, as well as forestry acts, these were no longer available. With some satisfaction, the *Echo* reported that Know-Nothings were not able to shut German settlers out of the homesteading act by implementing a lengthy residency requirement. Those who declared their intention to become American citizens could still obtain 80 to 160 acres in this way. Lastly, the paper considered land purchases direct from railroads to be the most preferable option: "This last method of land acquisition has the advantage that one is to some extent certain of his neighbors, while a German who occupies federal land elsewhere occasionally discovers later that he is surrounded by Negroes and nativist squatters."[20]

German farmers in Arkansas had access to better conditions for land purchase than many other farmers in the state who were suffering from anaconda mortgages, which will be discussed below. The railroads allowed a payment system if at least a quarter of the price was given in a down payment, and they had up to six years to pay off the loan. Most settlers could obtain the farmland itself without too much economic difficulty, but the down payment left few resources for the outlays required to establish a successful farm, such as the expenses of equipment, livestock, and seed. Thus, many German farmers in Arkansas found themselves in debt initially. In order to pay off their debts more quickly, some immigrants supplemented income from their farms by working as day laborers for other established farmers or by selling their garden vegetables. Jonathan Wolfe explains, "Even with a considerable debt to overcome, it was the usual thing for the immigrants to be out of debt after five or six years."[21] This bootstrap mentality appears in a pro-immigration pamphlet, written by Carl Meurer and published independently of the *Echo*, that mentioned the practice of selling surplus produce in nearby cities. In describing the success of a couple who immigrated to Little Rock with no financial resources, Meurer noted that the couple worked hard to save enough money to buy a farm and then clear the land: "The first year was certainly not a bed of roses. But today they have a beautiful, debt-free farm and are prosperous."[22]

While some German farmers acquired land directly from railroads, the *Echo* additionally records a secondary real-estate market for established farms among the settlers. These ads (listed in their entirety and in translation in appendix 2) frequently mentioned the amount of land available and whether any of the property was forested, the quality of the soil, the presence of wells, and how much of the land was fenced. They described buildings such as homes, barns, and stables that had been constructed, as well as plantings of vineyards and orchards. The distances to the nearest church and school were given. In one instance, the advertising farmer was also willing to sell equipment and livestock to the next owner. Other ads reveal that land holders were open to leasing the land or even bartering work on the land in lieu of payment. After one successful sale, the *Echo* published a rare legal notice in English, perhaps to assure the new owner that the German-speaking community was aware of his recent purchase from a German farmer: "Publication. To whom it may concern. Notice is hereby given, that the property on my former farm in Shoal Creek, Logan Co., now is in possession of Arthur Miles, is mortgaget [*sic*]. To-wit: 2 mules, one bay mare, 4 cows and young cattle, molasses mill and pan, one farm wagon and one spring wagon. Wm. Kuckartz."[23] Generally, the practice of advertising existing farms in the *Echo* allowed German farmers to find fellow German-speaking tenants or owners to replace themselves without introducing a perhaps-unwelcome element in the tight-knit rural community, thereby preserving linguistic continuity (Hermann Wellenreuther advances this theory in his examination of German American broadsides during the colonial period).[24]

German-speaking farming communities in neighboring states were in contact and could be regarded as one intended audience for these ads. As noted in chapter 2, a Benedictine priest from Missouri published a letter in the *Echo* intended to draw more immigrants to his own town, and the migration could naturally flow in either direction.[25] The *Echo*'s frequent satirist, Spottvogel, highlighted a friendly rivalry with German farmers in this neighboring state when he discussed an article he read in the Missouri German-language newspaper *Der Hausfreund* (The friend of the family) about how bad the soil allegedly was in Arkansas. He crowed that local farmers had already farmed red soil for twenty years with good results and proclaimed the soil to be miraculously productive with the use of a little fertilizer. He further noted the *Hausfreund*'s complaint that Missouri was getting no rain. Since there had been plenty of rain in Arkansas in recent weeks, Spottvogel suggested the *Hausfreund* should come to Arkansas and let himself get rained on.[26]

The *Echo* reported generally positive experiences of German American farmers in acquiring land in Arkansas. But the editors were certainly aware of the enormous problem presented by anaconda mortgages. These mortgages required farmers to promise revenue from future crops to obtain on credit supplies needed in the short term, such as seed—the supplies were exorbitantly priced. These costs typically could not be covered once the harvest was sold, thus putting the farmers further into debt each year. The landholders could additionally demand that farmers with anaconda mortgages grow cotton, a widespread cash crop, the overproduction of which led to falling prices. The *Echo* published an editorial decrying these mortgages, in response to a letter from L. Altheimer to the editor of the *Arkansas Gazette*. The *Echo*'s editors agreed with Altheimer that, while repealing the mortgage law would cause difficulties for one or two years, the situation would then greatly improve, as farmers could become independent and diversify their crops. As farmers gained financial stability, they would in turn pay shopkeepers with immediate cash in exchange for their wares, which would improve the overall financial situation of the state as a whole. Aside from these pragmatic arguments, the editors viewed anaconda mortgages as a moral issue and described the situation in emotional language, accusing the cotton wholesalers of holding farmers *bei der Kehle* (by the throat) and stating, "Across the whole country, at every intersection, are stores, I mean traps, that suck the lifeblood out of the unsuspecting farmworker." The editorial further argued that the current state of agriculture differed from the customs of the early years of Reconstruction: "Without a doubt, some readers will still remember what a splendid business was done in the fall of 1868, when after the disastrous harvest of 1867 no merchant was in the position to give credit to any farmer, who nevertheless cultivated a rich harvest."[27]

In another editorial, the paper discussed proposed solutions to the problem of farmer debt. The editors, who overall were circumspect regarding capitalism and supported workers' rights, also viewed the existing agricultural economic situation critically. The editorial noted proposals to institute a 2 percent national loan rate, but the writer felt it was unsustainable. He did believe a reduction of the rate from 10 to 5 percent should be achievable. Again, the paper framed the strategy in both moral and economic terms: "The capitalist who loans money to the farmer at 10 percent knows very well himself that this interest of 10 percent does not stand in a just relationship to the work and trouble of the farmer and to its yield. He knows that the farmer gets deeper into debt with it and loses his property. No farmer can swing 10 percent out of his enterprise."[28] The *Echo* editors offered a possible solution from Germany and described a system in Prussia of small regional savings-and-loans banks run with public funds. Those in the community decided who received the funds, so they knew who was reliable and could be trusted to repay. Although Germany had a national borrowing rate of 5 percent, the editors asserted that these institutions were able to make money available at an even lower rate, usually around 3.5 to 4 percent. The editorial noted that there were many more private banks in Germany, which made it easier for farmers in the Rhineland, Westphalia, or Trier to get the money they needed without paying usurious rates. Germans felt they knew viable solutions, brought from Germany, to the question of restructuring of the agricultural-economic system in the United States. But this would be one of many cases in which they felt unheard by English-speaking Arkansans.

German farmers' biggest criticism of Arkansas agriculture was an over-reliance on cotton as a cash crop, and it was a fault in the system that they actively sought to change. They were not the only ones in the state to realize that cotton was a problem. In 1884, the Brothers lodges organization, a group attempting to unify farmers in matters of self-interest, was also advocating that farmers increase crop diversification and plant crops for their own use, rather than producing the cotton that fed into the corporate agricultural system that benefited large landholders and cotton wholesalers. Carl Moneyhon estimates that by 1889 "almost 45 percent of all harvested acres" in the state were used for cotton production. Additionally, railroads were proponents of crop diversification, as low cotton prices also negatively impacted their business; for instance, the Iron Mountain Railroad encouraged the planting of fruit trees in the 1890s.[29] The *Arkansas Gazette* published numerous articles in 1892 on the need to reduce the reliance on cotton. Although others were aware of the cotton dilemma, German readers of the *Echo* seemed to believe that they were the only ones with the resolve to implement solutions. They did not acknowledge that native farmers might be interested in diversification but lack the resources to plant any crop except the cotton demanded by their creditors.[30] Instead, the general impression was that American farmers were fundamentally deficient due to a lack of agricultural education. A February editorial contrasted German agricultural methods with those employed in their new country:

> Also the farmers who immigrated from Germany or Switzerland twelve or fourteen years ago to Arkansas have brought with them the intelligence and competence tried and tested in the homeland. Many of these same ones come from wine regions and understand viniculture, which would be the most profitable crop here, if this same crop were not prevented by Prohibition. The farmers in Arkansas have to contend with unusual difficulties, against which it is difficult to advance. Many a brave German family was submitted here to great privations while working hard and came into debt through it. But nevertheless it is not to be doubted that here the Germans will overcome all difficulties.[31]

The editorial further explained that crop rotation had been practiced in Germany since the ninth century. But the paper was not as critical of American farmers in general as it was of fellow southern farmers: "On the other hand, we also do not want to do our American farming colleagues an injustice. In the northern states there are already many farmers in high crops and the agricultural department of the government in Washington is bustling and successfully endeavoring to promote progress."[32] A June editorial, though, did not distinguish between southern and northern farmers, declaring all American farmers not up to the task of implementing diversification: "A trained farmer is necessary to raise a diverse harvest, one who does not simply live for the day, but rather who knows how to divide his time and his land. And the average American is not yet able to do that today."[33]

In countless editorials and letters to the editor, Germans portrayed themselves as battling the Goliath of big cotton on their own. They considered the cotton issue to be more than a crop problem; many felt that the crisis was exacerbated by large farms in southern Arkansas that benefited from exploiting black labor, much as had been done before slavery was abolished. On January 8 and 9, 1892, an agricultural meeting was held in Memphis that included many high-ranking delegates from Arkansas, among them the governor and agricultural commissioner. The group encouraged less cotton production, more planting of other crops, and entreated buyers and bankers to help in the enterprise of changing the nature of agriculture. While Germans advocated for all of these measures, an editorial the following week argued that the resolutions of the Memphis meeting would largely come to naught, due to the plantation system in place in south Arkansas: "These large plantations, which even now only afford a few thousand Negroes a meager life, would become, if parceled, the highlight of the state in the hands of German settlers. However, as long as they are used for cotton production, the overproduction cannot be regulated." The editorial ended by questioning why these great men did not instead focus on repealing laws which would enable the establishment of viniculture. A letter from P. W. S. in Morrison Bluff the following week agreed with the editorial that large plantations, rather than small farmers, caused cotton overproduction.[34]

German-speaking farmers could do little about large-scale cotton production in south Arkansas in 1892. But small producers still discussed making voluntary efforts to plant less of this cash crop, reasoning that fewer cotton bales in the state would lead to higher prices for local farmers. There were so few German farmers among the total farming population that this minor reduction would have made a minimal difference, especially in the context of the global cotton market's influence on prices. The *Echo* kept readers informed about the global market and regularly reported on international prices, surpluses, and the status of the growing crop in other countries, such as India. Despite plans to reduce cotton planting and promises to do so, many farmers were less than honest about their actual practices; if every other farmer planted less and the price sank, those who surreptitiously planted more would benefit from the better prices and also have more salable product. In reporting on an *Arkansas Democrat* article urging farmers to voluntarily plant less cotton, the *Echo* reflected the farmers' own cynicism: "(Leichter gesagt als getan! Anm. d. Red.)" (Easier said than done! Comment of the editor).[35] One farmer urged Germans to plant both cotton and other crops.

> My dear farmer brothers! Leave speculating to the capitalists. Plant corn, cotton, wheat, etc. Be confident, one will always need clothes and bread. If you have more corn than you need and can't sell it well, then give it to your cows, chickens, and pigs. Then you will get more milk, butter, eggs, bacon, and good pork. Be assured that the storekeepers will look around to see where they can sell the farm products.[36]

The editors again could not resist adding a comment: wheat, they observed, grew well in states like Illinois but would probably fail in Arkansas's semi-tropical climate. Elsewhere in the paper, Conway correspondent J. L. remarked on another problem with cotton besides market prices—the demanding nature of the crop. He urged German farmers to believe

Southerners who referred to cotton as a thirteen-month crop; some farmers were still picking cotton in March, when the traditional month for harvesting and ginning was January, with a new crop going into the ground in April.[37]

Germans in the state of Arkansas were carrying on in the tradition of German American farmers dating back to the colonial period who regularly practiced crop rotation.[38] If the German farmers wanted to move away from cotton, the question was what alternative crop to plant. Some native Arkansan farmers attempted to move to corn production.[39] Overwhelmingly, though, the *Echo*'s readers' answer to the need for diversification was viniculture. Germans realized that a crusade against Prohibition was a needed first step if wine production was to establish itself in the state, as was discussed in chapter 2. Yet many articles and letters to the editor treat as an inevitability the political necessity of winning over the native Arkansans to the benefits of converting cotton fields to vineyards, and so they carried forth with specific instructions on how to establish vineyards and produce wine.

Early on, the *Echo* staff realized that not all German-speaking immigrants came from wine-producing parts of Europe. In light of that, a February editorial argued that getting started in viniculture should be easy enough. The paper assured readers that even if they had never raised grapes before, they could procure a sound book on the subject and teach themselves. The *Echo* urged them to experiment, since experience was the best teacher, and also recommended asking neighbors who had already established vineyards about their best practices. Farmers were told to start with 500 to 1000 vines, planted in long rows to allow plow access, and that vines should not be farther than six feet apart.[40] The newspaper also helpfully directed readers to Mr. Ignatz Fritz, a farmer living four miles outside of Paris, who had 1,500 grapevines for sale, should readers decide to take the proffered advice and switch to viniculture immediately.[41]

The *Echo* was eager to contribute to the education of would-be German grape farmers by publishing a lengthy series written by Charles Frings. These articles, which ran over six issues in February and March, began with a historical perspective on wines, noting Roman storage methods as outlined by Plinius and Dioscorides,[42] and moving through wine production in the seventeenth century. Then, shifting from a historical to a scientific perspective, Frings gave a basic overview of the processes involved in creating wine, offering a detailed account of all the stages of wine, how microbes eat the sugar provided by the grapes, and what role heating and cooling play. He noted that German wines were rarely considered drinkable before they had aged for at least three years, unless the grapes happened to have an incredible amount of sugar in them. In their new homeland, aging time presented a less significant barrier in moving the product to market: "With American wines, however, the adage 'time is money' prevails!"[43] In subsequent installments, Frings went into great technical detail about the individual components of the process, utilizing a variety of specific cultivars and other fruits, and the peculiarities of wine production in America.[44] The *Echo* supplemented Frings's advice by providing exact recipes throughout the year for some of these non-grape wine varieties, including gooseberries, blueberries, and rhubarb.[45]

The *Echo* further encouraged German farmers to become winemakers by featuring successes in the field. Three separate farmers—Mr. Hoffmann of Avilla, Mr. Lenggenhager of Collegeville, and Mr. Bohn of Bryant were mentioned because they made a visit to the *Echo* office in Little Rock to discuss wine production. The paper praised the first two German speakers for abandoning cotton to instead plant wheat and produce wine; Mr. Hoffmann noted that he had already made an experimental foray into the market by producing fifteen barrels the previous year, most of which were already sold by March. Mr. Lenggenhager was new to Arkansas but had the impression that most Germans were not going to plant cotton in the upcoming season, so he would also concentrate on wheat and wine. And Mr. Bohn brought a sample of his wine, which the staff deemed excellent. The paper noted that Germans should bring only the best wine of this sort to market so that Arkansas developed a good reputation for wine; wine of lesser quality could be reserved for home use. For farmers unwilling or unable to sell wine on their property due to three-mile laws, the editor recommended a specific agent of his acquaintance in Little Rock who could sell wine by commission.[46]

In May, an anonymous reader suggestion from Logan County called for some sort of quality control to be established for the fledgling viniculture scene, especially if the farmers hoped to develop an industry that could export beyond the boundaries of the state. The reader suggested that a group with experience in wine production should get together and create a set of rules that would then be published, giving other experts a chance to weigh in and perhaps expand them. Then, there should be a meeting to ratify the wine statutes of all of those who were interested, who would sign them and agree to abide by them. The group could print common wine labels that would serve as a kind of guarantee that whoever produced the wine was abiding by the common statutes. The pages of the *Echo* leave no indication whether this idea found resonance within the German community, and it was not mentioned again in 1892.[47]

The heart of the German community's obsession with viniculture was a firm belief that it could supply a successful alternative model to cotton. Grapes were not, however, the only crop that German-speaking farmers considered, and the *Echo* was an enthusiastic supporter of experimentation. Alternate crops earning mentions included spring barley, wheat, ramie, buckwheat, sorghum, corn, oats, sugar cane, and sweet potatoes. Some of these crops were being grown as feed for animals, either for the farmer's own use or for commercial production.[48] Tobacco was seen as a possible alternative if enough Germans planted it in concert to yield a crop large enough to create a market. Again, the *Echo* offered a farmer from its own community as a forerunner in this experimentation: Mr. Wiermann of Alexander, who reported that he had experience with tobacco being a good cash crop. The newspaper helpfully relayed Mr. Wiermann's very specific planting instructions. It noted that Commissioner Locke of the agricultural department had offered to procure tobacco seeds for any farmer who wanted to try it. The crop was reputed to sell for a high price, and the paper dared to dream that Arkansas could someday rival Virginia in production.[49]

One important alternative crop successfully developed by immigrants, discussed by both Felton Freeman and Simone Schede, was rice. Both scholars place its widespread adoption later in Arkansas history, around 1905–20. Henry W. Young, the son of Germans who immigrated to Arkansas in 1901, described how his family originally farmed oats for livestock feed but then converted to rice production around 1910–12. But the *Echo* shows that immigrants were already considering rice as a crop in 1892.[50] From October to December, as farmers contemplated what had worked and what they should try next, the *Echo* highlighted rice cultivation in a series of articles. It began by mentioning a German farmer, W. Lori, on the outskirts of Little Rock who had heard from "older settlers and Negroes" that rice had once been grown as a crop in the area. The paper printed his exact planting instructions, and further informed readers that there were two types of rice: a water crop that required irrigation, and a mountain crop that had more nutritional value. This initial article stirred interest, and in a follow-up, the *Echo* reported that Mr. Lori would be willing to sell rice plants to others curious to try it. A reader complained that the article had given too positive a view of rice, since farmers had no way to get it cleaned and hulled. The editor responded that lots of rice used to be grown in the state and gave a method for hulling. In December, the *Echo* followed up by publishing the article "Ein Aparat [*sic*] zum Enthülsen von Reis" (An apparatus to hull rice), which included a rough drawing, so that every interested farmer could build his own device. The article stated that it made rice-hulling easy enough for even a boy to do.[51]

To aid experimentation, the *Echo* eagerly reported on conditions around the state and on national and international developments in agriculture. Correspondents contributed updates on local conditions. N. from Spielerville wrote in June that garden vegetables were generally thriving; corn and cotton, which had been a little behind, were catching up in the warmer weather. He noted that some vintners in the area were worried about grapevines, but N. was optimistic about the plants. Similar reports followed from Charleston and Pocahontas. Severus from Pocahontas attributed agricultural good news to the German virtue of industriousness: "And indeed, our German farmers here are all without exception entrepreneurial and active people, who do not know idleness and never slothfully place their hands in their laps. Pray and work, God helps always, that is their principle, and it is worth money."[52]

In July, the editors stepped in with a general report on the state, noting that some areas had gotten too much rain and other areas too little. The cotton harvest was reported to be about two weeks late in development and thus not looking particularly good. Wheat had already been cut, and oats were in the process of being cut and had yielded a better harvest in some places. Fruit crops were reported as being extremely rare for the year—even tomatoes. Bee-keeping had also not yielded much. The editors predicted that the harvest overall would be *eine mittelgute* (a mid-good or decent one). In August, the agriculture commissioner's report provided more concrete figures regarding the harvest. Wheat and oats were said to be good, corn average, and cotton only at 75 percent of its potential harvest.[53]

Cotton dominated the rest of crop reporting for 1892. In mid-September, the *Echo* noted that Texas had a larger harvest, but Arkansas was close to its production and had better-quality cotton, judging by the first bales sold in Little Rock the previous week. By the end of September, there was a decidedly less optimistic tone. The *Echo* stated that everyone had planted more cotton than last year, in spite of promising to plant less. Then, two floods washed two separate crops away. Throughout the fall, the *Echo* alerted readers to the price of cotton, giving prices in various Arkansas cities and noting that the price was rising and advising readers to consider holding on to their harvests before selling. It provided readers with cotton-crop data for Texas, Missouri, Virginia, Kentucky, Kansas, and the

Oklahoma territory. In early December, it reported that the price of cotton had fallen by three-eighths of a cent. The *Echo* believed this decline to be evidence that speculators were at work, since it in no way reflected supply and demand. Reports from Malvern and Poplar Bluff alleged that cotton was only bringing in a third of the price of the crop in the previous year. By mid-December, it was said that many farmers were holding on to their cotton, awaiting higher prices. Shortly before Christmas, the paper reported that most cotton had been picked, prices were steady, and the city of Paris had done well. That issue also brought hopeful news that India's disastrous cotton harvest, due to lack of rain, was expected to lead to higher cotton prices in the United States. Earlier in the year, the paper had been similarly optimistic regarding world trade developments: the proposed Nicaragua canal would hopefully help Arkansas farmers, since it would facilitate cotton exports to Japan, a market which—it was claimed—preferred American cotton to Indian cotton.[54]

The *Echo* was additionally interested in news of technological and research advances in agriculture at national and international levels. One story reported on successful irrigation methods developed in the American West, and a report from Memphis told of a man who had purportedly developed a machine to harvest cotton. Initial research on growing crops with electricized soil had solid results. An agricultural research station in Ohio shared information about the best wheat cultivars. Experiments in South Carolina with planting tea had been successful. And the *Echo* shared information on French experiments using Chinese ramie in various products, including as fibers in monetary bills.[55]

Animal husbandry was another agricultural option that German farmers considered at the time. Atkins correspondent P. R. reported: "Many of our farmers are going into raising chickens with full force. A local firm exported eggs and chickens last year in the amount of $1,000, and it says that this year it wants to send out three times as much."[56] In one amused note, the newspaper reported that a long-time tavern keeper, John Drees, was passing on his establishment to fellow German W. Haibach, in order to go back to his real love, raising chickens: "He lives eight miles west of the city and is thoroughly happy and confident of his success."[57] Reports on hog farming were mixed. First, a note reprinted from the *Texarkana Democrat* proclaimed that farmers who raised hominy and hogs would be among the most well-off in 1893 and ended with an encouragement to readers to try it. Farmers might have been put off by three further news items, though, one of which reported on an incident near Poplar Bluff. Police discovered pigs that had been stolen from farmers in the form of one thousand pounds of pork in the possession of three men, whom they arrested. Two more stories described how wolves had been poaching pigs from farmers in Sharp County, and in one humorous case near Ozark, the dogs who were meant to hunt down the wolf got scared when it bared its fangs.[58] Finally, the editor showed the same enthusiasm for experimentation in animal husbandry as in crop selection. In February, the *Echo* reported on a farmer's feeding experiment with two cows: the cow fed hulled oats mixed with hay gave more milk than the cow given wheat bran mixed with hay. The paper urged readers to do their own testing to see if it was worth spending more on certain kinds of feed.[59]

As much as experimentation was praised, a few items from the *Echo* spoke to its unpredictable nature. A February item advised that farmers could get seed samples from the Agricultural Department or from members of Congress for free; the federal government spent $3 million dollars on this program every year, so the farmers should make use of it. But a few weeks later, a humorous item mocked the same seed program: when farmers were asked to report back to the government on their results, one wrote that the onion seeds he was sent produced great poppies, which served as a delicious seasoning in soups.[60] Reporting at the end of the seasonal experimentation in September and October was decidedly less humorous, when it was noted that farmers were disappointed when sorghum and wheat did not bring in as much cash as expected, due to falling prices.[61]

German speakers were certainly interested in finding a viable economic alternative to the dominance of cotton. Among other strategies, they undertook a practice that provided a degree of economic autonomy and great pride in self-sufficiency. This was the establishment of a home vegetable garden for personal use. In certain regions of Germany, the lower classes traditionally grew their own food in kitchen gardens to subsidize the insufficient wages they earned in agricultural work performed for others. This custom was so widespread that at least one source credits German immigrants with introducing the idea of kitchen gardens to the United States. The idea to grow one's own livestock food as much as possible, rather than buy feed, was well-established in Germany by the early nineteenth century. Farmers developed the practice of supplementing grain with root vegetables to feed animals kept in stalls throughout the winter; the manure produced by these animals was then used as fertilizer in the spring.[62] The situation German settlers encountered in Arkansas made their insistence on self-reliant farming all the more unusual, as Kenneth Barnes notes: "Cotton dependency had so increased that by 1880 the region no longer produced enough food to feed its people but had become a net importer of livestock and grain."[63] The Germans, however, continued to set aside part of their land to grow food to be consumed by themselves and their animals. Carl Moneyhon estimates for this era "that a family of five in the South might spend as much as $292 on food alone during a year."[64] Barnes, who mentions that the Holy Ghost Fathers near Morrilton established their own facilities to produce wine and process cotton, corn, and lumber, also theorizes that self-reliance "protected the immigrant farmer population from the higher prices charged by local Protestant operators."[65]

A number of articles throughout 1892 underscored the need to grow one's own food. One editorial began with the question, "How can the farmer in Arkansas cover the loss of income resulting from the low cotton price?" The *Echo*'s advice was first not to spend money on anything that one could grow or produce himself: "It cannot be difficult for the German farmers; they are used to producing food for the family themselves. Nevertheless, those farmers who up to now have only planted cotton and corn and have bought most of their groceries in the store will find it difficult to adjust to the new circumstances. But it is necessary nonetheless." The editorial went on to recommend poultry and cattle as necessary expenditures that pay for themselves and noted that cattle were helpful because they additionally provided fertilizer for crops. It suggested raising pigs for income but cautioned the reader that one must start with good stock.[66] A March editorial on the problems created by speculation in the cotton market again called for farmers to grow items used for daily consumption, in addition to cash crops that could be diversified and sold for the most money. In May, the *Echo* offered a concrete plan on how to raise enough food on two to four acres to feed a family of six to eight. One acre was to be devoted specifically to vegetables and a half acre to berries and grapes. The fruit was intended both for the family's immediate consumption and for later use, as revenue from selling these fruits at the market would offset the cost of sugar for canning. Finally, dairy products—including milk, cream, butter, and "sog. Cottagekäse" (so-called cottage cheese)—were suggested as an alternative to regular meat consumption, and farmers could sell surplus of these items to others.[67]

As previously mentioned, the option to turn comestibles produced for the family into an additional cash crop in nearby towns was also found in a German pamphlet published in 1894. It claimed that the growing season extended through "the week of Christmas" and mentioned success with strawberries, apples, "wine," corn, wheat, vegetables, and potatoes as crops.[68] In the *Echo*'s inaugural year, multiple advertisers offered to trade farm products for store items or to sell farm products in their establishments on a commission basis. Grocer J. Kaufmann in Little Rock advertised, "Feed and grain as well as all farm products are sold on commission," which a later issue revealed to be 5 percent of the market price. Competing grocer E. Schift in Little Rock was willing to buy from farmers directly: "Highest prices are paid for agricultural products."[69]

A November article indicated that the transaction between local stores and farmers was less than ideal. Farmers complained that they could not capitalize on smaller quantities of products, especially butter. The editors found this strange, since they estimated that Little Rock imported more butter yearly than all the German farmers put together could supply. The paper theorized the farmers were producing butter of inferior quality, and it urged farmers to create a union that would organize production and enforce standards. The article gave practical tips: milk and cream should not be left out or allowed to get old; butter had to be washed properly; and farmers had to pay attention to what the cows were consuming, which could affect the taste of the butter.[70]

There is limited evidence that some German settlers relied on hunting to supplement their families' diets. A February news item reported successful hunts, telling readers that 131 deer were shot during the last snowfall near Big Flat in Baxter County, along with too many turkeys to count. A reader letter from Dixie thanked the editors for publishing the hunting laws of Missouri and requested the hunting laws for Arkansas. An August news item alerted readers that deer were abundant in Ouachita County, where the season had just opened. Germans' documented enthusiasm for hunting in the state of Arkansas goes back to its days as a territory, when German author Friedrich Gerstäcker expressed great excitement and wonder that he was allowed to shoot wild animals for food and their skins, since the privilege of hunting in Germany was reserved for the wealthy, who hunted animals on their own land but denied their subjects the privilege of doing so.[71]

The fall of 1892 brought reduced cotton prices, reinforcing the value of home gardens. The *Echo*'s pages communicated a sense of superiority. Civis, writing in late August from Pocahontas, shared the following news: "Our Germans are all doing well, and the happiest thing about it is they do not throw themselves head over heels into debt, but rather raise all food products themselves, 'live at home and go in the same place to eat' [provide for their own room and board]."[72] December reporting from Malvern and

Poplar Bluff stated that cotton was only bringing in a third of the previous year's price; the editors appended the observation that the speculators must again be manipulating the market. The paper still distinguished between the regular farmers in the state and the German farmers: "The other consequence [of the downturn] is dire times for the farmers who raised none of the necessities of life for themselves, but rather counted only on their cotton. Many smaller stores will go bankrupt. Last week, ten went bankrupt. It is a serious lesson for our farmers to raise first the foodstuffs needed for consumption at home and only then products for the market." This perception that Germans were better off than their English-speaking neighbors because they were smart enough to plant their own food does not reflect research into Arkansas agriculture of the time. Carl Moneyhon explains that English-speaking farm families of the same period also grew their own food, with the exception of consumer goods such as coffee, sugar, and salt, which the German settlers would also have had to purchase.[73]

Fruit served a dual purpose for the Germans: they were certainly interested in it for home consumption, but it was additionally an up-and-coming cash crop in Arkansas. In January the *Echo* provided a number of concrete recommendations for early and midseason varieties of apples, as well as those that could be stored over the winter. Specific varieties of peaches, plums, pears, edible crab apples (*Kirschäpfel*), grapes, cherries, strawberries, and blackberries were suggested, with the cautionary addendum to begin with small quantities of different kinds of fruit to test their productivity in local soil before increasing plantings. The article recommended against planting gooseberries, currants, and raspberries in Arkansas, as those fruits did poorly in dry soil; it expressed the hope that a canning factory could be established. The June 23 issue reported that this ambition had in fact been realized in Harrisburg in Poinsett County, with $10,000 of capital stock. *Echo* advertiser Edmund Craig saw the benefits of promoting fruit for commerce and advertised the materials needed to make strawberry boxes. In May, the *Echo* announced from its Little Rock office that 1,196 crates of strawberries had been shipped from the capital city.[74]

Carl Moneyhon's research also reflects growing interest among the Germans and other Arkansans in producing fruit for the market : "In 1880 not a single one of these counties had been among the top five producers of fruits and berries for market. By 1900 three of the top five, Washington, Benton, and Madison Counties, accounted for nearly 35 percent of all such goods grown in Arkansas."[75] Arkansas's weather proved especially challenging to the immigrants for fruit production. In the spring of 1892, cold and snowfall in late March destroyed the chances for good peach and plum harvests, while causing apple and pear blooms, as well as young vegetation, to freeze. In October, the *Echo* reminded readers that fall was the time to buy and plant fruit trees so that they would have a chance to develop roots before the hot summer, unless there were a sudden cold snap as had happened in the spring.[76]

In addition to general discussions about alternatives to King Cotton and suggestions for what crops farmers should experiment with next, the *Echo* advised on general planting practices and the treatment of specific cultivars found to be successful in Arkansas. First and foremost, Germans believed themselves to be pioneers in Arkansas agriculture in the use of manure as fertilizer. In his 1894 pro-immigration pamphlet, Meurer recounted a story about English-speaking neighbors who ridiculed a German farmer in 1878 for the supposedly filthy habit of collecting cow manure and admonished him to stop; but once they saw the increased output of his crops, they adopted the practice.[77] Along these lines, the *Echo* published a lengthy commentary on the importance of natural fertilizer. It reminded readers of the old German farming proverb that summarized manure's ability to resurrect soil that had been judged infertile: "Wo ist Mistus, da ist Christus" (where there is dung, there is Christ). It recommended that cows be kept in stalls with plenty of hay spread around to catch waste. This had the positive side effect of not attracting the attention of English-speaking neighbors who might question the direct handling of cow manure, but it also prevented another precious animal resource from being lost: urine, which the article praised for being rich in the phosphoric acid necessary for the development of seeds. As alternatives to straw, the *Echo* also suggested collecting "straw from the forest," presumably pine needles; another efficiency the paper suggested was using sawdust to soak up cow urine and then using the dust as mulch for vegetable beds. In April, there was speculation that cotton seed might be worth more as fertilizer than the bolls were worth as a cash crop. The editors were so convinced of the necessity of fertilizer that they cautioned farmers to cultivate only as much land as they could procure manure and urine for. One solution to a scarcity of natural fertilizer was chemical fertilizers, which the *Echo* praised alongside manure and urine for their efficacy and ease of use.[78] There is mixed historical evidence as to whether the Germans actually caused fertilizer to become more widely used in Arkansas. Carl Moneyhon comments, "As late as 1900, for example, only 10 percent of Arkansas farmers used fertilizers." Still, another group of minority farmers working the land during Reconstruction was aware of the advantages of natural fertilizer. Kenneth Barnes reports that black farmers coming from South Carolina during Reconstruction knew that the soil would benefit from fertilizer but considered guano too expensive for their agricultural practices.[79]

The *Echo* provided its readers with recommendations for various cultivars that were suited to Arkansas and specific instructions on how to plant them. In over thirty articles, readers learned how to grow asparagus, beans, cauliflower (although with a warning that it was a difficult crop in Arkansas), cucumbers (in pots), green cabbage, horseradish, kohlrabi, mushrooms, onions, popcorn, potatoes, rhubarb, red beets, sorghum, spinach, St. John's rye, tomatoes, and wheat. Farmers with sufficient space could use the paper's instructions for pansies, which are in fact edible but were more likely raised as ornamentals by those less reliant on garden kitchens for subsistence. Flower lovers learned how to turn rose shoots into transplantable starts. Gardening in Arkansas required knowledge of how to deal with inevitable pests and diseases, so other articles addressed thwarting moles by using bone oil, dry gooseberry sticks, and gooseberry vinegar mixed with dung; combatting pea weevils; preventing bee swarms; protecting trees from aphids; getting rid of rainworms; ridding fruit trees of caterpillars, snails, and fungi; attacking corn weevils; and preventing the spread of disease by following correct protocol for washing out planters between uses. The paper instructed readers on how to keep up with the important task of maintaining farm machinery, including cleaning and applying enamel to metals. This type of advice extended to the home with recipes for a material that could be used to patch an oven and the tip not to store sewing machines in cold rooms.

The *Echo* provided concrete instructions for the care of animals as well. The most frequent topic was poultry-raising: the molting process, poultry diseases, distracting hens so they did not become bored and pull out their feathers, combating chicken lice, and how to use heracleum (cow parsnip) as feed. Most information concerned chickens, but there were additionally articles on training ducks to lay eggs indoors and feeding peas to doves as an occasional treat. The *Echo* covered the basics of raising swine, weaning piglets, and measuring their growth. Farmers interested in keeping milk cows learned the importance of exercise for young cows, establishing a milking and feeding schedule, and treating swollen utters. There was a wealth of information on horses: how to treat mange, a warning of a horse disease spreading in Poplar Grove, how to water a horse, protecting horses' hooves, estimating the age of a horse, the causes of colic in horses, and even a report about a farmer in Saxony using coffee to restore a horse to health. Apiarists among the Germans read about how to repair hives and about an experiment on how long bees could live without food. Finally, there were two general articles regarding illness. One instructed farmers to relocate sick animals outside as soon as there was enough grass available in the spring and to acclimate animals away from winter food slowly. A second explained how to administer liquid medicine to animals without harming them.[80]

Readers were provided with instructions on how to conserve the food they had raised for themselves and their families. A column entitled "Items for the Common Good" was a regular feature and included many food-preservation and -storage instructions. Notably, the column's title is not gendered. German-language publications of the nineteenth century regularly had dedicated columns with content "for the ladies," and while the *Echo* occasionally addressed female readers directly and made it clear that women were doing the cooking, information on food preservation was presented as generally useful. The paper does not give hints about which of these techniques belonged to which gender's work realm in the German home. A few examples of preservation methods follow. To preserve tomatoes in gallon stone jugs, readers were advised to cook the tomatoes and pour them while still boiling into jugs that had been warmed in advance with boiling water. Then the jug was immediately covered with a thick cork and sealed with a mixture of beeswax and resin. In a method formulated by the French agricultural ministry, potatoes were kept from sprouting in storage by soaking them in a solution with 2 percent sulfuric acid. Walnuts could be preserved with 90 percent spirits. Grapes were supposed to be layered in a barrel alternating with ashes, with ash being the top layer. The idea was to preserve them for the winter, but the article claimed this would keep the fruit edible for eight to ten months. Onions had to be covered with hay or straw and stored in airy, dry environments to prevent rot, or alternately they could be kept in bags or nets near a heated oven. Flour similarly required a cool, airy room for storage, but it could not be stored near the onions or other strong-smelling foods, as it would pick up their odors.[81]

The *Echo* additionally published advice for conserving meat and other animal products. Meat that could not be cured in a smoke room or smoke house ("im smoke-house") could be painted with *Holzessig* (pyroligneous acid), but the editors recommended against using this method more than two or three times. Meat could then be smoked after the acid treatment but had to be hung out in the air until the acid was dry. The paper suggested that bacon and ham would last for a year if first wrapped in paper and then put into a chest in a dry and airy place. Each piece was covered in ashes to prevent insects from laying eggs. Bratwurst could be kept for several months; as soon as they were stuffed, the skins were cleaned, and the sausages were put into an earthenware jug. Heated lard was poured over the sausages so they were covered entirely. As the sausages were removed for consumption, the lard had to be reheated and everything completely covered again. One recipe for conserving eggs for several months at room temperature indicated soaking them in a mixture of ethyl alcohol, glycerin, and salicylic acid. Readers were warned that some old cheeses could become poisonous and that this seemed to happen with those made with *quark* (a German dairy product similar in consistency to thick sour cream) in which the whey had been left sitting out too long. The *Echo*'s advice was to avoid old cheeses of this sort. If butter became rancid, readers could add some milk or buttermilk to it and then wash and salt as if it were fresh butter. The *Echo* reported on experiments to determine whether or not fresh butter benefited from washing. Unwashed butter was perceived as better.[82]

Baking advice assisted readers in making use of new ingredients or new ways to prepare foods that were ubiquitous in their adopted southern home. The *Echo* suggested its readers use buttermilk in biscuits and gave a recipe for cornmeal muffins. Pie crusts were included, with the editors opting for the German-English hybrid term *Piekruste* for the American pastry, although the paper developed a recipe that used less lard. It recommended using a marble slab to keep the dough cool during rolling. Instructions for planting rhubarb, a vegetable grown in German-speaking countries since the mid-nineteenth century, included the note that it was better known as "pie plant" in Arkansas. One recipe for chocolate cake included "frosting" in quotation marks, using the English term for this finishing touch, which was likely unknown to the German settlers. Other baking stories were of a more general nature. A recipe for baking powder noted it was better to make one's own since there had been so many stories of counterfeit versions utilizing ammonia or alum. The paper advised readers that bread tasted better and kept its moisture longer if left in the oven an additional five minutes with the door cracked open.[83]

Articles on cooking provided instruction on how to make German favorites. There was a recipe for stuffed cabbage, in which a meat mixture was wrapped in cabbage leaves and then boiled. *Frikadellen* (meatballs, or fried meat patties) were touted as a delicious way to use up food that was going bad. The case of liverwurst that fell apart when it was being cut was diagnosed as having been overcooked. A little vinegar in water when boiling tough meat tenderized without influencing the taste, and instructions on how to cook bacon safely, with salt in the pan, so as to avoid a fire were given. Gelatin desserts were a popular recipe repeated in various flavors: lemon, raspberry, and apple-quince. Another article gave instructions for small dumplings to put in meat sauce. There was a recipe for lentil soup with breadcrumbs, and readers were told how to prepare dried white beans. Parsimony in cooking was lauded in the pages of the *Echo*. Readers were admonished not to throw away the shells of fresh peas but rather to cook them down to yield flavoring for soups. And, while it is possible that men were also involved in preserving some foods, the editors left little doubt about who was preparing food in the German settler household with this note: "A frugal housewife, who considers in advance what should be cooked, always asks first: what foods do we have on hand? . . . and attempts to prepare nutritional dishes according to what is found present. But in a household where 'the will of the people' is the kitchen master, the daily question tends to be: 'What would we like to eat? What dish are we yearning for right now, as expensive and difficult to obtain as it might be?'"[84]

Other articles focused on what must have been curious foodstuffs for the settlers. "Pop-Korn" or "Puff-Korn" was touted as a national dish *bei den Yankees* (among the yankees). The newspaper noted it could be grown like regular corn and recommended two cultivars, Illinois Schneeball (snowball) and Premium-Pearl. There was an ode to maple syrup reprinted from another German American newspaper, *Die Woche* (The Week). Another article asked, *Haben unsere Leserinnen schon von cottolene gehört?* (Have our female readers already heard about cottolene?). The cottonseed oil product was described in comparison to butterine and oleomargarine, but it was purported to be even better, as it was more digestible than animal fats and could be conserved for a year before becoming rancid. The *Echo* told readers of a farmer in Plymouth, California, who invented strawberry pots by drilling holes in a regular pot.[85] Food items were additionally recommended to female readers as beauty aids. Hair could be colored brown with fresh green walnut shells, but one had to be careful to avoid getting it on the skin. Lace could be dyed with coffee, but for blondes, tea was recommended as a dye, since the color was said to suit them better.[86]

German settlers believed foodstuffs and nutrition played a role in health and wellness. The *Echo* suggested a number of home remedies. Stinging nettle was advocated as a way to clean out mucus in the chest and lungs, for cleansing the stomach, and to cure rheumatism. Recipes were given for stinging nettle tea, salad, and vinegar. A tincture of eucalyptus and juice of black currants was advised for combating fungus that caused wet coughs. Mustard-oil tincture, following a sweat, was good for rheumatism. As a general preventative against bacteria and microbes in the mouths of children, naphthol sugar was supposed to be mixed with honey and held in the mouth as long as possible. Chlorate potash was reputed to stop pain quickly in teeth with cavities. One article promoted moderation in eating and drinking: "Man lives from that which he digests, not from that which he eats." The author went on to explain that the most nutritious choices were those that could be digested well and thus actually used by the body.[87]

The *Echo* published many articles of a practical nature regarding farming and homesteading in its inaugural year, but the editors did not limit themselves to the mechanics of farming. The paper offered many observations on the politics of agriculture in editorials. In these commentaries, the editors showed a keen interest in both state and national farming developments and were aware of positions held by the Arkansas Grange, the Farmers' Alliance, and the Agricultural Wheel. The editors were less interested in specific governing bodies and bureaucrats, but the paper did mention them in two instances. In February, the *Echo* reprinted a story from the German American newspaper *Katholischer Hausfreund* (Catholic friend of the family) explaining the purpose of the federal Agriculture Department to foreign-born readers. The author stated that the agency's goal was to combat sicknesses and diseases of plants and animals, and that it printed books and brochures regarding its research findings.[88] At the state level, the *Echo* endorsed John D. Adams for the position of Arkansas Agriculture Commissioner. When he died only four months after being elected, the paper lauded his replacement, George M. Chaplaine, noting he was a former member of the legislature and lawyer by trade but owned a farm in Lonoke County and was generally known as a *sehr gebildeter Herr* (a very well-educated gentleman).[89]

The editors primarily addressed two fundamental issues of agricultural policy: speculation in the commodities market and protectionism in tariff strategies. The *Echo* saw these issues as symptomatic of a larger problem with the American system: the hindering of the proper functioning of a free-market economy, which affected farmers disproportionately. On the supply side, the paper argued, farmers could not demand more for their goods, as the monopolists who cornered markets did, because there were too many farmers to act in concert. On the demand side, they could not buy goods for less because of protectionist trade tariffs that the editors believed assisted only rich producers, who hoarded profits instead of sharing them with the government in the form of taxes or disbursing some of the profits to their workers. The two primary editors during the initial year, Carl Meurer and Friedrich Hohenschutz, were both staunch Catholics, and this fact is reflected in their use of the strongest language possible to condemn the American system in the editorial "Die gekreuzigten Farmer" (the crucified farmers).[90]

The editors were particularly galled by short selling, a practice through which speculators on the stock market, who did not yet own the commodities themselves, could affect the prices to the detriment of farmers, who actually produced and were in physical possession of the goods. The title of one editorial referred to short selling: "Das Börsenspiel mit dem Schweiße des Bauern" (The stock market game with the sweat of the farmer). In a later news report regarding the wild overestimation of the fall harvest, the *Echo* noted that farm product prices were expected to improve, which would be beneficial since wheat prices had sunk low enough to make growing the crop unviable. The article's author could not resist adding that the farmers would have to wait to see how they would be compensated for their labor, while the speculators, who did nothing in his estimation, put the profits in their pockets. In another article, the paper referred to the "rapid accumulation of capital without work." It noted that although the practice of speculation was legal in America at the time, it was a punishable offense under Germanic law code. The author quoted from two leading cultural leaders of the fourteenth century, poet and craftsman Hans Sachs and leading humanist Desiderius Erasmus, discussing both men's disdain for the practice as evidence that Europeans had long realized that speculation should be banned. A correspondent from Switzerland wrote to thank the *Echo* for truthfully examining the problems with speculation in the American market, claiming that news of overproduction had been kept secret by speculators in the previous year, which hurt the Swiss spinning mills. Throughout the inaugural year, the *Echo* called repeatedly for the passage of the Hatch Act of 1892, which aimed to eliminate short selling.[91]

In addition to opposing the practice on ethical grounds, the *Echo* argued that speculation was bad economically. It stated that a prosperous nation could not be established by a few thousand millionaires, but rather by a farming class that was debt-free and thus independent, counting its wealth in self-reliance rather than riches. And when commodity prices were held artificially low, the entire economic eco-system was endangered. While some consumers might be pleased with low prices for farm products in the short term, those prices meant that farmers were not receiving much for their crops and thus could not buy as many consumer goods themselves. This in turn would impact the retailers and ultimately the wholesalers. The *Echo*'s position throughout the year was that one and only one political party would be able to reform American democracy in a way that would allow farmers to fairly compete in the marketplace. While the paper was sympathetic to the agendas of Arkansas's various agricultural parties, the editors did not believe those parties had done much good in affecting change: "Years ago, the Farmers' Alliance wanted to help, and now the People's Party wants to help. It can only help the farmer if it can ensure that he receives more for his products and has to pay less for that which is necessary [for him to buy]." The *Echo* firmly believed the Democratic Party was the best hope for farmers, and the editors had little sympathy for farmers who voted for Republicans: "They themselves fashion the noose with which one hangs them." The editors further argued that part of the problem lay with how the American system created an inherent rivalry between rural and urban populations: "Rarely does a child of the city become a farmer. Yes, the lads in the city look down on the farmer with a certain contempt. And even a portion of our press often seems to be predisposed to ascribe less intellect to the farmer than to city residents and to speak in a dismissive way about the 'country uncles.'"[92]

The *Echo* opposed tariffs, and specifically the McKinley tariff of 1890, as much as it did speculation, for the damage it believed they caused all members of society. Editorials argued that the problem of increased prices for consumer goods particularly impacted farmers. In the piece entitled "Der Nutzen des Schutzzolls" (The benefit of the protective tariff), the author stated that farmers who could not understand why they were not climbing the economic ladder in spite of good crops should buy a copy of the McKinley tariff and study it. He lamented that small farmers were not represented in Washington, where industrialists deployed their lobbyists. He then included a long list of items that farmers had to purchase, such as pieces of clothing and household items, claiming that the tariff had increased the prices of those goods from 25 to 150 percent, which amounted to a hidden tax on the farmer. The editors railed against those in power for always talking about American industry as though it were in its infancy and needed to be fed and supported. This claim was countered by comparing American industry profits to those of England, Germany, France, Russia, and Austria, with the conclusion that industry in the United States generated almost twice as much profit as its closest competitor, England. The author asked rhetorically if it were not time to start weaning the "baby" from the bottle before it sent everyone to the poor house and declared, "Tariff reform is the only salvation for the bulk of American farmers."[93]

The *Echo* additionally included extensive reporting on specific problems that the farmers among its readers were experiencing, with flooding being the largest challenge of 1892. The first flood reporting was from the May 19 issue, when the natural disaster was front-page news. Crops currently in the ground were ruined, and there was concern that the land might not dry quickly enough to allow for a replacement planting. In Arkansas, farmers had to move their cows to higher ground using cow cars, although this plan was hampered because many rail lines were washed out. The Arkansas River was flooding the bottomlands, but those in the mountainous regions were not spared, as usually harmless creeks overflowed. A June 2 report speculated that the Mississippi appeared to be changing its riverbed near Memphis and that Bradstreet estimated damages in five states of $32 million.[94]

A reader letter by P. W. Sch. from Morrison Bluff put a human face to the misery. He stated that May was usually the month when things improve and everything is fruitful, but the wind was terrible and many a housewife did not know what she was going to put on the dinner table. P. W. reported that the floods simply added to the misery, which was especially true for farmers in the bottomlands, who lost both their entire crop and their homes. He described how one of his acquaintances, whom he referred to by his *Echo* correspondent name of "Goldfisch," had to be rescued by boat from his home. He joked that he was going to start thinking of other names for Sweet Home like "Wet Home." P. W. finished his letter by noting that settlers who had purchased farms on higher ground could take solace in the knowledge that, while the bottomlands might have better soil, they lived in a healthier area under somewhat less dangerous conditions. An editor's note a week later noted that *unsere Farmer* (our farmers) were having a hard time of it, but the author hoped that the warm weather would improve the situation greatly. He noted that the German farmers did not lose much in the floods and could still plant corn: "One will have to do some saving this year, and the Americans who grew up here in this country will have a much harder time of it than our fellow countrymen." The editorial ended on a positive note, with the author admonishing settlers not to panic about the flood damage, since too much rain was better than too little. He encouraged readers to take the long view: even in the Mississippi valley's worst flood year, 1844, there was still a good harvest. Revealing a native's understanding of Arkansas's weather, the writer finished with the hope that the flooding not be followed by a drought and that the rainy nature of the summer continue, with alternating days of sun so that crops could grow.[95]

Agricultural issues provided a central focus for community building, as the German settlers sought advice from one another about what practices and cultivars proved successful in their new home. Roman Catholicism was another major unifying force that brought *Echo* readers together. A majority of the newspaper's readers were Catholic and proudly so. But the editors expressly stated that they did not wish for the *Echo* to be regarded as a Catholic paper, and they did not want to be understood by others in Arkansas as only Catholics. Catholics knew they were a religious minority in Arkansas and felt the burden of that status in issues such as Prohibition. In 1851 a Presbyterian minister wanted to publish an anti-Catholic screed in the venerable Little Rock newspaper the *Arkansas Gazette*. Its founder, William Woodruff, refused to print the material, and he explained why: "'These columns are not designed, and we trust never will be perverted, to the persecution of any class of our countrymen, who hold different tenets of religious faith.'"[96] In spite of this impassioned position, however, the situation had changed four short years later. In 1855–56, the *Arkansas Gazette* indeed ran anti-Catholic guest articles by Protestant preachers in a serialized format.[97] Also in 1856, the nationwide American Party, referred to as the Know-Nothings, attempted to make inroads in the state. The party found that its signature national platform of railing against immigrants and Catholics was less effective in a state in which neither population was large. Though the party's overall showing in Arkansas was not a success, well-known politician Albert Pike contributed an anti-Catholic pamphlet to the discourse, and party members were successful in securing positions in Little Rock city government.[98]

There is some anecdotal evidence of positive interactions between Catholics and other denominations in the state. Jonathan Wolfe cites an account by a Catholic priest stationed in Charleston who reported that his English-speaking Protestant neighbors were respectful and friendly.[99] Wolfe theorizes that Catholic identity is what helped forge individual settlers into a more cohesive group, whereas Protestant German-speaking immigrants tended to migrate in organized groups and were acquainted with one another before leaving Germany.[100] The *Echo* certainly played a role in forming this Catholic group identity. Catholicism became to some extent a shortcut to establishing the unified German community that early German immigrants desired. But the Catholic core of this community was not exclusionary; they welcomed German speakers of other faiths. Ironically, in providing a group identity, Catholicism alienated these Germans from many native Arkansans at the same time. In light of that earlier sense of alienation, the quick assimilation of subsequent generations is notable.

The biggest event of 1892 for Arkansas's Catholics was the *Jubiläum*, the twenty-fifth anniversary of the service of Bishop Edward Fitzgerald in the state. German-speaking Catholics felt a special kinship with Bishop Fitzgerald; he had immigrated from Ireland as a teenager, and his mother was German. He was equally appreciative of the settlers, as they provided him with a flock in an area that previously had few Catholics. Immigrants made up substantial numbers of the total Catholic population in Arkansas, and Fitzgerald himself had organized the recruitment of the German settlers in cooperation with the railroads. During the dedication of the German-speaking church in Morrilton, Fitzgerald was emotionally moved to the point of speechlessness after hearing a German boy speak as part of the event. A German speech was included at the consecration of the cathedral in Little Rock in 1846 as well.[101] The *Echo*'s coverage makes it clear that German-speakers saw themselves as pivotal to the event. The *Jubiläum* was publicized far in advance, and the actual event was front-page news in the February 4 edition. The *Echo* included four separate drawings to commemorate the special occasion, a rarity in a newspaper that was composed primarily of print. This was the first time the paper included images that were not part of advertisements: a large representation of the bishop himself, the interior of the cathedral where the celebratory Mass had taken place, and smaller images of the exteriors of both the old and new cathedral buildings. The *Gazette* ran these same illustrations, so it is possible that they were provided by the diocese, although the celebration only warranted coverage on pages 5–6 in the English-language press.[102]

The *Echo*'s reporting portrayed the bishop's time in service as uniquely helpful to German immigrants, although the Polish-speaking Catholic community was at least mentioned. The article afforded only one line to his provenance and then carried on with his education as a priest and his career highlights. It discussed how there was no real organized Catholic presence in Arkansas prior to the Civil War, and certainly no bishop, so that when Fitzgerald arrived, he was greeted by only a few framed buildings and a *Log-Kirche* (log church). Reconstruction was summarized in one brief sentence: "The land was ravaged by war, and the Republican government made great mistakes." The author noted there were few Catholic immigrants initially but praised the establishment of Subiaco Abbey, after which the surrounding area became filled *mit arbeitsgewohnten Deutschen* (Germans accustomed to work). The bishop was praised for his own hard work in recruiting priests to the area and for occasionally returning to his own priestly labors, hearing confessions and giving last rites as the need arose. The Logan County churches and Catholic schools (Spielerville, Paris, Morrison Bluff, Shoal Creek, Prairie View, and Caulksville) were given the honor of being listed individually, but other German-speaking Catholic churches were also mentioned (Charleston, Fort Smith, Altus, Coal Hill, Hartman, Oppelo, and Dixie), as was Father Eugene Weibel's *Colonie im Norden des Staates* (colony in the north of the state, meaning his work with parishes in the Pocahontas and Jonesboro areas).[103]

Apparently, rival paper *Die Staatszeitung* criticized the *Echo*'s front-page coverage of the celebration, although there are curious references to *Staatszeitung* editor Phil Dietzgen attending the event and trying to pass as a fellow Catholic. The author of this article, correspondent and frequent Dietzgen critic Spottvogel, condemned the other German paper: "You 'Catholic saints', (verbatim from the insult register of the *Staatszeitung*) the *Staatszeitung* will teach you morality! It has become more Catholic than you in the last fourteen days." While there are no editions of the *Staatszeitung* extant from this year, the *Echo*'s response indicates that Dietzgen mocked the attendees for allowing themselves to celebrate with alcohol and dancing, after attending the Mass in the cathedral earlier in the day. Spottvogel ended his letter by saying that he anticipated the rival editor attending further events of other denominations in his sheep's clothing, implying that Dietzgen had no morality of his own and was only reporting on the event in an attempt to increase his paper's readership. The account that Spottvogel's letter gives of the *Staatszeitung*'s attack is indeed strange. If Dietzgen were attempting to appeal to Catholic readers of his own paper by attending the bishop's jubilee and reporting on it, it makes little sense that he would then mock Catholic readers for celebrating with drinking and dancing. Even if he were specifically criticizing the *Echo*'s staff, Catholic Germans reading the *Staatszeitung* would have seen nothing wrong with toasting the bishop's tenure in this manner. It was one of many skirmishes in the battle between these two Arkansas German-language papers in 1892.[104]

The *Echo* was so enamored of Bishop Fitzgerald that it reported his appointment as administrator of the Diocese of Dallas in November with a degree of melancholy reluctance. The editors understood that these new duties might take Fitzgerald away from his position in Arkansas: "It would be a heavy loss for the Diocese of Little Rock, if it were to lose Bishop Fitzgerald, who has done very, very much for it." But Fitzgerald was to remain in Arkansas with the Catholic German settlers long enough to celebrate his fortieth anniversary as their bishop, shortly before his death.[105] Bishop Fitzgerald was not the only clergy member the paper followed. News of clergy appointments and initiations was regularly included, such as ceremonies for novices and initiates at Subiaco Abbey and at the Benedictine convents in Fort Smith and Shoal Creek, clergy transfers from one parish to another, and Father Eugene Weibel's travels abroad to recruit new priests to the state of Arkansas. The *Echo* passed along information regarding teachers and curricula for Catholic schools in the state, and published weekly items from correspondents regarding local events in parishes, including Subiaco's election of a new abbot, mission gatherings, celebrations of Catholic holy days and feast days of patron saints, the dedication of new churches, and the building of other new facilities.

The *Echo* saw itself as a unifying force because it created a virtual community among its readership of German settlers. But the newspaper acted as a physical unifying point as well: readers who had business or were visiting friends and family in Little Rock frequently stopped by the headquarters. The editors always noted when friends and readers called. These items usually included the name of the visitor and some bit of wisdom the visitor had to share or information on the person's business or wares for sale. The paper used a notice about a visit from Conrad Elsken to promote his candidacy for Logan County treasurer. There were calls of a social nature: young men introduced their new brides to the staff, others stopped by on their way out of town to "take the cure" for health reasons, and a few readers were headed to or returning from visits in Germany. In some cases, these trips to the *Echo*'s office were a form of reciprocation. Editor Carl Meurer's daughter asserted that the paper's success in recruiting and keeping advertisers was due in part to her father's constant travels around the state to build and cultivate relationships with various establishments, sometimes including overnight stays at the homes of businessmen.[106]

Meurer strove to create the sense of a close-knit community by reminding readers to frequent the German businesses that advertised in the *Echo*, not simply because they were advertisers of the newspaper but because they were part of the German community. Accordingly, an ad told readers, "Whoever comes to Paris should not fail to visit Cravens & Sohn. They are always pleased to see their friends, irrespective of whether they are shopping or not." When a cobbler opened a new shop, a news item referred to him as *Unser strebsamer Mitbürger* (our ambitious fellow citizen), along with an editorial comment that disclosed he had purchased an ad, lest someone question the purity of the paper's intentions in passing along news of German business dealings. One news brief late in the year read more like a local testimonial.

> Mr. Je[o]seph Schmeltzer, the beloved bartender of Sol. Johl, and one of our young ambitious Germans, has for a long time now tinkered with the thought of opening his own place. Finally, he has found the opportunity. He wants to try his luck at the beginning of the new year at [the corner of] Markham and Scott streets and open the Warehouse Saloon there for the public. We wish the young family father luck in his venture and vouch to the public in advance that the service will be the most courteous and the drinks the best in "little Joe's saloon."[107]

The paper reported on German-owned businesses being sold to other Germans, or in the case of one saloon, coming into German hands again after having been sold to an American: "Earlier, when it was run by John Drees, it was a popular meeting point for Germans and sports people. Then it went into the hands of G. Britton, who sold this week to Tony Heibach. Tony is known and liked as an ambitious young man and will completely renovate the saloon, so that one can drink there with complete peace of mind." This final comment was possibly a reference to fellow Arkansans' dislike of German settlers' drinking habits, with which a fellow German could identify.[108] Geo M. Zeller & Co. in Paris publicized that it was the oldest and largest German establishment of its kind in Logan County, and the Wisconsin-based John A. Salzer Seed Company advertised with the claim that it was the only German seed cultivator in America.[109] Some companies not owned by Germans made special efforts to appeal to the German settler community: businessman D. L. Gray gave notice that he had moved and asked his German customers to follow him to the new address; and insurance company Murrell & Mizzel noted in a larger ad: "A clerk of the firm, Mr. C. Hohenschutz, speaks German and will give information, also per post when desired, in the German language."[110] Occasionally, news items mentioned German-owned local businesses that were not advertisers in the newspaper, such as a dance held in F. Roßner's confectionary that was located under Concordia Hall or a false fire alarm in Hoff's bakery.[111]

The *Echo* reported on gatherings of Germans around the state, some of which were related to holidays. On New Year's Day, there was an event in the German Catholic Casino that incorporated old and new traditions. The committee promised a *Christbescheerung* [*sic*] *der Schulkinder* (a giving of gifts by the Christ child, here to the school children, which traditionally takes place on December 24 in Germany) with apples, nuts, and candy for all the children. Afterwards, the children were to perform a three-act play. The ad promised that a few items would be raffled off, and coffee, cake, and mocha would be served, all for an entrance price of twenty-five cents.[112]

The June 2 edition included a report on *Gräberschmückungs-Tag* (Grave Decoration Day), which was held in bad weather but saw a good turnout nonetheless. It is unclear from the brief mention whether the Germans were participating in the local American tradition of Decoration Day, since it is also a custom in German-speaking countries to tend graves meticulously like miniature gardens. This is a case where a European tradition likely coincided nicely with local Arkansas customs. Germans enthusiastically celebrated the founding of their new homeland on July 4. Festivities in Altus included a Mass as well as performances by a men's choir from Fort Smith and a band from Spielerville. The affair described by a correspondent from Prairie View was much larger and included a beer tent, lemonade stand, a luncheon, and a brass band performance. After a break in the afternoon, the girls of the community staged a play entitled *Im Spital* (In the infirmary) and the boys a play entitled *Kleider machen Leute* (Clothes make the man).[113]

The *Echo* informed readers it could celebrate another American holiday, Columbus Day, in the capital city at a discounted rate being offered by the railroads. The editors reminded their German audience of the importance of the World Expo (to be held the following year) in highlighting Columbus's achievement as well as in events taking place across the country.

> As the commemoration of the 400-year celebratory anniversary of the discovery of America through Christopher Columbus, it should exemplify the cultural progress of the "new world" in the 400 years since the white race has taken possession of it. Through the admirable accomplishments of this culture, which will be portrayed for the visitors of [the Expo], it will itself truly be the most noble and beautiful exultation of the commemoration of the heroic sea voyager and discoverer of the new world.[114]

German settlers in Arkansas in 1892 believed they had much to offer to this celebration of white cultural progress. Churches served as ready-made concert venues for musical events. At the end of February, the choir of St. Andrew's Cathedral repeated the concert they sang in honor of the bishop at his jubilee celebration, and the *Echo* reported that it was well-attended and enjoyed by all. In May, correspondent Lucius wrote from Paris to report on a cultural event that featured two short comedies produced by the youth of the local Catholic church, who were accompanied by the brass band of Paris. Lucius noted the group's hope to undertake similar productions in the future. In June, there was a notice regarding a zither concert by Professor John Stahrl, who was playing a benefit to assist the local church, and the St. Anna Academy of Fort Smith advertised its final exam, which apparently was accompanied by a program for which prizes were given out. These cultural events were often open to all in the local communities, whether or not the attendees could understand German. Sometimes, this resulted in grumbling from the German-speaking attendees, but others clearly viewed such performances as a chance to flaunt their cultural heritage for the locals. Severus, writing from Pocahontas, made this clear in his description of the celebration of a local wedding, attended by a mixed group: "The melodies of our beautiful, immortal folk songs rang out powerfully through the silent night, which allowed the Germans here in this far-away, emotionless country to come alive anew and moved the Americans to speechless amazement and wonder."[115]

In February, March, and April, German settlers had the opportunity to come together to take part in balls in Little Rock, one at the St. Andrew's school hall and two at the venue of Sarlo's hall. The latter two were fundraisers for the *Kriegerverein* (veterans' association). Other groups organized festivals and invited the *Echo*'s readers to attend. In April, a large turnout was expected for the *Turnerfest*, an event organized for May in Hot Springs by the Turners, a gymnastics group (discussed later in this chapter). The paper speculated that the attendance would be great due to half-price travel provided by the railroads and the mobilization by the citizens of Hot Springs, who had managed to convince local hotels to offer a discount to those attending the festival. Fort Smith hosted a celebration of a more local nature to honor the patron saint Boniface, particularly appropriate given that Boniface was an English monk who had traveled to Germany in the eighth century to work as a missionary.[116]

Evidently, German speakers took part in activities organized by the larger community as well. In June, *Echo* readers could choose from a number of events, such as two excursions in the vicinity of Little Rock: one was a train trip to Palarm, a township in Faulkner County where the machinists were holding a picnic, and the other was a ride upriver on the steamer *Anna B. Adams* during which refreshments would be available. Each trip cost fifty cents. In June, a "baby show" was organized in Glennwood Park, and children of German immigrants appeared in the list of winners among the sixty participants, alongside the names of the companies, including a number of German-owned contributors, that had donated the prizes. A baseball game between the *Arkansas Democrat* newspaper and the staff of Quinn's Dry Goods, an *Echo* advertiser, was announced for the Fourth of July, and is the only mention of this American sport in the paper's inaugural year. Another competition was held in August: a *Preisgehen* (walking competition for prizes) held in West End Park in Little Rock and open to all. It consisted of a four-hour daily walk for seven days straight, and the prizes consisted of a percentage of the entrance fees and medals.[117]

The biggest event of the year for the German settler community was without a doubt Maifest (May festival). In 1892 it was held on May 23 in West End Park in Little Rock, although notifications regarding the event started to appear in early March. It was planned in a cooperative effort by three major German organizations: the Little Rock chapters of the *Turn-Verein* (the Turners), the *Zither- und Gesang-Club* (zither and singing club), and the *Krieger- und Landwehrverein* (veterans' association, literally union of warriors/soldiers and militia, often shortened to just *Kriegerverein*). Men paid an entrance fee of fifty cents, whereas women were admitted at no charge. The *Echo* noted that organizing and staffing the event required a considerable amount of work, and that those involved should be compensated for their labors. The morning featured a parade including floats decorated with allegorical themes, and after that, attendees were promised every sort of game, dancing, and concerts. The event was regarded as a major show of German unity: "The May festival unifies the whole of Germandom from city and country.—Everything, which German speakers from over there have brought with them in comfortable sociability and German custom, should be brought to bear here." Later in the same issue, the *Echo* noted, however, that the May festival was enjoyed by the city at large and not just the German speakers: "In order to honor the Germans, local businesses will close their doors to permit their employees to take part in this German festival." Indeed, the festival committee advertised the event with the slogan: "For all Germandom and its friends!"[118]

In reporting on the event afterwards, the editors reinforced the idea that the May festival was a general endorsement of German culture. The first sentence of the review proclaimed the *Maifest* a success, noting, "Our English-speaking fellow citizens" had given an "approval of Germandom through their multitudinous participation." The editors reported that it was a financial success as well, with all of the costs covered and a small amount left over, so that the organizers were planning an even grander event for the following year. Lest readers think the editors were being wholly uncritical of an event designed to celebrate German identity, the *Echo* noted that the string music for the dance had been a mistake and that brass instruments should always be employed for dances in open areas.[119]

The May festival was planned by a group of German organizations (*Vereine*), but such *Vereine* partook in activities beyond event-planning. Previous scholarship on Germans in Arkansas has noted that the immigrants tended to form groups based on shared interests, such as music; one group, the Turners, is often mentioned by name. An examination of the *Echo* reveals how great a role these Vereine played in assisting German community members to organize around a common purpose, to support each other, and to interact. These groups were not simply created in response to the need to interact with fellow German speakers in an overwhelmingly English-speaking state. Rather, the Verein tradition was one that the settlers brought with them from Europe.[120]

The Verein culture was so widespread in Germany that the *Echo* paid tribute to it with a number of jokes. One poked fun at the German penchant for creating a club around seemingly any interest group: "—new flowering of the German 'association dairy': in Malstatt-Burbach, an organization for heads of organizations, and in Auerbach im Breisgau there is even a mother-in-laws club!" Another joke was entitled "Geographic Explanation" and featured a boy asking his father why one was always talking about European *Festland* (which means "continent," but translated literally is "fixed land"). The father called the boy stupid and explained that one only needed to read the paper: "'Schützenfest, Turnerfest, Sängerfest. D'rum heißt halt Europa ein Festland'" ('Marksmen' festival, gymnasts' festival, singers' festival. That's why Europe is called a festival land').[121] In berating his son, the father revealed his miscomprehension of the term *Festland*, assuming it referred to all of the festivals (German: *Fest*) organized by the Vereine.

The three groups mentioned in the joke—marksmen, gymnasts, and singers—were the three most popular types of clubs in German American communities nationwide. The *Echo* espoused the nobility of Vereine in an editorial statement in January 1892. It argued that God put into man's heart the desire to associate with others, and several people working in concert to achieve a common goal could solve problems too large for one individual. Thus, the *Echo* proclaimed it only natural that more and more Vereine were appearing.[122] There was some contemporaneous national discussion among German communities about whether the various Vereine assisted immigrants with the integration process. Some argued that it did, since it introduced newcomers to Germans who had been in the country longer, while others felt that Vereine negatively impacted assimilation, as they exposed new settlers primarily to other Germans. It is clear, however, that the German American press across the nation and German-language activity clubs existed in a symbiotic relationship. The press dutifully announced group activities and events, and high levels of participation in German-speaking clubs allowed new immigrants to continue using their native language and thus provided an automatic reading public for German newspapers.[123]

The *Echo*'s editor made a much more direct appeal to the Vereine to unite in common cause by producing content for the paper. After praising Josef Glanzman of Altus for submitting the first contribution regarding the history of the German settlements around the state, the paper took on a reprimanding tone when noting that other submissions had apparently been promised but not yet written: "What has become of the great plans of the state assembly [meeting of all Vereine]. Don't the individual Vereine want to attend to carrying out their plan? We call for the gentlemen presidents to take the matter into their own hands so that contributions come [in] and we can work further. We ask that photographs of churches, schools, and assembly halls be sent in to us with the descriptions."[124] This lack of cooperation within the Vereine is perhaps reflected in a reprint from another German American paper called the *St. Joseph Volksblatt*: "Vereine and lodges all have lovely principles on paper, but unfortunately there is often so much harm wrecked in and through the same due to dog-in-the-manger jealousy, as well as through intrigues of small men who would like to be important, that many a decent man is forced to withdraw [from the organization]." On a lighthearted note, the commentary concluded that the family of a man who has given up his Verein was often delighted that he was no longer spending all his time and resources on it.[125]

Vereine in Arkansas in 1892, as represented in the pages of the *Echo*, fell roughly into the following categories: mutual-protection societies, organizations centered around a common interest or hobby, groups with a focus on the Catholic church, clubs revolving around an occupation, and fraternal organizations. The mutual-protection society most prevalently mentioned in the *Echo* was the national *Deutscher, Römisch-Katholischer Central-Verein* (German Roman Catholic Central Union, abbreviated DRKCV). As part of its larger mission, this organization provided death benefits in the form of payouts to the families of deceased members who had contributed dues to its insurance scheme. The national secretary of this Verein's board of trustees, H. J. Spannhorst, regularly submitted reports regarding the identities of widows and orphans who had received funds from the organization, as well as the amount each was given, which averaged around $1,000 to each widow. These accounts listed the total debts, assets, and liquid holdings of the group. Apparently, not all DRKCV members participated in this mutual-protection insurance product. In January, the *Echo* related news of the death of Anton Schmeden of Caulksville as a cautionary tale. The paper noted that Schmeden had been sick for only five days before succumbing to a lung infection at age thirty-six, leaving behind a wife and four small children. In light of this tragedy, the *Echo* encouraged all men in the DRKCV to enroll in the widow and orphan fund. Similarly, the Arkansas *Krieger- und Landwehrverein* voted almost unanimously to join a national campaign offered by their umbrella organization, *Der deutsche Kriegerbund von Nord-Amerika* (the German Veterans League of North America). This voluntary coverage would provide surviving relatives with $300 upon a member's death, but the national organization needed 1,500 members to commit to the fund to make it financially feasible.[126]

The *Echo*'s readers also had the option of insuring themselves against fire. Locally, two separate social organizations, the *Liederkranz* and *Grütliverein* (Song Circle and Foresters' Association, both discussed below) announced they had decided to offer fire insurance as a common product. Both groups were rural in nature and explained that by joining forces with other country dwellers, they could lower the costs of coverage, given the greater danger to urban structures located in close proximity to each other. In the May 19 issue, in the *Vereinsnachrichten* (Verein news) section, the *Echo* published what essentially amounted to an advertisement under the heading: "Constitution of Hillsdale, mutual protection society against fire." The multicolumn article started with an introductory letter by J. W. from Hallbur, Iowa. It is cast as J. W.'s response to a friend who asked about the organization and requested a copy of its constitution. J. W. gave a testimonial for the organization and outlined the officers' responsibilities. He warned, however, that the society could not insure against tornado damage, because that would result in insolvency. This was an odd caveat; the very first paragraph of the constitution established the official name as the mutual protection society against *Feuer, Blitz und Tornado* (fire, lightning, and tornado).[127] Another news item from this group relayed a discussion from Morrilton about when to have the yearly *General-Versammlung der Unterstützungs-Vereine* (general meeting of the aid societies), although it is not clear which other organizations might have fallen under this umbrella. The planners proposed having it on the same day as the Columbus celebration (October 12). That way, participants would not have to make a separate trip. And since the first cotton harvest would presumably have been gathered by then, attendees could afford to be away from their farms for a few days. Organizers realized that, aside from time considerations, members had to consider the financial burden of planning to attend; accordingly, they reported that J. Snyder had written to Saint Louis to inquire about any planned fare reductions for the trains.[128]

Hobby-centered organizations comprised another major category of the Vereine. Several of these were focused on music, which is unsurprising given the largely middle-class makeup of the *Echo*'s readership. Bourgeois German families in the nineteenth century placed great emphasis on having music in the home. Children were instructed in both vocal and instrumental performance, and home concerts were frequent and included children and adults. In Arkansas, the Silver Cornet Band of Paris played at a variety of events, including a gathering at Subiaco, a First Communion reception, and a meeting of the United Confederate Veterans, not only in their own town of Paris but also in Caulksville and Fort Smith. Two Vereine featured in the *Echo* were dedicated to music: the *Liederkranz* (Song Circle) and the *Zither- und Gesang-Club* (Zither and Song Club), the latter of which had Little Rock and Collegeville chapters. The Zither and Song Club organized a singers' festival in Collegeville for their fellow singers, who arrived by train and wagon and were served lemonade, beer, and wine. The Little Rock club gave a portrait of their organization to the Collegeville chapter. Earlier in the year, the Little Rock group hosted a large masked ball in the *Vereinshalle* (organization hall) at the intersection of Second and Sherman streets.[129]

Nationally, many German clubs were dedicated to the sport of marksmanship or to an interest in the military, and Arkansas proved no exception. The *Echo*'s weekly column on Vereine recorded the existence of two groups for German speakers interested in shooting sports: the McCarthy Light Guards and the *Schützenverein* (Marksmen Club). An individual named Wipple, a member of the McCarthy group, won first prize in a competition in Omaha and received a gold medal worth $50; it was noted that those who could not travel to Omaha were planning a reception for those who did. The *Schützenverein* was a new club formed in March 1892, and its officers included prominent members of the German community, including Georg Wehrfritz, who was elected president, and Dr. Jungkind, who served as treasurer. In August, Little Rock members traveled to Hot Springs to take part in a shooting competition. The *Krieger- und Landwehrverein*—part of a larger umbrella organization—included a small poem with news from the group; the poem ended with the declaration: "And if again the call goes out: 'To weapons,' then you will fight bravely for Columbia's [America's] honor." A separate organization was interested in preserving the United States politically, the *Rechtsschutzverein* (Rights-Protection League) of St. Scholastica. In late August, the group met and decided unanimously not to vote for the candidate Harvey, who was running for an unspecified office in Logan County, and they planned to urge their fellow Germans not to vote for him either. P. T., an *Echo* correspondent from Prairie View and a member of the *Rechtsschutzverein*, said he would not elaborate on why Harvey did not have their support, since the reasons were well-known. But, he noted, it was important to vote for Harvey's opponent rather than refrain from voting altogether, to prevent dire consequences, "[lest] the Germans in the county be terribly embarrassed and be fully stripped of the little political influence which they have enjoyed up to now." The letter ended with an admonition to the reader to remember, "unity, all for one and one for all."[130]

One of the organizations in the Arkansas German-speaking immigrant community that is best remembered today was the *Turnverein* (gymnastics society), whose member were often referred to as Turners. This sport and social organization was an import from Germany; it also carried political associations in both countries. The international movement was founded in 1811 by Friedrich Ludwig Jahn, whom members referred to as *Turnvater Jahn*. Jahn was inspired by Roman historian Tacitus's descriptions of the Germanic tribes and by a need to train youth in his native Prussia after Napoleon's victories in Europe. He sought to create an organization that would allow Germans to develop their bodies and minds in harmony. Jahn's teachings grew in popularity but were feared by local governments as socialist and nationalist, since a united Germany would have necessarily required the many small principalities to yield their own power. The group was outlawed in 1819, and Jahn was arrested and imprisoned. The movement itself continued to exist, however, and became a driving force, along with student groups and the urban population, for democratic demands in the failed 1848 revolution. Many of these would-be revolutionaries, known as Forty-Eighters, fled to the United States and brought Jahn's ideas with them.[131]

In its American incarnation, the organization was principally focused on gymnastics and physical fitness, but political undertones remained, primarily opposition to slavery, Prohibition, and nativism, especially in the antebellum period. At that time, the organization was made up largely of

Forty-Eighters, many of whom had an interest in various forms of socialism. In the time preceding the Civil War, the Turners were more focused on politics than sport. In addition to opposing slavery, some members called for changes to American democracy in the form of a direct election of senators, direct public voting on issues via popular referenda, and US participation in international bodies of law. Politically engaged members were additionally interested in reforms to the nature of work through the implementation of child-labor laws and other policies to protect workers, and through a greater availability of affordable land. Some Turners felt that the group should avoid politics. This led to a division in the organization during the years 1856–59, with one group following a more apolitical course, although the sides reunited after the Civil War. Unlike other Vereine, the Turners were able to establish a national organization by calling for regional meetings instead of one large national meeting, which most delegates would not have been able to attend. If the Arkansas Turners had any political interests, it is not evident in the reporting on the group in 1892. Jahn himself designated how the organization's gatherings in Germany were to be structured, with a combination of religious, sporting, and social elements. The American branch of the organization dispensed with the religious aspects, however, since their primary aim was to foster unity among Germans in America, who were often of different faiths. The physical fitness portion of the program usually included both individual competitions and group demonstrations of gymnastics ability. Furthermore, German scholar Heike Bungert postulates that the German Turners in the United States tended to be younger and less well off than immigrants who belonged to marksmanship groups, since the former required the athletic ability of youth and the latter required funds necessary to purchase weapons and ammunition.[132]

Jonathan Wolfe largely describes the Turners in Arkansas as a social organization: "Among the best-known and most accepted German organizations in Little Rock was the Turn Verein. It figured prominently in the social life of the town. Its balls and picnics were always well publicized by the local press and reporting often shifted into a robust, exuberant vein."[133] The *Echo*'s reporting in 1892 shows the organization in its prime; planned events included a masked ball in February, a competition for which six hundred individuals traveled by train to Hot Springs (the *Echo* printed the winners' names), and a ball and group gymnastics demonstration on December 26.[134] A major milestone for the group was the construction of its own hall in this year; the *Echo* reported on all stages of the project. In January, the group announced its intentions and called for the submission of designs; the winner would receive $100 in stock options and the runner-up, $25. By March, the organization had formed a building committee consisting of Fred. Roesch, John A. Jungkind, Fred. Roessner, Fred. Wolters, and W[ilia]m Zeisler. The architect was Casp[ar] Kusener. The group laid the cornerstone in June, but they were still meeting in the hall of the Knights of Pythias at the time of their annual meeting in September. The new building was dedicated on October 21, with both a program and a parade. The ceremony included an address in English by Morris Cohn, a prominent Little Rock attorney, and one in German by Georg Dörner. The day concluded with a ball and a gymnastics demonstration, during which, the *Echo* remarked, a small child stole the show when attempting to imitate the adults. Both Turners and members of other Vereine attended the celebration.[135] The hall would serve as a gathering place and cultural center for local Germans until February 1914, when the *Echo* had the sad duty of reporting that the structure had burned to the ground. In April 1914, however, the *Echo* provided readers with an artist's sketch of the design for the building's replacement. The drawing was entitled "The German home," reinforcing the enduring importance of the Turners for the German-speaking community.[136]

Aside from general announcements regarding the local Turners in the club information section of the paper, there was a rather curious short editorial on May 5 entitled "Exercise and the Gymnastics Societies." The first section of the opinion piece reaffirmed the newspaper's commitment to equal representation of all German organizations in the state and to work for their "harmony, influence, and honor." It further discussed the importance of exercise, especially for city dwellers. The author stated that children and young men needed physical exertion as a break from the mental rigors of the school and work, and that exercise kept the body healthy while also strengthening the mind. In the second section, the Turnvereine were initially praised, though the antireligious bias of the American chapters was taken to task. The third section then showed a marked difference in both the tone and content, as the author suddenly shifted to a discussion of Rome's purported fall due to materialism, of politics, and of the Turners' role in this realm.

> But materialism is the doctrine according to which our monopolists and monied barons consider it to be permissible to oppress their fellow men and make them their slaves, according to which the socialists and radicals make the state the tyrant of all, and the

> anarchists want to destroy the rich with dynamite. Now it is up to the Turners to decide like Hercules at the crossroads whether they follow the temptations of the deceitful doctrine of materialism, the antithesis and mortal enemy of the German spirit, or [whether] they want to place themselves as German men on the side of justice, which grants work its honor and fitting compensation, and forbids the oppression of weaker fellow men. However, justice is based alone on natural laws, from which our forefathers created the old German law and which agree with the fundamental truths of Christianity.

While the abrupt change likely was in reaction to a specific matter, it is not clear if the *Echo* was commenting on the role of Turners in national discourse or in local politics. The following issue of the paper included a note that a local Turner had taken exception to the editorial. The critique itself was published in the *Staatszeitung* and the complainant was referred to only by the initial "D," suggesting that *Staatszeitung* editor Dietzgen was the offended party. The *Echo* was not concerned about potential fallout from the Turners: "We hardly believe that the Turners endorse such bluster. There is no reason for it."[137]

For those seeking moral leadership, there were a number of Vereine dedicated to supporting the local churches and to fellowship with other believers. Some organizations appear in the pages of the *Echo* merely because of announcements of participation in church celebrations such as the Mass, officer elections, and sponsorship of events such as picnics and dances. These organizations include *Die katholischen Ritter* (the Catholic Knights), *Männerverein St. Scholastica* (Men's Club of St. Scholastica), *Die Sodalität der Jungfrauen an der Kathedral-Gemeinde* (the Sodality of Virgins [unmarried women] of the Cathedral Parish), and the *St. Fidelis-Verein* (St. Fidelis Union). The pages of the *Echo* contain details about a few other organizations as well. The *Brüderschaft der christlichen Mütter* (Fraternity of Christian Mothers) in Fort Smith was a local chapter of a national Catholic women's organization founded in 1891. They wrote to the newspaper to report that their membership had tripled in one year, with 11,000 members in 146 chapters. The Fort Smith group had formed an auxiliary altar society that made monthly contributions to the upkeep and costs of running the parish. Correspondent JHK from Saint Vincent wrote to report that the *Maria-Hilf-Verien* (Mary Aid Union) had held its first patron-saint celebration in German American style, with the dedication of a new American flag followed by a play put on by members of the community. The announcement of the *St. Paulus Frauenverein* (St. Paul's women's organization) in Little Rock stands out as the only non-Catholic religious organization represented in the *Echo*. The newly formed group invited all evangelical women to join them in Christian fellowship, assistance to the sick and ailing, the decoration of the church, and the support of missionaries.[138]

Most numerous by far were the St. Joseph societies. Jonathan Wolfe comments, "By 1890 there was a St. Joseph Society in every Catholic German settlement in the state." Each community's *St. Joseph Verein* was in turn allied with the statewide organization, which was itself part of the national DRKCV.[139] The group's largest project in 1892 was assisting with the preparations for the bishop's jubilee. The DRKCV urged all local Vereine to plan to participate in the festivities: "Though such participation has a double purpose: 1. [It] should bestow upon the ecclesiastical prince the honor due and the Vereine ought to show that they know what the Bishop is due. 2. The Vereine manifest in this way their strengths, flourishing, and unity, and show that they are a factor that must be reckoned with." The group even offered to find substitutes if there were remote chapters that could not send their own representatives yet could send in their flags to be carried by local members. Later in the year, the North Little Rock chapter of the group became embroiled in controversy when it underwent a split, apparently brought on partly by *Staatszeitung* editor Philip Dietzgen. The discord among the factions of the St. Joseph Verein was so great that the bishop disbanded the local chapter, and a representative of the national organization wrote to the parishioners appealing for unity. The upstart group laid claim to the treasury, and the matter was ultimately settled in court in favor of the renegade members, an outcome that vexed the *Echo* editors greatly and that Dietzgen viewed as a personal victory.[140]

Other groups in the German settler community were organized around occupations, such as the *Krieger- und Landwehrverein*. In January, it postponed a planned ball out of respect for its vice president, a forty-seven-year-old named Max Kutzleb who died suddenly and left behind a wife and eighteen-month-old child. Two issues later, the group announced the rescheduled concert as a family affair, meaning no entrance fee, and shared news that the well-liked Peter Biehl had been elected by a vote of twenty to three to take over Kutzleb's office. A ball was held on Easter Monday to raise money for the organization. The group sent a Mr. Langreck as the Arkansas delegate to the national meeting, held in Kansas City in August. Less information is preserved in the *Echo* about the *Grütliverein*, the Swiss name of which indicates a group dedicated to clearing forest lands. Besides their plans to offer fire insurance, the group also wrote in to announce their newly elected officers. Equally little is preserved about the *Deutscher Farmer-Club*, which is represented by a single entry contributed by Anton Wohlfahrt of Alexander, Arkansas. Wohlfahrt informed readers of the *Echo* of the organization's plans to combine their harvest festival with a Columbus event, which would feature music, dancing, and card-playing for those not inclined to dance.[141] The *Obst- und Weinzüchterverein* (Fruit-Grower and Wine-Producers Association), unlike other groups that offered social programs, was strictly a professional organization. Its goals included efforts to repeal Prohibition laws and to make Arkansas a flourishing viniculture market (as discussed in chapter 2). The Saline County chapter was reported to be considering building a toll road from the border to the county seat of Benton. The Collegeville chapter was intent on discussing a new road tax, exploring the possibility of setting up a fire-insurance mutual-aid scheme, and finding candidates who would support its views for the next election. The report of a June meeting of the Collegeville group revealed that the county judge they had invited to their meeting was convinced of the viniculture argument. The road-building issue was discussed, and everyone agreed that the best way to proceed was to raise funds with a tax and then build the roads with convict labor.[142]

*Echo* readers were apparently less interested in established fraternal organizations, but the paper included one mention of the Knights of Pythias to note that the local group had just returned from a meeting in Kansas City, where it won six prizes. It is unclear whether the meeting was regional or national. The editors offered a note of thanks in German to the Young Men's Christian Association for a copy of its publication, so there were apparently German-speaking YMCA members among the paper's readership. One unusual entry noted the formation of a new society in Little Rock, holding its first meeting at a school of dance: "'Unabhängige-Jünglings-Gesellschaft'" ("Independent Young Men's Association"). The name of the organization is given both in German and English, so that readers were initially uncertain if this was a group formed primarily by English speakers at which German speakers were also welcome. Only a week later, the *Echo* announced that the meeting included a ball so successful that no one went home until the early hours of the morning. Again, the name of the group was given in English, but the participants in the event and the officers who were elected indicate the organization was likely being run by German speakers or those of German heritage: Beinberger, Stiel, Wexner,

Riff (a Little Rock barber and *Echo* advertiser), Spitzenberger, and Ostrich. In September, the paper ran a one-line announcement that the bishop attended a meeting of the *Jünglingsverein*. If this is the same organization, as is likely the case, it would suggest that the members had ties to the German Catholic community. It might also indicate Bishop Fitzgerald's support of the group as an alternative to Masonic lodges, given the "independent" in the organization's name. Beginning in 1890, the bishop forbade his flock from joining such organizations, and Masonic groups are noticeably absent from the *Echo*'s pages.[143]

Jewish community organizations are not represented in the pages of the *Echo*, although some Jews were members of the *Turnverein*, and *Echo* readers likely knew them from interactions there. Carolyn LeMaster mentions a number of Jewish groups that had been established by 1892, including the Little Rock Club, later renamed the Concordia Association, founded in 1864; B'nai B'rith chapters founded around Arkansas between 1866 and 1879; and a Pine Bluff Jewish social club called the Mendelssohn Club, mentioned in a local paper in 1876 but perhaps defunct by 1892. There was certainly other news reported from German settlers in Pine Bluff.[144]

While formal organizations allowed Germans to create smaller groups based on shared interests within the larger German community, in times of difficulty, German speakers still felt an overarching sense of duty to all members of the diasporic community. Jonathan Wolfe describes how German settlers were known for assisting others who had fallen on hard times, and he theorizes that this support perhaps allowed German immigrant communities to retain members who would otherwise have been forced to return to Europe or seek their fortunes in other states.[145] It is clear from the *Echo* that settlers admonished each other to purchase insurance policies so that each family could be self-reliant in times of calamity; providing a financial cushion for one's family in time of death was seen as a basic responsibility, not something to be left to the group. In cases of illness, though, there was no payout, and the *Echo* then appealed to the German-speaking community at large. In February, readers were informed that Paul Masur's wife had been sick for months, and the illness had progressed to temporary mental instability. The family's address was published with the appeal, "Noble-minded philanthropists are urged to see to the needs of the hard suffering family." A week later, a second notice indicated the German settler was uncomfortable accepting charity outright: "Paul Masur, who has been put in a terrible position by the illness of his wife, asks to be supported through offers of work. He has his express wagon at 2nd and Louisiana Street." Another family was suffering as well, in this case due to the illness and eventual death of its mother. The editors informed *Echo* readers that Mrs. John Hilt had been buried, and the wording of the announcement implied that the family was enduring hard times precisely because they had come to Arkansas.

> The family is originally from Bohemia, and came from Cincinnati to settle here. They established themselves at a homestead six miles from Argenta. The land is bad, and four family members came down with typhoid fever. The father and two children are still healthy but completely destitute. They have been living off of cornbread, and the mother has died. Noble-minded persons are asked to support the family, which is completely impoverished.[146]

The *Echo* additionally called upon its readers to help their fellow Germans in cases of accidents or natural disasters. In one case, correspondent Goldfisch wrote from Sweet Home to describe how local settler F. G. Bauer lost his horse, which was only five years old, in an accident. The editor appended a note to mention that the *Unterstützungs-Verein* (aid society) of Morrison Bluff had helped Bauer and called on other Vereine in the state to do the same in similar circumstances. Multiple disasters occurred in the state in May. On May 12, the *Echo* reported that a tornado had struck the St. Joseph Colony of the Holy Ghost Fathers in Morrilton, damaging the new church building, the monastery, and the cotton gin. The editors mentioned that the destruction of the church, which had been built only the previous year, was an especially great loss. The next week, correspondent G. B. gave a more detailed account of the calamity. He noted that they were thankful that no lives were lost; while a tenant farmer had been found in the rubble of a stall and was injured, his four-year-old son was found playing as though he had no idea of what he had just lived through. Local residents believed they were spared because they had attended church in Morrilton that day for a celebration; the monastic church would otherwise have been full at that time and the loss of life great. G. B. mentioned that the buildings were only partially insured, so local German speakers had already taken up a collection to assist with rebuilding efforts.[147]

Editions published in late May and early June featured multiple stories on community efforts to assist victims of flooding. The *Echo* reported that Louis Blass and Thomas Lafferty were in charge of the committee for the support of the flood victims. They had solicited funds by walking through Little Rock's downtown and asking everyone they saw for donations. The editors noted that the committee had received many donations, including a contribution of one thousand pounds of meat from the Cedaky Packing Company in Omaha. The paper further admonished anyone who could contribute to do so. Edmund Craig, a regular *Echo* advertiser, took up this call; he donated 1,500 packets of seeds, which were included in a shipment of agricultural supplies sent to the flooded region of Arkansas. Both the editor and correspondents drew attention to the fact that poor, black families who had lost everything needed aid the most.[148] While the *Echo* reported on attempts to help flood victims, it was again attacked by the *Staatszeitung*, which reported that John Kaufmann, one of the founding members of the *Echo* Publishing Company, had contributed only $1 to the relief efforts. The *Echo* responded angrily that Kaufmann did not think it necessary to publicize all of his assistance and assured readers he was helping in other ways. Kaufmann had suffered his own losses, including many hundreds of acres of harvest along with the buildings on the farmland that had been washed away. The paper noted that he had provided the black families who were affected with immediate necessities *ohne Aufsicht auf Wiedererstattung* (without the likelihood of repayment). By June, the many requests for aid were apparently taking a toll on the average German speaker, who nevertheless thought it important to keep giving, according to one reader's letter. J. L. reported that the priest at Morrilton was calling for donated funds to help rebuild the church. The local *St. Joseph Verein* had already depleted almost all their reserves to aid the sick in the community, but they managed to donate ten dollars as a group, which amounted to roughly seventy-five cents per member. He further called on other Vereine around the state to follow their example and contribute to the rebuilding effort.[149]

After examining how the *Echo* chronicled Germans' interactions with each other at state and community levels, we now turn to consider how the paper depicted the individual German family. Both editorial content and reader opinion supported traditional roles for women as mothers and keepers of the home, but already in 1892, there was evidence that attitudes were beginning to change regarding women working outside the home. Though the editors knew that the *Echo*'s readership included women, very few articles addressed them specifically—a total of three during the entire inaugural year. Two articles were published in a column entitled *Für unsere Damen* (For our ladies) and featured a pattern for crocheted baby shoes and slippers followed by a pattern for knee warmers. In September, an article that featured housekeeping tips was explicitly marked *Für die Hausfrau* (For the housewife). Generally, though, these sorts of articles were published under the designation *Gemeinnütziges* (Items for the common use), indicating that there were probably some German households consisting only of men who had not yet married or widowers who could benefit from the occasional tip.[150] In an article about the difficulty of putting on a jacket for which the lining had come loose, the writer mocked the knowledge of bachelors in comparison to the wisdom of housewives in addressing such a calamity: "'Of course that would happen to a bachelor!' our married female readers call out, because what woman would not immediately reattach the first unraveling stitches on the lining, if only the dear spouses would indicate the damage right away."[151] These small items in the *Echo* aimed toward women were almost afterthoughts. By comparison, in larger markets the German American press appealed to women with publications dedicated solely to what were considered women's interests. *Die Deutsche Hausfrau* (The German housewife), founded in Milwaukee in 1904, included not only household tips and items on fashion and the American way of life but also international news and serialized fiction (the last two types of items were of course also found in the *Echo*).[152]

Not surprisingly for 1892, the *Echo* expressed the general attitude that women were intellectually, morally, and physically inferior to men. For example, a schoolboy reminiscence on the pleasures of learning Latin gendered the subject in an uncomplimentary way: "Latin, my [dear] ladies, is namely not as easy as French and needlepoint." Middle-class boys were taught Latin, as the study of the ancient language was the sine qua non for German university studies, whereas girls learned French, which was considered an asset in polite society. Another item, an epigram, proclaimed, "Women often need more time to do nothing than men need to work." And many articles indicated that German women needed protection, both physically and spiritually, in coarse American society. One article complained that there was a conspiracy in Fort Smith to take women and girls, who were traveling alone and had arrived in the night by train, to disreputable hotels. The paper applauded the city council's steps to protect the weaker sex from such *Lasterhöhlen* (dens of iniquity). The general criminal element in America bothered the editors, who frequently reported on sensational trials and lamented that women, especially unmarried ones, were allowed to watch the court proceedings. Another news item detailed the case of Amanda Rosson, a fifteen-year-old who was sent to prison in Ozark after being accused of maiming another girl, Georgiana Smalley. The paper noted that this was the first female inmate in a long time, and remarked that the Rosson case echoed an incident that gained much national attention in both German and English language papers alike in 1892.[153] That incident was the case of lesbian Alice Mitchell, who slashed the throat of her girlfriend Freda Ward, purportedly determined that no man should be allowed to marry Ward if she could not. Mitchell was sentenced to a sanatorium for the crime, but the *Echo* considered the root cause of the crime not mental illness but the immorality of the American school system. It cautioned readers about the need to give German girls proper instruction so they could avoid a similar fate.[154]

A number of articles in 1892 revealed German men's fear that their wives and daughters would become radicalized by immersion in American culture and would adopt the attitudes of English-speaking women. In a December editorial entitled "A Comparison of American and German Women," the *Echo* argued that the cause of women's rights was indicative of the misguided goals of the American education system and accused American women of raising their children only for starring roles in the crime pages. Its linkage of the role of women in American society with a general cultural depravity is worth quoting at length:

> American women of the so-called educated classes generally possess, as a result of their backward upbringing, no real understanding of their feminine vocation. This is where their vehement pursuit of and insistence on emancipation, that is equality with men, on the right of women to vote and on the participation in the affairs of men in politics, legislation, and governance comes from; this is why they feel themselves called to agitate for the fraud of prohibition and waste a lot of time reading newspapers and novels or engage in writing themselves, while they often do not entirely possess the necessary education to fulfill their feminine duties. This false position of American womankind means much disaster for the families and for the nation, because the order established by the Creator does not let itself be subverted with impunity. It is therefore understandable that American women, who have been led astray by false goals, look on German women, who have remained true to their calling, with contempt. A haughty "lady" even called German women "cooking animals" in a written text. In defiance of these miseducated American women, we Germans are allowed to view our women with justifiable pride, who have remained true to their calling and who find their happiness in making those who belong to them happy in [their roles] as spouses, mothers, and housewives, and who raise well-behaved daughters and sons fit for military service for the fatherland.[155]

This editorial is striking not only because of its assertion that women should be proud of their role as mothers but also because it indicates the militarism that permeated German society in the second half of the nineteenth century. The editorial went on to praise Germany's ability to raise sons who could defend themselves against the *streitsüchtigen französischen Nachbaren* [*sic*] (combative French neighbors). From this German perspective, women's continued dedication to their proper rolls was critical not only to civil society but also to national defense. The end of the editorial was equally noteworthy. Although the piece had just criticized women who regarded themselves as authors, it singled out one female writer for praise: Henriette Davidis, who was known for her books on cooking and housekeeping and who had died around fifteen years earlier. Davidis was extolled for helping women fulfill their natural calling, and the article included her poem "Die Hausfrau" (the housewife), which admonished women to industriousness, loyalty to their husbands, parsimony, charity, temperance, and piety. The facts that Davidis had become a bestselling author in spite of her gender and had switched publishers so as to obtain better compensation were not addressed by the newspaper.[156]

A March editorial against women's emancipation linked it both to the detested French rivals and American radicalism, therefore making it decidedly un-German. The article began by blaming the French Revolution for first introducing the concept to the world stage, before again accusing American women of being the most ardent supporters of the movement and thereby abandoning their families. The *Echo* argued that women's natural place was in the home, because God had made men and women physically different: "The man is born to rule due to stronger bodies and mental strength." Physical superiority, however, also obliged men to provide sustenance and protection for their wives and families. The editorial then focused on the special calling of a woman as the heart of the family: "For this reason, the Creator has equipped her with the necessary mental aptitudes, with the loving concern for spouse and children, for the preparation of food and clothing, and for the many small needs of the family. But above all the good wife holds close to her heart the raising of children to be religious and fear God." The editors ended with an anecdote that seemed out of place, given the paper's usual animosity toward France. It claimed that Napoleon once asked an old woman what he needed to raise good, highly principled men, and her enthusiastic but simple answer was "mothers."[157]

About a month and a half later, another essay addressed young women directly. It advised them to be happy with their material possessions, such as clothing and furnishings. It recommended that those who were discontent with their lot should go to the houses of poor women to see how they were starving and clothed in rags. This was perceived as the cure for materialism: "Then you will greet your spouse with a grateful heart and learn to appreciate his self-sacrificing efforts through which he endeavors to create a comfortable home for you. Arrange your expenses in such a way that the mind of [your] husband is not continually distressed by concerns over sustenance—thus will his loyal [female] helper promote happiness of the home more than through vain glamour." This article was clearly addressed to readers in the middle and upper-middle classes, who were concerned with establishing "a comfortable home" and did not actually have to be troubled about the necessities of subsistence. The author indicated that the husband might worry about putting food on the table if his wife did not fulfill her role in spending the budget wisely. Other items in this same vein included a joke about men who had to buy their wives and daughters new spring hats (they could at least be proud of themselves for subsidizing the silk-ribbon industry), and an anecdote in which a young woman, rather than taking seriously her husband's explanation of his business's low revenues, tried to trick him into buying her a new dress.[158]

The sentiments found in the *Echo* were obviously not unusual for 1892, but what made them distinctive was how the paper claimed the "woman's place is in the home" argument for a larger part of German identity in distinction to the ostensible moral bankruptcy of American identity. An October essay clearly tied the issues together, complaining that Americans were only interested in making money, regardless of how it was acquired, and they therefore raised their children to view financial gain as the foremost goal. The paper argued that Germans knew that work was a duty given man by the creator, and this included the high honor found in women's work; as a result of this knowledge, German women did not interfere in the manly sphere of politics, for example.[159]

Given this focus on women's roles, marriage was naturally a topic for the *Echo.* Jonathan Wolfe comments regarding marriage in German immigrant communities: "Records of marriages show that the German preferred a German for his spouse. This was carried a step farther by over half of those married between 1878 and 1890 in the Arkansas River Valley colonies. They chose their mates from the people living within a radius of ten miles of the church where they worshipped, and also chose someone from the same region of Germany as themselves."[160] Wolfe's observation that German speakers tended to choose other Germans as marriage partners did not necessarily indicate that Germans simply chose spouses from circles of familiar acquaintances. At least one correspondent, Severus from Pocahontas, mentions this practice as a deliberate strategy, and again, this article deserves to be quoted at length:

> Just as in general the survival of humankind is conditional on certain factors and in absence of the same is called into question, so also the future of pure German settlements here in America is dependent on several terms or conditions, without which [the settlements] gradually lose their initial character and disappear and merge in the general throng of people of the new world. Because when a German community does not let itself be concerned with keeping together among one another, to preserve and maintain their German disposition, the good qualities which they brought with them from the old homeland, in a nutshell if it does not direct its attention to raising German youth, then it is at the very least questioned and the seed grain of death for Germanness is planted in the community in question and will result in ruinous fruits as a result for them and their descendants. In order to avoid this, it is above all necessary that Germans marry their countrymen and -women, and no longer be intent on chasing after the Americans in the insane belief they would stand on a higher level of civilization through this practice.[161]

German settlers in Arkansas were concerned about the possibility of losing their cultural identity through assimilation, and they saw intermarriage within the German community as a way to combat this loss.

Two other articles regarding marital trends are noteworthy. In one, the paper reported with disdain on a women's group in New York that was debating the question of whether or not young women should marry. The reporter stated that those with "Mrs." in front of their names seemed to be more tolerant and asked: "Are the Misses so willing to condemn marriage and men because they do not want to have them or simply because they cannot procure any?" In another, an actress was chastised for requesting a divorce because she was no longer in love with her husband. The author was aghast at the implications for society if this argument were to become a trend: "If every man and every woman who 'no longer loved' their other half would regard that alone as sufficient grounds to divorce . . . we'll break off [the thought]—the perspective is too . . . too terrible." Conversely, the *Echo* reported on a case in Arkansas that presented a satisfactory reason for divorce. In spite of a general disapproval of vigilante justice in the paper's inaugural year, the *Echo* noted with a sense of satisfaction that a German living in Argenta by the name of J. Lemmer had been taken from his home into the woods and given twenty lashes by twenty-five men, *Weisskappen* (white cappers), because Lemmer had brutally beaten his wife again. Apparently, the abuse was frequent, since the article indicated that Lemmer had earned *seine Hiebe* (his blows). Only some of the men were masked, and although Lemmer recognized a few of his attackers, he did not dare identify them for fear of receiving another beating. Even more curiously, the cause of the abuse was his wife's defense of a young black boy, whom Lemmer had attacked because the boy had accidentally almost hit the man's dog while throwing a rock. The *Arkansas Gazette* reported on the event as well, noting that John Lemmer was both a German and a "well-known character" and that the white cappers could not be found. The reporter added, "They seldom are, when their work is in a good cause—and North Little Rock citizens seem to think John deserved what he received." The *Gazette* additionally noted the wife was filing for divorce.[162]

If women were called to be wives, the *Echo*'s perspective was that they were equally called to be mothers. The coverage of this topic featured a sentimental tone. A poem entitled "Muttersegen" (Mother's blessing) published in February was a tribute written by an adult son to his mother. Although she had long since died, even *in der Fremde* (in a foreign land) and *ganz allein* (completely alone) the speaker could remember the feel of her hand on his forehead and her words, and it was as though she were still tucking him in. Thus, the blessing in the title was both the nightly benediction and the feeling of being cared for that the man carried with him throughout his life. Another article, "Mutterliebe" (Mother's love), reinforced the idea of valuable self-sacrifice from a mother's viewpoint: "A larger and more important thing than we mothers often suspect and believe is put into our lowly hands, namely the development and upbringing of the youth, therefore of the future of mankind."[163]

In spite of its stated importance, the *Echo* had only two articles to offer its female readers in this mission, one of a philosophical and one of a practical nature. "Der Penny" (The penny) was written from a male perspective and was quite critical of women and child-rearing practices in the middle and upper-middle urban classes. It claimed children were bribed with a penny for good behavior but did not stay good for long after spending the coin at the candy store, returning with sticky faces and hands. Women were also chastised for spending hours going shopping and then eating sweets, which led to indigestion and pitiable husbands listening to complaints. This article was almost certainly reprinted from a German-language newspaper in a larger urban market, rather than having been written for settlers in rural Arkansas, but it reinforced the idea that some women were not living up to their full potential as wives and mothers. The practical article regarded teething in children and was written by a mother of four children in Berlin. It contained detailed information that would have been helpful to young immigrant women living in rural environments who likely could not turn to older female relatives for immediate advice. Further, the author told mothers not to panic if a child did not walk by the age of one and to give it plenty of opportunity to crawl outside, which was likely less helpful in rural Arkansas, which had a greater abundance of snakes and insects than the well-kept parks of nineteenth-century Berlin.[164]

Overwhelmingly, the worldview the *Echo* presented in 1892 was that women, relegated to the domestic roles of wife and mother, had no business in spheres such as politics. A February editorial highlighted the fear that women's participation in politics necessarily meant abandoning their traditional roles: "In a short time, they make themselves noticeable as temperance witches and howling wenches in a most unfeminine way; shortly after they put on airs as priestesses of suffrage, stick their noses unbidden into politics and neglect spouses and children, kitchen, and cellar." An October article, after proclaiming that God gave Germans the duty to work and not merely to chase after wealth like Americans, reinforced the notion that German women's roles were in the private sphere: "German women look for and find the highest honor in their feminine occupations, they do not want to interfere in the affairs of men, in politics." A week earlier, an editorial had grouped the suffrage movement in with a long list of other undesirable political efforts and declared that fighting these developments had given Germans common purpose in the new land: "In this lies the secret of the German character, which explains the otherwise so unintelligible unity of the Germans: where it is essential in this land to fight unjust laws against natural rights, Prohibition, the right to women's suffrage, [and] state tyranny."[165]

Given this general attitude, the paper was, unsurprisingly, quite critical of efforts by American women to campaign for the right to vote and for Prohibition, both of which were well underway in Arkansas and nationally by 1892. Arkansans' interest in suffrage dates to 1868, and two women's journals that were launched in 1884 and 1888 also called for suffrage. In 1892 federal judge Isaac Parker ruled that civil rights should be available to married women, a development the *Echo* chose not to report or comment on.[166] In fact, the attempt by women to gain the right to vote at the local level went generally unnoticed in the German paper, which was much more concerned about another political cause taken up by women in the state—the attempt to ban the sale of alcohol. The editors and readers were especially galled that young women were being allowed roles in Prohibition efforts. In January, correspondent Geo. A. complained that eighteen-year-old "girls" were busy attempting to "destroy" local representatives over the Prohibition issue. Further, he used the word "girls" in English, likely to distinguish the young women whom he identified as agitators, external to the immigrant community, from German-speaking young women. A July news item from Clarksville indicated that the prohibitionists were preparing for the fall election, in which the banning of alcohol would be on the ballot. It was reported that their tactics included holding picnics and barbecues featuring preaching and singing, and the *Echo* notified readers that "young girls" were being allowed to hold speeches. In its national reporting, the newspaper linked the issues of women's suffrage and Prohibition. It lamented that a committee bill recommending an amendment to the constitution for the right of women to vote had passed 3–2, but noted that *gute Vernunft* (good reason) had prevailed in Iowa, where the newly elected governor had pledged to repeal Prohibition laws that had already been passed. The *Echo* also satirized women involved in politics. For example, in the first of two items published in May, it called Lady Henry Somerset a *Temperenznärrin* (temperance fool) and reported her declaration that Prohibition would dominate over the silver question and tariffs in the near future. It mockingly quoted her as saying, "'I have every prospect then of being elected as American water empress,'" referring to the idea that prohibitionists would ban every drink except water. Another item on the same page ridiculed women campaigning for suffrage in the state house of New York. It noted that in past years the House passed a bill for women's right to vote and the Senate rejected it, only for each chamber to reverse its role the following year. Considering that behavior, the *Echo* argued, it was no wonder that suffragettes viewed all men as a "wretched, deceitful band of hypocrites." Unsurprisingly, the *Echo* did not reprint a July news item from the *Gazette* on the selection of Kate Cunningham of Little Rock as a delegate for the People's Party national convention; Cunningham had said she would reserve her support for the party until she was sure of their platform stance regarding suffrage and equal rights for women.[167]

Curiously, the *Echo* did publish a number of positive items about women in politics and the treatment of women in general. In the same edition that mocked politically active women in New York, the very next news item was entitled "A Triumph of the Fair Sex in the Political Area Is Reported from Cheyenne in Wyoming." The brief article highlighted two women, Theresa Jenkins and *Frau* (Mrs.) Carleton, who were elected as representatives to a state delegation. It noted that Jenkins was the wife of a businessman, but the author additionally mentioned her personal merits: her career as a schoolteacher, her political activism of ten years, and her ability to give the keynote address to a public of fifteen thousand people. Similarly, the article referred to Mrs. Carleton according to her status as the daughter of a known elder in Salt Lake, but its reference to her as a *Geschäftsfrau* (businesswoman) who helped in her husband's business, rather than as a *Hausfrau* (housewife), is noteworthy. The editorial page of the same issue included the article "Freie Gedanken" (Unfettered thoughts), essentially an attack on the religions of Confucianism and Buddhism as compared to Christianity. The piece first argued that the eastern religions did nothing to acknowledge the ennobling power of work or support the rights of workers. The article then argued that these religions also did not advocate for the emancipation of women: "The girl is without rights by the Chinese, she is raised and regarded only as a commodity. The husband buys his wife. Thus, she is also his full, complete property. She must do what her master wants and if she resists, then he can have her be whipped by the police department. Yes, he can rent her to another, as one rents a house or a horse."[168]

A few news items underscored that German women were to remain home, yet reported cases of non-German women in the workforce in a neutral manner. One item noted that there were 6,335 female postmasters in the United States, with Pennsylvania having the most and Alaska having the fewest. (Although, the German paper did not reprint from the *Arkansas Gazette* the news that their own state had 122 postmistresses.) Two other reports stated that female dentists were very popular in London and were making *ein Heidengeld* (a fortune) and that it was women, not men, who served as freight loaders in Japan. Such coverage might lead a careful reader to wonder why the *Echo* was undermining its own arguments that women belonged only in the domestic sphere. Another brief story outlined the pecuniary rights of women in response to a court ruling: the court held that women could not be compensated for work they did in their husband's business. But a woman did have the right to compensation for work performed for others, through paychecks issued to her rather than her husband, and she could buy and sell land from and to her husband. Admittedly, these were all filler items and likely did not carry the same weight as relentless editorials.[169]

But some evidence indicates that not as many German settlers as suggested by the *Echo*'s coverage held the conviction that women should stay in the home. One reader letter actually advocated that young German women be allowed to seek employment outside of the home and offered the unusual argument that allowing girls to work kept them out of trouble. Regular correspondent Severus began with a complaint that the *Randolph Herald* had been berating German Catholic settlers frequently because of their opposition to Prohibition. Most recently, though, the *Herald* had attacked German farmers for allowing their daughters to seek employment in the cities. Severus retorted, "Whoever claims that work is a disgrace and a degradation of the female gender, he can let himself be buried with his opinions. Work does not demean human beings but rather ennobles them, and we were all born for it, not just the male gender." He added in parentheses that the case of the murderess Alice Mitchell showed that work would be good for English-speaking girls as well, and postulated that idle time led Mitchell to a mania that resulted in the murder of her friend. He also predicted that if all the German-speaking girls were to quit their positions in English-speaking families immediately, there would be an uproar. Young women also helped out in German-speaking families. There were two advertisements by Max Heiman and J. W. Thomas specifically requesting German girls to help out with childcare and general housework; each ad ran for a number of weeks, after which a successful candidate was presumably found.[170]

The *Echo*'s advertisements reveal a number of women working outside the home, but all in industries that would have been regarded as safely within the realm of women's work, such as fashion, hospitality, and midwifery. Advertisements carefully noted the marital status of working women, who were listed as *Miß* (Miss), *Frau* (Mrs.), and occasionally "Mrs." in English. Miss Trazzare was a seamstress in Little Rock with New York connections who specialized in women's clothing, such as suits, evening wear, and traveling clothes. She addressed women directly in her ads: "Ladies will allow me to inform them that I am thoroughly equipped for the manufacture of spring and summer suits." Mrs. T. Kuttner was pursuing a similar clientele in advertising her finery store, offering items such as hats, lace, ribbons, and feathers in Little Rock with both German- and English-speaking store assistants. Another item apprised readers that Mrs. Gans would be moving to new premises under the Masonic Temple, presumably the first floor, and that she would be offering her existing inventory at greatly reduced prices. This is possibly a reference to Bluma (DeYoung) Gans, whose life as a successful businesswoman in the Little Rock retail sector is detailed by Carolyn LeMaster. However, LeMaster gives her husband's first name as Jacob, and the *Echo* advertisements otherwise refer only to the millinery and fine goods establishment of Gus Gans.[171] Women in hospitality included Mary Woestman, proprietor of a boarding house in Fort Smith, and Mrs. S. Erber, who ran the City Chop House restaurant in Little Rock. Mrs. Erber had apparently made a name for herself among German speakers in the city. In the birth announcement for her son, her husband is identified according to his wife's career, although her name as the mother is not mentioned at all: "In the family of H. Erber, whose wife runs the well-known City chop house, a little boy has arrived.—Mother and child are well." Mrs. Erber ostensibly continued working after the June birth of her son, as the Chop House continued to be a regular advertiser throughout the inaugural year. It was also not unheard-of for mothers in Arkansas to continue their employment after childbirth. The *Arkansas Gazette* published a proposal in March 1892 from a "kind-hearted, pious lady, with several small children of her own" to find a centrally located house so that she could take care of other children whose mothers work outside the home.[172]

The *Echo* mentioned the woman who helped deliver Mrs. Erber's baby as well, and she happened to be another female entrepreneur. Mrs. Friederike Schmand advertised her services as both a midwife and a female doctor for women and children. She additionally took in female boarders who were *Frauen, die in stiller Zurückgezogenheit wohnen wollen* (women who want to live in quiet privacy). German women living in Little Rock could choose another midwife and *Echo* advertiser, Mrs. Elisabeth Müller, to help with their deliveries. It seems Little Rock was a large enough market to allow for this specialization, whereas women in Paris were treated by a male doctor, E. L. Harley, who assisted in childbirth and treated wounds. German women could have preferred a midwife for any of a few reasons: their inherent trust of being treated by another woman, the lower fees, or modesty.[173]

Although the *Echo* published much other information on medicine, there are no articles regarding pregnancy or childbirth. Hermann Wellenreuther, whose research focuses on German American broadsides of the colonial period and early democracy, also finds few broadsides on these topics and speculates that the information was passed down from mother to daughter. Other *Echo* articles on women's health similarly avoid gynecological issues. This editorial decision was likely due both to the reluctance to publish such information in a morally conservative middle-class newspaper in America and to the background of the editorial staff, since publishing on topics related to reproduction and sex was forbidden by morality censors in Germany. The very few articles that were targeted toward women's health tended to be demeaning. An item in February proclaimed that women were more disposed to being obese because their bodies naturally stored more fat and their lungs were made inefficient by lack of physical exertion. The author suggested that women avoid fatty foods and alcohol and engage in more activities that increase lung capacity. Another article in the same issue, entitled "Warm Feet Are the First Condition of Wellness," claimed that women were more prone to health problems caused by cold feet, such as migraines. Finally, in July the *Echo* published an advertisement for Mount Nebo that was targeted specifically to German-speaking women and children in Little Rock, who were encouraged to seek out a healthier and cooler summer residence in the two-thousand-foot altitude. This ad is indicative of the common belief among Germans in the nineteenth century that mountain air possessed unique health benefits.[174]

The *Echo* continued the long tradition of the German American press in assisting immigrants in treating their own medical ailments and in adapting remedies to a different culture and climate. In 1769 John Tennant published the work *Ein jeder Sein eigner Doctor* (Every man as his own doctor) for colonial Germans. In the 1760s and 1770s, famed German publisher Christoph Sauer made room in his almanac for descriptions of local herbs and their medicinal applications. Unlike German American publications of an earlier period, the *Echo* does not contain advertisements for medicines concocted by local doctors that were intended for specific ailments. Instead, patent medicine is advertised next to home remedies. The *Echo* certainly received considerable revenue for these mail-order medications, especially from the Charles A. Vogeler Company in Baltimore, which offered a line marketed under the name Dr. August König in Hamburg including *Brusttee* (chest tea, that is, tea for respiratory health), *Kräuterpflaster* (herb patches), and *Tropfen* (drops) as well as "St. Jakob's Oil," which was touted as a cure for rheumatism and neurological pain. The newspaper accepted advertising revenue from Hood's sarsaparilla and pills as well. These ads all touted the miraculous nature of the remedies being sold and offered testimonials complete with pictures of satisfied, and presumably healthy, customers. There was an ad from the Nature Remedy Institute, a patent-medicine company based in Chicago, looking for "reliable" German speakers to assist with marketing and sales of their products.[175]

Nevertheless, the newspaper staff attacked those who hawked sham remedies in their midst. In July, the *Echo* warned readers about a local patent-medicine seller who was using *Negern, welche er hypnotisirt* (Negroes, whom he hypnotized) to demonstrate an alleged cure for addictions to alcohol and tobacco. The editors cautioned that no such cure existed and that one could seriously damage one's health by imbibing these potions. When another case surfaced in December in Little Rock, the author could barely contain his exasperation: "Although we have enough doctors and even an over-abundance of patent-medicine men wandering about, who can make the blind walk and the lame see with their hocus pocus and their bottles, there are still quacks around. A black man, H. Gray, was fined $5 on Thursday morning because he was practicing medicine." The *Echo*, though, also reported on an apparent medical miracle with very little fanfare when it described the case of a young lawyer, J. A. Watkins, who had been found lifeless on his bed due to gas inhalation from a line that had not been fully turned off and was revived: "An electric battery was applied, and the blood circulation started up again."[176]

Given the cholera outbreaks and a global flu epidemic, 1892 was a banner year for health concerns. Regarding cases in the United States, experts refer to a three-year epidemic, beginning in 1889 and culminating in 1892, with the highest number of fatalities occurring in the final year. Epidemiologists note the difficulty that even doctors have in distinguishing between flu and other respiratory ailments such as pneumonia. It is uncertain, then, if German families were in fact always dealing with the flu when they reported as much in the *Echo*. In the lead story of January 21, 1892, the *Echo* stated that the flu continued to claim victims, although more in Europe, where the English heir to the throne, Prince Albert Victor, and two Catholic leaders, Cardinal Manning and Cardinal Simeoni, had died during the week. Each of these prominent flu victims was remembered in a long biographical feature. A week later, a dispatch from Saint Petersburg noted that the czarina was recovering from the flu. Locally, the first report of 1892 was from a Paris, Arkansas, correspondent writing on January 11, who stated that the flu was everywhere; an accounting of flu cases became a regular part of correspondence from German communities in that year. One reader even penned a poem about the epidemic, billed as humor: "Trotz dem Quinin, trotz den Pillen, Thut die Grippe Manche killen" ("In spite of the quinine, in spite of the pills, the flu still kills some"—the verse rhymes in German).[177] Dr. W (likely Dr. Nic Weny, who was an advertiser in and cofounder of the *Echo*) contributed a feature on the flu in January written especially for the newspaper, giving its history and offering home treatments.[178]

In addition to illness, German immigrants were acutely aware of the danger posed by accidents, since each issue brought news of the injured and dead. Overwhelmingly, accidents involving the railroads were a top cause of death, with twenty-three incidents reported in the *Echo* in 1892. Deaths and injuries were caused by collisions between freight and commuter trains, between trains and animals, and between trains and horse-drawn wagons. Many were seriously injured while trying to jump onto moving trains, including a man trying to avoid paying a toll to cross a bridge and a doctor hurrying to get to a patient. Streetcars accounted for a number of deaths, such as a particularly gruesome story of a toddler whose legs and skull were crushed by a streetcar but who lived for a time after the accident. The paper complained that the city council should limit the speed of streetcars in Little Rock. Drownings in rivers were reported as a frequent cause of death, whether of children or teenagers who were swimming or of passengers in buggies who tried to cross creeks after rainstorms and were swept away. Workplace accidents, caused by industrial explosions or malfunctioning machinery, and construction mishaps were high on the list of causes of death or dismemberment. There were additionally a number of unusual accident cases reported in 1892. When three hundred young people gathered to go sledding at the hill on the end of Seventh Street, the result was two broken legs and serious back injury to a *Miß* (Miss) Tigh. A woman and infant were burned to death in a domestic accident apparently caused by sweeping too closely to a fire. Ex-governor Elias Conway died a terrible death by burning on the morning of February 28. When locals noticed his house was on fire, they discovered his head in the fireplace and his face *bis zur Unkenntlichkeit entstellt* (disfigured beyond recognition). In Goshen in Washington County, the schoolhouse accidentally exploded during the Democrats' victory celebration, killing a man and two children. There was also an accident involving fireworks and horses for Election Day celebrations in Little Rock.[179]

German immigrants to Arkansas encountered natural hazards in their new home as well. In April, a correspondent from Conway told of how a German settler had been bitten by a water moccasin while repairing storm damage with his son. The family attempted to treat the wound by enlarging it and applying carbolic acid before taking the victim to a doctor in Conway, who approved this course of treatment but said there was nothing to do but wait. From a bite above the foot, the man's entire leg had swollen within forty-eight hours. The correspondent stated that, to his knowledge, this was the third case of a German being attacked by a water moccasin and requested that Dr. Weny contribute an essay about what to do in the case of snake bites. Responding to this request, the *Echo* promised an article the very next week from Dr. Weny regarding animal bites in general and how to treat them, with a special emphasis on snake bites. The resultant article was entitled "Poisonous Bite Wounds" and discussed bites by insects, snakes, and rabid animals, noting that none of these were rare. Farmers were particularly at risk given the *Unmasse* (vast quantity) of poisonous snakes in Arkansas, the first three examples of which the author listed in their English translations: water moccasins, cotton mouths, copperheads, and rattlesnakes. Settlers had to be careful of spiders as well. A September news item revealed that a Bentonville man lay near death after being bitten by a large spider—which his family believed to be a tarantula—and receiving an initial and inaccurate diagnosis of rheumatism of the hips.[180]

While accidents were part of daily life in 1892, the *Echo* believed that one risk to health could easily be avoided: addiction. As discussed in chapter 2, German settlers were convinced that the benefits of medicinal uses of alcohol firmly outweighed the potential risks of addiction, since they saw the root of addiction as the lack of morality prevalent in American society: "That is why the Americans raise so many miserable slaves of their passions. . . . Only a better education is a sure remedy, not only for alcoholism but also against all other vices." Similarly, in an article regarding tobacco dependency, the *Echo* accused cigarette-addicted youths of being more difficult to treat than heroin addicts, as the latter group, according to the paper, at least knew to be ashamed of their addiction. The article ultimately placed the blame for this health scourge on the way in which the American government limited the rights of parents to raise their children as they saw fit, noting that US children could even bring up their parents on charges of child abuse in cases of corporal punishment.[181]

The *Echo* offered items directed toward preventative care. One article promoted good sleep habits as the key to health and offered a cure for insomnia: placing a moist hand towel behind one's neck. Dr. Weny, the paper's medical expert, contributed another article explaining how the use of appropriate clothing could influence health. For example, wool (or flannel) was believed to be the best for undergarments because it retained heat, especially for those with rheumatism and teething children. A March article offered more general health advice. Daily exercise and deep breaths in good air were important. Sleeping rooms in particular needed to be aired out. Skin was cared for by bathing and cold rinses, which encouraged "hardening" (*Abhärtung*) or resilience. Drinking water was seen as a digestive aid. The paper recommended a glass in the morning upon waking.[182]

Several articles indicated that part of maintaining good health was keeping a safe and clean home and provided tips on this topic, for example, a combination of a liter of water and a teaspoon of turpentine oil set to boil was thought to prevent others in the household from contracting airborne illnesses. A solution of prepared aluminum water was to be kept on hand in case of fire, or milk could be used to smother the flames of a petroleum fire. Readers were discouraged from using celluloid buttons due to their high flammability. Mosquito bites could be prevented by applying either a solution of borax or caraway seeds cooked in wine or vinegar.[183] Some tips concerned the running of a household. One told readers to sift ashes at the bottom of the fireplace grate to retrieve smaller pieces of coal that had fallen before being burned and to moisten coal lightly to prevent it from falling in the first place. The paper noted that someone who had tried this had reduced his coal usage by half. Cleaning tips abounded, and instructions were given for eliminating spots on parquet floors and carpets; cleaning knives and the oven; cleaning specific types of clothing such as felt hats, leather gloves, fur, gemstones, flannel, wool, silk, straw hats, and men's collars; removing oily spots from books; making whitewash and indoor paint; polishing steel and iron; removing stains from all manners of fabric due to food, ink, tar, or ironing stains; tanning hides; caring for leather products with oil; cleaning upholstered furniture, feather beds, and lamp cylinders; cleaning doors and windows painted with oil-based paints; making a pin cushion for sewing; controlling bugs with aluminum applied to the walls or a direct spray of vinegar if they could be seen; eliminating fleas with a variety of methods; preventing ant infestations in the home; getting rid of moths in closets; softening hard rainwater; drying out wet boots with dry oats; and polishing boots. Other items gave tips for "better living"—practices that were not strictly necessary for daily life but improved the home. Directions were given for overwintering camellias indoors, growing hyacinths and tulips indoors in the winter, turning white roses yellow with picric acid, cleaning flower pots, dying curtains with rhubarb, repurposing wine glasses or fruit bowls with a broken foot as indoor planters, using denim or ticking rather than gingham for more durable aprons, and bronzing plaster of Paris figures. Several items may seem simply curious to present-day readers, such as instructions on the proper way to carry an umbrella or cane in a crowd—vertically and not horizontally.[184]

The *Echo* offered its readers practical advice in other areas, such as avoiding scams that were making the rounds and how to achieve and maintain financial stability. One warning involved fake coffee beans made of rye that were being offered in both the United States and Europe. Counterfeit foods would not have been unfamiliar to the German speakers, since the peddling of fake or diluted foods and beverages stretches back to the Middle Ages in Germany, as did laws prohibiting such behavior, with punishments ranging up to torture and death. A month after the warning about counterfeit coffee, the *Echo* printed a notice regarding a swindle that was more specific to its readers' new surroundings. A pamphlet from the "Cherokee Colonization Company" was circulating, promising the right to buy land for a $2 fee sent to the company. The *Echo* investigated and warned its readers not to throw away their money. A more serious scam that targeted German speakers directly was a letter sent to a German's home that offered to send him $6,000 in counterfeit money in exchange for $400. The newspaper noted that this offer was nothing but a scam, and it advised its readers to turn over any similar letters directly to the police.[185]

Readers received finance advice as well. Financial stability was a matter of German pride and one of the reasons that the politicians of Arkansas wanted to recruit more German-speaking settlers to the state. Indeed, the words for both "debt" and "guilt" are represented by the same word in German: *die Schuld*. Living within one's means is tied linguistically to moral virtue. Altus correspondent P. U. attributed the prosperity of the German community to intrinsic values that made them superior: "Even here in the country, the farmer can make something of himself with hard work and frugality. Not only in relation to domestic matters but also to religious, Germans know how to do things easier and better." Advice reprinted from the German-language periodical *Der Bergmannsfreund* (The miner's friend) admonished readers to be content living within their means and to avoid debt at all costs. The article compared debt to rust that could quickly spread and cover a piece of metal, or to the act of purposely putting a louse into an animal's fur, with the interest being the louse's sharp teeth continually biting the animal. Instead of taking out loans for items one could not afford, Germans were advised to build their businesses and wealth slowly but securely and to live within their means: "Your business be small, but solid; small your trade, but honest; small your status and craft, but virtuous; small your house, but clean and not mortgaged; small your estate, but not buried under debts." The article concluded with a cautionary proverb, which rhymes in German: *Borgen macht Sorgen—Schuld ist Ungeduld* (borrowing creates worries—debt is impatience).[186]

The *Echo* contributed to solidifying German identity in large and small ways in its inaugural year. The availability of railroad lands allowed Germans to establish close-knit communities on neighboring farms and to do so under favorable economic conditions, escaping the anaconda mortgages that they knew were ruining other farmers in the state and which the paper condemned as economically untenable and unjust. Agricultural topics drew readers together as they considered solutions to problems presented by the Arkansas climate and soil, while at the same time enforcing a group identity since they considered themselves superior to the native American farmers. One of German immigrants' greatest criticisms of the agricultural system they found in Arkansas was the overreliance on the cash crop of cotton, and they discussed possible alternatives to provide a more diverse market within the state. They far preferred developing a viniculture industry in the state to supplant cotton, and the newspaper gave detailed instructions on how a farmer could establish himself in wine-making. The paper and correspondents reminded German speakers that house gardens provided food for one's family and animals regardless of the vagaries of the cotton crop and market prices. Animal husbandry was discussed as another way to introduce a revenue stream not based on cotton, with the added benefit that animal waste could be repurposed as fertilizer for plant crops. Based on the record in the *Echo* of 1892, Germans were unaware that crop diversification and home gardening were remedies also proposed by native Arkansans; rather, Germans believed they held the key to a better system that the English speakers did not understand. Reporting included stories on harvests, market prices, and technological innovations in agriculture. Editorials took stances against speculation in commodities markets and protectionism in tariff policy. Flooding additionally created great problems for German- and English-speaking farmers alike in 1892.

Catholicism provided another unifying force for readers in the newspaper's inaugural year, but the *Echo* did not regard itself solely as a Catholic newspaper. It solicited news items from other denominations and often referred to broad Judeo-Christian values in editorials. The major Catholic event of the year was the celebration of the twenty-fifth anniversary of the service of Bishop Edward Fitzgerald in Arkansas. The settlers shared a special bond with the bishop, who had managed to recruit more Catholics to the southern state by targeting German speakers in an arrangement with railroads seeking buyers for their lands. The paper included frequent Catholic news from local parishes and reports regarding clergy placement, as well as more general news regarding visits of Germans to the capital city and developments regarding German-owned businesses.

Settlers gathered for various festivities and holidays throughout the state, including those unique to German speakers, such as *Maifest* (May festival), as well as those celebrated by English speakers, such as Columbus Day. They were careful to portray themselves as both belonging to the white majority culture and as being uniquely positioned to elevate it aesthetically. While English speakers attended these events, they were not always greeted with open arms. Throughout the year, local Vereine, or clubs, provided fellowship with other settlers organized around common interests, ranging from target shooting to singing to gymnastics. The tradition of organizing in Vereine is one that originated in Germany and was transported with much success to Arkansas. Some of these groups, such as the Turners, had connections to larger national organizations. The *Echo* appealed to a general sense of community among German speakers when it solicited funds for individual families who had fallen on hard times and for victims of larger calamities such as tornadoes.

The *Echo* serves as a record of how German speakers interacted with one another in the state and local communities, but it provides information on how German settlers related at the family level as well. Editorial content and reader opinion reflected the dominant attitudes of the time regarding women's proper place in the home as wives and mothers, but there is some evidence in the pages of the newspaper that these roles were beginning to become more flexible. German speakers were proud of the contributions made by women in their community, yet they feared that American attitudes regarding women in politics and the external workforce would influence German women. Nevertheless, some articles published in 1892 offered favorable depictions of women working outside the home, and there were a number of female entrepreneurs represented among the *Echo*'s advertisers. Unsurprisingly, settlers preferred to seek marriage partners within their own linguistic and cultural community. Medical care was frequently a matter for the family, and the newspaper provided readers with home remedies for injuries and illnesses as well as information regarding preventative care. The editor warned about quack medical practitioners and cures and provided general advice on how to avoid financial scams and secure fiscal independence.

# Arkansas Echo.

Allgemeine Zeitung für Wahrheit und Klarheit auf politischem und socialem Gebiete.

Jahrgang 1. | Little Rock, Donnerstag, den 18. Februar 1892. | Nummer 8.

Wochenrundschau.

Telegramme.

Kabeldepeschen.

Inlaendische Nachrichten.

A typical front page of *Das Arkansas Echo*, February 18, 1892.

# Arkansas Echo.

Allgemeine Zeitung für Wahrheit und Klarheit auf politischem und socialem Gebiete.

Jahrgang 1. Little Rock, Donnerstag, den 4. Februar 1892. Nummer 6.

## Zum 25jährigen Bischofs-Jubiläum des hochw'sten Bischofs von Little Rock.

Alte Kathedrale.

Bischof Edward Fitzgerald.

Neue Kathedrale.

Inneres der Kathedrale.

Ad multos annos!

The front page of the special issue honoring the jubilee celebration of Bishop Edward Fitzgerald's tenure in Arkansas, February 4, 1892.

# Arkansas Echo.

Allgemeine Zeitung für Wahrheit und Klarheit auf politischem und socialem Gebiete.

Jahrgang 1. Little Rock, Donnerstag, den 2. Juni 1892. Nummer 23.

Subiaco Abtei. Spielerville P. O., Logan Co. Ark. von der Südwestseite.

## Subiaco-Abtei.

Subiaco von der Nordostseite.

## Bischof Spalding

Marienkapelle auf dem Hügel.

## Telegramme.

## Kabeldepeschen.

## Ein Weichkohlen-Trust.

## Die anwachsende Hochfluth.

## Gedankensplitter.

The June 2, 1892 edition featured several illustrations of Subiaco Abbey on the first page.

Die große

**Iron Mountain Route**

mit ihren vier täglichen

**Schnellzügen**

offerirt dem reisenden Publikum die schnellste und directeste Route zu allen Punkten in

**NORD, SÜD, OST** und **WEST**.

Zweimalige tägliche Beförderung

von

**LITTLE ROCK** nach **MEMPHIS**

über die bekannte

**Bald Knob Route.**

Kein Wagenwechsel von

**Little Rock nach Kansas City**

über die

Neue Waggener Route.

Die kürzeste Bahn erfordert die wenigste Zeit nach

**Kansas, Nebraska, Colorado**

und dem

**GROSSEN NORD-WESTEN.**

Bei den Touristen beliebt für Reisen nach

**Texas, Mexico und Californien.**

Gut eingerichtete Wagen, elegante, freie Chair Cars.

Die feinsten

**Pullman Palast-Schlafwagen**

auf allen durchgehenden Zügen.

**H. C. TOWNSEND,**

G. P. T. A.

**St. Louis, Mo.**

A close-up of the fonts used in publication from an Iron Mountain railroad ad, February 4, 1892, 8:5.

Der Ausstellungspalast

eskultur.

An example of one of the many illustrations of buildings from the World Expo published throughout the inaugural year, September 16, 1:3–5.

One of only a handful of editorial cartoons from 1892, which were all published in English and reflected the paper's allegiance to the Democratic Party, October 7, 3:5–6.

# Arkansas.

— Die Staatswahlen sind am 5. Sept., nachstehend das demokratische Ticket.

## Staats-Beamte.

Gouverneur:
Wm. M. Fishback, von Sebastian.
Secretär.
H. B. Armistead, von Franklin.
Auditor:
C. B. Mills, von Monroe.
Treasurer:
R. B. Morrow, von Sebastian.
Attorney-General:
James P. Clarke, von Phillips.
Superintendent für Public Instruction:
Josiah H. Shinn, von Pulaski.
Commissionär für Staats-Ländereien:
C. B. Myers, von Pulaski.
Commissionär für Agricultur:
John D. Adams, von Pulaski.
Associate Justice Supreme Court:
W. E. Hemingway, von Jefferson.
Prosecuting Attorney, 6. Judicial Circuit:
W. H. Pemberton, von Pulaski.

## County-Beamte.

County Judge:
W. A. Compton.
Sheriff:
Anderson Mills.
County Clerk:
John Brodie.
Circuit Clerk:
E. A. Ramsey.
Chancery Clerk:
Isaac J. Hicks.
Treasurer:
J. B. Cowpland.
Assessor:

A partial list of Democratic candidates endorsed by *Das Arkansas Echo* for the 1892 elections, September 2, 4:3.

*Top:* An advertisement for J. V. Zimmermann, watchmaker and jeweler, October 21, 2:6–7.

*Right:* An advertisement for H. Struckhoff, selling steamer tickets to and from Europe, March 24, 8:6.

*Top:* An advertisement for Ben S. Thalheimer, dealer in horses and donkeys, February 4, 5:6–7.

*Left:* An advertisement for Edmund Craig & Co., offering mowing machines, February 4, 6:6–7.

**Rose City Candy Fabrik,**

Bäckerei und Conditorei,

**beste Qualität Waaren, billigste Preise,**

**J. G. Leiser,**

Little Rock, Ark., 215 West 5. Str.

An advertisement for the Rose City Candy Factory, a bakery and sweets shop, March 24, 7:6–7.

**Subiaco College, Spielerville, P. O. Logan Co., Ark.**

Die Anstalt steht unter der bewährten Leitung der Benedictiner. Präsident: Hochwürdigster Herr Abt Ign. Conrad O. S. B.

**Gründlicher klassischer und commercieller Cursus. Beste Gelegenheit für Musik.**

Schulgeld und Kost $15 per Monat.

Für Genaueres wende man sich an den

Schul-Eröffnung 3. October.

**Hochw. H. Präfecten.**

An advertisement for Subiaco College, September 23, 3:4–7.

An advertisement for Union Machine Works and Foundry with German proprietor E. C. Wehrfritz, February 4, 1892, 6:6–7.

An illustration for Hood's Sarsaparilla, August 5, 5–6. Patent medicine ads used illustrations from the English language press with the copy text translated into German.

CHAPTER 4

# Reaching Out Beyond the Immigrant Community

## *German Speakers and Arkansas*

IN 1989, Sister Herbert Huber published an index of topics covered in *Das Arkansas Echo* under the title *Arkansas Echo 1892–1906: An Arkansas German Language Newspaper*. The goal of the index was ostensibly to give English-speaking researchers some access to the publication and an idea of what issues had interested the German settlers, but Huber also drew a number of general conclusions about the newspaper. One of these included this statement: "Rather surprisingly, the editorials dealt more with international and national areas rather than state or local issues; this changed the nature of the project."[1] In a similar vein, Jonathan Wolfe writes of German settlers, "Schools and religion received emphasis from them, yet broader questions such as politics or the economy were not even mentioned. Concentration of effort to preserve a foreign culture in Arkansas tended to emphasize parochial concerns."[2] But this is decidedly not the case with content the *Echo* published in its inaugural year. Reporting, editorials, and correspondent letters show German settlers who were deeply interested in what was going on in the state of Arkansas, in the English-speaking communities that surrounded them, and in how it would affect their lives and fortunes. The *Echo* provided vital information that helped German speakers understand the economy and politics of Arkansas.

As discussed in the previous chapter, the *Echo* offered extensive information regarding agriculture. Yet farming was not the sole occupational pursuit and interest of readers. While there is a common belief that most German settlers to Arkansas were farmers, Wolfe concedes that immigrants also included teachers, craftsmen, and those who ended up in the business sector after their attempts at farming were unsuccessful. Regarding the immigrants of the 1870s and 1880s, Wolfe offers this unflattering assessment: "The fact that they did not know the language, combined with their ineptitude in commerce, allowed some of them to be shamefully swindled."[3] The *Echo* clearly shows that some settlers had overcome linguistic difficulties by the 1890s, and many were entrepreneurs or tradesmen, as the advertisements show. The paper attempted to assist these readers in acquiring knowledge of local customs necessary for business. The era from 1880 to 1890 was a period of great economic growth in the state, including the development and expansion of the transportation, timber, and mining sectors. Carl Moneyhon writes of the contributions that one German business, Union Machine Works and Foundry, made during this time, offering "essential services and goods."[4] The historical record does not mention that this business was owned and run by a German, and that would have surely caused consternation among the staff and readers, who were obviously proud of the company's proprietor, and Little Rock city council member, E. C. Wehrfritz. The paper referred to him as *unserm Maschinenbauer Wehrfritz* (our machinist Wehrfritz) when relaying his firm's contributions to the building of a new canning factory in the capital city that could produce ten thousand cans a day. Readers were regularly informed of local business dealings and governmental developments and regulations that would prove useful, whether or not they were directly employed in commerce. Once farmers had raised their animals or produced their crops, they were deeply interested in economic factors external to the community, such as the availability and price of transportation necessary to move goods to market.[5]

One particular interest was the development of natural resources, including minerals and natural gas. In January, readers learned that the state geologist, John Casper Branner, was mapping zinc formations in Marion, Boone, Baxter, and other counties in north Arkansas. A few years earlier, in 1888, Branner had come under great public criticism for publishing a report revealing that gold speculation in the state was not supported by actual geologic formations; the report resulted in the loss of $113 million in investments. Whether the German paper was unaware of the English press's disdain for Branner or simply was enthusiastic that more resources would eventually be found (and more immigrants potentially drawn to the state), the *Echo* affectionately attached the possessive "our" to Branner's title (*unser Staats-Geologe*) and made a note later in the year when Branner left the state for a professorship at Stanford. A week later, the *Echo* reprinted an article from the *Arkansas Gazette*, which quoted W. F. Winner, *ein Kapitalist von*

*Kansas City*, about the zinc-mining industry, the mineral's transportation on the White River, and its eventual use in England. Winner encouraged investment in a railroad line up to the mining area in south Missouri and north Arkansas. More speculation followed. An enthusiastic report from April told of "Silvery City" in Montgomery County, where Commissioner Locke was quoted as having found two dozen deposits of valuable types of ore in the most remarkable combinations he ever had seen. Locals asserted that the Elnora deposit would have been worth $100,000 within twenty-four hours of discovery if it had been found in Colorado. German readers who wanted to verify good deposits were urged to send samples to the government.[6]

The same issue brought news of discoveries of salt, natural gas, and oil at Magazine in Logan County. The *Echo* reported the oil field to be at least ten miles long and stated that a rail company was already planning a line to the location. The editors hinted at the downside to natural resources as an economic driver—they are not renewable once extracted—when they noted that the machines to be used at Mount Magazine "in order to exploit the petroleum sources there" had come through Paris in the previous week. Natural gas was found in Morrilton by a well digger, and happenstance similarly resulted in the purported discovery of gold in Scott County. Hunters were said to have accidentally found gold after one of their dogs chased an animal into a cave. Again, the frenzy for found wealth came over Arkansans, and the *Echo* reported that hundreds were camping in the area, causing the men who made the initial discovery to guard the cave continuously with rifles. By October and November, the *Echo* had resumed a more enthusiastic tone regarding natural resources, reporting about oil and coal near Paris and declaring: "Logan County is approaching a rapid boom." This pronouncement was surely a matter of pride for those who founded the paper, given its initial incarnation as *Der Logan County Anzeiger* (Logan County Gazette).

The *Echo* reported on the incorporation and activities of mining companies, including the Little Rock Mining & Smelting Company, the Kellogg mines, Melrose Mining and Diamond Drill Company, and the Petit Jean Oil Company. Existing mining operations were singled out for recognition. One article reported that three hundred miners had marched for two weeks from Oliver Springs and Briceville in East Tennessee to Arkansas. They had been forced out of work because of the use of convict labor in the mines there. Half found work at the Quita mine about three miles from Russellville, and the rest were employed by Stiewel & Company in Coal Hill. The author mentioned that more immigrants from Tennessee were expected and proclaimed, "All will find work in Arkansas and bring our coal business to an upswing." This was followed by reports of coal discovered near Conway and of eight coal mines in operation around Russellville.[7]

The *Echo* also covered in detail the opening of new factories, mills, and other production facilities around the state. Perhaps because the paper was located in Little Rock, readers learned more about new facilities in this city: a canning factory to be opened by Thomas Manufacturing Company, a feather bed and mattress factory planned by Pulaski Manufacturing at Broadway near the Arkansas River, a stave factory, and an ice factory built by Anheuser-Busch. Other parts of the state reported successes: an operation for preserving fruit in Harrisburg, a brick factory operated by a Mr. Toyle in Fort Smith that employed fifty workers, the Red Cypress Shingle Company in Parksdale, and a broom factory in Pine Bluff. One entry made clear that negotiation was sometimes necessary to draw economic development to a city. The *Echo* reported that Pine Bluff was supposed to receive a new workshop for the production of rail cars for the Saint Louis and Southwestern Line, but only if the city could contribute $25,000 to the building of the facility. At the time of publication, the Chamber of Commerce had already raised $15,000. In December 1892, controversy erupted in a conflict between cotton oil mills located in Little Rock and Conway. The paper reported that agents of the Little Rock mills were attempting to put the Conway Cotton Oil Mill and Gin Company out of business by bringing in raw materials and selling at extremely low prices, possibly to try to flood the market. The paper criticized this behavior as an attempt to establish a monopoly in central Arkansas: "It is said that the trust companies do this everywhere where there is an oil mill that does not belong to the trust. They will not have success here. The oil mill here has contracts with almost all the farmers in the county for seed, and the farmers want to keep the local mill running."[8]

Other articles addressed real estate, whether the purchasing of land, renovations, or new construction. Most of these stories came from central Arkansas. In January, readers learned that Captain Jas. R. Miller had decided to build a four-level building at the corner of Markham and Scott; the existing buildings would be torn down, and the Tennessee Brewing Company had agreed to occupy a corner of the planned building. Other new construction in Little Rock included a large new building on Second Street next to Hotel Richelieu, rumored to be the new headquarters of Trust & Savings Company, as well as the new home of the Turners. For this German financial organization, the paper listed the trustees and members of the building committee as well as the architect. Those interested in auctions were alerted that they could purchase lot six on the corner of Fourth and Spring Streets at the courthouse on July 2. Another news story merely hinted at new development, noting that an "Eastern capitalist" had suggested to the citizens of Jonesboro that they procure an opera house and electric lights, although the story did not report whether the capitalist had offered to supply the funds for the endeavor.[9]

The biggest news story regarding real estate in the 1892 *Echo* was the establishment of what is today known as MacArthur Park in Little Rock. The land for the park was owned by the federal government, which had constructed numerous military buildings on the property that had fallen into disrepair by 1892. When the Tennessee Brewing Company expressed an interest in the land, some leaders grew concerned. Congressman William Terry helped broker an exchange of a considerably larger property of one thousand acres, as long as it would be held in perpetuity as a public park for the citizens of Little Rock. But these eventual plans were not widely known at the time, and a number of articles illustrate how Germans living in the capital city followed the transaction closely while it was under way. The first note regarding what the Germans would come to call the *Stadtpark* (city park) was a brief news item stating that bills to create a new military post in Little Rock had been introduced first in the Senate and then the House; it mentioned a sum of $50,000 to be spent on the development, and the stipulation that the thousand acres for the new military post had to be located no farther than ten miles from the city. In return, the citizens would receive the current arsenal land for use as a city park.[10]

Most of the other reporting during 1892 on this issue concerned attempts to find a suitable spot for the thousand acres to be traded. In April the *Echo* noted that an unnamed company with significant holdings in west Little Rock was buying up farms at good prices in an attempt to attract a bid for the military post. The reporting made it sound like a fait accompli, with an additional promise of an electric rail line to be built out into west Little Rock to serve the base. By May, the editors already seemed discouraged by the glacial process of selecting a site, beginning a news item with *Es hängt von Little Rock ab!* (It depends on Little Rock!). The article stated that the city government needed to move forward more decisively lest it jeopardize its opportunity to receive both a new city park and military post from the federal government. In June, the paper told its readers that a general had arrived to inspect six possible sites for the post, with the final selection requiring the approval of the Secretary of War. A City Park District was formed after a petition was turned in with over one thousand signatures of leading men in the city, some of whom were nominated as park commissioners. By the end of the year, the options for the military post site were narrowed down to a decision between Nubbin Ridge or Pulaski Heights; Pulaski Heights was ultimately rejected because it was too close to an existing sanatorium and there was concern that the waste from the military post would end up in the Arkansas River. Apparently German speakers were confused about whether or not the new tax for the city park had to be paid immediately. The paper informed them that, though there had been several lawsuits filed regarding the legality of the tax, the issue had been settled by the courts and payment was due in the Real Estate Building by January 1.[11]

German speakers in Little Rock in 1892 were additionally interested in the military as a source of revenue because of the militia drills taking place in the city. A practice skirmish in Clinton Park in August was put on by three hundred soldiers. The soldiers were housed in tents, and the *Echo* reported that they were welcome guests in the city; it listed all of the companies taking part and where they were from. It considered the militia troops to be capable, given their training, but voiced uncertainty about their readiness for war—this was likely more than a mere offhand remark, given that the Brooks-Baxter War had taken place eighteen years earlier in Little Rock. Some of the older German settlers surely remembered the street fighting that had occurred. A week later, the *Echo* ran another assessment of the drill sent in by a correspondent calling himself simply *Ein alter Soldat* (An old soldier) that included a lengthy summary of the maneuvers themselves, a critique of the bad food served, and a mention that the governor had visited and received a fourteen-gun salute.[12]

The *Echo* regularly featured reporting from city council meetings. There were, of course, the usual controversies and bickering attendant to local governments, many pertaining to personnel decisions. In January the fire department struck because its chief, Robert McKay, was threatened with dismissal due to a complaint by the electric streetcar company (he was ultimately allowed to continue in his post). The city council voted to convert the volunteer fire department into a paid one, with positions for twenty-nine men. In June Mayor Fletcher got into a shouting match with Dr. Taylor, who had been denied the opportunity to speak on behalf of his petition. The city collector, Sides, was suspended and ultimately replaced and arrested after discrepancies were discovered in his accounting. Police chief Sanders resigned after accusations were leveled against him; one of the *Echo*'s advertisers, Ben Thalheimer, claimed the police had never returned the $25 in bail that he had paid on behalf of another man, Mr. Meyer. By a particularly tense December meeting, the police chief had still not been replaced. When the mayor was asked why, he said it was no one's business. During the same meeting, it was decided that city employees who did not pay their debts would be fired. The *Echo* took an interest in local politics down to the level of the election of new school-board members, even though many German children attended Catholic schools with instruction conducted in German. Readers were informed when and where elections would be held and provided information to determine their ward, and the paper announced the results following the election.[13]

The *Echo*'s reporting shows that Little Rock was modernizing, with new utilities, improvements to roads and bridges, and an emphasis on hygiene, while at the same time struggling with some aspects of the transition. The city passed a new water ordinance that allowed for ten more miles of pipe to be laid with one hundred more hydrants for the fire department. The council voted to spend more money on electric lights and to establish a city morgue and city hospital, after an inmate was found dead in the local jail. The area of the city that could be used for cattle-grazing was extended, although a few months later, the city council announced that the position of cow catcher was being eliminated. An electric streetcar caused two accidents, and the paper expressed hope that the city council would enact a speed limit for streetcars, to give other vehicles time to get out of their way. The paper asserted a train wreck occurred because the city council had forbidden the use of train whistles within city limits. Plans for new city wards and pavement and improvement districts frequently made appearances in the *Echo*'s pages, as did Pulaski County's plan to create a toll bridge over the Arkansas River. The city council sent a petition to the governor to ask that convict labor not be used to build roads in Little Rock. Citizens sent a petition to the mayor regarding the problem of improperly cleaned stalls at the Southern Oil Company that resulted in swarms of flies and a terrible smell that they feared could be a public health hazard. Due to the risk of cholera, the mayor ordered that standing-water pools be dried up and disinfected, weeds pulled, and alleys cleaned. Finally, there were conflicting opinions presented to the city council about whether or not Argenta (which would eventually become North Little Rock) should remain a part of Little Rock or become its own city.[14]

While the majority of reporting on local politics was dedicated to goings-on in Little Rock, the *Echo* published a few articles regarding governmental decisions from other cities around the state. Readers learned that the city council of Fort Smith would allow cows to run loose within city limits, a pronouncement that was respectively championed and scorned by those on opposite sides of the issue. The Fort Smith Chamber of Commerce appointed a committee to discuss building a street through the Cherokee Bottom on the Cherokee side of the river. The city council of Pine Bluff decided to tax all bars $600 in order to pay off the debt of the water company, arguing that this would allow enough water to be delivered throughout the city and that insurance rates would fall as a result. The *Echo* speculated that licensing fees for bars in Brinkley ($2,000) and Des Arc ($2,500) were not intended to benefit the public good, but rather to make it impossible to run a profitable establishment serving alcohol, resulting in de facto Prohibition.[15]

The *Echo* informed readers about new developments in transportation and their effects on commerce. One major development in 1892 was a plan of the Executive Committee of the Arkansas River Commission to make the waterway navigable year-round, from its opening in the Mississippi to Fort Smith. The editors strongly favored the plan and urged readers to advocate for it with neighbors, as petitions were circling in affected communities: "We are calling the attention of our fellow German citizens to the great benefit which this river correction will bring to all. Especially our farmers and the owners of coal properties on the Arkansas River will benefit from the inexpensive water freight, and many places will profit from it." However, revealing an understanding of Arkansas politics and promised improvements, the editors closed with the sentiment: "Let's hope that the project is realized." In the next two months, readers were informed of its progress. The Board of Trade in Little Rock urged immediate passage of the Torrey Bill in Congress, since it would help Arkansas pay for the necessary work in clearing the river. Several prominent Little Rock citizens traveled to Washington, DC, to convince lawmakers to back the plan. A meeting of the Arkansas River Commission was held, and the secretary presented data regarding how much freight was shipped on the Arkansas and the railways as well as how much agricultural acreage and timber land the state possessed; it elected a delegation to send to Washington. The lobbying efforts had paid off by March. The House committee for rivers and harbors allotted $250,000 of the total $20.7 million expenditure for the Arkansas River improvements and additionally gave $20,000 to improve the Ouachita River.[16]

The German newspaper was additionally interested in international developments that would assist farmers and others in transporting products to market. An October news item noted that a planned Nicaragua Canal, a project that was never completed, would be good for Arkansas farmers, since it would mean that cotton could be exported more easily. The editors enthusiastically supported the project and outlined the reasons why in a lengthy editorial, providing readers with numerous export and import statistics. A Nicaragua Canal would be helpful in increasing United States exports to Latin America, as it would shorten shipping times by several weeks and avoid the most dangerous parts of the sea voyage. Further, the editors believed it could open Asian markets to American goods and products. The argument was steeped in paternalism regarding "lesser" Asian cultures, but the paper asserted that America could serve as a better trading partner than Europe: "The inhabitants of India, China, and Japan will gradually be permeated by the advancing spirit of Western civilization. The seclusion, which rejected for long years the approach of European advances, is yielding little by little to the influence of modern thought. Just and honorable trade with American commerce will open the extensive and valuable markets of the East." Although frequently critical of American capitalism, the editors in this case backed their adopted homeland: "In the competition for a worthwhile price, the shorter route should make it possible for the Americans to conquer their European rivals." The editorial further envisaged direct trade between the farmers and producers of the Mississippi valley and the Asian markets via the canal.[17]

While rivers could be advantageous for shipping, they were often a hindrance in moving goods to market, and so the building of bridges was another major transportation topic in the *Echo*. Extensive reporting was devoted to the opening of a new iron bridge across the Mississippi, which was referred to as "the king of rivers," as well as to all of the festivities planned from May 11 to 14 to celebrate the opening. Several thousand attended, and the opening parade featured police, military, bands, German and Polish Vereine, and famous guests and politicians, whom the *Echo* listed by name. The paper concluded the parade description with ethnic pride: "Our citizenry will give much credit to the Germans for this lovely participation." The report went on to describe other elements in great detail: how the engineers tested the load, how the governors of Arkansas and Tennessee participated in a mock wedding ceremony between their states, the firing of canons from the river, a parade of elaborately decorated bicycles crossing the bridge, an evening parade, the excursions of the second day, and the concluding fireworks. Other bridge projects were only in the planning stages but nevertheless of great interest to *Echo* readers. In April the Little Rock city council was given a petition from several citizens to turn the city and its surroundings into an improvement district for the purpose of building a free bridge over the Arkansas River. The editors stated that all the candidates for the county judge position were in favor of a free bridge, which they felt could and should be built with county funds. The issue was mentioned again in October after the Little Rock Bridges Company was incorporated with the Secretary of State's office with the intention of building a toll bridge. Until this occurred, a new ferry would be in operation from the north side of the river from Newton Avenue to the beginning of Main Street. German speakers living in Logan County had better luck with bridge financing, as the *Echo* reported the County Levying Court had approved $2,000 for the construction of an iron bridge over Short Mountain Creek near Paris.[18]

German settlers found the roads in Arkansas to be particularly vexing, and the contrast between European roads, which had existed since the Middle Ages with some already constructed by the Romans, must have been jarring. In a humorous letter from Morrison Bluff submitted by Silberfisch, the correspondent described an arduous journey to the train station so filled with problems with sandy roads that he felt he was "quite in a proper African sand desert"; he wished he had had a camel, especially when all the oil in the travelers' lamps burned out because the journey took far longer than expected. The editors viewed such difficulties of travel on Arkansas roads to be an impediment to recruiting other immigrants and retaining newcomers in the state. While the paper generally opposed the practice of convict leasing by private corporations, it supported a plan to allow the state government to use convicts as a work force for new roads. The *Echo* argued that the prisoners would not be competing against workers in the free market, since there was no money to pay for such labor in any case. The 1892 elections were a cause for optimism that the state might begin to take the need for roads seriously, but the editors again had low expectations regarding Arkansas politics: "The candidates for the office of governor are all three in favor of building good roads in the state. Now, will the next legislature deliberate regarding the best ways and means for this or waste its time with nonsense? We'll see, and hope for the best."[19]

In October the paper published an extremely detailed report on the meeting of the commissions for agriculture and mining that seemed to indicate progress was being made. The *Echo* shared with readers plans to raise funds for road building, basics of street construction and drainage, a proposed timetable, the use of state and county convict labor, and the need for users to switch to wide-wheeled wagons, since the use of thin-wheeled wagons led to damage. The committee was scheduled to present its proposal to the legislature. The editors saw a special role in this cause for fellow newspapermen, who, they believed, should explain the issue to readers and reinforce the importance of infrastructure. The editors preferred a more top-down method to creating a linked interstate road system than what they saw in the plan: "This road building plan might be good; it very much depends on the implementation, and in this regard, we have a number of concerns. It would appear to us to be better and more secure if initially the state had begun with the use of convicts to build end-to-end state roads, onto which the counties could themselves connect their county roads, as requested and desired, and through the awarding of state advance money."[20]

Railroads affected daily life on both personal and professional levels, and the paper provided information on developments in passenger and freight lines. In each issue, the *Echo* included the timetable for daily passenger trains, giving morning and afternoon departure times for routes from Little Rock to Fort Smith, Texarkana, Memphis, Saint Louis, Helena, Pine Bluff, and Arkansas City, as well as the return trips. The *Echo* alerted readers whenever a line was offering discounted rates for certain events, such as the Turner meeting in Hot Springs or a special exhibit in Saint Louis. Settlers could read about the newest developments regarding new routes opening and closing and new rail companies being incorporated. The editors, ever critical of monopolies or potential monopolies, wrote with enthusiasm about a planned route from Little Rock to West Plains, an enterprise with capital of $3.5 million. Although the Iron Mountain Rail Company was an advertiser of the *Echo*, the paper told its readers, "The railroad will additionally depress the freight prices of the Iron Mountain Rail, since it will be a competing railroad. At any rate, it will contribute to the boom in the state and much to our rose city." The German settlers apparently had noticed what others who needed to move freight in Arkansas knew; the railroads often acted as monopolies, and competition was welcome.[21]

A month earlier, though, the *Echo* ran a glowing report about the contributions of the Iron Mountain Shops in Argenta, proving that the paper's coverage could be as fickle in this regard as it was in others. The story discussed an invention by the chief of the car department: a new wagon door that offered an easier closing mechanism that was nevertheless extremely tight. It further mentioned that the Argenta shops employed one thousand workers. The author speculated that if Little Rock would give a subsidy, the company would be willing to build railcars in the shops as well, which would lead to hundreds more jobs and more money spent in the local economy.[22]

The paper covered business dealings of the railroads, including problems they faced, such as calamities, legal proceedings, and strikes. For instance, heavy rains in April left two stretches of the Iron Mountain route in Little

Rock dangerously washed out, and a stock car train at Poplar Bluff ran off into the river, an accident from which neither personnel nor freight were recovered. Taxes were another railroad issue. The Chancery Court ruled in favor of the state and against the Little Rock and Memphis Rail Company in the amount of $45,000 for taxes, and the Iron Mountain Railroad settled with the state for $250,000. Another legal case held important ramifications for German farmers. W. L. Cravens, an *Echo* advertiser, sued the Missouri Pacific Rail Company when they refused to take responsibility for several bales of his hay that they had been transporting when they caught fire. The Supreme Court decided that because Cravens had entrusted his freight to the railroad, the company was responsible for it and had to pay compensatory damages.[23]

Iron Mountain Railroad contended with strike threats during the *Echo*'s inaugural year. Already in 1883, a strike was broken with the help of law enforcement, and sixty to seventy-five workers were terminated. In 1886 a more serious strike threatened the company, but it failed as public pressure mounted. Carl Moneyhon discussed the role newspapers took in strike actions in Arkansas around this time.

> Many nonunion Arkansans saw what was taking place as somehow vaguely un-American. Newspaper editors frequently criticized strikers, especially when their actions involved violence, accusing them of being anarchists. They blamed these actions on the large number of ignorant foreigners that they believed had filled up some of the unions and explained their actions as a failure to understand American civilization.[24]

If German settlers were responsible for encouraging workers to strike, the *Echo* gives no evidence of it; the editors would certainly have been appalled at this assessment of their countrymen, since they frequently editorialized on the ideals of democracy. The paper was, to be sure, interested in the protection of workers' rights. But it had no qualms about accepting advertising from Iron Mountain after its role in breaking the strike of a few years earlier. Reporting on possible strike actions at the company in 1892 was neutral in comparison to some of the paper's strident lectures regarding capitalist abuse of the everyday worker. On August 5, a news item detailed that the workers in the roundhouse of the Iron Mountain Workshops had threatened to strike if the new foreman, Elkins, were not replaced. An update one column later explained that after a strike had been looming for a few days, Mr. Reardon, who had traveled from Saint Louis, was able to resolve the situation via a conference with the affected employees, who then all returned to their work.[25]

Later that month, there was another threatened work stoppage regarding unequal pay raises among the boilermakers: "The boilermakers had demanded a pay increase because individual workers among them had been given one. As their desire was not consented to, they went on strike. On Monday, the matter was considered in an assembly and explain[ed] that sufficient reason to strike had not been presented and that the boilermakers had acted rashly. All strikers returned to work." In the original German, the writer used the passive construction *nicht willfahrt wurde* for "was not consented to." This rather unusual construction, typically used to refer to a monarch's granting privileges, hinted at the unequal relationship between the employer and workers. Nevertheless, the paper emphasized that the strike intentions were peacefully resolved.[26]

Near the end of the year, a final peculiar case regarding worker unrest and Iron Mountain appeared in the pages of the *Echo*. On December 19, nineteen black convict laborers, who had been working near Helena for the Iron Mountain Rail Company, became ill; four died. The next day saw ten further victims and two more deaths. In addition to these black victims, the paper reported that a Captain Dunlap and a white warden were ill. For the *Echo*, the cause of the mysterious illnesses was clear: "The workers there were disgruntled and attempted to remove the convicts. Nevertheless, they were not successful. . . . A medical investigation of the dead identified arsenic poisoning." The *Echo* article is noteworthy for its identification of the negative ramifications of convict leasing and its sympathetic portrayal of the victims. In describing the transport of the victims to Little Rock, the paper noted: "On the way, an additional convict died, and a number more became sick. The trip was a terrible one, the ill groaned and moaned from the beginning to the end." The *Arkansas Gazette* also suspected that the cause of the incident was disgruntlement over convict leasing and further noted that the contract had been canceled and the men returned to prison as a result. But the English-language paper was far less considerate of the terrified prisoners who remained, referring to them as "zebras" and mocking their relief at being returned to the penitentiary: "As the train pulled out, they cheered lustily as if they had been set at liberty." These contemporaneous accounts omit the opinion of the medical authorities behind the scenes. While the local papers suspected sabotage, the acting assistant surgeon general and supervising surgeon general in Little Rock were more concerned about a possible cholera outbreak at the Helena camp, which the arsenic poisoning might have inadvertently exposed. One of the first questions officials asked was whether the convicts had been in contact with immigrants. This was not the case, and so the officials instead focused on the deplorable unsanitary and crowded conditions of the camp and prisoner transport. The *Echo* gives no indication that contagious disease was being considered as a cause of the illnesses and deaths and that if so, immigrants were the suspected cause of the contagion.[27]

An April news item reprinted from a Fayette, Missouri, source should have made clear to German immigrants that convict labor was essentially the continuation of slavery after the Emancipation Proclamation. The first sentence bluntly stated, "On the 29th of the previous month, three Negroes were sold in Fayette, Missouri in accordance with the law against vagabonding." The article further described how after a trial and guilty sentence, the men were turned over to the sheriff. The auction, in which local farmers engaged in bidding to obtain the work of the black men, was described as lively. The newspaper reported the amounts that the men sold for, commenting that the money went to the county treasury and that "the delinquents [would] have to work for the entire period of their sentences without pay and for only their foodstuffs."[28] The *Echo*'s editors, who otherwise routinely championed worker's rights and decried uncompensated work, made no comment on this article.

In addition to reporting on business developments in the state, the *Echo* kept readers informed of numerous small practical matters pertinent to settlers running businesses, from assessments of which business partners were considered reliable to explanations of governmental matters such as permits and taxes. A regular item in the paper was a notice of those banks and businesses in danger of failing or that had already failed. In July the President of Magnolia and Gate City National Bank in Texarkana had gone missing after the bank closed its doors. The *Echo* assured immigrants that it was the first bankruptcy of a bank to occur in Arkansas since 1874, and the "fugitive banker" J. G. Kelso was apprehended in Pine Bluff by October. A similar case occurred in Hope in September, when the bank owner, a Dr. Crosset, sold the bank and left town. The new owners discovered only forty-five cents in deposits when they expected $120,000. In July a report of a bank failure in Texarkana turned out to be only a rumor circulated by the banker's business rivals. Other business closings were a more frequent occurrence. Most of these announcements stated whether the sheriff had been involved in seizing property, whether a receivership had been established, if garnishments had been applied, and the amounts the company had in assets and liabilities. Occasionally, reasons for bankruptcy were offered such as the poor price of cotton or the inability to collect accounts due from customers. *Echo* advertisers were not immune to the bankruptcy trend, and the paper had the unhappy duty at different points throughout the year of alerting its readers to bankruptcies of Peitz & Snyder, a store offering groceries and clothing; Pollock & Hirsch, a furniture store; and the Davis Reinmann Company, which dealt in livestock and carriages. Due to the numerous business closings and the economic downturn, a committee was formed in Little Rock to ask landlords to reduce rents across the board by 25 percent.[29]

Arrests, lawsuits, and judgements related to business dealings appeared in the *Echo* as well. Arrests included two cases of postal clerks, one of whom had opened and kept registered letters. A fruit seller was arrested and fined $3 after blocking the road and refusing to move until he had waited on his customers. Another man was arrested, fined $1,000, and sentenced to thirty days in jail for selling hops tea without a license. A more serious incident occurred when a farmer near Yellville tried to collect on a small personal debt and was stabbed to death by the debtor, who then fled. Lawsuits affecting businesses included two cases in which the families of workmen who had died on the job sued the employers of the deceased. G. M. Stucky of Fayetteville received a judgement of $700 in damages against the Frisco train company because his horses had been scared by the train and had run off. And the *Echo* was delighted to report on a court date for its adversary, Philip Dietzgen. Dietzgen showed up in court after suing a Mr. Lessing, who served as guarantor for a $50 note to Friedrich Niehaus three years earlier. Niehaus contended the loan had been paid back, which Dietzgen denied. The *Echo* noted the matter would be heard before the circuit court but did not report back on the outcome.[30]

Other business difficulties in 1892 included property damage, loss of goods in transit, and theft. Transportation mishaps were responsible for some of the losses. When the steamer *Eugen*, property of the Memphis and Arkansas River Packet Company, sank, all of the personnel and passengers could be saved, but the cargo of cotton and cotton seeds was lost. Two separate train incidents in Little Rock were responsible for the destruction of a milk truck near the double bridge at Nineteenth Street as well as $5,000 in damages to the gas company offices. As a result of flooding around the state, a lumber mill washed away, the building housing a cooperage fell into the river, and rail and telegraph lines were damaged; a November tornado swept away businesses, goods, and a post office near Fayetteville.[31]

Some articles reported on more unusual problems for businesses in the state. In the bakery of Otto Solf, a frequent *Echo* advertiser, a young baker was playing with a gun and pretending to shoot one of his senior colleagues. Around the time the senior baker admonished him to stop playing with the gun, it went off, and the older man was struck in the head. Although the wound bled copiously, the senior baker was thought to be fine and had already returned to work. In November the establishment of the jeweler Bulard in Searcy was leveled by a dynamite bomb, and the explosion also damaged the nearby courthouse. No more information was provided regarding the sensational incident, with the relatively short item concluding simply: "No clue of a perpetrator." In December the *Echo* offered a cautionary tale about counterfeit money involving the establishment of Gershner: A boy identified as E. Baldwin was sent to the saloon several times to purchase whiskey with a dollar coin, until the barkeeper became suspicious, bit into the coin, and found it to be a fake. The boy had been sent to purchase the whiskey by a warden in the state prison, and subsequently both the boy and warden were arrested. Theft and burglary were frequent topics of news items. Almost weekly, German settlers read of safes being burgled and merchandise being stolen from businesses, with goods as diverse as cotton, chicken, cigars, empty sacks, groceries, postage stamps, tools, watches, and whiskey being taken. Due to the crime epidemic in the streets of Little Rock, a nervous clerk at one of the businesses that advertised in the *Echo* found himself in trouble for shooting at police officers in a case of mistaken identity. Two policemen were searching for a burglar in an alley when Norton, a clerk in Lescher's shoe shop, approached. One of the policemen attempted to ask him if he had any information and was promptly shot by the terrified clerk, who assumed he was being attacked by robbers. The paper explained the incident thus: "He had been addressed suddenly, and scared to death, he had naturally shot far beside [where the policemen were standing] and he ran into a house and shut the door. The police followed him, obtained entrance, and arrested him." Though he had not injured the officers and evidently had a reasonable motive for shooting, Norton was kept in jail overnight and charged with carrying a concealed weapon and firing a gun with the intention to kill.[32]

By far, the biggest hazard to commerce as reported in the pages of the *Echo* was the danger of fire resulting from accident or arson. Some accidental fires were caused by bales of cotton spontaneously igniting while awaiting shipment, either by train or by boat. In a March fire in Clarksville, the highly combustible cotton—145 bales' worth—had help from a machinery spark and resulted in the destruction of an entire train platform. The Capital

Hotel suffered a fire sparked by a defective chimney, and lightning produced by a heavy thunderstorm in Malvern struck the wall of wires in the telegraph station, badly injuring the telegraphist. In addition to fire resulting from natural causes, arson was a widespread problem. Arson or suspected arson was reported in fourteen cases in 1892; targeted businesses included pharmacies, hotels, grocery stores, stalls, and a women's finery store. Some of these incidents perhaps resulted from business rivalries or personal vendettas, but a February reprint of an item from the *Commercial Bulletin* hinted at another reason. It reported that 1891 saw much more fire damage than 1890, but that 1892 should be safer, since the economic forecasts were better. The editors chastised the *Bulletin* for accusing those who lost property in fires of being the perpetrators.[33]

In April the *Echo*'s editor questioned whether anarchists could possibly be at work in Little Rock. A milk man saved Fletcher's Drug Store from an arson attempt by discovering a pile of paper and wood shavings coated in petroleum on the front steps. A follow-up article in July reported on a fourth attempt to burn down the same drug store. This time, the arsonists had broken down the back door at four in the morning and set fire to oil on the premises, but the fire department was still able to extinguish the fire. A Swiss man, J. B. Suters of Conway, experienced losses of uninsured livestock and equipment in the amount of $1,000, and the editor commented that it would be good if arsonists could be apprehended and made to pay restitution to their victims. A more unusual story of arson was reported close to the new year, when a drunk man set fire to a stand selling fireworks, and passersby had to dodge the suddenly erupting Roman candles. Fire damage was often extensive; the close proximity of buildings allowed blazes to spread easily and the fire-fighting capacities of the time were limited. Fire reports generally listed several businesses as being damaged or destroyed. A spectacular fire in Malvern, which the *Echo* claimed was the largest ever seen there, burned the store of B. and H. Berger to the ground, along with all of its contents, since Malvern had no fire department. Damages were an astronomical $75,000, but insurance covered only $36,500. In another Malvern case, the owner of Clark's brickyard was more fortunate, as the citizens were able to lend a hand and successfully put out the fire resulting in only $3,000 worth of damage, all of which was covered by insurance.[34]

The *Echo*'s reporting in its inaugural year sought to assist German speakers in their interactions with state and local governments. Readers in Conway and Logan Counties were notified of how and where to pay taxes. These notices listed townships requiring tax payment, locations, and dates of collection and reminded property owners to bring their quarterly tax receipts when paying. One typical announcement, reprinted in several issues in March, discussed levies and incorporated an English term that readers would encounter: "The taxes must be paid on April 10. After April 10, a 1/4 dollar penalty will be added to every dollar [owed]. The tax levy (making an 'assessment') takes place in the first half of June, and we will additionally call attention to it." Notices for Little Rock property owners subject to grading district and sewer district taxes appeared in June, with instructions on whom to pay and the July deadline for payment. The editors kept readers informed about possible future taxes as well, reporting in September that the Little Rock city council was discussing a new tax policy that would bring in $80,000 through the taxing of all property at ten mills. The paper additionally explained what happened when citizens did not pay taxes at all. A news item from June told readers that land seized due to nonpayment had been sold at public auction earlier in the week; ownership of unsold lots reverted back to the state.[35]

German speakers paid funds to local government in the form of licenses. Little Rock residents were warned that those who had not paid a license for their dogs could have the dogs impounded, again using a mixture of German and English for clarity: "Steuermarken sind auf der City-Clerks-Office zu haben" (Tax stamps can be obtained at the city clerk's office). In December, the Little Rock city government made significant changes to licenses for professions. Mobile fruit peddlers saw an enormous rise in annual license fees from $25 to $150. Commissions and futures brokers, who previously had to pay no taxes, would be required to pay $50 and $500 respectively. Poultry dealers received a reduction from $25 to $8, and those selling other meat from $50 to $25; an added provision exempted farmers from buying a license if they offered meat from cattle they had raised themselves. Theaters would have to pay $5 in taxes for every performance, and those who organized dances, a frequent occurrence in German Vereine, were responsible for turning over $10 for regular dances, $15 for those requiring formal attire, and $25 for masked balls. The editor did not offer readers any explanation for the hefty increases in licensing fees for some professions and reductions for others. However, in July, the paper reported that brick-and-mortar establishments had complained to the city council that fruit and vegetable peddlers should have to pay more in licenses because they were damaging the business of established shops.[36]

In other financial matters, the paper announced the value of government-issued scrips in Pulaski County and Little Rock. Readers were told that banks would pay dividends on July 1: 4 percent for the Exchange Bank, the Bank of Little Rock, and First National Bank and 5 percent for the German National Bank. But the editors perhaps did not understand much more about banking than their readers. The paper printed a retraction a week later, noting that an "error had occurred" in the reporting, and it was incorrect that the banks would be paying dividends on July 1: "The previous year's dividends were intended and, to be sure, the First National Bank and the Exchange Bank had twice declared dividends, the last of which were paid on June 1, while the Bank of Little Rock and the German Bank had only declared yearly dividends."[37]

Germans interacted with their new government in the court system as well, and the *Echo* tried to inform readers about local laws and justice. Readers were told when local circuit and probate courts were meeting. One story involved a boy who was arrested for shooting sparrows, and his mother told law enforcement he would not be allowed to have the gun again. The item closed with a caveat to readers that boys who had air rifles or bean-shooters on the street could be arrested and punished. A more serious case involved theft and destruction of property at the home of German Nic. Fässler. Fässler was away from his farm working at the coal mine in Russellville due to depressed cotton prices, and his wife went to church seven miles away, leaving the oldest child, an eight-year-old girl, in charge of three younger siblings. Three local boys came into the house, stole $18 that had been set aside to pay bills, and dislodged the stoppers of two barrels of wine, which spilled out about a hundred gallons that had been produced only the day before. When the girl attempted to replace the stoppers, one boy picked her up and threw her across the room. There were three trials: The boys were acquitted in the first, even though the young daughter could identify them as the attackers. In the second, Fässler prevailed and was awarded $100 in damages. A third trial was held after the judge in the case admitted he had received death threats, after which the verdict was changed again, with Fässler both losing and being ordered to pay $131.50 in total court costs. He was forced to pawn property to cover the debt. The most notable part of this lengthy article was the commentary on how the German farmer attempted to obtain justice in what was clearly a corrupt system.

> Fässler and an American of English descent attempted to bring the matter before a grand jury. All believed that the facts of the case were as narrated above, but the legal action had to be dismissed due to insufficient evidence. (In this there is a warning for our

> fellow countrymen: first see if there is enough evidence and then bring suit. We have made inquiries of honorable men regarding the matter and would have helped the man to obtain his rights, if something could be done about it. The Editors.)[38]

While this was presented as a cautionary tale to other Germans, it is not clear from the *Echo*'s reporting what Fässler could have done differently, and the warning to be gleaned between the lines was perhaps not to put too much faith in the local courts, in which threatened violence rather than evidence could determine the outcome of a trial.

Regardless of the unfavorable news regarding business closings, the calamities of fire and theft, and the challenges of dealing with government entities, the *Echo* finished its 1892 reporting on Arkansas's economy on a positive note. A late December editorial proclaimed, "In spite of the bad harvest and the depressed business transactions, the hope for improvement has risen very much recently. New trains and factories are being built in the state, and that will bring work and earned income."[39] Of course, the looming economic crisis of 1893 would prove this optimism to be unfounded, but Germans were very much considering themselves a part of the future of the state, which they were beginning to regard as their own. The Chicago World Exposition planned for the following year provided ample opportunities to showcase the good to be found in their chosen new home. Throughout the year, the *Echo* kept readers informed of the preparations and what would be included in Arkansas's representation. Friedrich Meyer created a special plaque that was sent to the World Expo. The plaque showed all twenty-two kinds of wood that grew in Arkansas and listed types known to Germans such as maple, spruce, pear, and ash, as well as native species, which the paper did not bother to translate, such as persimmon, pecan, sassafras, hickory, and Bois D'Arc. Readers were informed that the wood produced in the state was useful in every kind of industry and that Arkansas had more forest than any other state except Texas. Other items described the collection of mineral samples for the exhibit and purportedly the world's largest white oak, on the White River, which was also to be transported to the Expo. While the state was rich in natural resources, the capital necessary to exhibit these wonders proved more difficult to collect. By January the citizens of Pulaski County had managed to raise only around $4,800 to cover the costs associated with representing the state at the expo, and in October, the *Echo* lamented that many counties had not contributed at all, which prevented the state from showcasing itself properly. This had been an important point in an earlier story, in which the paper argued that while the Arkansas building was not the largest at the expo, it featured beautiful ornamentation. The paper promised to publish drawings of the World Expo buildings, roughly one per week during the fall months, so that readers could appreciate "that even our state is represented in a dignified way at the exhibition."[40]

John Lucey, an ex-Confederate whose accounts of immigration to Arkansas are therefore unsurprisingly problematic in some ways, noted that the Chicago World Exposition was an ideal opportunity to present the positive aspects of the state in the hopes of attracting more immigrants. The *Echo*'s coverage of the Expo does not have the cynical undertones of a newspaper that undoubtedly championed the promotion of immigration; it has the tone of a local paper proud to highlight the good to be found in the area. The same year, the paper published a quotation from Father Eugene Weibel, a missionary to the state who frequently made trips back to Europe to bring more German-speaking clergy and nuns to Arkansas. It is indicative of the German settlers' attitude toward the state as a place they were already a part of and to which they could contribute greatly.

> I believe in the future of the state of Arkansas. It is not only the state and the land, which make the people, but rather the opposite: it is the people who make the state. Thank God, Arkansas has obtained a healthy, vital seed in German immigration, which, carefully tended, will grow into a mighty tree. I hope confidently that the *Echo* will take a stand for the equality of various nations in regard to the church, for the rights of Germans in state and church, and the denominational school. (The '*Echo*' will wholeheartedly take a stand for this. [editorial note])[41]

Indeed, political news and editorials featured heavily in the newspaper's reporting in its inaugural year, as the *Echo* sought to make Germans aware of their rights and assist immigrants in defending them in a politically turbulent year.

German settlers have played a role in American politics since the colonial era. A 1777 broadside by Andreas Emmerich does not show an interest in American-style freedom but rather in maintaining law and order and in fidelity to a monarch, appealing to Germans to remain firmly on the side of the British who were, in his view, only subduing a rebellious colony. Benjamin Franklin argued that German immigrants were fundamentally unsuited to participate in a democracy. After the Revolution, though, Germans did embrace the ideals of a constitutional democracy, and this embrace showed in the views espoused a century later by the *Echo* staff. The majority of Germans tended to be moderates in the early days of the American republic. The failed 1848 revolution in Germany led to an influx to the United States of more politically engaged immigrants in the second half of the nineteenth century. These Forty-Eighters were virulently opposed to slavery and tended to favor the Republican Party. Yet American Germans have generally held a wide range of opinions and affiliated with both major political parties. Willi Paul Adams argues that the German immigrants were less successful in working together as a political group than the Irish, divided as the former were by social class, religious views, and regional differences, and agreeing essentially only on matters concerning the availability of alcohol and the need to teach German in schools. The Civil War did not serve as a unifying factor among Germans either, as Walter Kamphoefner notes:

> Complex considerations regarding a wide range of issues including slavery, prohibition, nativism, and religious freedom drew German settlers to both the Democratic and Republican parties, depending on which issues were most important to them: not a monolithic political force. Not just southern slaveholders, but also many of the impoverished, immigrants, Catholics, or tipplers (sometimes all wrapped up in one) felt threatened by Republican "do-gooders" with their tendency to improve people whether the ostensible beneficiaries felt the need for it or not. In both the North and South, the issue of nativism clouded the issue of Unionism.[42]

Jonathan Wolfe observes that Germans in Arkansas tended to be supporters of the Democratic Party during the antebellum period, but Kenneth Barnes's research has shown that white Democrats in Conway County were not certain that they had the vote of immigrants in the chaos following the Civil War, especially because poor whites were working together with newly freed blacks in political matters. German immigrant papers, particularly in the first half of the nineteenth century, were deeply reliant on financial support by the political parties, as politicians sought the patronage of new voters. By the time of the *Echo*'s publication, however, most German-language newspapers had come to rely on an economic model that required editors to satisfy subscribers and advertisers rather than political parties. This meant that the newspapers were reflective of a broader segment of local German sentiment, although a subgenre of radical newspapers from the political fringes existed in larger markets.[43]

From its very beginning, the *Arkansas Echo* was a paper deeply aligned with the Democratic Party. Its founders chose to register it in Ayer's *American*

*Newspaper Annual* as Democratic, whereas the rival *Arkansas Staatszeitung* was registered as independent. Years after editor Carl Meurer's death, his daughter, Mary, was interviewed about her father's life and career. The interviewer stated that Arkansas has a strong Democratic tradition and asked if her father's paper followed that mold. Meurer began her response by noting her father's friendship with a leading Republican, and after a somewhat faltering attempt to clarify his beliefs, agreed with the researcher's revised characterization of the *Echo* as "independent or politically neutral." But in its inaugural year, the *Echo* would prove to be not only an ardent supporter of the Democratic Party but also a paper deeply invested in discussing political topics, from philosophical generalities to specific policies.[44]

Already in February, the editors reported that they had received letters complaining that the paper was either too liberal or too conservative, and they felt it necessary to address the newspaper's political direction. It is worth quoting the editorial at length, as it reveals an aspirational political direction from the outset. The editors regarded their Democratic allegiance not as blind devotion to a single political party. Rather, they claimed that the paper's link to the party was fundamentally American in nature.

> True freedom and liberalism can only spring forth from the ground of natural law, which corresponds to the fundamental truths of Christianity and Judaism. . . . Many, yes almost the majority of people have been blinded by the lies of our modern materialism, unamenable to an understanding of natural law, upon which alone the freedom of nations is based. Thomas Jefferson, the erudite third president of the United States, was an enthusiastic authority and admirer of natural law and was therefore considered a very liberal man. And justifiably so! Because the source of true freedom was known to and sacred to him. He therefore founded the Democratic Party on the natural human rights, on whose principles even today the confidence of the best and most insightful men of the Democratic Party are agreed. The *Arkansas Echo* also counts itself as a supporter of these principles, although it does not consider itself bound to agree to the errors in judgement of the Democratic Party. We therefore regard ourselves as entitled to be allowed to uniformly rebuff the irreconcilable accusations that we are too liberal or not liberal enough.[45]

The paper would make good on its promise not to follow the judgement of the state Democratic Party blindly. However, the bias toward the party increased throughout the election year of 1892, to the extent a statement made in a July editorial was hardly supportable: "Up to now, the *Echo* has acted neutrally in the election campaign." For example, when the paper published the platform of the Democratic Party in June, it declared, "The platform of *our* state convention first thoroughly heckles the Republican administration." After the election was over, the paper observed of Logan County, "*Our* entire county ticket is elected." A November article on victory celebrations around the state noted a banner that said "We done our best!" The editors added, "The *Echo* can say the same thing in reference to its work for the Democratic Party."[46]

One issue that transcended party loyalty was an opposition to nativism; in this way, the Arkansas *Echo* was typical of nationally circulated German American newspapers. An editorial proclaimed, "Among both Republicans and Democrats there are fanatics who want to put an end to European immigration. Now, if one of such nativist candidates faces a reasonable and in the noblest sense impartial candidate, then the American of German parentage will surely prefer the latter." It is telling that while the editors defended the right of other Germans to immigrate, they also employ the phrase "American of German parentage" in this political discussion. In most contexts, settlers refer to themselves as Germans and their English-speaking neighbors as Americans. In embracing the democratic process, the German settlers demonstrated a measure of acculturation, as they came to view themselves as Americans first. Yet some reader letters do contain some critiques of the local Democratic Party. In a scathing letter from Prairie View, reader P. J. expressed his disdain over the behavior of two Logan County Democrats, which he characterized as immoral if not illegal: Judge Harvey allegedly engaged in shady business dealings regarding price-fixing in the selling of county script and profited personally. The county treasurer, whom the judge was supposed to be supervising, had additionally misplaced $8,000 in funds, and the deficit had been ongoing for five years with no action taken. P. J. chastised the local Democratic papers, the *Paris Express* and the *Paris Times*, the latter of which was co-owned by the judge's son. He accused them of ignoring the charges against the judge, and instead praising him for his competence. P. J. noted that discontent over the situation was why the People's Party had been heavily recruiting among Democratic voters and went so far as to encourage his fellow Germans to vote for the Republican candidate in the race, in order to teach the Democratic Party a lesson. He believed the Democrats should choose candidates with more integrity in the future and stated that the Germans could live with a Republican county judge for two years. In this case, the editors printed the critical letter without comment.[47]

A week later, G. H. from Oppelo in Conway County shared a similar story of dissatisfaction with the Democratic nominee. He described a complicated case in which the local German community felt a farmer had been cheated in the purchase of railroad land ten years earlier; a third of the 120 acres allegedly purchased were in fact owned by the state. The German had been paying taxes on the land the entire time and had built buildings on the now-disputed acres. The writer felt that the land commissioner, C. B. Myers (referred to by the German speakers as Meyer) was not supporting the German in his claim and ended with: "And Meyer is on the Democratic ticket again. Are we supposed to vote for him again?" While the *Echo* printed the letter, including its criticism of a sitting Democratic official, the paper still directed readers to vote for the Democratic nominee. The paper's argument was that perhaps one of Myers's clerks, rather than the commissioner himself, had committed an error that led to the situation, and that the complaint should have been brought to light before the Democratic ticket had already been established. The *Echo* later reported on a different incident in Oppelo that illustrated how difficult it was to find an alternative to the two major parties. A Reverend Birmingham of Morrilton had announced he would give a talk supporting the Farmer's Alliance. Shortly into the speech, he began to complain about both parties. The audience shouted accusations that he was a liar and threw eggs at him, and he was forced to escape through a side window and spend the night in the woods before leaving town the next day on a freight train. The story is additionally noteworthy as the only episode of political violence the *Echo* chose to report during the troubled election year of 1892.[48]

In another case, readers urged their fellow German speakers to vote for a Republican candidate on his own merits, rather than simply as a protest vote against an unsavory Democratic nominee. S. A. Williams was a Republican candidate for the position of State Auditor. The enthusiasm for Williams reflected settlers' irritation that Arkansas politicians did not take them seriously as voters and underlined the *Echo*'s admonitions that Germans should become more involved in politics and work together as a group. The first correspondent from Fort Smith, S. P., praised Williams's work as mayor of that city and said he could personally vouch that German was spoken in the candidate's home and by his wife and children. S. P. regarded the candidacy as an important chance for Germans to vote for one of their own.

> I'm no political junkie but I would also like to see a German man among the high state officials, who recognizes that we Germans

> also pay taxes and that we are also entitled to something more than simply to pay and work. . . . One has so often made the Germans the loveliest promises and afterwards saddled the individual counties with ignoble prohibition laws that they [the Germans] now for once unanimously should vote for a good capable German who will earn us respect.[49]

Frequent correspondent Civis, also writing from Fort Smith, added his thoughts a week later; Civis believed that Williams had so much experience that his political affiliation should not matter. He urged his fellow Germans to vote a straight Democratic ticket with the exception of Williams. A third letter endorsed Williams in the next issue: F. V. expressed his disgust with politicians who would allow an entire industry (viniculture) to be destroyed simply to appeal to *einer gewissen Klasse von Menschen* (a certain class of people). He asked his fellow readers: "Are we simply going to take all of this?! I hope not!" F. V. went on to list the considerable experience Williams would bring to the office, as he had served on the Fort Smith city council nine times, as mayor for two years, and as the president of a construction company for nine years. In spite of the Germans' enthusiasm, Williams was not successful in his bid.[50]

The case of S. A. Williams's political campaign was unusual for another reason. The *Echo*'s rival, the *Staatszeitung*, apparently took exception to the support Williams had received from *Echo* readers. This is strange because the competing editor Dietzgen was, according to the *Echo*, "as he freely declares a well-paid and therefore commissioned spokesman of the Republican Party and supporter of the candidacy." Unfortunately, there are no extant copies of the *Staatszeitung* from this period, but the *Echo* alleged that Dietzgen's attacks on Williams supporters were libelous, and the *Echo*'s response was couched in emotional language that elevated the dispute to a danger for the entire republic, if anarchistic forces sowing hate and discord were allowed to come to rule. Perhaps Dietzgen suggested that *Echo* editors and readers had ulterior motives for supporting Williams's candidacy; the *Echo* editorial staff protested that Williams was a personal acquaintance of those endorsing him and that the *Echo*'s support for Williams would mean more in the German community than that of a "ball of paper printed with trash." Additionally, Williams was not the only Republican whom the *Echo* praised. In August the paper published the names of those candidates on the fusion ticket between Republicans and the People's Party. It noted that there were not a lot of independents represented but conceded, "The names of many who are known as good citizens are on the ticket." Thus, the *Echo* likely felt justified in taking the moral high ground as an independent judge of which candidates were suited for office regardless of party.[51]

Another divergent political opinion was offered by an anonymous contributor who submitted an article entitled "Ob's geht?" (Could it work?). It was penned in response to an earlier story about whether the government should follow the proposition of the Farmer's Party to loan farmers money at 1 or 2 percent and was structured as an imaginary debate between two German farmers: Hans and Fritz. The topics covered are astonishingly wide-ranging, including the Israelites, Henry VIII, and the need for coordinated international monetary policy, but several interesting perspectives emerged regarding politics. First, Hans accused Fritz of provoking the editor to stir up trouble, while Fritz replied that the editor wrote to him and said he did not mind "misguided" ideas like national farming loans being debated in the open. Fritz believed that the erroneous articles likely came from the Farmer's Party office in Washington, which hired writers to spread their ideas by sending boilerplate stories to regional newspapers. Second, the fictional German speakers decided that the moneyed class that controlled politics would not allow the existing system to be reformed, even though Germans agreed with the basic idea that farmers instead of lawyers and merchants should "have the profit from our sweat and work." The duo debated a local attempt by German farmers to raise the funds to take the means of production into their own hands by establishing a cotton mill and gin. Not enough Germans had the cash to invest, and no one was willing to take out a loan, but they would have perhaps considered a low-rate federal loan. After this concession, though, the article puzzlingly shifted position to mock the Farmer's Party's proposal to create a loan program. One farmer said he did not understand where the money for the loans should come from and that one would have to ask the "bigwigs" of the party. The other replied that he did ask, and the answer was, "Make it!" Finally, this article shows that the *Echo* hoped to be an opinion maker among the German settler population: "Hans: 'Nonsense! The farmers only borrow as much money as they owe; the money would immediately flow into the pockets of the capitalists, and they would of course speculate with it; thus says the *Echo* and I am in complete agreement with it.'"[52]

Political opinion among German settlers in Arkansas was not as unified as one might think from reading the pages of the *Echo*. While the editors and readers did not regard themselves as blind party loyalists, they were extremely enthusiastic in their support of the Democratic Party, both nationally and locally. There are indications, though, aside from the *Echo*'s dispute with the *Staatszeitung*, that not all Germans voted this ticket or voted at all. Kenneth Barnes mentions two German Americans who had been active in Republican politics around this time, Charles Wahl and Harry Coblentz, but notes that they left politics and moved away, fearing violence due to their political affiliation. The above-mentioned F. V. opened his letter with the statement, "The fact is that we Germans of Arkansas worry about politics little or not at all. At least, one only very rarely hears about a unified presence of Germans." Indeed, the editors addressed discord among German Americans regarding politics with an article ostensibly about the traditional German day celebrations held in many communities around the state. They noted that some had called for German days to be canceled in the contentious political climate: "The contrast between the Democrats and Republicans is said to be too sharp as to be able to be bridged over in such a way. It is alone certain that the German American voters vote those party candidates who conform to reasonable demands, so may considering solidarity with tribesmen [fellow Germans] influence his deliberations to a certain degree." The editors further called on all German American newspapers to examine their own parties' ranks and work to eliminate nativists from the ticket, although they did not call out any particular politicians by name. As readers of Saint Louis German American papers, the editors were perhaps aware that Germans in that city were beginning to shift their support from the Republican Party, which Germans preferred during the Civil War due to German opposition to slavery. Saint Louis Germans worried that new black voters, already courted by the Republican Party through its enfranchisement initiatives, would back nativist elements of the Republican Party. When it came to supporting candidates who were good for German interests, the *Echo* reported that no less than Carl Schurz, an ardent Republican who served in the Senate and as Secretary of the Interior under President Rutherford B. Hayes, had been part of a group of German Americans who penned a letter outlining the reasons why German Americans should vote for Cleveland, a Democrat.[53]

Regarding local politics, there are other clues that the *Arkansas Staatszeitung* supported Republican positions, in spite of its declared independent affiliation, or perhaps the editor merely saw politics as another venue in which to continue the ongoing feud. In April a reader made light of the brawling nature of the *Staatszeitung* when discussing possible gubernatorial candidates in a sarcastic tone, commenting that Files would be a possible rival to Fishback: "But because the *Arkansas Staatszeitung* has promised to give Mr. Files a piece of its mind, there will be little left of our Files, when this one is done with him." A July article mentioned a complicated dispute between a German named Gerhard Morgner and Pulaski County judge Jacob Erb. *Staatszeitung* editor Dietzgen had apparently published a favorable article about Erb, and while the *Echo* attempted to give a more nuanced view, it admitted that its account of the confrontation was incomplete. These two German papers remained on opposing sides of this issue involving the elected official.[54]

An August article directly accused the *Staatszeitung* of favoring protectionist tariffs. In a rare move, the *Echo* reprinted the exact words from the competing paper, of which no copies are extant today: "'All of Europe most fervently wishes for the victory of democracy [*sic*—the Democratic Party] so that the high tariff is reduced and the manufacturers of Europe again can compete with the domestic ones. If that happens, then America will be flooded with European goods and hundreds of thousands of workers will become destitute or will have to work for starvation wages.'" The *Echo*'s response made its irritation palpable: "With that, one is supposed to get goosebumps [in fear of] the evil Democrats. And the Germans are all supposed to be so clever and all vote Republican!! And the *Staatszeitung*, or whoever was dictating to it, cries further that what was said above cannot be disputed, it is absolutely true! Only it is of course not even strange that it is not true." Once the election results were known, the *Echo* conspicuously suggested that the political positions taken by the *Staatszeitung* were adopted solely because they were paid to publish them. It triumphantly reported the Democratic victories in Pulaski County and then asked tauntingly if voters had perhaps not read *die gut bezahlten Artikel* (the well-paid articles) of the *Staatszeitung* that advocated for the Republican Party. The item ended by reminding readers that the *Echo* supported Germans aspiring to political office no matter what their affiliation: "Would the *Staatszeitung* have fought like this and so praised the German candidates, if they had not been well paid for it? Whoever reads the *Echo* and the correspondence contained within the same will appreciate the attacks of the above[-named] paper."[55]

Arkansas saw significant political developments in 1892. The Democratic Party attempted to reassert or solidify its control around the state, after Republicans and especially black candidates and voters had made inroads during Reconstruction into a system that had been controlled essentially by one party for the majority of the state's history. The *Echo*'s editors and founders were undoubtedly convinced by the Democratic Party's platform, but they had no illusions about who was in control of the state politically. Already in July, the *Echo* was attempting to help Germans understand that the primary elections, rather than the general election, determined who would actually be in power: "The primaries are on July 16; to these, every citizen should go who wants to make use of his right to vote. Above all it is a matter of nominating the right men. Once the candidates are nominated, there is nothing more to be done. The primaries are the main thing." By siding with the Democrats, they were voting their conscience regarding the matters that mattered most to them, but they were also supporting the inevitable winning side.[56]

The groundwork for the political outcomes of 1892 was laid a year earlier. The Election Law of 1891 purportedly reformed the voting process to eliminate fraud and to avoid calls for federal oversight of state elections. These changes made it possible for local Democrats to control the casting of ballots and to disenfranchise illiterate voters, who had to appeal to elections judges for assistance in marking a standardized ballot, rather than relying on color-coded ballots produced by political parties, as had previously been the case. This measure served to eliminate opposition to the Democrats from candidates supporting agrarian voters and especially disenfranchised black voters, while a smaller percentage of illiterate white voters were affected. The 1892 election marked a landslide victory for the Democrats, unsurprising given that the 1891 law had been designed for this very outcome, and the Democratic Party maintained political control in Arkansas for decades to come.[57]

The *Echo* was overwhelmingly in favor of the changes implemented by the 1891 law. It was seen as a way to avoid the unwelcome outside influence of what they routinely referred to as the "Force Bill," in actuality the Lodge Bill, which they vehemently opposed. The proposed bill would give the federal government power to ensure that elections held at the state level were fair and free. Primarily, Germans were concerned that nativist elements in the Republican Party would use this as an excuse to limit voting rights of immigrants. Indeed, as Willi Paul Adams comments, German supporters of Grover Cleveland must have felt vindication when the new Democratic president vetoed a law that would have required a reading test of new immigrants (albeit in their mother tongue). However, the *Echo* readily adopted the racist language of white southerners who opposed the bill, believing that federal forces would unfairly influence elections to ensure that more black candidates gained power. In June an editorial discussed the upcoming state convention of the People's Party; it argued that the party should make an alliance with the Democrats, as it was too weak to constitute a political force on its own. Its main concern regarding cooperation between the

People's Party and Republicans was the potential for such a union to affect black suffrage: "If [the People's Party] goes with the Republicans, then that will soon be the end of it, because Arkansas does not want Negro rule and cannot endure it. One should be especially careful in light of the threatening declaration in the Republican platform of Minneapolis, which wants to protect the free vote of the colored in the South, probably with the Force Bill proposed in the last Congress." In September, the *Echo* reprinted and translated into German a speech by Judge James F. Read, Sebastian County Democratic committee chair, which it declared to be superb. Read praised the Democratic candidates on the tickets and attacked the opposition.

> [The Republican Party] comes with the McKinley Bill (high customs tariff) in the one hand and the Force Bill, which means bayonet and negro rule, in the other. The Republican reconstruction regiment is still like a gaunt ghost in the memories of those who lived through these days. But that period of terror would not be comparable to that which would come over Arkansas with Negroes as federal marshals to implement the provisions of the Force Bill.[58]

This language is striking in comparison to an earlier part of the speech, in which the translator used a more neutral term for black Arkansans: "Our schools are flourishing and equipped with abundant teaching materials both for white [students] and for colored [students]." The linguistic practices of the *Echo* regarding race are discussed in chapter 5, but it can be noted here that the word "Negro" is always used in regard to the so-called Force Bill.[59]

Another example came a few weeks later, in an editorial that again conflated the fear of black rule in the South with the fear that a bill requiring federal oversight could hinder immigrants from voting; an attempt to secure their own franchise allowed the *Echo* staff and readers to justify undermining voting rights for black Arkansans. The editorial first attacked those who argued that the "Force Bill" would only affect the South: "Even if alone the South would be affected, if the proposed law, so warmly recommended by Harrison, could have no other effect, as to bring the South under the rule of Negro scum and the carpetbaggers, this would be a national disaster." The article implied that immigration official John J. Davenport in New York used tactics to suppress immigrant voting, by confiscating papers under the pretense of investigating whether they were genuine and returning them only after the election: "They cannot use such tricks against native citizens, and thus the first result of the bill would be that federal officials, namely the political agents of the ruling party, would hunt everywhere for the naturalized citizens of the opposition party, find fault with their papers, arrest them, and would otherwise prevent them from voting." Of course, these methods were remarkably similar to the voter suppression tactics actually used against black citizens in Arkansas during the 1892 election, but this language makes clear that the German American editors felt the Lodge Bill represented an existential threat to the German-speaking community.[60]

A proposed poll tax was another major issue regarding suffrage in the state during the *Echo*'s inaugural year. Using the control afforded by the new voting law, Democrats pushed through an amendment to the Arkansas constitution in 1892, although historians doubt that the number of votes required for ratification were actually cast.[61] Under this new law, voters in future elections would be required to show that they had paid a $1 poll tax before being given a ballot. This further suppressed would-be voters who were poor and/or non-white, since the amount was equivalent to roughly a day's wages. Additionally, proof of payment had to be obtained from the local sheriff's office instead of from the county clerk, offering often-unscrupulous local law enforcement another opportunity to intimidate those who sought to cast ballots.[62] While the *Echo* wholeheartedly endorsed many of the modifications proposed by the Democratic Party regarding election changes, they did oppose one provision that was eventually removed from the law. An article from July both made fun of the "third party" for complaining that the new regulations were unjust and conceded that they had a legitimate concern regarding the numbering of ballots and the recording of corresponding names: "For what other purpose could this be except to allow the ruling party to later be able to check how the individual citizens have voted. And that is alleged to have already happened in the bid for appointments [to office]. The provision to furnish the ballots with numbers should be deleted. As long as it still stands, the voter is influenced, and the vote is not a secret one."[63]

If German voters were concerned that they could be affected by the provisions in the 1891 bill and the constitutional amendment passed in 1892 meant to hinder black voters, the *Echo* gives no indication of that fear. As Jeannie Whayne and her coauthors observe, the provisions lacked an English-only requirement that similar legislation in the North contained, so that it was not obvious that immigrants were being targeted.[64] The paper did its best to prepare voters regarding what to expect in the voting booth.

> Every voter receives a ballot at his polling place, Democratic or Republican, whichever he wants. With this, he goes into one of the partitioned areas and looks through it, strikes the names of

> those not suitable to him and in their place writes others in the empty space on the ticket. If he cannot do this himself, then one of the election judges will help him. Each man has five minutes and no longer.[65]

But readers' actual experiences likely differed from this description. For example, one tactic to disenfranchise black voters was to clear the polling place for up to twenty minutes under the pretense of election judges assisting a single voter. The *Echo* similarly did not raise an alarm concerning the proposed poll tax on the ballot, but rather depicted it as a way to prevent voter fraud.

> There is a proposal to vote about an amendment this fall, which gives the right to vote only to one who pays his taxes. It is only appropriate and fair that one who does not contribute to the upkeep of the government should also have no voting rights. Then, too, will the mischief of voting multiple times at different poll places, as was purportedly frequently the case earlier by the blacks, be prevented through this [provision].[66]

Another argument made in support of the tax, that funds raised would go to support public schools, naturally did not appeal to German voters, who supported their own German-language parochial schools. Yet it is noteworthy that they made no complaints about a tax that would not benefit them.

The newspaper's lack of concern regarding literacy could hardly have aligned with Germans' actual experiences on voting day. Correspondent Civis wrote in a general election discussion that Germans in the Pocahontas area were excluded from grand juries due to their language skills, and that interpreters had to be called when Germans testified in court: "But out of all 23 candidates, it only occurred to one that a great injustice is happening to the Germans here, namely none of them is appointed to the position of election judge or clerk, moreover that there are many Germans here who can understand no English, who can neither read nor write, above all the older ones." A brief note in the election coverage two weeks later declared the new system a success, even though protested by some: "The elections went quietly in Paris and the participation was low in all townships. A majority of the people appeared to be pleased by the new voting method, while others took issue with it and some did not even want to vote for that reason."[67]

An election article in the *Arkansas Gazette* offered another interpretation regarding the low turnout, stating that a lack of desire caused some not to vote: "The reduction in the vote is mainly from indifference on the part of colored voters and some foreigners who did not understand the new law or could not read or write English and refused to vote, though every opportunity was afforded them to do so." The *Gazette* went on to state: "Everything perfectly quiet here, and the new law works like a charm. Everybody delighted with it." The similarities between the two accounts are significant, as if the German paper is merely parroting the positive English-language coverage. It is furthermore implausible that Germans did not understand that the voting reforms were designed to disenfranchise their fellow black Arkansans, whether or not the *Echo* chose to report this fact. Kenneth Barnes notes that a song circulating in the areas where Germans lived at the time of the election made it clear that this was the intent; while some Germans could not understand English, there were certainly many among the *Echo*'s staff and readership who did. Barnes found that Democrats in the September 1888 election used election fraud and violence to disenfranchise black and Republican voters in Morrilton and Plumerville. Intimidation, a stolen ballot box, and ballot-box stuffing occurred in Conway County and elsewhere in the state in the November 1888 election, in cities and a county where there were a significant portion of *Echo* readers. Only one item published in the *Echo* mentioned that fewer blacks had voted in the 1892 election, and the explanation offered, that blacks were voting merely out of a sense of short-term self-interest, was blatantly racist: "The Negroes kept away in many cases. There were neither cigarettes nor whiskey there, and therefore nothing in it for them."[68]

Regular contributor Severus indicated in a letter that he also did not take black Arkansans seriously as political participants. He began by making fun of the non-Democratic parties: "Even though some Republicans are haunting around here and even the People's Party attempted to build itself a nest in which the newly baked candidate was supposed to lay his eggs, both made—as was to be anticipated—a pathetic fiasco and had to depart with hung heads." He characterized the response to election results as general jubilation and hinted that it was obvious that the Democratic victories were not good for black fellow citizens: "Even an old Negro with gray hair was swept away by the general ecstasy and got so excited about the future Democratic government that he ran through the streets and shouted with a loud voice: Hurrah for Cleveland, to the annoyance of the fellow members of his community." Although Severus addresses race, his support of Cleveland was economically motivated as well; he described Cleveland as a champion of the people, whereas Harrison was a "minion of the financiers."[69]

The coverage of the *Echo* reflected general opposition to the non-Democratic parties for both pragmatic and racial reasons. The newspaper informed German settlers in July, well in advance of election season, that a splitting of the vote could have only one consequence: "Thus we have three parties in this year. The Democratic, the People's Party, and the Republicans. If the last two had gone together, then they perhaps would have had some success, but in this way, it means the absolute victory of the Democrats." Other political parties might have appealed to the *Echo*'s readers, if the paper had not been so staunchly Democratic. In June the editor admitted that not all of the People's Party's ideas had been bad ones, even if it encouraged fellow German settlers to stay away: "But the so-called People's Party has put up, next to many sensible demands, so much absurd[ity] that one would do better to keep his distance from it." Four years earlier, both the Union Labor Party and the Agricultural Wheel championed causes that interested the Germans, such as regulation of laissez-faire capitalism, tariff reductions, better roads, and an end to convict leasing. In the 1888 election, the Agricultural Wheel supported John G. Fletcher as a gubernatorial candidate for the Democrats; when Fletcher's name was again mentioned in 1892, the *Echo* welcomed him as worthy of consideration. However, part of the Wheel's 1888 platform included support for a Prohibition amendment, which was a non-starter for German settlers. Not that their opposition to Prohibition was taken seriously by the Democratic Party. An August editorial declared that it was time to explain to their fellow English-speaking Democrats that they could no longer tolerate the tyrannical laws of the prohibitionists. In its quest to be regarded as nonpartisan, the *Echo* dutifully reported on the Prohibitionist Party state convention in May, even if there was obviously no chance their readers would be voting for the party. Opposition to the Republican Party was based on the issues of immigration and financial policies, but race played a large role, as this editorial comment showed: "We Germans cannot become good friends with the Republican Party and its system, especially because here in the South it supports itself with Negroes."[70]

For this reason, a group of German voters from Saline County was especially angry with a Democratic candidate for county clerk by the name of Evans, whom they referred to as a *Bursche* (boy). They wrote in to the *Echo* to report his alleged words at a campaign rally, which were given both in English and then in a German translation that immediately followed: "'If I am defeated, I will be proud of it, because I will be defeated by the germans [*sic*] and the niggers. If I am elected, I will be proud of it, because

I am elected by the better element.'" In this case, they were willing to throw their support behind the other two parties to teach this particular Democratic candidate a lesson.

> Now should the Germans stand together and demand from the Democratic candidate an explanation that they equate the Germans with the Negroes, and regard them as the worse element. If we proceed in concert, then we have the elections in our hands in Saline County, Democrats and the united Republicans and People's Party members are almost equally strong; wherever we throw our votes, there the victory will fall.[71]

Three weeks later, a follow-up story reported that Evans had denied saying the words printed in the *Echo* but had not met their unspecified demand (perhaps some sort of oath renouncing the statement), so they concluded he must have made the statement.

Another candidate found himself in trouble with the Germans after the election. While the German settlers in the previous example wanted to be seen as part of the majority white in-group, they had not forgotten their immigrant past and realized how precarious a situation future countrymen would be in if they allowed anti-immigration rhetoric to flourish. A reader letter from Conway described how Representative Hugh Dinsmore began by praising both the Germans and Irish for being model immigrants but quickly transitioned to the assertion that America should be closed to Italians, Spaniards, Poles, Russians, and Chinese. He singled out the Russians for special ridicule, declaring that they expected to find money lying in the streets and believed they could eventually become president. After these last statements, the audience, which had applauded after every line of the speech in support of the Democratic Party agenda, suddenly fell silent. The letter did not state the reason explicitly, but the Germans who feared Know-Nothings in the Republican Party were surely shocked to hear this rhetoric from one of their own party. The letter writer concluded, "It's only too bad that the man was not standing on the shores of America with an efficient club four hundred years, three weeks, and three days ago, so that he could have hit the Italian-Spaniard Columbus over the head. If a schoolboy were to babble such rubbish, one could laugh about it, but a member of Congress should, to put it mildly, show somewhat more tact."[72]

Without question, editor Carl Meurer was able to influence which election issues became most important to *Echo* readers. It is therefore important to examine the aspects of Meurer's biography that shaped his thinking. Meurer saw himself as the champion of working men. His interest in their plight was not academic, but related to his own life experiences. Meurer's father had been an entrepreneur, selling wholesale groceries to other small-business owners, but his untimely death left Meurer's mother with four small children to care for. As a young adult, Meurer spent time working in a factory that produced woolen cloth, where workers regularly put in ten- to twelve-hour days. Meurer did well in this work and became indispensable to the owner, due to his knowledge of the factory's operations. It was such a productive relationship that the owner both offered his daughter's hand in marriage and promised to make Meurer his successor in the factory, but Meurer was not prepared to convert to Lutheranism from Catholicism, a precondition of the offer. Instead, he immediately left town to seek his fortunes elsewhere.

After being denied a government position, Meurer began to travel around Europe. Meurer's biographer, Gregory Kehres, regards this time in his life as pivotal to the formation of his political views: "On these travels he had his mind set on learning the conditions of the laboring man and farmer by personal observation and by taking jobs himself. In Italy he took lessons in painting, and did manual labor to pay for these lessons as an employee of a great landlord. He was put to work at digging drainage ditches together with other laborers."[73] After a suggestion about how the work could be done more efficiently, Meurer was invited to dine with his employer, who "asked Meurer why he, an educated man, was doing the work of a common laborer. Meurer replied that he had in the past given much study to the social questions and had applied for this kind of work to study the lot of the laborer. He did not hesitate to ask the proprietor the pointed question how he could reconcile such scanty wages as he was paying his employees with his conscience." Meurer was not moved by the employer's answer, which was that he believed his employees were fundamentally happier than he was, in spite of his many material advantages.[74]

While still in Germany, Meurer put his political opinions into practice when he was recruited as a speaker for the Catholic Centre Party, which opposed Chancellor Otto von Bismarck and his anti-Catholic policies. Meurer recalled that during one of the speeches, he was forced to make a quick exit through a back door to avoid arrest. Kehres further suggests that Meurer's time as a farmer gave him opportunities for reflection on sociology, history, theology, and philosophy through reading Socrates, Aristotle, Tacitus, Albert the Great, St. Thomas Aquinas, and the Bible. Kehres notes, "He gave careful study to the social theories of Karl Marx, compared them with Catholic principles, and drew his conclusions."[75] Kehres's characterization of Meurer is indicative of how the editor's views regarding many topics cannot be easily categorized; he was, for example, familiar with Marx's theories, but decidedly not a Marxist.

Meurer's political thoughts, and thus the thoughts that shaped the editorial page and the paper at large, were often quite complex. While the work was unattributed, it is not hard to imagine that one particular editorial series from July 1892 was shaped by Meurer personally and captured the nuances of his thought particularly well. The overarching theme was that the German peoples had developed a just economy under the guild system, and when Roman law was introduced, it began to undermine the social fabric. The immigrant paper harbored a tremendous disdain for the excesses of capitalism as practiced in the United States, which allowed robber barons to accumulate vast sums while leaving others in abject poverty. The language used in the editorial at times seems appropriated from socialism. It asked of the capitalist, "What does it concern him, whether his workers live well or terribly? . . . And nevertheless he takes monstrous usurious interest from his capital at the costs of the consumers on the one hand and at the cost of the muscles and bones of workers on the other." Meurer could not, however, be regarded as a socialist; his was a middle-class paper, and he walked a fine line. He clearly worried about violent clashes in the streets if enough workers decided to rebel against the political and financial circumstances with armed force; this same article refers to the *Blutscenen in Pittsburgh* (bloody scenes in Pittsburgh). It went on in a pessimistic tone, "And that is the reason for the dull fermentation among the worker masses which allows one to fear revolutionary outbreaks. But in order to beseech these, the capitalist will by no means consider reinstituting the human rights that have been trampled in the dirt."[76] In a separate article, the editor expressed dismay that a "well-meaning friend" slipped him a copy of an international German-language anarchist newspaper wrapped in a copy of a well-known Catholic German newspaper. The former had the word "truth" written across it, while the latter had "hypocrisy" scrawled across it. The editor opined, "We also see the abuses and wish for serious corrective action. We also defend the Christian tenet that work is the only way to create value and that the created value belongs to the worker. But to murder and rob a number of fellow men in order to eliminate the present evils, that we consider to be a greater wrong than the currently existing system." He ended by suggesting that the friend should sell his possessions and distribute the money among the poor if he were really so concerned with social change.[77]

While the editors were in favor of workers' rights, this did not automatically translate to support for unions. The paper explored the historical origins of worker compensation in another section of this editorial, subtitled "The Upheaval of all Relationships through Roman Law," which argued that the pre-Roman Germanic guild system served to ensure fair working conditions because it coupled a just wage and secure employment to mastery of the field in which one was working. Modern unions were depicted as a corruption of the initial system meant to protect workers against unscrupulous bosses: "No longer competence in labor and the completion of an examination, but rather the payment of the dues into the till qualified [one] for membership in these unions. And therefore every union drags along a multitude of less qualified workers, helps them to a good income, and protects them against the capital as much as it can. Naturally the better workers must suffer in this way." This editorial was part of a larger series on Roman law. In the last installment, industry and the rise of machines were blamed for the contemporary economic malaise, and the author argued that problems with capitalism in its existing form were due to heathen (Roman) ideas about work being applied to a Christian construct. In a separate editorial regarding rights and duties under natural law, the editors stated that it was incumbent upon workers to equip themselves with multiple skills and be flexible in the workplace, lest a new invention make the one skill they possess useless.[78]

The greatest political guiding principal found in the *Echo* in its inaugural year was a fixation on natural law. The editors were careful to distinguish between *natürliches Menschenrecht* (natural law) and *Naturrecht* (law of nature). The former was used to refer to the divine rights endowed to men as outlined in the Constitution, and the latter was the survival of the fittest and strongest as outlined in the theories of Darwin. The editors conceded that the law of nature did in fact exist among animals, but they were loath to have it applied to humans, who possessed reason, understanding, and free will. Ideally, these qualities would lead to the application of the golden rule and man treating his fellow man in a worthy manner. The *Echo* lamented that the contemporary age saw men acting in a way that was even lower than the animals. The paper argued that one animal could not force another animal to work for him nor make food too scarce for another because he was hoarding it for profit. The editors additionally believed that men were entitled to what they termed a natural right to work and earn a fair wage, which was being denied by capitalists. One editorial argued that an idyllic system of natural work had existed in Germany among the guilds during the medieval period, when enough resources existed to ensure that even widows and orphans had been provided for. Still, the *Echo*'s call for more just employment in this and other editorials was not a call for more radical political action. A November editorial proclaimed of communism, "And today this communism still exists not only in the minds of half-educated men, but rather indeed among the animals, where it belongs to be sure. No wonder that people who regard themselves only as refined beasts also want to introduce the laws of the same." Rather, the *Echo* advocated for capitalism itself to correct course. Another article praised the Pullman company for building its own town and taking care of its workers, arguing that this was also good business practice (although it should be noted that the town created by Pullman would be the scene of strikes due to wage reductions a mere two years later).[79]

In the summer of 1892, the *Echo*'s staff had reason to be concerned regarding capitalism as it was practiced in America. A July news item reported that labor disputes in Idaho between union and nonunion miners had led to a two-hour gun battle with four fatalities: two union members and two company men. The paper covered all of the news emerging from Pennsylvania during the Homestead Strike. Reporting from Pittsburgh was initially positive and stated that around three thousand steel workers were protesting for higher wages. The atmosphere was depicted as celebratory and nonviolent. When federal troops were called in, city fathers urged those not from the area, including purported anarchists, to leave. The soldiers' greatest problems were reportedly heat and malnutrition, while the strikers were either going fishing or staying home. As the strike dragged on, the paper informed readers that other workers were losing their jobs due to the strike, but some were nevertheless striking in solidarity with those in Homestead. The situation grew more desperate as union strikers allegedly murdered two Pinkerton employees. Although this story was tailor-made for the *Echo*'s preferred narrative that capitalists were unjustly exploiting workers, the paper reported the outcome of the story as a sobering reminder that a violent overthrow of the existing system was not the answer. When an assassination attempt was made on plant manager and Carnegie associate Henry Clay Frick, the *Echo* referred to would-be assassin Alexander Berkman (spelled Bergman in the *Echo*) as a clear madman and noted that his actions had not helped the workers. A news item stated that one of the imprisoned leaders of the Homestead strikers expressed happiness after being released from jail and learning that Frick was recovering.[80]

Another important overarching political theme was disdain for and mistrust of the wealthy, which resulted in a number of general attacks on the rich and specific policy stands. One lengthy poem was entitled "Money Governs the World." The rich were portrayed as having achieved success only through morally repugnant means, and inherited wealth was criticized. According to the poem, wealthy men, who were often idiots and drunkards, were regarded as wise and "jolly," and the wealthy were even considered to be more holy than regular men. The poem finished with the assertion that Adam would be appalled to see how his descendants treat one another and lamented the loss of Christian regard for one's fellow man: "That you instead of a Christian / Are only a money man, / Nurture pride and greed / Only honor money." An editorial declared that "justice" was the watchword of the election season, in the sense that the wealthy should finally be held accountable for their behavior: "[The rich] snatch for themselves the benefit of all the inventions of the human spirit, the plundering of all natural resources, as well as the exploitation of the manpower of the people, in order not only to live in princely glamour and luxury, but also in order to exercise power over their fellow citizens through the unassailable influence of their immense fortunes." The paper worried that hoarded wealth was causing economic downturns and that capitalists' only motivation for reinvesting in the economy was to acquire further profit. Another article drew parallels between the contemporary situation and what Aristophanes had attacked in ancient Greek society, signaling that the wealth imbalance was part of a human cycle that could be rebalanced in the upcoming election.[81]

The newspaper's strong stance against laissez-faire capitalism was reflected in a number of concrete political positions. Similar to other German immigrants across the United States, German settlers in Arkansas were highly skeptical of the idea of free silver, even though it had been endorsed by the Democrats in 1890. In letters to the editor, editorials, and a reprint from Saint Louis German newspaper *Amerika*, the general tone of the *Echo* was one of mistrust. Germans in Arkansas assumed that this was a scheme invented by the wealthy to further cheat the poor and working classes, arguing that the less well-off were the ones who actually used silver as currency. One article saw parallels in the debate over the gold standard abroad and proclaimed that long before Jay Gould was using his *trügerische Tricks* (deceitful tricks) to amass millions, the gold profiteers in Britain were at work, robbing the system so that they could clothe their women in diamonds. Another editorial took up a discussion begun in the *Arkansas Democrat* regarding income taxes, with the hope that a more just tax policy could be created that would prevent the rich from finding loopholes to avoid paying their fair share.[82]

The subject of tariffs was the most prominent *Echo* topic regarding the intersection of politics and economics. Seventeen separate articles made the argument that protection tariffs ostensibly intended to preserve jobs were actually injurious to workers. It was claimed that the Republican Party initially sold the tariffs as a method to pay off war bonds and only pivoted to the pro-worker argument once their wealthy allies were profiting. Articles alleged that producers were not passing on benefits to workers when tariffs led to higher prices for goods, while fewer exports of goods resulted in lost wages. In turn, workers who were being paid did not have access to cheaper goods from abroad and had reduced buying power as well. Farmers additionally lost the ability to sell their products abroad due to retaliatory tariffs. An August editorial decried "Three evil T's: tariffs, trusts, and tramps," linking the first two examples of capitalism run amok to the creation of the third. The article invoked Adam Smith's argument that protection tariffs and monopolies were harmful and were not to be tolerated by the state. A quotation from Johann Wolfgang von Goethe's play *Faust*, the quintessential story of the negative consequences of a pact with the devil, was included for good measure. Tariffs were the topic of a cartoon published in English during the inaugural year, when indeed only a handful of cartoons were included in the *Echo*'s pages at all. A worker was depicted reading a sign that stated, "The tariff is not a tax it is a protection to the workingman." A businessman was shown picking his pocket while he read. The caption explained, "This is the way it 'protects' him."[83]

The *Echo* criticized local capitalists as well. In April the newspaper noted that those who had come to Little Rock for horse racing were spending a lot of money. The editors groused that money abounded for luxury and celebrations and admonished "the citizens of capital" to remember that wealth was generated via the hard work of farmers and to tone down their celebrations. A month later, a gathering of bankers in Little Rock raised the ire of the paper for a similar neglect of those who worked with their hands and generated value. The news item first noted that the amount of deposits that bankers "worked" with, sarcastically including the quotation marks around the verb. It further clarified that it was not against wealth per se, but rather against wealth enjoyed by those who had not earned it: "Where work is given its fitting honor and pay, as happened in earlier times, everything is right. The existence of class difference must be and is beneficial for all. But the current condition is a mockery of justice, for too many people want to lead an idle lavish life and on top of that amass great riches. This can only happen through deductions from the earnings of work." The banker W. S.

McCain was quoted as saying that it is not the lawyers and legislators that make the laws but rather the bankers, and the *Echo* thus suggested that one should start approaching bankers about fair wages.[84]

In addition to the previously discussed topics of Prohibition and German schools, three other local election issues were of particular interest to German settlers: the selection of Germans to serve on grand juries, the need for better streets in the state, and the abolition of the practice of convict leasing to private parties. Reader Civis complained that Germans were rarely selected for grand juries, and a correspondent from Paris noted the selection of Leop. Strobel, a German from Spielerville, for a grand jury as important news. Equally vexing was the fact that Freemasons seemed to the Germans to be well-represented in the legal system. One letter from Conway reported on a murder trial in which the defendant, Bob Williams, was a Freemason, and the presiding judge, Vaughn of Little Rock, revealed to the jury that he also was a Freemason. The reader complained, "Although now for twelve years a large number of Germans have lived here, none of them has yet been a jury member. Before elections one always promises us, 'That will change, if you will vote for this one and that one.' But it has always stayed the same." Another anonymous letter from Conway noted that *The Wheel* newspaper published a story saying that the jury commission was considering allowing Germans to serve. He argued that he and his countrymen were good citizens and that the courts in their existing configurations were overrun with Freemasons.[85]

The *Echo* brought the issue of convict leasing to the forefront because a private company was using convicts to work on Little Rock streets, including Markham, in an area of town where there was a high concentration of German immigrants. The prisoners were watched over by guards with weapons, and Germans feared that an escape attempt could lead to shots fired into groups of nearby innocent citizens. Settlers additionally believed that only the state, not private enterprise, should profit from convict labor, since the state bore the costs of incarceration. Finally, the Germans complained that employing convicts in this manner was depressing wages and depriving honest men of the opportunity to do the work. This general fear was supported by a concrete example from the neighboring state of Tennessee, where the use of convict labor to displace regular workers earning higher wages had led to violent labor unrest. In August the *Echo* became annoyed with the *Arkansas Democrat*'s general attitude toward the matter, when the English-language paper voiced skepticism that the state's politicians would have the courage to end the practice of convict leasing, even though the general public supported its abolishment. The *Echo* chastised its journalistic colleagues for giving up the cause so easily. It noted that, while those profiting from the practice would obviously oppose its cessation, the government existed to enact reform. For its part, the *Echo* reported which candidates pledged to end convict leasing. It encouraged its readers who were citizens to write letters directly to the governor to advocate for its end. In November the paper felt vindicated and assured that its opposition was a majority stance, when it reported that the deadline for new leases had come and gone with no bids being submitted. This was an error that the *Echo* corrected in December, observing that four offers had been submitted and the governor had rejected them all as insufficient. New bids could be submitted in May, but the paper remained hopeful that the legislature would put an end to the practice.[86]

Germans were not entirely against the idea of putting convicts to work in service to the public; they merely objected to the existing system of renting their labor out to private companies. As previously discussed, the settlers regarded convict labor as the solution to a pressing problem in the state: the need to create better roads. They expressed puzzlement that the problem had not yet been solved. The *Echo* argued that roads were vital for attracting new residents and tourists to the state. A report on the meeting of the Collegeville Fruit Growers Association pointed out the necessity of roads to aid in shipping goods and in building commerce. Readers were warned, "One must also not expect to get good paved roads for nothing." Germans seemed to be in general agreement that tax increases would be necessary to accomplish this goal, but the paper proposed structuring the new tax based on property adjacent to the road; it complained that rich urban dwellers frequently owned land in the country but were not asked to pay tax on their rural properties. The counties were suggested as overseers for the convicts who would conduct the labor. One item noted that a ball and chain was used in Germany to keep prisoners from fleeing, and recommended its use in Arkansas as a way to prevent prisoners from escaping into nearby forests when building county roads. Germans saw themselves as experts in road construction and hoped that they would be able to contribute their knowledge to the process.[87]

In October the paper announced a meeting of the road-building commission in Little Rock at which comments from all around Arkansas would be collected. The editor urged English-speaking German immigrants to attend. The *Echo* was especially concerned that the need to fundraise millions of dollars was being discussed in relation to the project, whereas the paper preferred a slower and more affordable pace to construction. They noted that this was the practice in Germany, and it resulted in a manageable tax burden. They praised Prussia's designation of streets as either local or state, so it was clear who should finance what construction. They proposed either starting with the road between Little Rock and Fort Smith or beginning on two major arteries reaching across the state at the same time, if the state would be willing to commit funds as well. The greatest concern, though, was that tackling the need for a network of good roads all at once would inevitably result in graft: "And if we start immediately with millions, then likewise nothing orderly will come about, but based on frequent experience, hundreds of greedy hands would be stretched out in order to get their share of the plunder. Therefore Festina lente!—More haste, less speed! Finally begin—but without rush!"[88]

With these issues and support for the Democratic Party in mind, the *Echo* did not hesitate to recommend candidates and voting stances to its readers. It saw election coverage both as a patriotic duty and as a possible way to encourage new subscriptions. In August it offered a special rate for the election season and through the end of the year of fifty cents paid in advance. It promised to keep readers informed about issues being decided and other matters, the latter presumably a reference to the ever-changing voting provisions. It admonished German settlers, who it claimed had moved to the state mostly in the previous twelve years, to understand the difference between their old and new homelands.

> We live here in a republic in which it is the duty of every good citizen to take as much of a share in public affairs as his work allows him to. Everyone must have time to educate himself about the questions which are to be decided through the elections and to go to the ballot box. Because if the good citizens neglect their duties for the common good, then the domineering and avaricious politicians will have an easy time.[89]

The *Echo* directly compared the political sensibilities of Irish and German-speaking immigrants. It claimed the former were ready to run for office the instant they departed from the ships that had brought them to America, whereas Germans were seemingly unwilling to become immediately active in politics: "But this also has the advantage that their judgement remains cool and unbiased and that they cannot easily be won over for one-sided party tendencies." The article claimed that this was the reason most Germans in the South had decided to support the Democratic Party after lengthy deliberation over which party most closely aligned with their values. It asserted that Germans could be loyal to the Democratic Party without regarding fellow citizens who were Republicans as enemies.[90]

Unsurprisingly, the vast majority of politicians that the *Echo* recommended in the 1892 election were Democrats, and the paper carefully noted which candidates were endorsed by the party itself. The *Echo* supported candidates at the national, state, county, and local levels (appendix 3 gives the complete list of these endorsements). It noted that two candidates, John W. Colquitt running for assessor and E. A. Ramsey for city clerk in Argenta, were popular in Arkansas because they had served in the Confederate army during the Civil War but did not take a stand on whether this would be a reason to vote for or against them. Despite the lament that Germans did not become as active in political life as the Irish, there were several German candidates, including Emil Baerlocher and Dr. Carl Flucks, who were praised as fellow countrymen who should be supported because they would share the readers' political interests. An endorsement of Beni F. Reinberger by several readers was entitled "Wacht am Rhein" (Vigil on the Rhine) and encouraged immigrants with the words, "Germans, wake up!" The candidate for state representative in the primaries was deemed worthy of support because "[he] himself has German blood, German mores, comes from respectable German parents, is a sound Democrat."[91]

Conrad Elsken, who ran for treasurer of Logan County, was another German Democrat endorsed by the *Echo*. The paper ran a flattering biography of Elsken as early as March. The profile featured an anecdote from 1884 of how Elsken worked for the Little Rock and Fort Smith Railroad Company and was ordered by his boss, a Mr. Weaver, to either collect debts owed by farmers or have them evicted. Elsken knew that farmers had no money because the previous harvests had been bad, so he contacted the Little Rock office directly to see if arrangements could be made on behalf of the farmers. Weaver promptly fired Elsken and threatened the farmers with eviction unless they made payment immediately. The farmers of the area went to the local storekeepers and threatened to leave en masse unless Elsken was rehired, and the storekeepers in turn put pressure on the railroad. When Elsken was offered his job back, he accepted on the condition that he would no longer have to report to Weaver and would be allowed to work with the farmers in the manner that he saw fit to help them pay off their debts. Both were accepted. Elsken was elected by a landslide, and he went on to serve four terms and became a leading figure in the Logan County business community.[92]

The *Echo* did note some voting irregularities, but they were presented as infrequent acts by the opposing parties. It informed readers that the Republican leader T. Grayson and two members of the People's Party had been arrested for intimidation in Prescott. In Lamar a candidate for the People's Party was condemned for being unprincipled because he voted in the Democratic primary. Political differences resulted in a "scuffle" in Conway on Saturday in which one man was wounded; he was nevertheless able to go to the polls on Monday to cast his vote. Two Democratic candidates who were defeated in Crawford County by representatives of the People's Party contested the results due to *Betrügereien* (cheating). Given the proximity of German settlers to the extensive fraud the Democratic Party was committing in Conway County and other locales around the state, it is inconceivable that the newspaper had no knowledge of their favored party's misdeeds, but none were reported.[93]

The national press did not possess the same sanguinity regarding the elections in Arkansas, and the *Echo* took exception to these unflattering stories. In October, it reported that Judge Jack M. Clure had deemed the state's new voting practices regarding illiterate voters unconstitutional. His proposed solution was to appoint two thousand supervisors to oversee the election judges to ensure that illiterate voters were in fact casting their intended votes. The *Echo* conceded that this development might result in riots, but it was incensed that the *Memphis Commercial* should depict it as a "reason for serious concern regarding bloodshed." The German newspaper noted exultantly that similar predictions of riots and spilled blood in Arkansas by papers in Saint Louis and Tennessee had proven baseless. It reported that the election had been largely peaceful, using the opportunity to reiterate the alleged necessity of the new voting laws to prevent fraud: "A few arrests were made, in the third ward of the city [Little Rock] several Negroes were arrested who wanted to vote twice, and one who wanted to steal a ballot. The US Deputies stayed outside of the polling places on the streets and did not cause any offence." Not until November was there a story regarding election-related violence in Texarkana, in which three men were shot to death. The *Echo* portrayed the event as a matter in which Democrats were divided, and the warring factions began shooting; two bystanders were also struck. Even this article concluded with the assertion, "In this year, the election campaign was therefore conducted rather fairly."[94]

Both the *Echo* and its readers delighted in the Democratic victories of 1892. German voters enjoyed early success during the primaries, when the *Echo* proudly reported that the *Arkansas Democrat* had noted that a unified German vote made the difference in Logan County. The editor added,

"That's right! Unity makes [us] strong." In September reports poured into the German-language paper from correspondents in Faulkner, Logan, and Pulaski Counties. In mid-October the *Echo* reprinted a humorous item from the *Paris Express* that announced the paper was collecting contributions to buy a gravestone for the People's Party. November brought correspondent letters from Little Rock, Fort Smith, Pocahontas, Atkins, and Paris about victory parties being celebrated locally. The *Echo* assured readers there was a conciliatory mood in the air and that even members of the parties who had been defeated joined in the merrymaking, which it termed "celebrations of the people and reconciliation." At a gathering in Atkins, candidates appeared to thank the German voters for their support. W. L. Terry said he appreciated that they had voted for him as a fellow Democrat and not solely because he was Catholic, since several other denominations had apparently refused to endorse him due to his faith. Judge Cravens thanked the crowd and noted that he had a German son-in-law. An editorial on "the duties of a democracy" stated that the victor usually receives the spoils of land, money, or both. It encouraged the Democrats around the nation not to take advantage of their new positions by selecting bureaucrats according to political patronage, but rather to install good civil servants. The paper contrasted this with the Republicans, who were alleged to have given mail carrier jobs to the party faithful, in order for them to purposely not deliver Democratic-leaning newspapers. The *Echo* felt much course correction was necessary. Given the paper's other stances on race, its remarks regarding the governance of Indian territory seem particularly uncharacteristic, although the editors were perhaps thinking of the area as potential new territory for the missions field and Christian conversions: "And the new administration should always keep in mind that the Indians are also human beings and are entitled to the religious freedom guaranteed by the Constitution."[95]

But a mere month after the election, the *Echo* was rehashing the political squabbling that had marked the election. The paper republished an item from the *Faulkner County Wheel* that stated, "We are not in the habit of swearing, but we would like to hurl such a load of curses against the Democratic Party that it would be damned for eternity." The *Echo* editor commented wryly that the Democratic Party had nevertheless won. The German newspaper also published an unflattering item on People's Party candidate J. B. Weaver. The article summarized a report, which happened to have been published by an executive committee of the Democratic Party, regarding his behavior during the Civil War. Weaver was alleged to have abused men, women, and children, tortured those whom he thought possessed money, shot men indiscriminately, and insulted women on the street. The editors added this comment to the "news" item: "A nice candidate for the People's Party!"[96]

In the 1892 election, the German settlers enthusiastically participated in the democratic process and were delighted by its outcome. Throughout the year, though, they expressed doubts about the efficacy of democracy as practiced in the state of Arkansas. In January correspondent Pionier wrote to complain about Logan County judge John H. Wilkins. Pionier claimed that Wilkins promised he would assist wine producers when he campaigned as a Republican candidate for office. But once elected, he instituted a three-mile rule for the county that essentially made commercial wine production impossible, without allowing those opposed to the measure to submit a petition against it. An August editorial addressed the problem of broken campaign promises in fervent language.

> Now, we Germans have, to be sure, already had to experience with bitterness and loss that even the best principles are not always capable of fending off the vile consequences of human weakness and delusion. Since our English fellow party members have, after we helped them fight to their victories, expressed some very undemocratic inclinations, both in the administration of government and in legislation, and in particular have tortured us with tyrannical Prohibition laws, which even charge the farmers with a crime for the selling of their home-made wine.[97]

Another editorial argued that the general public was in favor of abolishing convict leasing to private parties, but the piece pondered whether the politicians in Arkansas would have the courage to go through with changing the policy. J. H., a correspondent from Collegeville, expressed cynicism more generally regarding politicians: "We as truthful and honest workers will also do the same in our home, will remain awake, and will not vote for bandits, who take away our bread basket or help wreak destruction."[98]

One major event in Arkansas politics during 1892 probably contributed to the negative attitude toward politicians. The trial of William E. Woodruff Jr. was a regular subject of reporting during the year. Woodruff was a former state treasurer who resigned in disgrace after it was discovered that he had misappropriated state funds and hidden a deficit of $43,857.17 through the use of scrips. Because some of the scrips had been stolen and were reported as such when they were presented to the German National Bank, a Little Rock bank founded by German immigrant Charles P. Penzel in 1875, the case was of particular interest to the German community. The *Echo*'s reporting shows that this case brought up aspects of Arkansas politics that confused the German immigrants. First, they could not understand why public opinion was apparently so divided over whether Woodruff was guilty of wrongdoing, when it seemed clear to them that public funds could not be used for private benefit: "But here the assumption seems to prevail that the position of surety gives the right to use the entrusted funds in any manner." Second, they could not fathom the desire to pardon Woodruff, as though he were a poor man who had stolen a bit of bread, as the editors expressed it. Third, they noted that the vast majority of the money disappeared between Woodruff's fourth and fifth terms in office, and they could not understand how public officials could be allowed to stay in office for so long without any sort of oversight. The editors admonished, "If the people of Arkansas do not change their Constitution so that the long terms of men are not hindered, men who have access to a copious retinue and have to manage large sums of public funds, then they also earn all penalties which flow from this dereliction of duty." In December, the editors informed readers that Woodruff had been arrested after a grand jury indicted him on three new counts.[99]

Stories regarding general lawlessness in the state additionally made frequent appearances in the *Echo* during 1892. The paper reported on a family feud between two families near Van Buren, the Horns and the Hatleys, that resulted in the killing of a Dr. Horn by William Hatley. Both men had apparently drawn their weapons immediately upon a chance meeting, and Hatley claimed self-defense in the matter. The editors described the region as a wild mountain area where officers of the law put themselves in danger while carrying out their duties. In another case of feuding near Pine Bluff, a seventy-six-year-old renter named Stewart shot to death the twenty-two-year-old farmer whose land he had been living on. A reader who submitted the item noted, "The outrage is very great, and it is easily possible that Judge Lynch takes the maintenance of justice into his hand." An update later informed readers that the young farmer apparently had whipped the older man because he could not pay his debts, and a lawyer had advised the renter to do what he must to protect his life. This is not the only time the paper mentioned the practice of lynching, a matter which will be further discussed in the next chapter. Generally, the paper rejected any actions that could incite violence, such as when it condemned the hanging of an effigy of Carnegie outside the courthouse in Little Rock. And in a story on a convict who had escaped prison after first evading justice by posing as a Union soldier, the editors condemned the system in the main: "These are the fruits of our wonderful judicial system, the enormous yet futile expenses of which wander from the pockets of the tax payers into those of the lawyers."[100]

Generally, the *Echo* focused on larger political topics, but there were a handful of stories that indicated that Germans were displeased with more specific aspects of how their fellow Americans were running things. There was grumbling that Germans would prefer the land that would eventually be developed into MacArthur Park be sold to a brewery company instead, which would bring jobs and revenue to Little Rock. The *Echo* quoted an article from the English-language *Paris Express* that described a petition calling for each county to have a treasurer who would hold funds meant for the public schools, thus eliminating the inefficient transfer of tax revenue back and forth between the state capital and the counties: "'That saves unnecessary expenses, and because the money would not be piled up in a large sum, burglars and civil servants are spared temptation.'" The *Echo* suggested that the next legislature should pass a law to set regular office hours for elected officials, as it was frustrating for citizens to go to an office to find no one there. Relatedly, the paper praised a county deputy clerk named McEvoy for providing transparency by moving his desk into the office of the county judge and making himself available to the public. Finally, the newspaper expressed consternation at the adopted country's traditions of shooting guns into the air and setting off fireworks to celebrate its independence: "The ridiculous manner in which the Fourth of July is celebrated costs a number of human lives each year, as though the otherwise so sensible Americans want to declare themselves independent of human reason each Fourth of July."[101]

The general consensus of scholarship on the German American press is that these newspapers succeeded in hastening assimilation, as they helped German settlers understand the ways in which civic life and commerce functioned in their new homeland in language that was accessible to them.[102] Yet Germans in Arkansas maintained an interest in European politics. The front two pages of the paper were generally dedicated to a summary of international news each week, with special attention given to German-speaking countries and especially the activities of former German chancellor Bismarck. But the *Echo* also helped German readers understand the kind of politics that were most important to them as settlers in Arkansas: local politics. The *Echo* provides definitive evidence that the German speakers were intent on creating a home for themselves in the state, no matter the circumstances under which they left Europe. No content in the *Echo* makes any mention of the idea of returning to Europe once the political or economic situation should change. It is obvious that the German immigrants who created and contributed to the paper were keen to shape politics because they regarded the United States as their country, too.

German settlers were in a unique position in a South transitioning from Reconstruction to Post-Reconstruction. They became landowners at the same time as many black and poor white farmers found themselves in circumstances of debt slavery. The readers of the *Echo* were Catholics who drank alcohol, and in 1890s Arkansas, where the Protestant majority favored Prohibition, *Echo* readers were ostracized for being Catholics. They were therefore eager to show themselves to be good Democrats (and by extension, good whites) and to fit into the dominant power paradigm in the 1892 election. They imagined their political power to an extent that outstripped their actual political influence in the state, which is perhaps why there is little evidence in the *Echo* that English-speaking Arkansans were alarmed by the German speakers conducting politics in German. Anti-foreign sentiments unmistakably circulated during the 1892 election season, while some candidates courted the German vote. Generally, though, the Germans were few in number compared to other constituent groups. That Germans were discussing civic and economic matters in their native language was likely due to a combination of two factors: some still had not mastered English at a level necessary for participation in wider civic life; and Germans were simply taking advantage of the existing linguistic community to discuss what would most benefit them as a group.

CHAPTER 5

# Encountering Diversity

## *Other Ethnic and Religious Groups as Represented in the* Echo

IN THE ARKANSAS of 1892, German immigrants tended to live in communities of fellow German speakers, but these enclaves did not represent impenetrable barriers. Readers of the *Echo* were aware of other ethnic and religious groups in their pluralistic new homeland, and the paper reported both national and local news about them. But the minority group that held the most interest for Germans in 1892 was African Americans. Around 1974, Mary Meurer, daughter of *Echo* founder Carl Meurer, stated that race relations were a nonissue among Germans, as reported in the paper. In a discussion regarding Carl Meurer's interest in social justice issues such as worker's rights, she was asked, "But as far as, let us say, racial equality goes, he did not touch that issue, did he, in the paper?" Mary Meurer's answer was a simple "No." The interviewer replied, "All right." Meurer then clarified her initial response: "We did not have the racial Negroes. They stayed in their place. We did not bother. We did not have any trouble with them." She then commented that there were separate Catholic churches for black Arkansans, before the interview shifted to other topics.[1] This assertion likely reflected Mary Meurer's own experience growing up in Arkansas, but it does not accurately describe the situation at the time of the *Echo*'s founding. German immigrants in 1892 were very much aware of and concerned about race relations. Many of these immigrants had established themselves in the state during the era of Reconstruction, from 1865 to 1880. This was obviously a period of tremendous change in the South, as federal politicians ostensibly sought to undo the structures of slavery and enact the provisions of the Emancipation Proclamation. Coming after the end of Reconstruction, 1892 was a particularly volatile year for race relations in Arkansas, and German settlers experienced the beginnings of Jim Crow laws, voter disenfranchisement, a rash of horrific lynchings, and a large black emigration from the state that came fast on the tails of an immigration after the end of the Civil War. In many ways, German speakers' impressions of black Arkansans were shaped by the racist ideology of white Arkansans; Germans adopted the language of southern racism, their coverage of black Americans was dominated by reports of criminal activity or blacks as victims, and they were concerned about the possibility of a race war. But some aspects of the *Echo*'s coverage of the black community in Arkansas reveal that Germans regarded blacks as fellow human beings and were especially troubled by the implications of lynching culture for the rule of law in their newly adopted homeland.

Much has been written on German immigrants' attitudes toward slavery and race relations in the United States in both the antebellum and postbellum periods. A brief summary of some of the prevailing attitudes held by German speakers prior to 1892 will offer some context, since immigrants to Arkansas were coming both directly from Europe and also from other parts of the United States. Germans in the Colonial period tended to oppose slavery. Albert Faust observes with pride that Pennsylvanian Germans held the first protest of its kind against the practice in 1688: "The system of Negro slavery was repulsive to the German settlers from the very start, and they were shocked to find that the Quakers remained indifferent toward this criminal abuse."[2] By the nineteenth century, however, some Germans in the South had become slaveholders, though to a lesser extent than the native-born population, as Ira Berlin and Herbert Gutman remark: "Immigrant workers generally remained suspicious of chattel bondage."[3] In Charleston, South Carolina, Germans even did business with slaves (illegally) prior to the Civil War and continued trading with blacks afterwards. Jeffery Strickland generally portrays a culture in Charleston in which Germans and blacks were regularly in contact with each other in daily life, in economic transactions, or perhaps in working environments or boarding houses. These interactions began in a neutral or sometimes friendly manner but with time, relationships deteriorated, and there was eventually targeted violence between the two groups.[4] The *Echo* presents little evidence of deep interaction between Germans and black Arkansans, which does not rule out the possibility of such interaction. However, when *Echo* editors and correspondents discuss black people, they do so in broad, stereotypical terms or by describing chance encounters on the street, rather than in terms of personal relationships.

As the nation approached a state of civil war, German immigrants could be found on both sides of the issue of slavery. In particular, the more recent immigrants, who came to America after the failed democratic revolution of 1848 in Germany, opposed slavery. This put them at odds with the Democratic Party. Older immigrants who stayed in the ranks of the Democratic Party condemned them as "'sentimental Negrophiles'" and "'White Niggers.'"[5] Nor was the Republican Party an ideal fit for these German speakers, given the number of former Whigs in the party and their general mistrust of Catholicism and immigration. While the two groups shared anti-slavery sentiments, the Germans were concerned about proponents of nativism and Prohibition within the Republican Party. Aside from moral issues regarding slavery, Germans opposed the Civil War for economic reasons. Potential white customers in the South could turn against them if they denounced slavery. Additionally, Germans knew from their old homeland's history that war brought economic peril, a lesson especially learned during the Thirty Years War in the seventeenth century. In addition to committing other atrocities, looting troops spread diseases and seized or burned stockpiled foodstuffs and equipment, leaving civilians unable to feed themselves in both the short and long terms. Generally, German American journalists were interested in the slavery question simply because it threatened national unity, which they thought was important to maintain at any cost. Carl Wittke's examination of the German American press of the time leads him to conclude that most German immigrants likely did not understand the concept of states' rights. And Faust argues that many Germans simply regarded slavery as an issue of no concern to them because it was an existing law, until the Kansas-Nebraska law of 1854 forced the issue, when a substantial number of Germans decided to oppose slavery. This stance did not necessarily reflect a concern for slaves, though. Berlin and Gutman note, "As in the North, this opposition to slavery took a variety of forms and did not necessarily assure sympathy for the slave. Hatred of slavery and the slave frequently became one."[6]

The case of the Hermann family of Arkansas, as told through their own diaries and letters, is illustrative of the conflicted feelings of Germans in the South. The family's sympathies lay with the North, but the family owned a slave and tried to pass as "good Southerners." Karl Friedrich Hermann was opposed to secession based on the threat of war, but he read political trends and remained silent to protect himself and his family. He observed that pro-secession forces had to resort to intimidation to obtain the desired outcome at the ballot box. He realized that while most Southerners were aware that Germans in the North were against slavery, his position as postmaster initially protected the family in the Arkansas community. Once marauding forces began appearing, his fears about his family's precarious position materialized quickly: "We were soon made aware of our plight; and to the best of our people the horrendous lessons of civil war were being learned. The terrorizing bands were outfitted in military uniforms; they committed deed [*sic*] of violence as if devils incarnate, and in every respect they were similar to the roving bands that plagued peaceful people during the Thirty Years' War." His wife Karolina expressed fear that German Arkansans would be conscripted into the Confederate army, and in 1862 she complained about the loss of her slave, which left her solely responsible for all the work necessary to maintain the homestead. She wrote, "Although we have been under some suspicion, we have generally been thought of as good Southerners. If Northern troops come in, we will have to reveal our true feelings, and after that is done we cannot, of course, continue to stay around here." A few weeks later, she reported, "Now it is generally known that our men are in a Northern camp, and for that reason we know we must expect to be plundered. In the evening robbers came to my house and took all the meat, bread, and apples." The family eventually left the state due to the losses and ongoing violence of the Civil War.[7]

By 1892, the suffering of the war had begun to recede from German Arkansans' memory, even if the aftereffects and the end of slavery would continue to impact German speakers and the state for generations. In December, the *Echo* felt the need to explain what the Freedmen's Bureau was in a news item. An elderly black woman in need of food and wood had come to town and inquired about the location of the Bureau. The article's author clarified, "The same [office] was established right after the war, in order to support the freed slaves, but it ceased operating long ago." In an editorial, the newspaper juxtaposed a characterization of the abolition of slavery as a result of the Civil War with an endorsement of presidential candidate Grover Cleveland as a protector of the everyman, thus: "But just as surely as the American people forced the abolition of black slavery from the haughty planters and slave holders of the South through the Civil War, so just as certainly will it prevent the creation of an even more curse-worthy white slavery from the pilfering of the people by the money princes who have emerged." Aside from these and a few other brief mentions, the Civil War was not directly referenced by the newspaper in 1892, even though the war was still very much a topic in the English-language press in Arkansas at the time.[8]

After the difficult period leading to war and the Civil War itself came the equally divisive period of Reconstruction. Just as Germans had not been united in support of or opposition to slavery, a variety of opinions regarding the process of Reconstruction and necessary steps toward repairing society were represented in the German press.[9] There is no reason to think that German speakers in Arkansas were more or less unified than their landsmen in other parts of the nation, but there is unfortunately no known record of the immediate German response to Reconstruction in the state. By 1892, however, the tide was clearly turning, and gains made by black Arkansans were being erased through a combination of violence and political chicanery. As Kenneth Barnes mentions, the 1891 legislature sent an unmistakable signal by replacing the portrait of George Washington in its chamber with one of Jefferson Davis.[10] The black population in Arkansas in 1892 was concentrated in the southern and eastern parts of the state.[11] Many of the counties where *Echo* readers were most likely found also had the lowest percentages of black inhabitants, 10 percent or less of the total county population: Craighead, Franklin, Johnson, Logan, Pope, Randolph, and Sebastian. But the populations of Faulkner, Perry, and Saline Counties were up to 24 percent black. In Conway and Pulaski counties, up to 49 percent of the population was comprised of black residents. Only one county in which known *Echo* subscribers lived also had a majority black population: Jefferson, where up to 75 percent of inhabitants were black. There were no known *Echo* subscribers in counties where white residents were an extreme minority (counties with a 75–100 percent black population). Generally, then, most of the newspaper's readers likely did not have many black neighbors, especially given Germans' preference, as outlined in the *Echo*, for selecting farmland next to other Germans. But Germans certainly interacted with black Arkansans and were keenly aware of the problematic nature of race relations in the state. A few counties among those with both black populations and *Echo* readers experienced racially motivated violence during 1892, especially during the election season, and the entire state was plagued by a large number of atrocious lynchings that year. And German speakers in Arkansas would have been aware of the legacy of the Civil War; in 1892, the United Confederate Voters established a chapter in Morrilton, a city in which *Echo* subscribers and correspondents lived.[12]

In examining how black Arkansans were portrayed in the pages of the German newspaper, it is important first to discuss the issue of what language and terms were used to identify individuals by race. A useful tool in this endeavor is the *Deutsches Wörterbuch*. The project was begun in 1838 by

Jacob and Wilhelm Grimm, best-known to Americans for their collection of fairy tales. The brothers also cultivated a deep interested in the origins of German language, literature, and culture, subjects which were first being treated as serious academic disciplines in the early nineteenth century. Both brothers had died by 1863, but the work on the sixteen volumes has continued, with the most recent edition published in 1999. The dictionary is remarkable because it not only seeks to define over three hundred thousand entries beginning in the early medieval period but also to document the appearance of the words in over four thousand sources. It thus gives researchers a sense of when words began to be used in common parlance, and most critically, during which periods of time these words were being used. The *Wörterbuch* entries for the words the *Echo* used to refer to black people provide some insight into which words German settlers would have brought with them and which terms they likely learned from anglophone newspapers and neighbors.[13]

The following are terms for black Arkansans printed in the *Echo* during its inaugural year, discussed in alphabetical order. *Afrikanisch* (African) is not found in the *Wörterbuch*, and it is rarely used in the newspaper; I found only two instances in my research.[14] In a news item regarding the purported invention of a machine that could pick cotton effectively, the writer commented that the machine could potentially have disastrous consequences *für die afrikanische Race der Südstaaten* (for the African race of the southern states). The use of English spelling in the term *afrikanische Race*—instead of the German word *Rasse*—is another indication that the editors incorporated this term from English-language sources. The second example is an editorial note appended to a report of an outbreak of racial violence in Guthrie, Oklahoma, in which German farmers were advised to locate their homesteads in areas not crowded *von afrikanischen Nachbarn* (by African neighbors).[15]

*Farbig* (colored) appears both as an adjective and as an adjectival noun in the *Echo* and is the second most frequently used descriptor. The *Wörterbuch* states that it is used to denote an object that is multicolored but also as a suffix to describe a color in relation to another object, such as *blutfarbig* (the color of blood) or *schneefarbig* (the color of snow). The entry associates it with a positive connotation from German poet Goethe, who described jewels using this word. The *Wörterbuch* does not record the usage of the word to indicate people with dark pigmentation, but German settlers would have heard the word "colored" used as a noun in Arkansas. It appears in equal measure in negative and neutral connotations in the *Echo*, and it is most frequently used neutrally in news reporting to describe accident or crime victims, occasionally with a hint of sympathy for the victim. In a negative way, it is used to describe criminals, especially in longer stories in which the writer uses it as a synonym for *Neger* (Negro). Very occasionally, it is used in a positive way, for example to describe the industrial school for blacks established by the Catholic Church in Pine Bluff or to indicate the mother of a newborn.[16]

*Mohr* (moor) is a noun known already to Old High German, a term used to describe the language from around 600 to 1050. It references Mauritanians, Ethiopians, or North Africans more generally. It is used in German Biblical translations about the retinue of the three kings who sought Jesus at his birth and was used in pharmaceutical work to indicate dark-colored powders. The entry contains neutral use of the term as a descriptor in opposition to whites, namely a doctor respected by whites and moors, as well as negative connotations, in which the punishment for a rapist was to color his skin as dark as a moor, or a reference to the devil as a "hell moor." I only encountered one example of this term in the *Echo*, used in a Christian context by a correspondent from Morrilton. The usage is quite odd, in that it at once attempts to be positive but is nevertheless insulting and paternalistic:

> Today, the first Negro pair was wedded privately: may they both remain true to their vows and form the core for a—even if small—black Catholic congregation. After past experiences one cannot have too daring expectations. It is a long, difficult task to wash *the Moors* white, especially because their preachers convince them that we are actually the blacks and they only have the dark color outwardly.[17]

This is undoubtedly a reference to the difficulty the Catholic Church had in convincing black families to attend Catholic services and to send their children to Catholic schools, when black preachers advised against doing so.

"Mulatto" is not found in the *Wörterbuch*, although the concept of an individual of mixed black and white parentage has existed in German literature since the Middle Ages. In the medieval German courtly epic *Parzival* by Wolfram von Eschenbach, the eponymous protagonist has a half-brother, Feirefiz, whose mother is an African queen and whose father is a German knight. The narrator describes Feirefiz as having checkered or spotted colored skin as a result, whether this is because the author was unfamiliar with the appearance of mixed-race children or because the description was for literary effect. I encountered "mulatto" once in my investigation, and it was used in an article on the infamous Henry James lynching of 1892 to describe the victim. Since the English papers described James as mulatto and since the German newspaper otherwise did not use the term, it seems likely that the *Echo* adopted the word from other reports of the event.[18]

*Neger* (Negro) was first used widely among the nobility in the eighteenth century, adapted from the French term (*négre*). It was used by leading writers such as Herder, Kant, and Schiller to indicate black skin, black hair, or those of African descent more generally. It was also used in a synonym for African slavery (*Negerhandel*). This term is by far the most often used by the *Echo*. In roughly 70 percent of its appearances, it is either a negative descriptor for those accused of committing crimes or used in a mocking context, such as in a story about a Faulkner County woman who claimed to be 119 years old and to have seen George Washington. It was a neutral descriptor 30 percent of the time, for example, in news items about accident or flood victims or to describe the Catholic school in Pine Bluff (*Negerschule*). Other articles used this word to refer to blacks who wished to emigrate to Africa or to describe a club in Chicago for black men and their white wives. There were only two instances with an apparently positive connotation. One is the aforementioned reader letter about a black Catholic couple being married, when it is used synonymously with *Schwarz* and *Mohr*. The other is a story that decried the back-to-Africa movement and described progress made by black Americans, which will be discussed below.[19]

"Nigger" is not found in the *Wörterbuch*. I encountered only a handful of uses of the word in *Das Arkansas Echo*. As discussed in the previous chapter, it was used when quoting a white politician. Twice, it was used by the staff to describe accused criminals, but these were not cases of violent crimes such as murder or rape, the allegations of which often led to lynching in Arkansas in 1892. Rather, one case described an attempt to pass a counterfeit check in a German-owned store, and another was a simple case of burglary. It was surprisingly used as a neutral descriptor as well. In one news item, remarkably similar to the January story that mocked the Faulkner County black woman for her age and claim to have seen Washington, a Poinsett County woman described as *die ältesteste Niggerfrau in Arkansas* ("the oldest nigger woman in Arkansas") was said to be 115 years old and to tell interesting details about Washington's life; the writer added a comment about her age being a refutation of the claim that Arkansas had a poor climate. In a November story, the term is used neutrally in a news item to describe a black man who managed to kill a large bear near Ouachita.[20]

*Schwarz* (black), similarly to *farbig*, is used as both an adjective and an adjectival noun by the *Echo*. The *Wörterbuch* contains many more examples of it being used as an adjective. The *Echo* follows this pattern of adjectival use, for instance in the terms "black woman," "black people," "black moor," and less often employs the word as an adjectival noun (for instance, "the blacks"). Of all the terms used by the *Echo* to denote race, it receives the longest entry by far in the *Wörterbuch* with a wide variety of uses, most often as a prefix. It is used to mean dark, in both a physically descriptive (dark night, dark forest, a color in opposition to white) and a metaphysically descriptive manner (gloomy, bleak, illegal as in "black market"). It is associated with evil when discussed in opposition to good, and with mourning and sin, but religious members of the Benedictine order were also referred to as "black nuns" or "black monks." In medical usage, it denoted afflicted skin and body parts, and this was the term used when referring to the plague as "the black death" (*der schwarze Tod*). In the *Echo*'s pages, it is the third-most used term for black Arkansans. Like *Neger*, *schwarz* is used primarily in a negative sense (criminal accusations), occasionally as a neutral descriptor (emigrants), and, in the two cases already discussed with regard to positive connotations of *Neger*, as a positive descriptor.

One extremely odd expression, *die schwarzen Kinder Chams* (the black children of Ham), is not found in the *Wörterbuch* and is used once in the *Echo*. It is unquestionably a biblical reference to the book of Genesis, when Noah curses his son Ham for a transgression. The exact nature of Ham's impropriety, whether sexual or merely involving nudity, is debated by biblical scholars, but in his curse Noah proclaims that the children of Canaan, Ham's son, would become servants to Noah's other descendants. This story was used by racists as a justification for slavery. The article in question is a reprint from the Fort Smith German-language paper *Das Arkansas Volksblatt*, and it is a negative portrayal of black families attempting to emigrate from Arkansas to Oklahoma (discussed later in this chapter). While the author uses the word *schwarz* as a synonym for someone with black skin without further comment, the overall tone of the article is extremely racist.[21]

A similarly bigoted term that appeared only once in the *Echo* is *Hottentot*, a colonial Dutch loanword used as a descriptor for black people whose culture was regarded as inferior; it referred to a nineteenth-century stereotype of Africans. The context is a joke in the form of a short fictional narrative. A man traveling through Africa is welcomed into the home of a prince of the Hottentots. He discovers he is out of ink when he prepares to write down his experiences, but he fortunately finds a full pot of ink in his room. The prince's aunt enters the room and screams, since the pot belongs to her—a European traveler told her it was *Toilettenwasser* (eau de toilette, or perfume). The man had already been condemned to death when a European captain who was nearby manages to convince the prince of the man's innocence. This rather lengthy and ludicrous set-up served the sole purpose of allowing for the creation of the compound word used as the item's title: *Hottentottenpotentatentantentintenattentat* (Hottentot potentate aunt ink assassination), which is supposed to be the humorous element, aside from the implicit insult of the European's gifting the African woman "perfume" which is in fact ink.[22]

It seems clear that the *Echo* was influenced by the terminology that English-language papers used to refer to black Arkansans. Regarding shifting language use and attitudes during the era of Reconstruction, Kenneth Barnes states, "Changes in language also reflected a more stridently racist attitude. Previously articles in the *Gazette* had customarily referred to African Americans as Negroes, coloreds, or darkies. But by 1889 terms such as *nigger* and *coon* began to appear with frequency."[23] The *Echo*'s coverage appears to reflect the attitudes of whites Arkansans at the time, even if the paper did not specifically use the overtly derogatory terms to the same extent. First-generation German immigrants, whether moving to Arkansas directly from Europe or from other American states, would not have had much contact with blacks in their homeland. While token Africans (or *Kammermohren*), many of whom had been taken to Europe against their will, were present as servants at German courts beginning in the 1500s as a way to show the power and influence of rulers, Germany did not have a large population of people from the African diaspora until the twentieth century. Therefore the average German of the mid- to late 1800s would not have encountered blacks in daily life before coming to America.[24] The words "nigger" and "mulatto" were not in common usage in Germany at the time, and the word *farbig* (colored) was used primarily to refer to actual colors rather than race in German. While *Neger* (Negro) was used by European German speakers to indicate race, its notable frequency in the pages of the *Echo* may have been the result of its being linguistically similar to, while more socially acceptable than, the offensive term "nigger." As the editors read English-language publications of the state, racist word usage presumably affected their interpretations of the events reported.

Similarities between the *Echo* and the English newspapers were not limited to word usage. Michael Dougan, in his comprehensive study of Arkansas newspapers over two centuries, concludes, "One of the most conspicuous aspects of late 19th-century reporting was in the treatment of racial news. Over and over, blacks were treated as subhuman. . . . When, in the early 20th century, Governor Jeff Davis preached genocide, he was merely fulfilling the rhetoric too many editors had come to deploy in their everyday coverage of news events involving blacks."[25] Carl Moneyhon observes that pseudoscientific racial theories circulating at the time lent support to bigotry: "By the middle of the 1880s, Arkansas's white newspapers increasingly referred to African Americans as racially inferior and demanded formal segregation."[26] Just as developments in election laws in 1891–92 shaped politics in the state for decades to come, another law passed the year before the *Echo* was established would lay the foundations for racial segregation in the form of Jim Crow laws common throughout the South at the beginning of the twentieth century. The Separate Coach Law of 1891 required railroads to segregate the races by providing separate cars for black and white riders and segregated waiting rooms. There is no mention of the Separate Coach Law in the 1892 *Echo* issues, presumably because it did not affect the German-speaking readers. They were frequent railroad passengers and certainly must have seen discrimination, but they themselves were not inconvenienced by it. The topic of legally enforced segregation, in any aspect of society, was not addressed by the paper during 1892. But the *Echo* did advocate for self-segregation, by stating explicitly that German speakers were better off living away from black Arkansans. The paper's crime coverage, discussed below, certainly gave the impression that self-segregation was the safest course of action.[27]

The *Echo*'s reporting on local and state events involving Arkansas's black population was shaped by the editors' and correspondents' general views on race. Coverage of the black community is bewilderingly contradictory, with attitudes ranging from sympathetic to extremely racist, often within the same story or letter. For example, a March article offered a remarkably positive take on the contemporary experience of black Americans. A reporter asked US senator Bruce about planned attempts to assist blacks to emigrate to Africa. This was presumably Blanche Bruce, a Mississippi Republican who was the first black man elected to a full term in the Senate. He answered that it had been attempted and failed four times previously and that only Bishop Henry McNeal Turner still believed it to be a good idea. The article quoted at length Senator Bruce's explanation of why he believed black emigration was unnecessary.

> The blacks in America are only Africans by their skin; their whole nature, aspirations, and thinking are American, and there's no more

> reason for them to leave the country of their birth and emigrate to Africa because their forefathers lived there than there is for any fresh[ly immigrated] or German American to go back to Europe because their ancestors lived there. If the progress of the colored people of the South were less satisfactory since Emancipation, there would perhaps be a pretext for the encouragement of emigration, but there are now one and one third million colored schoolchildren in the public schools, 37,000 in private schools, 8,000 in parochial schools, which makes 1,370,000 schoolchildren. There are further seventy institutions of higher learning for colored people, over 7,000 colored people are being trained as teachers, hundreds are studying theology, medicine, and law; in spite of the disadvantages against which they had to struggle, the colored people alone in the state of Virginia have managed to accumulate property in the value of $15,000,000, and in Louisiana, Mississippi, and South Carolina, they would have had even better results to show, if the census had taken the property of colored people into consideration. The Negro will make something of himself with time; one simply has to leave him alone and give him the necessary opportunity.[28]

The article's author is careful to translate the senator's statements into the subjunctive mood, which in German indicates to the reader that they are reported speech. This is a neutral way of reporting that clearly denotes the opinions of the speaker, which the reporter may or may not necessarily agree with. It is noteworthy that the *Echo* editors did not comment on the content of this particular story, in contrast to their frequent editorializing on topics they felt particularly passionate about. From a modern perspective, Bruce's statements are obviously complicated. The post-Emancipation experience of African Americans in the South was not as ideal as he portrayed it; historians argue that he was out of touch with his black contemporaries in the South, while his office afforded him a life of privilege in the nation's capital. Nevertheless, the *Echo*'s article offered German-speaking readers a remarkably positive image of black accomplishment and potential as described by a successful black senator.

The article quoting Senator Bruce was published roughly a month after an editorial in the *Arkansas Gazette* proclaimed blacks to be inferior, although it is not clear that the *Echo* article was printed in response. The editorial starts with a description of a lecture by a Cornell professor: "During his lecture Prof. Jenks mentioned some of the blunders of the inexperienced reconstruction legislators in the South, and also the low moral tone, as well as the humble material condition of many of the race today, in proof of his estimate of it as 'an inferior race,' and one incapable of advanced, civilized self-government." The *Gazette* followed this editorial with a letter purportedly by J. C. Duke, the editor of a black Pine Bluff newspaper (coincidentally also named the *Echo*), whom the *Gazette* praised as an "intelligent Negro" for allegedly admitting that his race was inferior. Duke later demanded a retraction because he had in fact not written the letter, which the *Gazette* then claimed had been written by another black journalist, the editor of the *Baptist Vanguard*. The retraction read as follows: "The *Gazette* unwittingly credited the *Echo* man with a larger share of enlightenment and sagacity than he is willing to acknowledge. That is all."[29]

A few months later, the *Echo* ran an editorial that provides a more typical representation of its reporting on black people. Even when the writer attempted to be sympathetic to the experiences or concerns of black people, the tone was patronizing, and much of what was written was either negative or overtly racist. The opening paragraph of a May editorial entitled "Die Neger" (The Negroes) illustrates this tendency.

> The Negro is a problem child of our commonwealth. That one dragged the poor blacks here from Africa to force them into slavery was an injustice, the consequences of which we have to deal and that agitates us to the obligation to do what we can for these children of the dark continent. Up until now, one admittedly looked after the Negro almost only because his vote in the elections is regarded as equal to that of the white man, because after all every vote counts. The dragging of the Negro into this sort of politics has to pull him down morally still more deeply. The Christian mission as well has only done little up to now for the black man, although here and there promising starts have been made. This quiet work of the Christian mission is the thing from which one can most likely expect the best success. Because the kind of white who lives in the districts that are most heavily populated by blacks does business of the cut-throat variety with mortgages and certificates of indebtedness, which are a bone-crushing burden for the Negro, who is economically frivolous by nature, and which also bog him down morally.[30]

After addressing slavery, vote pandering, and anaconda mortgages, the editorial went on to allay fears of a race war by arguing that immigration was making the white population grow at a faster rate than the black population, and it made the stunning assertion that black birth rates were not higher "because the same [the black population], similarly to a transplanted tree, cannot possibly thrive in a foreign country as well as on its native soil." The editorial suggested that white immigrants were not as hindered by living in a foreign land, implying that African immigration was inherently doomed to failure. The author made the patently racist claim that the black population was decreasing because of "the filth in which the Negroes put up [with living]" and a higher risk of contracting tuberculosis. The writer commented on attempts to assist blacks through immigration to Africa or out of the South to other parts of the United States. This sentence regarding the back-to-Africa movement could be a clue that the editorial was taken from another newspaper, not published in Arkansas, since the author mistakenly assumed that the US government was paying for emigration to Africa and that not many blacks were moving away from the South. Other than this editorial, the *Echo* commented routinely on black emigration from Arkansas as well as on a scandal in which black people had paid themselves for passage to Africa only to be cheated out of the money.[31]

The editorial concluded that the best method for assisting the black population would be intraracial self-reliance and uplift. It reported on a conference in Alabama called by Booker T. Washington regarding this issue and attended by five hundred black farmers, workers, and preachers. The tone of the piece again swung wildly, applauding blacks who were attempting to find a solution for their own community and accusing them of being their own worst enemies. A black attendee, described as a farmer and "reverend" (the English word was used in quotes in the midst of German text) allegedly stated that blacks were like children in their inability to manage money, spontaneously purchasing items such as a buggy even if they did not own an animal to pull it. The article also criticized the practice of planting only cotton. The editorial included a quotation attributed to an elderly black farmer and published in English to reinforce the claim that someone from the black community had actually made the statement: "'We got too many Sundays and not 'nuff work days. We'se too lazy . . . . .WE must raise more meat and bread. We can raise corn, pumpkins, peas, wheat, hogs and cattle, but we don't. We stick to cotton, and cotton is starving us to death.'" But black farmers in debt often had no say in what they planted, as their creditors insisted they plant cotton as a cash crop. The *Echo* editors would have known that. The dubious claims of the quotation, along with the "eyewitness reporting" from Alabama, make it likely that the editors reprinted the story from another source. Yet the editors did not hesitate to offer their readers this racist interpretation of the challenges black Americans faced.[32]

The *Echo* staff felt it important to assert that they as immigrants belonged to the white majority. An article entitled "Weiße und Schwarze" (Whites and blacks) examined census-bureau data and stated explicitly, "Finally, we want to take a quick glance at the color of our population and to be sure, we understand in this connection all non-whites as 'colored', whether they are of African descent or also Chinese and Japanese or Indians as the case may be." It happily reported that overall population had increased in the United States in comparison to France and noted that the "colored" population was down due to a reduction in non-European immigration and the "dying off of Indians."[33] Another article made it clear that German speakers understood that European immigrants were not immediately accepted by the dominant Anglo-Saxon culture. The editorial lamented that the Know-Nothing movement of the 1850s had gained traction again and vowed that Germans would fight against this force.[34]

Because Germans counted themselves among the predominant white culture, one of their fears in 1892 was that of a race war, understood as an unprovoked attack in which large numbers of black Americans would target white neighbors. Certain historical events in Arkansas might have reinforced this fear of race violence. In an 1868 incident, white men confiscated weapons from black freedmen; a white man was killed in the incident, but he had been involved in attempting reconnaissance on the freedmen and so was not an innocent bystander. In December 1868, Governor Powell Clayton declared martial law to attempt to put a stop to politically and racially motivated killings. In 1881, another confrontation between blacks and whites escalated into violence on the streets of Morrilton. During the 1890 elections, rumors circulated that blacks had secured weapons to use if Republicans were not elected and that they had threatened to burn down Plumerville and Morrilton—both in Conway County, where German-speaking immigrants lived.[35]

In 1892, the *Arkansas Gazette* reported two incidents that directly spoke to white fears of an armed insurrection by blacks. In May, as part of the coverage of the Henry James lynching, a story described an anonymous black man who had allegedly revealed plans to send twenty-five men to Chicago to obtain dynamite for use in large gatherings of white people. No reference to this threat appears in the *Echo*'s pages. Perhaps the *Echo* editors felt reassured by the *Arkansas Gazette* editors' assessment of the situation and felt no need to worry their own readership: "This is regarded only as a threat from some despicable negro, for they must know as well as every white man knows that such a course would result in the speedy extermination of the colored race in this city, or any other community where such a thing would be attempted. But no such thing could occur. The negroes have too much sense, and have too much at stake to ever endorse such threats."[36] In September the *Gazette* reported on a threat of "an uprising of the negroes" in Thornton (Calhoun County) due to protests against the new election law: "They swear to kill every white man, woman and child in the township."[37] Later in the issue, though, the paper asserted that a single white man, known for troublemaking, had incited blacks in the county to riot. Two days later, the *Gazette* stated a member of the group had written proof of the oath to kill whites and that the remaining at-large members were being hunted down by the local sheriff.[38] The absence of these two incidents in the *Echo* is curious because of the clear fear German settlers had of a potential attack by black Arkansans.

An incident the *Echo* did cover was the demand by white citizenry that all blacks vacate the city of Paragould within three days, after a white man named Monroe Pulley was murdered. While the *Gazette* did not clarify how the crime inflamed racial tensions, the *Echo* reported that six black men were accused of the killing. The *Echo* also described the terroristic threatening in a way that implied that only the white residents were legitimate citizens of the town: "In Paragould, the Negroes have been called on by the citizens to leave the city." As the *Echo* had a correspondent in Jonesboro, some German speakers were surely aware of the actual details of the event. Strangely, another attempt to evict blacks living in Lonoke County in 1892 was not reported in the *Echo*. Other items in the German paper, though, alerted readers to signs of growing racial unrest. In an incident in Monticello in June, a young white man *aus bester Familie* (from one of the best families) beat a black man because the latter would not move from the sidewalk to make room for him. The writer commented, "Racial hatred is increasing and can yield terrible fruit." In a report about the aftermath of a lynching in Paducah, Kentucky, an *Echo* article described how "around midnight an armed mob of 75 Negroes suddenly appeared and opened fire on the [white militia] men standing around the jail." Consequent *Echo* reporting indicates that the Germans could sense coming racial violence, but their fear was that whites—including they themselves—would be the victims; they did not acknowledge that the power in post-Reconstruction Arkansas was still firmly in the hands of white supremacists. Racial violence continued to be widespread throughout 1892, and incidents reported as race wars followed in 1896, 1897, and 1899.[39]

Part of what made *Echo* readers uneasy was reporting, typical for the time, that portrayed black Arkansans primarily as criminals. Each week,

German-speaking readers were confronted with numerous reports of black suspects—most of whom were identified solely by race and not by proper name—who were accused of committing or attempting to commit assault, burglary or theft, murder, rape, rioting, or who had escaped from custody. This reduction of all criminals to a monolithic racial identity (usually *Neger* or "Negro") led to the impression that black people as a race were perpetrating crimes or being accused of them, rather than individual suspects. Most white criminals, by comparison, were identified by name. One exception was made in order to publicly shame an alleged lawbreaker, a black man named Fisher accused of mugging a white woman on the street and stealing her pocketbook: "Fisher was a waiter at the Richelieu Hotel, and therefore not in need, but rather committed an insolent street robbery." It also allowed a white man, Dr. Hudspeth, to figure as the hero of the story, as Hudspeth apprehended Fisher and held him until police arrived. Another news item reported that *unbekannte Spitzbuben* (unknown scoundrels) had broken into the house of German immigrant Al Schaeder; the report included the assertion that police believed "the thieves are nigger boys." This was one of the few uses of the racist epithet in the German newspaper.[40]

One incident stands out from the quotidian crime stories in reflecting what many white Southerners at the time feared: that black domestic workers, who had access to their families and homes, could exact revenge for harsh treatment. A black cook named Edith Gordon (who was unnamed by the *Echo)* and her husband were arrested for poisoning seventeen people at a boardinghouse on Rock Street. Initially, she herself claimed poisoning symptoms, but a doctor examined her and pronounced her healthy, after which the pair admitted that the husband had bought two packages of rat poison that she had mixed into the food she prepared. Curiously, the *Echo* reported that it initially seemed the suspects would be lynched, in keeping with the pattern of violence during the rest of the year: "Though because no direct evidence existed against the imprisoned Negroes, the people departed again."[41] This observation invites obvious follow-up questions: why was the couple arrested in the first place, and why did they admit to the crime if there was no evidence? It is improbable that the white crowd would simply wander off, when many white mobs in 1892 lynched black Arkansans with little or no proof of alleged wrongdoing. The *Echo* did not report the speculation that the Gordons meant the poisoning as retaliation for the Henry James lynching. The *Arkansas Gazette* had reported on this element of the story, while noting that the investigation was ongoing and the police were not convinced of the couple's guilt. Both papers were cryptic in their stories of the case's resolution. After sensationalized coverage at the outset, the *Gazette* later printed a very small note: "The Grand Jury dismissed the charge of attempted poisoning against Edith Gordon yesterday. She had been bound over by Justice Peay in the sum of $500." The *Echo* gives no direct evidence that its readers employed black cooks or nannies. After all, one reader letter (discussed in chapter 3) described how German girls themselves obtained jobs as domestic help, and the *Echo* also published want ads for individuals specifically seeking to employ German young people for childcare or manual labor. There were several advertisements for boardinghouses, so readers could potentially imagine themselves in the position of the poisoned boarders. The *Echo*'s publication of this story undoubtedly contributed to ever-present concerns among Germans about a race war.[42]

Most mentions of black Arkansans in the *Echo* that did not depict them as perpetrators of crime recounted incidents in which blacks were instead victims of crimes or of accidents. These stories were most often reported in a neutral tone, although some were sympathetic toward black victims, and at least one mocked the victim. Accidents included drownings, especially in rivers, or deaths or injuries in the workplace. Several of the latter were particularly gruesome, including a young boy who was electrocuted when standing too close to a steam vent that was also in the proximity of electric lights, and a black man, identified as H. Moore, whose body was cut in half when he fell onto a saw. Another worker named Jackson was injured when the flywheel of the steam engine he was operating caught and thrashed him, breaking his leg. S. McNeil of Poplar Grove was presented as a medical curiosity. He had suffered severe burns to his head that prevented the skin from growing back. The injury was covered with a bandage that, when removed, directly exposed his brain. Black men who were injured at the workplace were given the dignity of having their names mentioned, which was generally not the *Echo*'s practice when reporting on black Arkansans. But in one case, a black man who was depicted as a hero in a workplace accident was not even named. He was hired by C. Lehmer, owner of a dairy, to clean out a well and ended up rescuing his employer when Lehmer leaned over to monitor the work and fell in headfirst. A few accidents were reported in which blacks were injured in accidents with streetcars or trains. One article is notable for its cruel mockery of a victim who was walking on the tracks and did not step aside far enough after hearing the streetcar's warning whistle: "The Negro did move to the outside of the tracks, whether he also believed the train would move over as well or whether he wanted to throw it off its track is not known." The man was not killed but suffered a broken arm and rib.[43]

The fates of other black victims of accident or crime were relayed with more sympathy. These included two workers in Little Rock who were trapped in a ditch cave-in during the laying of waste pipes (one survived), and a man who died in terrible pain after mistaking strychnine for quinine. The survival of a black worker who was gravely injured by a fall from the scaffolding of the Capitol Hotel was described as *fast ein Wunder* (almost a miracle). In an incomplete story that appeared across two issues, the writer took a sympathetic view of a black man from El Dorado, whom he identified as a victim of murder. The story describes how white murderers ambushed (*aufgelauert*) the victim after he testified to a grand jury that the men who eventually killed him had kidnapped his children to force them to work off an alleged debt. A posse sent to apprehend the perpetrators was shot at and a deputy sheriff was injured. The *Echo* never mentioned the case again, and it remains unclear whether justice was served. Another article appeared that sympathetically reported on a "poor, hardworking Negro" named Cargler in Little Rock, whose ex-wife apparently burned down his small dwelling after injuring his eyes the previous week in an attack with a fork.[44]

Another way in which the *Echo* moved beyond crime-centered reporting of black Arkansans was its coverage of black religious life. An article about the jubilee celebration of Bishop Fitzgerald noted that four black girls from the black school in Pine Bluff took part. Two news items reported on the deaths of black preachers: One described a preacher who was on his way to hold a service in Murfreesboro but was thrown from his pony and drowned when he tried to cross the Little Missouri. Another account told of W. G. Johnson, who suddenly left a prayer service he was leading and did not return. The congregants finished the service without him, and when they exited the church, they found him face down in a puddle of water. The *Echo* reported that he was believed to have passed out in the puddle; an autopsy found that both of his lungs were filled with water. A final story reported on what must have been a curiosity for German-speaking Catholics: the baptism of several hundred black Baptists, largely women, in the Arkansas River. The author described how the cold water caused discomfort and cramping among several participants. The event was apparently of great local interest, with a crowd of five to six thousand in attendance and roughly fifteen to twenty people observing from boats on the water. M. H. from Morrilton complained in a letter about the challenge of converting black Arkansans but noted that German missionaries to Africa had a harder time: "Many are called, few are chosen, is especially true of the blacks." This condescending attitude appeared in a report on a German school in Togo, in which a teacher complained that his African pupils academically lagged behind German students: "'The boys show a stronger inclination to stealing and lying, for singing and gymnastics they express the greatest interest.'"[45]

While the previous chapter discussed the *Echo*'s coverage of politics in general, the paper's reporting on black Arkansans' involvement in the political process yields particular insights into the racial attitudes of German settlers. Kenneth Barnes reports, "By the later 1890s, the idea of African Americans participating in politics had become merely an amusement among Conway County Democrats." This statement unequivocally applies to coverage in the *Echo* in 1892. One news item began, "In the legislature of Arkansas, one chases off boredom in a number of ways." It described how a black legislator took exception to being spit upon by a white man watching from the gallery. A different article included an exceptionally mean-spirited portrayal of another black legislator that reinforced the idea that the Republican Party was the party of the uneducated black man. It is worth quoting at length:

> In the People's Party convention, there were eight colored men, while the Republican consisted of three-fourths Negroes. The ideas of these people were characterized by one of them, a colored shoemaker by the name of Bradford; he said he had not had time to learn how to speak properly, since he was born before the war, and the Democrats had not given him the opportunity to receive an education; they had kept him working continuously up until this day. I am a black Republican, and we black Republicans have to lay all prejudices aside this time and win; we yield this time to the whites, and we'll be up the next time. I am in favor of entering into a confusion (instead of fusion) with the other party. I have always been in confusion. We black fellers have to sit quietly and keep our secret. Let the nigger stand still this time and observe this horse trading-electioneering. Two years from now, then we'll put the black man in.[46]

The quotation is offered without commentary, and the editors apparently trusted readers to draw the appropriate conclusions about the dangers of voting for a fusion ticket. Long after the election, a paragraph in December again mocked blacks who were frightened by shooting stars, after which an elderly man allegedly commented that the heavens were celebrating the Democratic victory. After this, it was reported that his neighbor remarked that he voted for Cleveland, since he felt betrayed by Harrison's promise of higher pay four years earlier.[47]

In the middle of this racially charged climate, a German-speaking correspondent by the name of A. Kind wrote a remarkable description of the Ku Klux Klan (KKK) from the immigrant perspective. Kind participated in *Echo* editors' request that each settler community around the state send in a description of its history; his was the only account published in the paper's inaugural year. It appeared in three installments. The first gave a general overview of Randolph County and the German speakers there. Kind noted that he used existing English-language histories but also spoke directly to the founding members of the German-speaking community. In the second installment, he took exception to a historical description of the county, which he quoted, that claimed while lawlessness had been an issue in the area prior to Reconstruction, justice was consistently carried out according to the law since. Kind argued that the opposite was true, noting that the KKK was still active in Randolph County, as in other parts of the state. He related a story of a KKK attack on a German speaker in his home; the man was able to escape. Kind explained that he understood the "club" to have been formed in 1868 in Georgia as a boys' club comprised of young men who simply wanted to have fun, before transforming into a terrorist group. He claimed that, though nearly the entire native white population of Randolph County had been in support of the Confederacy, many were nevertheless glad that the Union still existed at war's end. He stated that German-speaking immigrants had been welcomed with open arms.

In the third and final installment, Kind told readers he was returning to the topic of the KKK because he had found and was able to interview a former member. He vouched for the truthfulness of this person and proceeded to tell the story of the Klan according to this former member, whom he identified by the initials F. v. G. It is probable that this alleged former KKK member was a German man who joined the organization in the aftermath of the Civil War, since a lower case "v" before a last name often indicates *von*, either denoting the area where one's family originated or noble status. The informant began with a bold statement.

> But no matter how atrociously the general public likes to portray the activities of these masked riders and quite justifiably was disgusted over their later monstrous deeds, so it must be recorded that this union did not come into being in order to play an arbitrary game with the weak, but rather solely to protect fellow citizens and to preserve them from the unjust oppression by the military of the United States. That is why we find that at the beginning of

> the 'Kuklux Klan' men from the best families were recruited and demonstrated an honorable character.[48]

F. v. G. argued that the KKK in Randolph County had been an omnipresent force after 1868, ready to stand up against roving bands who committed atrocities during Reconstruction. He described the colorful outfits that KKK members wore while patrolling, including striped pants and fake beards, although he mentioned the "steeple-shaped hats" as well. He claimed membership was so widespread that whole schools could be emptied if word came that the assistance of the group was required. He noted that once law and order were reestablished, there was no need for the self-policing and that the honorable members left the organization, since it began committing the very sorts of brutal acts it had sought to prevent and was declared to be a terrorist organization and outlawed.

Kind offered what he saw as an obvious connection between the KKK as it existed during Reconstruction and the *Femegerichte* (Vehmic courts) of the fourteenth and fifteenth centuries. This was a period of extreme lawlessness in parts of Germany after the medieval feudal system had begun to deteriorate, and roving bands terrorized civilian populations. The courts were known for their secret deliberations and exercise of swift justice by hanging. They similarly suffered from abuse of authority and the commission of atrocities they had been formed to punish. Kind contended that the period of Reconstruction was a period of even worse lawlessness than had been seen in Germany during the *Femegerichte*: "Every man did or could do what he wanted, no law found recognition or was followed, since the state did not have the power in its hands in order to enforce its authority." He even argued that the early KKK members were owed thanks for restoring order, although he stated again that the group lost its way and was justifiably outlawed in 1889. Not all German speakers may have agreed with Kind's characterization of the KKK. A few weeks after the last installment was published, a cryptic note directly addressing Kind appeared in the *Echo*. It said that he was of course being attacked by the *Staatszeitung* as a correspondent of the *Echo*, but that this was by no means a mark of shame, since the rival paper had in the meantime defamed more German speakers than could fit into the largest hall in Little Rock. There is no acknowledgment that the content of his story could have caused the controversy.[49]

This depiction of the KKK, a known terrorist organization, as essentially a charitable protection league is essential to understanding Germans' interpretation of the extreme, racially motivated violence they witnessed in 1892. According to the sentiments recorded in the *Echo*, German speakers felt themselves under threat of attack from either black Arkansans or white outsiders who sided with blacks. At the same time, the KKK showed Germans how a vigilante organization in the South could represent both protection and threat. Germans were enamored of the law and wanted to live in an orderly society. Yet several items from the inaugural year illustrate how Germans were frustrated by the American justice system and might have understood a perceived need for alternative forms of punishment for crime. Even so, they were frustrated and frightened by the climate of lynching in 1892 Arkansas, as it was not reflective of the orderly society that they expected to find in their new homeland. Conway correspondent J. L. related a story that was published by the agricultural *Wheel* newspaper. The prosecution of a group of men who stole a single bale of cotton ended up costing taxpayers $1,600. J. L. commented, "In this instance one would truly like to ask: 'Who is the thief? The state or these men?'" Correspondent T. from Paris wrote about a vigilante case gone wrong. A posse of men were going to punish a known domestic abuser, Brewer, but the men became so drunk that they decided to wait until the next day. One posse member, Young, went to the wife-beater's house anyway and tried to arrest the man alone. He was killed, and Young was arrested for the murder. In the same county, a grand jury was deadlocked in another case in which a landlord shot his tenant. T. asked, "Is it a wonder that one daily reads about Judge Lynch in the newspapers with such a justice system?!"[50]

German immigrants understood lynching to be the inevitable result of a broken justice system, and they thought that the only possible remedy for the problem was to reform the system. They did not acknowledge concretely, or perhaps did not fully understand at the time, what historians today document about the rash of lynchings occurring in the state: lynching was a way for the white majority to reimpose the power structure of slavery by inflicting violence that went unopposed by the state. German reporting of the time, however, bought in to the stereotype perpetrated by the contemporary white press that lynching most often resulted from retaliation for sexual violence of black men perpetrated against white women. When news was reported that a black man was accused of attacking a white woman or girl, it was often accompanied by the statement that a lynching was expected. Yet the paper additionally included examples of when a white man was murdered in this way and when a black mob lynched a black man accused of a sexual crime against a black victim. For example, one report described how a white man in Perryville identified as Stewart was accused of raping an eleven-year-old girl. He was being held captive in a jail but was restrained, as the jail was not regarded as particularly secure. One morning, the body of the deputy sheriff who had been guarding him was found in his cell. The theory was that Stewart tricked the man into loosening his bonds by claiming they were too tight, then hit the deputy with a piece of wood but found no key on him with which to escape. Stewart claimed the deputy sheriff had been thrown into his cell after being murdered, which was not believed: "The embittered citizens, though, hanged him from the first convenient tree." In two cases, both the perpetrator and victim were black. Describing the case of Robert Donnelly, accused of raping a twelve-year-old girl at gunpoint, the writer began the story by saying that blacks had lynched "one of their own," reported that the alleged rapist had confessed to the crime, and asserted that there was not a single white person in the lynch mob of 250. In December, it was reported that a black mob was prevented from lynching J. Morrison, who also went by the alias Chas. Williams, after he infected his eleven-year-old victim with syphilis.[51]

German speakers were concerned that lynching was a uniquely southern problem and wondered what that meant for society at large. A March article stated that a man in Memphis claimed to be responsible for the alleged crime committed by "McCoy" (Edward Coy), a particularly brutal lynching case that took place in February (discussed below). The Memphis admission was likely not true, since Coy alleged that the "victim," who was a married white woman, had actually been a consensual lover. Nevertheless, this fear regarding lynching—that an innocent man might be murdered by the crowd—was raised by the Germans. They were additionally concerned about similar vigilante behavior exhibited in Memphis and New Orleans: "There must be a terribly crude element growing here in the South which is developing an appetite for such atrocities. If a murderer has earned death, that does not mean that a crowd of people has the right to punish him." In this way, *Echo* reporting differed from *Gazette* coverage. At least one researcher believes the *Gazette* pointedly notified readers of other lynching incidents from around the South in order to normalize the behavior. The *Echo*'s disdain for barbarism was reflected in another report about the Coy lynching, in which the writer grimly noted that it was "genuinely American" that a man named Mathews had taken wood from the stake on which Coy was "roasted," fashioned a police button from it, and presented it to Chief of Police Sanders as a token of esteem.[52]

In May, June, and July, the *Echo* editors addressed the issue of lynching directly in several editorials, quoted here at some length in order to let the German settlers' opinions speak for themselves. The first was entitled "Gerechtigkeit und Lynchjustiz" (Justice and lynch law). The editorial began with an assertion that the pursuit of justice was one of the founding principles of the paper and took a firm stand against lynching: "We condemn the lynch law exactly as much as every person who loves law and order must." The editors added that they were tired of the platitudes about how terrible the situation was: "Nothing will be improved with clichés; they only serve as insincere excuses in order to avoid improvement and the stoppage of evils." The editors predicted that what happened in Little Rock, when not even Governor Eagle could prevent the lynching of Henry James, would bring the state into the national spotlight. Yet they rejected the inevitable lamentations of officials: "But this hypocritical ado might well lull to sleep the conscience of these gentlemen, but it does not erase the blot which dishonors us in the eyes of all civilized nations." The article concluded with the assertion that lynchings occurred as a reaction to the shortcomings of a corrupt justice system, that it was the state's obligation to correct the injustices, and that, while lynching could not be justified, the people could only be partially to blame for violence.[53]

The June editorial was part of a larger discussion of Germanic versus Roman law and the need for legal reform in the United States. It began by praising the British system for the quick way in which it carried out the death penalty and deriding the American system for waiting to execute the guilty. The most notable section is a reprint of two excerpts taken from the *Southern Post Journal*, which are additionally printed in a slightly smaller font size to alert readers that it was quoted material.

> The brutal acts of violence committed by Negroes against white women, which have become virtually epidemic recently, have produced a mood in the southern states which foreshadows nothing good for the blacks. Any chance event could set off the up to now suppressed spark to a blaze and then there might be a horrific bloodbath. The honor of our women must be protected, cost what it will, and no sanctimonious complaints of northern philanthropists, who understand nothing about the state of affairs, can change anything about it.[54]

An editorial note followed, explaining that the *Echo* had cited the articles to illustrate the need to create a better justice system that would make lynching unnecessary. But the *Echo* editorial never quite fulfilled this stated purpose; it argued for an overhaul of the American legal system, but it did not tie it to the sentiments expressed by the *Southern Post Journal.* One is left, then, with two possible interpretations of this quoted material. First, the German settlers feared lynching was getting out of hand and could lead to wider violence; second, they were aware of the southern obsession with preventing any sort of racial mixing, so that the rape of a white woman by a black man would be considered a capital offense. (The editors did uncritically accept the assertion that rape was the cause of most lynchings.) The editorial additionally observed that those who were taking part in lynching were often wearing the clothing of the respectable middle class, and that the general public seemed to be uninterested in forcing a change that would make lynching unnecessary. Finally, it blamed the practice on the fact that there were so many untrained lawyers in the United States and how easy it was to become a lawyer compared with the process in France and Germany. Lawyers were said to be primarily concerned with their own self-interests rather than in fundamentally restructuring the justice system.

The July 22 editorial, entitled "Gewaltthaten" (Violent acts), attempted to place the southern lynchings in a wider context of violence. It could not justify the actions of miners in Idaho who used powder and dynamite when talks to negotiate wages failed, just as lynch mobs could not be justified in lynching black men who attacked white women. The editorial then shifted its tone, blaming the black lynching victims whose extralegal deaths it had just condemned: "Because as long as the colored beasts commit crimes and the proper courts allow a dearth of necessary speed, the endangered whites will always form a mob and 'take the law into their own hands.'" This euphemism is notable because the *Echo* generally avoided the language that sometimes appeared in the English-speaking press to disguise violent acts, such as "a general clean-up of the area'" or "neck-tie party." After this comparison to lynching, the editorial then abruptly turned back to the topic of worker violence.[55]

The *Echo* editors addressed the general practice of lynching in a year when specific cases were a regular part of weekly reporting. Several cases of particularly gruesome events are illustrative of the *Echo*'s coverage. The first of these happened in February and was noteworthy both because an entire family was killed and because the murders involved a dispute over property rights, rather than the reason sometimes given for lynching, black sexual violence against white women. The head of the household was Hamp Biscoe, a black man who had farmed for ten years on property that he had purchased under a squatter's rights provision. The man who had shown him the land appeared six or seven years later and demanded a $100 fee, which Biscoe did not pay. A court sided with the plaintiff and ordered the Biscoe farm sold to pay the debt, but the farmer refused to leave. Later, Biscoe threatened a neighbor who had pulled down a fence and attempted to cross the Biscoe land, and a warrant was issued for his arrest. A shoot-out occurred between the farmer and a deputy attempting to serve the warrant, who also tried to convince Biscoe not to escalate the situation; Biscoe's wife, thirteen-year-old son, and infant were in the house where he had barricaded himself. After the shooting began, the deputy, Biscoe, and his wife were injured, and the rest of the posse went to town for reinforcements. These men managed to arrest Biscoe and took the entire family into custody. That night, the family was being held in a house when a lynch mob arrived and dismissed the guards. Some of the guards were black and attempted to summon help from a local church, but by the time they arrived on the scene, the farmer, his wife, and their teenage son had been shot, while the infant only had a scratch. The son lived long enough to describe how his parents had been gunned down and who the apparent attackers were. He reported that his mother had hidden $220 in her stocking, which the men took.[56]

*Echo* coverage of the event began on February 18, and the story started with the assertion that three murders had been committed in Lonoke County on February 7. The overall tone of the story was one of sympathy for the Biscoe family. Biscoe was described using the word *Farbiger* (colored), a term often used in a more positive or neutral way than *Neger* (Negro), and the coverage at one point referred to him as the "farmer." Other stories involving crime almost exclusively referred to blacks by race, whether they were the perpetrators or victims. The beginning of the land dispute is described in this way: "A colored man, Biscoe, had a small farm, which he industriously worked for ten years." This would likely have resonated with the *Echo*'s readers, many of whom were small-scale farmers who would have seen themselves in the adverb *fleißig* (industriously). The attack on the family painted a tableau that would have been culturally familiar to Catholics, used to seeing Mary portrayed with the infant Jesus: "[They] murdered the farmer, his pregnant wife, who had an infant at her breast, and the approximately fourteen-year-old boy." The author expressed outrage at the theft of the money and bewilderment that the family was killed even though the deputy was only injured. He added that Biscoe was known to be suffering from mental problems brought on by the belief that his land would be stolen from him: "(Therefore why the desire to arrest him on the grounds of an insult?)" After the facts of the story were reported, the article concluded with an additional comment: "That is no case of a lynch court, but rather a shameful murder to commit robbery, and the murderers deserve to all be hanged along with their accomplices." In the same issue and on the same page, but one column later, a very short paragraph offers some revision to this story, apparently obtained after the initial story had been set in the frame. This account reported, on the testimony of one Squire Sidall, that thirty masked men had shot the family, that no money had been taken, and that the boy did not testify to the identities of the perpetrators before he died. However, the German text made heavy use of the modal verb *sollen* (to be supposed to) as well as the present subjunctive mood, customarily used by journalists to report claims that the journalist may not believe, so that the overall effect conveys the sense that the author regarded the second version with skepticism. The reason for this disbelief would have been obvious to Germans who followed the *Gazette* reporting on the crime. The *Gazette* first stated that Biscoe and his whole family had been shot by a named deputy while resisting arrest and that the mother had given the son a weapon to fire on deputies, but later radically changed its narrative to report that unidentifiable men wearing women's bonnets to mask their faces had shot the family later.[57]

The very next issue of the *Echo* contained news of another gruesome lynching, but the reporting in this event took a decidedly different tone. Edward Coy, a mixed-race man, was accused of raping a married woman, Julia Jewell, after finding her at home alone. Coy allegedly fled the scene; once caught, he was escorted back by fifty guards. Nevertheless, a crowd of one thousand people managed to lynch him by tying him to a stake, dousing him with coal oil, and demanding that Jewell light the fire, which she apparently hesitated to do. Several reports indicated that this was not, in fact, a case of rape, but that Coy and Jewell had been lovers and that she was forced to accuse Coy of rape. Coy himself insisted, as he was being burned alive, that they were in a relationship. The *Echo*'s reporting did not reflect this critical fact, whether because it was not known or by omission. This account embellished the details of the attack. Coy was said to have gained entry to the house by pretending to want to sell the farmer pigs, then attacked his wife, tried to strangle and rape her, then took her to the stall and raped her multiple times. Here the wife is portrayed as a brutalized victim who gladly takes the torch when it is offered to her. The story ends by saying that Coy burned for ten minutes before dying and that the crowd size was estimated to be between four and six thousand. This version portraying Coy as brutal attacker was reinforced a week later. In a March 3 news item from Missouri describing another alleged rape of a white woman, the *Echo* compared the event to the "atrocity and punishment of the Negro Coy" before reporting the details of the new case.[58] But the *Echo* chose to omit the claims of the *Arkansas Gazette*, which stated Coy "had four wives, killed one and deserted three more" and asserted, "Even the negroes say that he was served right."[59] A slightly different tone was taken by the *Echo* as well on March 17, in a report that another man claimed to be the perpetrator of the crime for which "McCoy" was lynched. This March 17 item questioned the brutality of the South where men took pleasure *an solchen Gräuelthaten* (in such atrocities). The case was mentioned again in June, when it was reported that another black man accused of rape had been threatened with the same treatment as Coy and thus turned himself over to authorities for protection.[60]

One of the more notorious lynching cases of 1892 was that of Henry James. James was accused of assaulting a five-year-old white girl who was the adopted daughter of a family for whom he worked. The lynch mob removed him from the state penitentiary where he was held, in spite of a large guard presence. On a prominent Little Rock street, the mob both hanged and shot him, a scene which Governor James Eagle came upon when arriving in the city. Eagle arrested one of the shooters, but the mob knocked down the governor and freed the mob member. The governor was rescued by his friends but sprained his hand in the incident. Eagle later lamented not that the lynching took place but that it happened in such a prominent place in the state's major city. And James's murder was certainly a public event, with large crowds gathering and souvenir seekers clamoring for pieces of the rope. In spite of the public nature of the lynching, the oft-repeated assertion that none of the perpetrators could be identified was given by the jury. The *Echo*'s reporting was notable for its narrative nature and for what the story included and omitted. The German newspaper missed a few critical details that likely would have been of interest to its readers. The alleged assault occurred when the girl was in the care of her grandmother, whereas the *Echo* story simply noted that she had been left in the care of a woman while her parents were in Hot Springs, making it seem as though the crime occurred because of improper supervision by an outsider rather than a member of the family. It neglected to mention that James's body was taken to Baer, an undertaker who advertised in the German newspaper, a fact that was part of the story because a large crowd attended the transfer of the body. The *Echo* article presented a contradictory attitude toward mob violence as it narrated how events escalated. Initially, the tone was neutral, as it mentioned that there were many distinguished men among the crowd and how the father of the victim was asked to identify James, so that an innocent man was not lynched. However, the assembled men, who were originally referred to in German as *die Menge* (the crowd), were then identified as *der Mob* shortly before the hanging was described. The lynchers were depicted as a dangerous force as they approached the penitentiary: "One of the leaders said: we're supposed to allow the shameful nigger to sleep here while the child he abused is dying? The men were generally terribly resolved to hang the criminal, come what may. The rage flashed in their eyes." The governor's actions were seen as positive in light of this violent mob. The *Echo* reported that the governor decided not to arrest the lynchers after he had heard the full story of the alleged crime and that his decision to move on was motivated by public safety rather than by fear for his own well-being: "He had surveyed the situation immediately and had seen that any interference would have to lead to awful bloodshed."[61]

In reporting the lynching of Eugene Baker, the German-speaking paper clearly sided with the victim, perhaps because no white woman had allegedly been assaulted and the black man was not even accused of a crime. A crowd of white cappers, who had been terrorizing black Arkansans by dragging them from their homes at night and whipping them, sometimes to the point of death, had commanded Baker to open his door. He fired on them in response and killed one of the attackers. He was arrested and taken to neighboring Drew County. Two men used the ruse of pretending to be a constable and his prisoner to gain entry to the jail, upon which they forced the jailer to release Baker to them, tied him to a tree, and shot him to death. Predictably, the jury found that no one could identify Baker's assailants. But two months later, a grand jury handed down indictments against a number of the band, including those accused of Baker's death. The *Echo*'s coverage of these events provided readers with further background. The paper refers to the victim by the more neutral term *Farbiger* (a colored man) instead of the word most often used to describe black Arkansans in crime reports, *Neger* (Negro). It alleged that the victim, whom the German paper called Becker (a phonetic spelling of the German translation of his surname—*Bäcker*), had already been whipped by the mob in the previous week, which would explain his willingness to fire on those attempting to break into his house. Further, the white man who was shot was alleged to have played cards frequently with Baker and to have recently lost a large sum to the black man. Other reported details included the fact that the white man had arrived at Baker's house in a disguise to obscure his identity and that Baker had been arrested and taken into custody "for his own protection." The writer made it clear that the jailer had not simply turned over his black charge, but that the ruse was believable because the alleged prisoner had recently been involved in a knife fight. The lynching was described as a barbarous act: "With revolvers trained on him, they compelled the jailer to hand over the key, forced their way into the jail, dragged Becker out, tied him to a tree branch, and shot him dead in a bestial manner." The article ended with the note that the citizens of Monticello were upset by the crime and that the sheriff intended to pursue charges against the perpetrators.[62]

Another prominent lynching covered by the *Echo* occurred in December, and in this case, both the victim and the perpetrators were black. G. P. F. Lightfoot was a Baptist preacher who had been collecting money in black communities to assist families in emigrating from Arkansas to Africa. When it became clear that his intention was to abscond with the collected funds instead of buying tickets as promised, a black mob attacked and murdered him. The *Echo*'s reporting of events was sympathetic to the mob, noting that many of the black families had sold all that they had in preparation for relocation to Liberia. Its account differed from those in English-language papers, though. The *Echo* neglected to mention that Lightfoot had attempted to force his way into a meeting which had been called to talk of reimbursement to victims of his scam, and that he had fired first on the crowd that ultimately lynched him. It further omitted the details of the fury-fueled attack. The *Gazette* reported that Lightfoot's corpse, which had been shot over fifty times, was slashed by the crowd: "Not satisfied, some jumped upon the prostrate and blood-smeared body, from which the vital sport had not yet departed, while others hacked his face, throat and hands with knives or razors." In the *Echo* version, some of Lightfoot's victims managed to recover $115 from the conman, and it states simply that his body was found with bullet wounds and a cut throat sometime later.[63]

A July story, however, did include a description of the fury of a black crowd executing a black perpetrator. This was the previously mentioned case of Robert Donnelly, who had raped a black twelve-year-old girl at gunpoint. The *Echo* carefully noted that Donnelly had confessed his guilt, and that "the furious Negroes" broke into the jail and hung him from the closest tree. Again in this case, though, it did not go as far as the *Gazette* in describing the wrath against Donnelly and how Donnelly begged for his life to no avail; the *Gazette* also stated that both blacks and whites agreed that the extralegal justice was well-deserved. Perhaps the German paper wanted to spare its readers the more gruesome details of the case.[64]

Many of the lynchings that made news in Arkansas in 1892 were covered by the German-language paper, but the *Echo* did not always report all of the same news as the English-language papers. An attempted lynching in Pine Bluff in February 1892 is not mentioned. It is impossible to say if this was because the *Echo* did not consider the event relevant news for its readers, some of whom did live in Pine Bluff, or because the editors were preoccupied with reporting on Bishop Edward Fitzgerald's jubilee. There is similarly no reporting on a Little Rock meeting of black preachers in 1892 concerning the increased number of lynchings, nor the resulting statement condemning the practice while also denouncing sexual crimes, which were sometimes given as the reason for vigilante justice. And the German paper typically did not follow the practice of the *Gazette*, which included editorial remarks about whether a lynching was considered justified or was to be condemned. Instead, the *Echo* usually gave only the details of the case, with the exceptions mentioned.[65]

It should be noted that Arkansas was associated with the concept of vigilante justice long before 1892. Author Friedrich Gerstäcker's first novel, *Die Regulatoren in Arkansas* (*The Regulators in Arkansas*, published in 1845 in Germany to wide acclaim), featured an extralegal posse hunting down horse thieves in Arkansas. The white posse turns over a fellow white man, a horse thief masquerading as a preacher, to the Native American whose wife the horse thief murdered to cover his tracks. Gerstäcker describes in gory detail how the Native American exacts his revenge by burning the murderer to death. This account was written fifty years prior to the racially motivated killings of 1892. However, in this case, the cruelty is perpetrated by a non-white member of the posse and is motivated by the heinous atrocities committed by the white victim of vigilante justice.[66]

A major development that resulted directly from the high levels of racial violence in 1892 was the emigration of large numbers of black Arkansans. The *Echo* and its correspondents certainly noted these departures. German-speaking immigrants and black immigrants to Arkansas had been in direct competition with one another in both the labor market and in society. In his research on the back-to-Africa movement in the state, Kenneth Barnes quotes from the "Liberia Exodus Arkansas Colony" delegates' statement: "Strangers from all lands, of a color different from ours, are preferred before us." This was not just the perception of black Arkansans; in the aftermath of the Civil War's upheaval, it was an openly discussed strategy to enlist immigrants from Europe to build up a white workforce and "maintain a 'Caucasian majority,'" as an 1867 *Arkansas Gazette* article summarized the approach. Governor Powell Clayton, who was in support of European immigration, stated in an 1871 speech that black Americans from other states should also be recruited as agricultural workers. This strategy was successful; as Jeannie Whayne et al. report, "Between 1870 and 1890 the black population of the state more than doubled." Kenneth Barnes estimates a near tripling of the black population for the same period and notes, "The rate of increase of the black population in Arkansas (46.7 percent) exceeded that of all other southern states." Black families settled on farmland near the railroad lines just as German immigrants did, and German speakers in 1892 certainly felt the tension between the two groups. One editorial reflected the presumption that blacks held a generally negative attitude toward whites.

> Therefore, a German farmer will make progress only with difficulty if he settles right in the middle of the Negroes. The racial feeling is so strong by these people that they regard an immigrated 'stranger' from Germany with mistrust. And in the life of every newcomer, circumstances occur that make the assistance of neighbors indispensable. If this help is refused in hostile coldness, then this frequently brings ruin to the abandoned family.[67]

The previously discussed political violence in Arkansas in 1892 and the years prior led to a reversal of the trend of black in-migration, and frequent news items in the *Echo* made note of these departures from the state, whether the groups of former black Arkansans were making their way to the neighboring state of Oklahoma or attempting to leave the country altogether and join other black Americans traveling to Liberia. One viewpoint markedly not represented in the *Echo* was concern over a potential labor shortage due to the departures. Although not expressed directly, German-speaking Arkansans could only benefit from such a development. But Germans did not view blacks as direct competition for individual jobs. Rather, as independent operators, Germans, who believed themselves to be more efficient farmers, contended they were struggling against the output from the sheer numbers of workers, many of whom had been slaves. An early March news item makes a point of mentioning that nine black emigrants headed to Liberia had formerly worked "on plantations in the southern part of the state" and remarked, "Many other Negroes in the state are said to have the same intention." The editors did not add any comment expressing concern about the departures. A week later, another brief report stated a steamer had brought two hundred black people bound for Oklahoma to Fort Smith, and that the boat would be making regular trips, since another fifteen hundred people from the same area intended to depart. Within one week, the *Echo*'s reported figures of black emigration increased from nine to fifteen hundred, but there was no remark about the rapid increases, even though both the editors and the typesetters had appended comments to many other straight news stories.[68]

In the following months, most other *Echo* articles maintained this descriptive manner, listing the number of black emigrants, their points of departure, and their destination, whether domestic or foreign. The *Echo* articles mentioned departures from Crittenden, Jefferson, and Philipps Counties. Conway County was not mentioned, even though a large group left Morrilton in the second week of March, an event that the paper or its correspondents surely were aware of. This was perhaps more in the model of English-language newspapers that purposely omitted developments in black migration or reported only on unsuccessful attempts to go abroad. A May news item took a less objective tone, though without declaring the occurrence positive or negative, and pointed out that migration was a trend in other southern states as well: "The immigration to Oklahoma among the blacks is quite amazing. Daily, they move through here in groups and almost all without any resources. Almost all come from Missisippi and Tennessee."[69] The *Echo* did not go as far as the *Arkansas Gazette*. A *Gazette* article stated that many farmers in Woodruff County were in fact pleased by the development, citing one farmer as saying: "When they are all gone, said one intelligent man from the North today, white people with means will flock to Arkansas from Iowa, Minnesota, and Wisconsin. We shall have better schools and better churches. Let the negro go to the land of his forefathers; let him go in peace. This is a white man's country, and the negro belongs in Africa."[70]

Two articles stand out among the more fact-driven reports. One is a reprint from the *Arkansas Volksblatt*, and its tone is vitriolic. The writer began by mentioning that over one hundred black Arkansans from Jefferson County and elsewhere in Arkansas had been attempting to emigrate to "Oklahoma, the promised land, where in their fantasies milk and honey flow." The steamer company from Pine Bluff, though, had forced them to debark in Fort Gibson, Oklahoma, two hundred miles from their intended destination, as the group had "neither money nor something to chew." It described how (Cherokee) Chief (Johnson) Harris allegedly hurried to the scene and arranged for the railroad to transport the group to Coffeyville, Kansas, with the costs covered by his tribe, "as it seemed to him to be the only way to get rid of the unfortunate horde." The inhabitants of Fort Gibson were described as equally glad to be rid of the black immigrants, bringing the group and the "junk that the Negroes were dragging with them" to the train station. The article ended with the observation that Harris expected to be reimbursed by the Indian agency, since Indian Agent Bennett accompanied the group to Coffeyville, and summarized the situation thus: "The Indians are laughing up their sleeves over the trick. Let those people there now see what they can do further with the Negroes. We're rid of them." In a single article, the *Arkansas Volksblatt* showed both an utter lack of empathy for fellow migrants of another race and insulted the Cherokee, who were depicted as being as unwilling as whites to welcome the black newcomers. Though this portrayal represented a radical departure from the *Echo*'s usual measured tones regarding black emigration, the editorial staff chose to reprint it without comment. The tone is much more akin to that of the *Arkansas Gazette*, which, with the headline "Dey's Gwine Da," described in a mocking tone how 236 "darkies" from Jefferson County had departed for the land being made available in the Cherokee Strip in Oklahoma, even if it would not be open for months, since they were quoted as saying they were starving in Arkansas in any case.[71]

The second standout article appeared in the next issue of the *Echo*. It was a more sympathetic portrayal of a group similarly stranded. The article stated that a party of 350 would-be black emigrants had arrived in Argenta via train from Tennessee, Mississippi and Alabama. Although they had paid $10 per person to a company that had promised to transport them to Oklahoma, they had instead been left in the *Sümpfen* (marshes or swamps) of Saint Francis County. After a week, they decided to attempt to travel on, some by foot and some by train. Those who had traveled by train were waiting for the other members of their group to arrive. The article noted, "They are in dire condition, many of them do not have necessary clothing. So that they can travel further, funds are being raised by their fellow tribesmen [fellows]." These are the only two instances that describe unsuccessful black migration; stories of blacks attempting to migrate to Liberia but who became stranded in New York that appeared in the English-language press were not published by the *Echo*.[72]

One aspect of German and black interaction in the state in 1892 is largely omitted: the German Catholic missionary outreach to black Arkansans. The German-speaking Holy Ghost Fathers, led by Fr. Joseph Strub, were heavily engaged with evangelization to the black population. They attempted to recruit black men as brothers and priests (possibly to serve as missionaries to Africa), opened schools, and established black Catholic communities. One of these schools was integrated and operated from 1883 to 1898; the white pupils were the children of German immigrants. The Holy Ghost Fathers were supported in this work by Bishop Edward Fitzgerald, and although the *Echo* editors were greatly enamored of the bishop, his interest in outreach to blacks is almost entirely absent from the paper. There is a brief mention of black children who participated in the bishop's jubilee, and then there is no other mention of German Catholic educational outreach until November. An article described how Catholic nuns were working hard in Pine Bluff at a *farbige Industrie-Schule* (colored industrial school) opened by Fr. Lucy in 1889. This school had produced items for the World Expo that had been inspected and praised by a representative of the *Arkansas Democrat*: "There, the boys learn trades and the girls sewing, knitting, and patching in addition to a thorough education. They say that every county should have such a school, in order to educate our Negroes to well-behaved, useful human beings."[73]

This portrayal of a segregated approach to schooling, organized by whites to make blacks productive members of society, stood in marked contrast to reporting on black victims of the historic flooding in 1892. In June farmers were involved in surveying the damage and attempting to rebuild. The *Echo* noted, "In Pine Bluff, most of the Negroes are back to work and are receiving seeds and the necessary sustenance. Yet there are still a number who do not want to work, but rather expect to receive assistance from the 'Gubment.'" Initial reporting of the floods showed sympathy toward black victims and described how one black family near Morrilton had drowned while trying to escape, while others were rescued from rooftops but lost all their worldly possessions. A week after the events, the *Echo* reprinted a report from a correspondent that again portrayed black farmers as those in need of assistance and white plantation owners as the saviors, helping connect black families in need with donations and assisting their own renters. A final note from December reinforced the idea that blacks in Arkansas could not take care of themselves: "According to the *Gazette*, there are 2,000 Negroes in the city without employment. They were driven from the country into the city by lack of work. Their prospects are poor to earn enough here to cover their subsistence needs for the winter."[74]

Black Arkansans were the ethnic minority represented most often, but the pages of the *Echo* also contain clues to Germans' perceptions of other minorities. Jeffery Strickland, in his examination of nineteenth-century German settlers in Charleston, South Carolina, observes, "Most scholarship dealing with the South during the mid- to late nineteenth century supports a black/white paradigm and ignores the racial and ethnic diversity in the region."[75] As it happens, Arkansas Germans were in close proximity to another group: the Native American population in neighboring Oklahoma. Germans did not seem to have much personal interaction with these tribes. They were, however, very interested in Native American affairs concerning land rights and government treatment of minorities. As in the case of black Arkansans, the German newspaper offered its readers both positive and negative portrayals of Native Americans.

The biggest story found in the *Echo* regarding Native Americans in 1892 was the opening of the Cherokee Strip in Oklahoma to settlers. The land run, which was the largest of four in Oklahoma, did not take place until 1893, but the German newspaper frequently reported on developments in the case. On January 14, readers were informed that the Cherokee Nation had ratified the treaty, and only Congress's approval was necessary to open the six million acres of land to white settlers. A week later, the *Echo* reprinted an article from the *Gazette* regarding Lovely's Purchase, which tried to make the case that Arkansans were owed some land from the Cherokee Strip due to historical developments. The area known as Lovely's Purchase was in northwest Arkansas, which Indian agent Major William Lovely had attempted to establish as a buffer zone between the warring Cherokee and Osage tribes. After a number of discussions and treaties, there was some confusion as to the ownership of the land, and white settlers in territorial Arkansas were resentful that they should be prohibited from settling on the agriculturally valuable land because of Native American claims. The creation of Lovely County in an area much larger than the original Lovely Purchase led Cherokee leaders to appeal to the federal government to protect their territory, and white settlers of the land were eventually compelled to move, but under such good terms that most were satisfied with the outcome. Lovely County ceased to exist after 1828. The article further quoted the *Memphis Commercial* in saying that it was far too late for Arkansas to protest the circumstances regarding the land held by the Cherokees, and the author of the article agreed. He believed the treaty was fairly signed and could only be disregarded if one did not regard the Cherokee Nation as a separate entity in the international understanding of the word "nation," although he protested that developments had been unfair to white settlers.[76]

The idea that Arkansans had somehow been cheated regarding the Cherokee Strip was brought up again in February. The *Echo* reported that Congress still had to act regarding the settlement of the land and that a *Ring indianischer Politiker* (ring of Indian politicians) was traveling to Washington to argue that Cherokee farmers should be allowed to choose land for themselves before it was opened to the general public. The *Echo* opposed this development, which did eventually come to pass. It backed Oklahoma farmers who were complaining about the monopoly on grazing fees held by the Cherokees, a right that was ultimately taken away in the treaty. Finally, the article again brought up the idea that Arkansans had somehow been cheated out of the land, and the author clearly regarded German settlers among those white neighbors referred to as "Americans": "Our representatives should therefore with all their power assert the rights of our state to this land, so that it may be opened as soon as possible as a part of the state of Arkansas under the homesteading law." Other reporting on the Cherokee strip included notes about prominent men interested in creating a new city there, the financial details of the plan that incorporated the purchase of additional land from the Comanche, Kiowa, and Apache tribes, how much land would be available, and when. One article foreshadowed the extreme nature of the eventual land run in Oklahoma by describing how in the opening of the Sisseton and Wahpeton reservation in North Dakota, some potential settlers sat in their wagons for twenty hours without food awaiting the start.[77]

The *Echo* did acknowledge that treaties between the United States government and Native American tribes were not always fair. A news item from Minnesota remarked that the members of the Fond du Lac reservation complained about their treatment by government agents. The tribe had not received their scheduled yearly payment, and the government agents robbed and plundered on the reservation and cut down forests on the reservation to sell the lumber. This sympathy toward the tribe was tempered by an editor's note that made it clear that another clergy member, described as a fanatic and presumably non-Catholic, had supported the Indian commissioner against Catholic schools for Indians in the area, meaning the support for the tribe was part of a larger disagreement among white Christian denominations. The *Echo* took the exact opposite attitude toward Native Americans in an editorial entitled "Die Neger" (The Negroes), in which the author claimed that the government's interaction with native tribes provided an example of how not to treat the black population: "The government not only made payment to the redskins for the land districts that were made free by them for settlement, through which the Indians received money for which they did not know any prudent use, but it also fed the redskin and is still feeding him today and through this practice makes him an idler and sluggard of the first order." Regarding matters in Arkansas, the *Echo* welcomed the appointment of Sam Peel to the post of Indian Commissioner and praised his experience.[78]

General attitudes toward Native Americans in the *Echo*'s inaugural year vary widely. In colonial times, German settlers most often viewed tribes as savages; German frontier farms typically served as the border between tribal lands and white territory, and they were subject to violent attacks. A single news item from 1892 reflected this attitude. It reported that a band of Yaqui Indians had attacked the Lacy family in Mexico during a meal. The wife was shot, but the husband was able to get to a tower constructed in the home for defense and repel the attackers. Within the United States, though, the situation looked more encouraging to German speakers reading the *Echo*. The paper stated that there were 250,483 Indians living in the United States, with the exception of the Alaskan territory, of which 50,000 were classified as warriors. Readers were assured that of these 50,000 *nur die Hälfte hat kriegerischen Sinn* (only half have a warrior spirit), although what exactly that meant was not clarified. The frontier mindset that settlers had something to fear from native tribes was so far removed that the paper published a joke about it, in which two not-very-intelligent German dialect speakers explained a popular show: "'Hey, tell me, Christian, why is that called 'Buffalo Bills Wild West?' 'Those are two Indians, Buffalo and Bills, they used to be wild west, but now they're tame.'" There was additionally some interest in Native American history. The *Echo* told its readers how flooding of the Red River near Hope had uncovered burial mounds that contained large skeletons, pottery, a pipe, and earthenware.[79]

Three other articles offered sympathetic or positive portrayals of Native Americans. A May article was entitled "Indianerlob" (Praise for Indians). It quoted extensively from the testimony of a South Dakotan farmer who had been living next to Sioux territory for seventeen years. He complained that white settlers routinely stole his oxen, but the Sioux were always able to find and return the animals. He reported that the Indians were so honorable that they never touched the settlers' plowing equipment or stores of grain and meat, even if they themselves were hungry. In June there was an acknowledgment that *unsere 'rothen Brüder' und Landsleute* (our 'red brothers' and fellow countrymen) were probably not joining in the general celebrations regarding the four-hundredth anniversary of Columbus's "discovery" of America. In September the paper offered a sentimental reminder of the portrayal of Native Americans by James Fenimore Cooper, whose works were well-known and appreciated in Germany. It examined census data regarding the six tribes described by Cooper and happily reported that there was much material prosperity and little conflict among the tribesmen, even if they still did not conform to white standards of marriage. The writer complained of the corrupting influence of *gesetzlose Weiße* (lawless whites) who were secretly providing the tribes with alcohol.[80]

Other ethnic minority groups are hardly mentioned by the *Echo* during its inaugural year, although there were a few. Stories regarding Chinese immigrants discussed events in Arkansas and nationally. A Hot Springs report told of a Chinese man who tried to cut his own throat while high on opium; a bystander was injured when he wrestled the Chinese man for control of the knife. In September the paper reported on a crackdown by the police in Little Rock against Chinese immigrants after the city passed an ordinance against opium smoking. Six Chinese men were arrested in a laundry and charged with smoking, but sentencing was delayed due to questions regarding whether the ordinance was legal. The article quoted a policeman who said he hoped it was upheld so that he could rid the city of opium smoking. An editorial note stated that opium use was known to be as terrible a vice as morphine and that it made users into violent criminals. Two items from California described the consequences of the *Verbot der Kuli-Einwanderung* (prohibition of coolie immigration), namely that the state was seeing a critical labor shortage. The clear implication was that legislation targeted against Chinese immigrants could benefit other nationalities, since the writer discussed how much trade the state engaged in with Germany. The German paper still found aspects of Chinese culture worthy of emulation, however. It noted that the Chinese were the most successful fruit growers in the entire world, and it offered readers a recipe for laundry starch that would replicate the famous sheen produced by the Chinese. This relatively sparse coverage resembles that of the *Arkansas Gazette*, which also only had four news items regarding Chinese immigrants in the state in 1892.[81]

Other immigrants are mentioned briefly in news stories. Two items included ethnic identity as a descriptor; the murderer of an Arkansas restaurant owner is labeled as "an Italian, John Ferseno," and the victim of a workplace accident in Little Rock is noted as "a Pole, Stevens." The *Echo* reported on a group of 150 Arabic and Syrian immigrants who had arrived in New York and were headed to Indiana to join countrymen, making special note of one of the group, a thirty-year-old who was traveling with the *Kleinigkeit* (trifling amount) of $10,000. On the opposite extreme was a group of *Zigeuner* ("gypsies") who were reported as begging in Conway, even though the group had good horses and wagons, which would indicate some measure of financial success. The women explained that they had lost everything in a fire and wanted to travel to Texas. A sarcastic editorial comment added that they must have had the same misfortune in ten other states and four territories, reflective of the historic German mistrust of Romani, whom they regarded as slothful. There was a feature on two Italian immigrants who became rich by cleaning the shoes of those arriving on passenger ships, and after becoming bosses themselves, paid a fair wage to those they hired to work for them; the writer commented expressly on the fact that they were living the American fairy tale of "getting rich quick" through hard work. Correspondent Civis made a point of including Polish farmers and businessmen among those from Germany and Switzerland in praising the contributions of immigrants to Arkansas during the previous twelve years.[82]

Jews were also among the German-speaking community in 1892. Carolyn LeMaster's work regarding the Jewish community, *A Corner of the Tapestry: A History of the Jewish Experience in Arkansas, 1820s–1990s*, is the most comprehensive source regarding Jews in Arkansas during this time. She notes, "The demographics of Arkansas Jewry in 1880 show that 95 percent of the Jewish immigrants to Arkansas between 1865 and 1880 were from Germany, and by 1878, half owned properties." Indeed, many of the names of *Echo* advertisers are recorded as prominent members of the Jewish community in LeMaster's work. Levy's Dry Goods was a Jewish establishment in Argenta that bought a single ad, although M. M. Cohn, a Polish Jew, regularly advertised his dry goods store in Little Rock; ads for Gus Blass's store selling clothing and shoes in Little Rock also made frequent appearances in the *Echo*. Gus Gans operated a successful millinery and fine apparel business in Little Rock from 1892–1908 and advertised in the *Echo*; the paper made note of the store's move in February to new location in the Free Mason's Temple. Ben S. Thalheimer was another major advertiser and German Jew who came to Arkansas by way of Philadelphia. He had a rags-to-riches immigrant success story similar to the one the *Echo* published about the Italian shoeshine brothers; Thalheimer also served as a Little Rock alderman. Louis Reinmann is mentioned by LeMaster as cofounding the Davis-Reinmann company in 1888, which provided a good deal of advertising business to the *Echo*. She does not mention that the company had to go into receivership in 1892, which the *Echo* reported in December. Reinmann apparently enjoyed better success after partnering with Louis Wolfort in 1898. Fred Sanders, a German Jew who became a photographer after struggling with subsistence farming in Mountain Home, advertised his business weekly in the *Echo* and contributed articles. Friedrich (Frederick) Kramer was a German immigrant, merchant, and former Little Rock mayor who died in 1896. He was not an advertiser, and in fact, the *Echo* recorded him as a character witness on behalf of Philip Dietzgen, the paper's major competitor, in one of the legal battles between the two organizations. Herman Kahn, a German Jewish immigrant, contributed greatly to Little Rock's growth after the Civil War and his sons were born in the 1880s, and the *Echo* reported in June that he had been elected president of an unnamed assembly organized to fight against Prohibition.[83]

These members of the Jewish community were clearly interacting with the non-Jewish German community in 1892, and most of them contributed to the success of the paper in the first year through regular advertising revenue. But the *Echo* never once mentioned the religion of these men. Perhaps the editors felt no need to. This would not have been odd in Germany at the time. Many nineteenth-century Jews had assimilated, were pillars of their community, had served in the military, and regarded themselves as German; not until the rise of the National Socialist Party did German society as a whole regard Jews' religion as more important than their nationality. It should be noted that there is no reporting in the *Echo* on events taking place at synagogues around the state, while Catholic events are covered heavily. For example, the United Hebrew Congregation of Fort Smith built a new synagogue in 1892, and judging by surnames, it would appear that there were a number of German speakers among the congregation, but the event is not noted in the *Echo*. The *Arkansas Gazette* in 1892 had stories on the Feast of Weeks celebrated at B'nai Brith, including a long description of the ceremony and decorations, the Jewish new year celebration, a Yom Kippur observance, and a Chanukah festival program.[84] There is, however, no record of animosity between Jewish German speakers and Christian German speakers. Two brief news items on anti-Semitism implied that it should not be tolerated. News from the city of Darmstadt came in November that Hessian civil servants had been urged not to have any contact with the anti-Semitic movement. In December a note from Paris that the notorious anti-Semitic politician Marquis des Mores had been injured in a duel was reported under the headline "The Consequences of Anti-Semitism of the Ruffian de Mores Tether Him to the Sickbed."[85]

The fact that Jewish Germans were regarded positively because of their ability to integrate in the majority culture is clear in a story that was actually about Seventh Day Adventists. The group was described as a small sect of forty to fifty members who wished to hold sabbath on Saturday, which no one opposed, and to be allowed to work on Sunday, which was causing problems. The writer noted that Jews were in the same situation: "The only difference is that Jews are reasonable people who comprehend that the friendly, fine relationship rests on the mutual respect of that which is sacred to those of other beliefs, which is a necessity among civilized people. That is why the Jews celebrate their sabbath undisturbed and also esteem the Christian Sunday." Jewish wisdom was referenced as well by the unattributed author of a submitted three-part series on education and religion. He complained that modern man wanted to reinvent the wheel continuously, thus proving the famous Rabbi Akiba correct in stating that everything existing had already been seen before. Other stories were less positive. A police report described a suspect who was arrested in Little Rock and wanted in Chicago simply as a Polish Jew. Similarly, the would-be assassin of industrialist Henry Clay Frick, was referred to as *Bergman ein russischer Jude* (Bergman a Russian Jew). The paper neutrally reported in a brief news item that Wolf Buschoff, a Jewish butcher in Xanten who had been accused of killing a Christian boy in a case of blood libel, had been acquitted. The neutrality of this short news item is significant since the charge against Buschoff was initially made by a Catholic, and it was sensationalized by the anti-Semitic press in Europe. There was another incident reported neutrally regarding a Polish Jew thrown out of a synagogue in Minnesota for preaching that Jesus Christ was the messiah. Finally, an article about the Hasidic sect led by the *Wunder-Rabbi* (miracle rabbi) in the city of Sadagora (present-day Ukraine) appeared in one of the last issues of the year. It discussed at some length the practices of the group, which had come to light as part of an Austrian tax-court trial and required regular followers to live in great depredation while the rabbi lived in luxury. The article is generally descriptive in tone. The author does revert to one stereotypical trope of the portrayal of Jews: "[The rabbi] indeed surpasses all others in his inventive spirit for business swindles and speculative gambling. And this impresses his subjects extraordinarily. They behold in his ability a higher divine inspiration." But it is clear from the context that this depiction refers only to the sect and not to all of Judaism. Notably, these less-than-flattering items regarding Jews were primarily regarding Eastern European Jews, and the Jews who established themselves first in Arkansas were from the Western European tradition, with Eastern European Jews following only later. It is not unreasonable to think that Arkansas Jews reading these descriptions of Eastern European Jews would therefore not consider themselves personally attacked.[86]

Reporting on other Christian denominations was composed largely of public policy regarding the administration of schools and Prohibition rather than on dogmatic differences, as was previously discussed. The Methodists were seen as foes, whereas German Lutherans in other states were seen as comrades in the school issue. The editors appealed to the German Lutherans in eastern Arkansas in Stuttgart for a story on their community, which had been founded around a decade earlier, but there is no indication whether any of these Lutherans ever saw the request in the *Echo*, and no other mention was made of the group. Generally, German Americans regarded American Protestants with suspicion because they did not require formal seminary training to serve as clergy. In the *Echo*, this attitude is reflected in a story about a Methodist conference in Omaha, in which a Bishop Forster's remarks against foreign language in schools and for Prohibition are reported. The title "bishop," however, is published in quotation marks. In March, the paper noted without comment that Th. J. Shelton, a pastor of a Christian church at Tenth and Louisiana Streets, whose congregation thought he was the second coming, had been divorced from his wife but filed for a new license to remarry her three weeks later. Another article proclaimed *Neu-England vom Heidenthum bedroht* (New England threatened by heathenism). Survey results revealed that half of the families in the region did not attend church on a regular basis. The writer of the article theorized that this was because Protestants spent a great deal of time urging sinners to repent and come to Jesus but no time talking about how one should live one's life after conversion.[87]

A few articles offered commentary on religions outside of the Judeo-Christian tradition, but the attitudes toward these religions were contradictory, as was the case with so many topics in the *Echo*'s inaugural year. An excerpt from the collected writings of Helmuth von Moltke, a revered Prussian military officer who clashed with Bismarck, argued that good can be found in all people: "Generally should not every pious prayer, whether it is addressed to Buddha, Allah, or Jehovah, reach the same God, before whom there is none? The mother, of course, hears the request of the child, no matter in what language it babbles her name." A later somewhat rambling editorial draws on these previously published thoughts of Moltke to argue, however, that Christianity improved civilization by helping to abolish slavery, emancipate women, and ennoble work. It argued that fighting among Christian denominations should be avoided, but that predominantly Christian countries had still made more progress regarding the treatment of women and workers' rights compared to "heathen" countries or those with "false Gods." Two months later, Christopher Columbus was praised for bringing Christianity to new regions of the world, but his mission was also described thus: "to garner treasures with which the struggle of Christian culture against the anti-cultural Islam could be victoriously concluded."[88]

German-speaking Arkansans shared many of the stereotyped views of other races held by white Arkansans, among whom they very much wanted to be counted. There is no evidence in the *Echo* of links between German entrepreneurs and the black population such as those found by Jeffrey Strickland in South Carolina. There is also no record of other sorts of interactions, for example at workplaces or in boarding houses, which is not to say they did not exist. The editors and readers of the *Echo* appeared to form opinions regarding blacks from public interactions rather than personal relationships. Reporting on fellow black Arkansans was heavily composed of crime reports that often did not even include the names of the accused, conflating the racial designation "black" with the identity of criminal, but the paper expressed sympathy for black flood victims and those fleeing racial violence. The *Echo* was generally opposed to lynching because it was perceived as both not American and too American. They regarded it as un-American because the practice did not conform to their imagined ideals of a democratic republic with a strong judiciary. It was all too American because the barbarism that accompanied these acts reflected the excesses associated with their adopted country. Part of the *Echo*'s opposition to lynching might have been because they were not as racist as other outlets. Vincent Vinikas notes, "To be able to accept the routinization of mob rule and mass murder in their society, whites had come to view blacks as the vicious and beast-like predators that they were portrayed to be in the racist literature of the day."[89] The *Echo*'s attitudes toward black people and the language the paper used to describe race reflect views found in white papers to some extent, although they did not display the same level of vitriol found in English papers or the German-speaking *Arkansas Volksblatt*, if the extant article published by the *Echo* is representative. There are no pseudoscientific racial claims that blacks were somehow less than human beings in the *Echo*. The editors and readers thought they were superior to blacks, but they also believed that blacks had been robbed of their culture, and did not want to suffer the same fate. They regarded themselves as superior to the Puritan white culture present in America, against which they constantly struggled in various crusades. There is at least one piece of evidence that the sentiment of some German Catholics would eventually further evolve regarding the practice of lynching; in 1901, Fr. John Michael Lucey was censured by the *Arkansas Gazette* for referring to lynching as murder.[90]

The *Echo*'s coverage of race was primarily focused on relations between the black and white populations, but other minority groups also appear in its pages. The Native American population was of interest primarily because of the land acquisition potential in tribal lands. The paper acknowledged that some tribes had been mistreated but argued as well that they had generally been made into idlers by government support. German speakers in Arkansas in 1892 regarded Native Americans more as objects of ridicule than as fearsome warriors, as they had been seen by Germans in the colonial period. Although immigrants themselves, the writers of the German paper took little notice of other immigrant groups, aside from a few mentions. Jews, considered in many situations to be an outsider group, were so much a part of the community that the paper rarely commented on their religious affiliation. German-speaking Jews were foundational in their support of the paper as advertisers in its inaugural year, and the editors often reflected on shared Judeo-Christian values, although the paper did not cover Jewish congregational events in the same way it devoted space to coverage of Catholic celebrations. Reporting on other Christian denominations was mostly limited to national conflicts regarding schools and Prohibition, with a few taunts regarding the lack of dogmatic rigor of American Protestantism, and remarks regarding non-Christian faiths were similarly of a general nature.

# Conclusion

*DAS ARKANSAS ECHO* was launched in what is widely perceived by scholars of the German-language press in America as the golden age of the field, a time when German-speaking immigrants across the United States were trying their hand at establishing small local papers. Carl Wittke reports that as the genre developed, many German American editors were forced to concentrate on the business side of publishing, focusing on advertisers and subscribers, and to move away from what could be considered controversial content such as politics.[1] In 1892, however, the *Echo* resolutely published strong opinions and attempted to mold the ideas of fellow immigrants and to produce a unified community via a linguistic space. We are left with a clear portrait of the German community in Arkansas in its own words and can examine their hopes, fears, and everyday life. The *Echo* is remarkable for its longevity as a paper with a small initial circulation, founded in a state with a relatively small number of German-speaking immigrants and in which two other German-language papers already existed.

Jonathan Wolfe notes that immigrants who had successfully established themselves in Arkansas were happy to assist fellow countrymen who were new to the state. This close cooperation and constant influx of new immigrants in the 1880s and 1890s contributed to the continued use of the German language and served to retard assimilation. Essentially, a new first generation was being continually introduced, even as those in the second and third generations were learning English. After the waves of immigration subsided, Germans assimilated remarkably quickly, a phenomenon predicted by noted German American statesman Carl Schurz. This is especially true for Germans in Arkansas, to the extent that almost all linguistic traces have vanished in the state, save for a few place and family names. Thus, the name of the *Echo* proved to be prophetic. The paper ceased to exist when it no longer had a German-speaking community to engage with, and it serves as an echo today of that community's attitudes and beliefs. Schurz, however, saw assimilation as an ultimately positive process. Germans might quickly become Americans, but Germans brought with them a culture and worldview that they believed changed the host country for the better.[2]

The German-speaking community of 1892 did not view itself as a linguistic population in decline, preferring to believe that more family members and friends would join it in Arkansas once the short-term hurdles of cholera fears and an increase in the cost of transport to America had been overcome. In the very next year, however, the financial crisis of 1893 occurred. Many scholars have noted that the turn of the twentieth century additionally saw an important trend that largely put an end to German American immigration: Germany's own rising fortunes as a result of industrialization, colonial exploration, and the creation of the social welfare state. At the same time, there was a decline in the amount of affordable American land available to immigrants. This did not stop Arkansas Germans from trying to recruit new immigrants. In 1894 *Echo* editor Carl Meurer published a pamphlet extolling the state's virtues to would-be recruits and discussed both successful immigrant communities and German-speaking individuals who had achieved the American dream.[3]

German-speakers in Arkansas navigated a dual identity, tied to both Europe and the South. As immigrants, they still had contacts in the home country, receiving news and mail. Some traveled back on occasion, and the community welcomed new members. Thus, it was not entirely a static group but experienced some flux and transit. It was also not homogeneous enough to enable one to discuss "the Germans" in Arkansas; one must examine their geographic diversity, as German-speakers who arrived with their own strong regional and national identities, as Bavarians and Swabians, as Swiss and Austrians. These traits were beginning to coalesce into a linguistic identity as German speakers in Arkansas with pride in their European homes, a consolidation which mirrors what was happening with German speakers across the United States. The *Echo*'s stated goal was to accelerate that process. It believed its mission was to forge a common identity and help establish a group that rallied around common causes, whether cultural, economic, or political. It made crusades of issues that were important to all German speakers regardless of origin: the fight against Prohibition, the preservation of German culture and language via separate schools, and calls for increased immigration. The fact that most readers were Catholic probably helped enforce an insular identity, but the editors very much welcomed German speakers of other religions. Although the Lutheran German community in

Stuttgart is conspicuously absent, many Jewish Germans in Arkansas helped to launch the paper by supporting it with consistent advertising revenue. The paper created a pan-Arkansas virtual community of German speakers, which could exist in spite of geographical separation across a rural state at a time when its competitor, *Die Staatszeitung,* was accused of creating division among German speakers in order to further its business model.

Previous scholarship in Arkansas history has regarded the Germans as an isolated group. James Woods remarks, "These two groups, German immigrants and Anglo-American natives, were segregated by nationality, religion, education, and most of all, language. Both sides were guilty of maintaining such separation for about forty years, at least until World War I. Germans tended to view their less-educated and less-cultured American neighbors with a disdain that bordered on outright contempt." To be sure, Germans did keep to themselves, producing three newspapers in their native tongue by 1892. The record preserved in the *Echo* shows that this was to some extent due to choice rather than linguistic necessity. It is clear that the paper's staff and many of its correspondents both spoke English and read English-language papers. They believed in preserving cultural traditions that they viewed as superior, but they did so because they thought their beliefs and heritage could fundamentally change their new homeland for the better. They additionally could not conceive of preserving this intellectual heritage in the absence of the language in which it had been transmitted to them. The *Echo* gives many indications that German speakers did not wish to recreate Europe in America; in many ways, they already regarded themselves as Americans and Arkansans, eager to embrace that which they approved of, such as the philosophical traditions of the founding fathers, and to change that which they believed they could improve, such as agricultural practices. Hermann Wellenreuther's assessment of colonial Germans is equally true of German speakers in Arkansas approximately two centuries later: "But this does not mean that they conceived themselves as 'strangers in their own land'; rather, they envisioned themselves as building a society that blended the possibilities of the New World with the social values and mores of the old and thus creating something that was their own."[4]

*Das Arkansas Echo* was a German American paper, but it was reflective of the American South and bears similarities to other community papers of the region. In his forward to Michael Dougan's exhaustive study of community newspapers in Arkansas, Senator David Pryor offers the following assessment of what these small local newspapers meant for the state and its development:

> Without these local newspapers, communities throughout Arkansas would have been denied not only access to news and commentary, but large segments of the population would have never experienced that central focal point that bound neighbors and communities together. The local papers told readers of current news, events on the horizon, and even who was visiting whom and where. They were the common denominator for rich and poor, rural and urban constituents.[5]

Pryor could just as well have been speaking of the *Echo*. Although it was circulated throughout the state, it offered a "local" paper for German speakers. It therefore featured many of the same topics discussed in other southern community papers. One major topic was agriculture. Germans fought against the established southern practice of planting cotton as the major cash crop and complained about the reliance of English speakers on practically indentured labor. The German speakers' preferred method of reshaping southern agriculture, by planting grapes and other fruits and establishing a viniculture to rival California's, put them at odds with the state's Protestant denominations, notably Methodists. They were also witnessing and experiencing many historical developments that would lead to the rise of the Jim Crow South. The year before the *Echo* was established, Arkansas passed a law requiring railroads to offer racially segregated passenger cars. The state was in a period of intense black voter suppression, both through semi-legal means, such as voter literacy laws and poll taxes, and through outright violence against black Arkansans and their supporters. In these matters, the paper's Democratically aligned editors supported the white establishment in its attempts to maintain social dominance in spite of Reconstruction. These German settlers made it clear that they were to be viewed as part of the white majority, especially after nativist politicians tried to associate German speakers with blacks. They believed that African culture and Native American culture had been actively destroyed, and they wished to avoid the same fate. The *Echo*'s editors and writers unambiguously adopted some of the racist attitudes and language used by the white society into which they had immigrated. But they were horrified by the brutal murders typical of lynching culture in 1892, as well as by broad disregard for law and order in what they had expected to be a functioning (and idealized) democracy.

The *Arkansas Echo* created a virtual community for German speakers who were navigating their own new identities as Americans while grappling with issues confronting all Southerners in the wake of the Civil War.

It secured its own future in doing so, astonishing in a state that had more examples of failed newspapers than successful ones, with many publications only lasting for a few issues or a few years. Fewer than 10 percent of newspapers launched in the nineteenth century were successful for more than two years. The paper was useful at the time because it provided a forum for the interests and activities of the German-speaking community in 1892. It is a useful tool today because it preserves a regional perspective on what most concerned German speakers, recorded contemporaneously in the members' own words. The editors offered content that they believed would be of the greatest appeal to subscribers in a very tight market that included two competing German-language newspapers, and reader correspondents delivered material from their own communities that they believed would interest all Germans in the state. The *Echo* was a survivor among German newspapers in the state, outlasting both of the papers that preceded it, *Das Arkansas Volksblatt* and *Die Arkansas Staatszeitung*. As a side note, it is interesting that the *Echo* and the *Staatszeitung* never consolidated into a single publication, as was the case with former rivals in other cities, in spite of all of the *Echo*'s discourse regarding the desire for unity among German-speakers.[6] The personal animosity between the editors, which had led to actual fisticuffs, was likely too great.

The *Echo*'s editors offered their own review of its inaugural year in a front-page item of the final issue of 1892. The year was regarded as negative in terms of weather, given the damage done by flooding and tornadoes, one of which destroyed the newly completed buildings of fellow German speakers the Holy Ghost Fathers. The paper offered a realistic outlook regarding the prospect of more Germans becoming Arkansans in the near future. It predicted that immigration would be limited by the unavailability of inexpensive mid-deck tickets, fears of cholera, and the efforts of US nativists. Overall, though, the paper's outlook was positive. The *Echo* saw cause for optimism in the state due to the possible development of mining and forestry resources and the election of Democrats nationally and locally. It is clear that the German speakers had begun to see themselves as Arkansans and wanted to help improve the state, and the front page is appropriately decorated with illustrations of the state's resources and scenery. The paper quoted Father Eugene Weibel, a German-speaking priest who ministered in northeast Arkansas, as saying, "Long live Arkansas, I believe in the land and its future." And the editors added their own good wishes for the state and German speakers' future in it:

May Arkansas grow and prosper in the coming year and everything shower our readers with blessings. May the long-hoped-for better and happier times begin and last with the new year. . . . Even God himself could not make us happy and content in paradise, if we do not want to be happy and content. We also therefore have to do our part to reach the targeted goal. So we can, in spite of the bad times, begin the new year with happy expectations. From all sides, efforts are being made to develop the resources of our lovely state. . . . The *Echo* will do everything in its power to help its countrymen and to instruct them and help them overcome the difficulties that they encounter.[7]

APPENDIX 1

# German Community Members Mentioned in the *Echo*

Each entry lists the individual's name, the reason he or she is mentioned, the date of the edition (e.g., 1–1 indicates January 1), and the page and column (e.g., 1:1 indicates page 1, column 1). Multiple publication dates for the same information, such as Conrad Elsken as the agent for *Das Arkansas Echo*, are not given; the first mention of a person's name in that function is that which is recorded in the registry. Some of the individuals listed may not have been German or Swiss nationals but rather speakers of German; some perhaps anglicized their names after arrival in the United States. Others might simply be acquaintances of German speakers. Names are spelled exactly as they appeared in the *Echo*, even if they do not reflect standard German orthography. See also appendix 2 for a listing of German-speaking businessmen and -women.

Ackermann, Herr (Mr.): resident of Bellmont who recently moved to Little Rock; he owned a tannery in Bellmont and intended to produce harnesses in Little Rock, 10–21, 8:4

Ahrens, J.: secretary of the local chapter of the *Deutscher, Römisch-Katholischer Central-Verein* (German, Roman-Catholic Central Union), 4–7, 5:3

Altenhöfel, Herr (Mr.): resident of Caulksville at whose house immigrants gathered after a First Communion celebration, 7–7, 3:1; thanked by Mathias Klein for the reception, 7–7, 5:4

Anger, George: groom in wedding to Maria Neumeier in Morrison Bluff, 2–25, 2:3

Arnold, Adolph: secretary of *Das Arkansas Echo*, 12–31–1891, 1:2; mentioned as recipient of a postcard from Philip Dietzgen that Dietzgen's former typesetter, C. Neff, intended to use to sue the *Echo* for damages, 8–5, 8:2

Asche, Georg: resident of Pine Bluff who was elected president of the *Pine*

who served as cashier of the *Obst- und Weinzüchterverein* (The Fruit Grower and Wine Producer's Association), although no first name given, 12–16, 5:2

Benedict, P.: former pastor of St. Edward's, visited Little Rock after spending the summer in Nevada, Mo, where the Benedictines bought a university from the Christian Brothers, 11–25, 8:2

Benner, H.: visitor from Atkins to *Echo* offices in Little Rock who reported that not as much cotton was being planted as in previous years, 4–28, 5:2

Bensberg, Chas.: proprietor of saloon in Little Rock whose establishment was found open by police because someone had forgotten to lock up, 12–16, 8:1

Benz, Otto: resident of Logan County endorsing fellow German Emil Baerlocher for the position of Assessor, 4–28, 5:2

Berg, Karl: father of newborn in Little Rock (child and mother not named in birth announcement), 4–14, 2:4

Berger, Henry (alternately listed as Heinrich): trustee in Phil. Ottenheimer bankruptcy case, 2–18, 5:6–7

Beske, Maria Antonia: widow from Spielerville celebrating her seventy-fifth birthday, 6–23, 7:4

Biehl, Peter: elected to position formerly held by Max Kutzleb in *Krieger- und Landwehrverein,* 2–11, 1:7

Biermann, Heinrich: employee of pharmacy run by Dr. Weny, congratulated for passing the state licensing exam to become full-fledged pharmacist, 8–19, 8:1; back in Little Rock after being absent for a few weeks due to health reasons, 11–18, 8:2

Binz, F.: resident of Logan County endorsing fellow German Emil Baerlocher for the position of Assessor, 4–28, 5:2

Binz, J. B.: resident of Logan County endorsing fellow German Emil Baerlocher for the position of Assessor, 4–28, 5:2

Binz, S.: resident of Logan County endorsing fellow German Emil Baerlocher for the position of Assessor, 4–28, 5:2

Blass, Louis: co-chair of the committee for the support of flood victims along with Thomas Lafferty, 5–26, 2:4

Block, Samuel: death notice for a Jewish German man originally from the Elsace region who was said to be one of the oldest and most respected members of the Jewish community and who had lived in Little Rock for 30 years, 7–15, 5:3

Bösch, Sr. Angelina: one of five new novices in Pocahontas welcomed by Bishop Fitzgerald, from Nottwyl in the canton of Luzern in the Diocese of Basel, 9–9, 5:1

Bohn, Herr (Mr.): a German farmer and wine maker from Bryant, who visited the *Echo* offices with his product, which was judged excellent, 4–14, 5:1

Bonaventure, Rev.: treasurer of *Das Arkansas Echo*, 12–31–1891, 1:2; honorary

typesetter Neff testified that Close had been with him from 9:00–11:00 on Sunday evening (when the crime occurred), 8–5, 8:2

Cohen, Albert: obituary for Little Rock resident who served in the Confederate Army; claimed he produced the first American manufactured sulfur to be used in munitions and worked afterwards as a clock maker, 12–9, 8:1

Cohn, M. (possibly Mathias Abraham Cohn or Morris Cohn below): Little Rock businessman recently returned from trip to New York; reported that there was no cholera there and that the city voted overwhelmingly Democratic, 9–23, 5:2

Cohn, Morris: Little Rock resident who gave a speech in English at the dedication of Turner's Hall, 10–28, 8:1

Conrad, Ignatius, O.S.B.: newly elected prior of Subiaco Abbey, 3–31, 3:1; mentioned in an ad for Subiaco College, 9–23, 3:4

Craig, Ed.: contributor of 1,500 packets of seeds donated to the farmers who lost crops to flooding in Arkansas, 6–2, 8:4

Cravens, W. L.: successful litigant in Arkansas Supreme Court case against the Missouri Pacific Rail line; the court ruled that the railroad was responsible for his cotton that had been destroyed in a fire in transit and that it must compensate him for damages, 12–30, 8:2

Culb, Dr.: doctor in Mammoth Springs who tried to flag down a passing train to visit a critically ill patient; he resorted to attempting to jump onto the express wagon and fell and broke a rib, 9–30, 5:2

D'Aujourdhui, P. Gall, O.S.B.: clergy member at Subiaco Abbey who announced youth meeting for September 27 in Morrison Bluff, 9–2, 5:3; supervising clergy of the *3te General-Versammlung der Jünglings-Vereine* (Third General Meeting of the Youth Organizations), 10–7, 5:2

Darscheid, J.: visitor from Conway to *Echo* offices in Little Rock, 6–23, 5:3

Darscheid, Mrs.: death notice for mother of seven girls, 3–24, 3:1

Demuth, Kathie: death notice for four-year-old, daughter of Wilhelm Demuth, died of diptheritis (membranous croup), 8–12, 8:2

Demuth, Wilhelm: father of Kathie Demuth, who died of diptheritis, 8–12, 8:2

Dengler, H.: farmer who submitted a version of a proposed anti-Prohibition petition to the *Obst- und Weinzüchterverein* (The Fruit Grower and Wine Producer's Association), 12–16, 5:2

Dietzgen, Ph.(ilip): editor of rival German newspaper, *Die Staatszeitung*, suing the Arkansas *Echo* Publishing Company, 2–18, 2:5; his correspondence with Matthias Bauer in a personal dispute was published by the *Echo*, 8–19, 5:2; mentioned as the sender of a postcard to Adolf Arnold that his former typesetter, C. Neff, intended to use to sue the *Echo* for damages, 8–5, 8:2; plaintiff in lawsuit against a Mr. Lessing, claimed that a $50 loan cosigned by Mr. Lessing was never paid back, 9–23, 5:2; involved in incident regarding postcards with alleged indecent material, 11–11, 8:2; beaten by *Echo* editor Carl Meurer in a physical altercation, 11–18, 8:1

Dörner, G(eorg): seller of *Das Arkansas Echo*, 12–31–1891, 1:1; gave speech in German at dedication of Turner's Hall, 10–28, 8:1

Dorm, Herr (Mr.): witness in the case between the *Echo* and the *Staatszeitung* who testified that the typesetter C. Neff had been with him Saturday night through Monday morning, 8–5, 8:2

Drees, John: former proprietor of saloon in Little Rock who sold his establishment to W. Haibach so that he could move eight miles outside of the city to pursue his former passion, raising chickens, 12–30, 8:1

Dreher, Carry: widow of H. Walter and daughter of one of the oldest German settlers in Little Rock, 5–5, 8:1

Dreher, Herr (Mr.): mentioned as one of the oldest German settlers in Little Rock along with Fischer, Forster, and Schaeder (no first names given), 5–5, 8:1

Duemler (alternately spelled Duelmer), H.: resident of Paris and delegate to the Third State Assembly of the German-Catholic Aid Societies of Arkansas (German title under "Bakes, M.") held in Altus and part of a five-member panel that decided that F. Krebs could not be seated as a delegate on behalf of the St. Joseph's Aid Society in Little Rock that had been dissolved by the bishop, 10–28, 7:4

Duerr, Maria Josepha: death notice for child aged two years and eight months; notice placed by father, Jos. W. Duerr of Morrison Bluff, 5–26, 8:2

Dunne, Herr (Mr.): participant in bishop's church consecration at Hoxie, described as being "of the Catholic Herold in Ft. Smith," 5–5, 7:1

Durst, H.: resident of Little Rock who was an individual competition winner at *Turnfest* (gymnastics festival) in Hot Springs, 5–19, 6:4

Duttlinger, Frau (Mrs.): resident of Little Rock who was attacked in her home but managed to fend off the attacker, who ran away, 10–21, 8:5

Ehrenberg, H.: owner of one of the most well-known and oldest whiskey dealers in the state, since 1866, forced to declare bankruptcy; also an agent for A. Kuhn's beer, 11–25, 8:1

Eichhoff, Geo.: purchaser of establishment of J. B. Shelby who intended to open a saloon on the premises, 1–28, 2:1

Eisenhardt, Carl: writer of letter to the editor in which he endorsed Beni F. Reinberger for state representative, emphasizing that he was one of the German's own community, 7–15, 2:6

Eisler, Charles: Ft. Smith resident elected to the committee for the sick of the *St. Josephs Unterstützungs-Verein* (St. Joseph's Aid Society), 8–5, 5:3

Eller, Johann: setter of *Das Arkansas Echo*, 1–7, 2:3

Elser, Adolph: agent for *Das Arkansas Echo*, 3–24, 4:1; resident of Altus elected protocol secretary of the Third State Assembly of the German-Catholic Aid Societies of Arkansas (German title under "Bakes, M.") held in Altus, 10–21, 5:2

Elser, Jakob: farmer in Altus whose farm was visited by L. Wilhelm and J. Huck of Caulksville, 8–26, 5:4

Elsken, Conrad: agent of *Das Arkansas Echo*, 12–31–1891, 1:1; visitor to *Echo* office in Little Rock, 3–24, 2:5; newly elected president of the *St. Josephs Unterstützungs-Verein* (St. Joseph's Aid Society) in Paris, 4–28, 7:2; announced meeting of *Deutscher-römisch-katholischer Unterstützungsvereine* (German Roman Catholic aid societies) as president, 9–2, 5:3; announced rescheduled meeting due to church building being destroyed by a storm and negotiations with Iron Mountain Rail for reduced fare to meeting, 9–9, 5:2; mentioned in a letter by correspondent "Spottvogel" in regards to on-going dispute with Philip Dietzgen, 9–30, 4:4; elected president of Third State Assembly of the German-Catholic Aid Societies of Arkansas (German title under "Bakes, M.") held in Altus, 10–21, 5:2

Elsken, Gerhardt (alternately Gerhard): resident of Paris and delegate to the Third State Assembly of the German-Catholic Aid Societies of Arkansas (German title under "Bakes, M.") held in Altus, 10–28, 7:4

Elsken, Henry: newly elected flag bearer of the *St. Josephs Unterstützungs-Verein* (St. Joseph's Aid Society) in Paris, 4–28, 7:2

Emrich, (no first name given): Little Rock store owner who suffered a burglary with significant losses, 10–14, 5:2

End, Sr. M. Meinrada: one of five new novices in Pocahontas welcomed by Bishop Fitzgerald, from Boswyl in the canton of Aargau in the Diocese of Basel, 9–9, 5:1

Erbach, Jacob: resident of Conway who visited Little Rock, 8–19, 8:2

Erber, H.: father of male newborn infant, noted that his wife runs the City Chophouse, 6–23, 8:2

Erber, S.: mother of male newborn infant, 6–23, 8:2

Fässler, Nic.: victim of burglary when he and wife were out but children were at home; three youths stole $18 and destroyed wine stores; three trials held, alleged threat of violence against judge, and sentence to pay damages against the youths reversed so that Fässler had to pay court costs of $131.50; he had to pawn possessions to pay the fine; editors noted it was a cautionary tale for other Germans, 5–19, 7:1

Faist, B.: secretary of the *Obst- und Weinzüchterverein* (The Fruit Grower and Wine Producer's Association), 12–16, 5:2; mentioned that he was a resident of Bryant and has additional copies of the anti-Prohibition petition, 12–23, 8:3

Feakele, R. V.: death notice for "well-respected citizen," 1–28, 3:1

Fergusson, Bessi: death notice for girl who died after sustaining injuries two weeks prior; a neighbor child set her clothes on fire, 8–26, 8:1

Fischer, Anton: resident of Logan County endorsing fellow German Emil Baerlocher for the position of Assessor, 4–28, 5:2

Fischer, Herr (Mr.), Sr.: resident of Logan County endorsing fellow German Emil Baerlocher for the position of Assessor, 4–28, 5:2

Fischer, Mr.: mentioned as one of the oldest German settlers in Little Rock along with Dreher, Forster, and Schaeder (no first names given), 5–5, 8:1

Fisk, (no first name given): Little Rock resident whose home was completely destroyed in a kitchen fire that spread to the rest of the house and the stall; he and his family were able to escape, 12–16, 8:1

Fleiß, Martin: new priest at Subiaco Abbey, 1–14, 2:1

Florian, Michael: death notice, 1–28, 3:1

Förster, Willi: groom in wedding to Elisabeth Rast (announcement prior to event), 4–21, 8:2; second report of wedding, 4–28, 8:1; mention of guests visiting the young couple at their home, 5–5, 8:1

Forster, (no first name given): mentioned as one of the oldest German settlers in Little Rock along with Fischer, Dreher, and Schaeder, 5–5, 8:1

Forster, Frank: businessman whose grocery was previously burglarized, a second attempt was thwarted, 8–12, 8:2

Foster, Frau (Mrs.): Little Rock resident whose stalls caught fire as part of larger arson event, 10–14, 5:1

Frauenthal, (no first name given): young murder victim, mentioned in story about escape from jail of perpetrator in Lonoke, 6–30, 5:3; murderer, Mulligan, sentenced to 21 years in prison, 7–15, 2:2

Frederick, H.: resident of Paris and delegate to the Third State Assembly of the German-Catholic Aid Societies of Arkansas (German title under "Bakes, M.") held in Altus, 10–28, 7:4; corrected in next issue to state that he was not one of the delegates, 11–11, 5:2

Frenken, Peter: groom in wedding to Gertrud Jungersfeld in Pocahontas, 11–25, 3:1

Frick, Heinrich: proprietor of the *Deutsches Gasthaus* (German Inn) in Little Rock, 1–7, 3:6–7; returned from New York to visit his relatives for the first time in six years, 8–5, 8:1

Friedheim, A.: vice-president of new liquor store in Little Rock, the Levinson-Friedheim Company, 7–29, 8:6

Friedrich, Julie: bride in wedding to Jos. Seiter in Morrison Bluff, 10–28, 7:2

Baerlocher for the position of Assessor, 4–28, 5:2; newly elected marshal of the *St. Josephs Unterstützungs-Verein* (St. Joseph's Aid Society) in Paris, 4–28, 7:2

Gisler, Katharina: bride in wedding to Burkhard (no first name given) in Charleston, 10–14, 4:3

Glanzman, Jos.: author of history of immigrants in Altus, 6–16, 2:4; farm likely mentioned (as Mr. Glanzman) in next planned visit of L. Wilhelm and J. Huck to Altus, 8–26, 5:4

Glaser, Gust.: author of opinion piece regarding the newspaper trade, 4–21, 8:2

Glöckler, (no first name given): youth who attempted to save the drowning son of Joe C. Schäder via boat but was unsuccessful, 6–23, 8:3

Goosen, Frank: groom in wedding to Elisabeth Komstedt in Little Rock, 10–21, 8:5

Grämer, Huber Frau (Mrs.): death notice for wife of Huber Grämer (first name not given); resident of Conway and mother of eight children, one of whom was buried with her, 10–7, 5:2

Grote, John: featured speaker at Assumption celebration in Altus, gave speech in English because of all the English speakers present, 9–2, 5:1

Grunert, Berthold: resident of Fort Smith elected correspondence secretary of the Third State Assembly of the German-Catholic Aid Societies of Arkansas (German title under "Bakes, M.") held in Altus, 10–21, 5:2

Guenther, Friedrich: resident of Paris and delegate to the Third State Assembly of the German-Catholic Aid Societies of Arkansas (German title under "Bakes, M.") held in Altus, 11–11, 5:2

Guenzel, Paul: secretary of St. Boniface chapter of Catholic Knights of America, 4–14, 2:3

Günzel, Theresia: newly elected president of *Brüderschaft der christlichen Mütter* (Guild ["Brotherhood"] of Christian Mothers) in Ft. Smith, 4–14, 3:2

Hahn, Gottlieb: Little Rock resident who sold his bakery business, 2–11, 2:2

Halter, Lorenz: groom in wedding to Maria Wüst in St. Vincent, 10–28, 7:1

Hamburg, Alph.: Lonoke resident whose horse panicked, buggy destroyed and man and five-year-old son severely injured, 8–12, 5:1

Hammelrath, Jacob: alleged victim of forgery regarding letter published in the rival *Staatszeitung*, 7–29, 8:2, incident mentioned again, 8–12, 8:1

Handmann, Emma: bride in wedding to Bern. Heinze on February 24, 3–3, 2:5

Hansen, H.: groom in wedding to Rosa Langhammer on April 27 (announcement prior to event), 4–21, 7:2; second report of wedding, giving new couple's home address as 807 Ferry Street, 4–28, 8:1; further report of wedding reception festivities, 5–5, 8:1

Hartmann, Anna: bride in wedding to John Heß in St. Vincent, 10–28, 7:1

Hohenschutz, Frau (Mrs.): member of community who took trip to visit in Germany along with her youngest son and daughter, 7–29, 8:2; traveled to Europe on the steamer "Veendam," Fr. Eugene Weibel made the voyage on the same vessel, 8–5, 8:2

Hohenschutz, Fred Jr.: Little Rock man accused but acquitted of carrying a pistol at the office of the *Staatszeitung*, 3–3, 2:5

Hohenschutz, Maria: bride in wedding to C. Meurer in Little Rock, 10–21, 8:5

Hoing, Gertrud: celebrated her silver wedding anniversary with husband Heinrich in Altus, 11–25, 3:3

Hoing, Heinrich: celebrated his silver wedding anniversary with wife Gertrud in Altus, 11–25, 3:3

Holmes, K.: death notice for prominent farmer in Altheimer; died at the age of 25 of malaria, 10–21, 5:1

Holpert, John: resident of Paris and victim of house fire who was greatly burned on hands and face trying to rescue household goods, 4–7, 4:5

Holtzman, (no first name given): Little Rock resident selected for committee to look for new city dump location, 8–26, 8:2

Homan, W. P.: president of Exchange National Bank, 1–28, 8:5–6

Howel, (no first name given): claimant in compensation case for $50,000; alleged that Storthz hit him in the face in such a way to make him lose an eye; altercation occurred in the office of Storthz' lawyer, since he and Howel were already engaged in another legal case against each other, 9–23, 5:2

Hoyng, Constantin: rented farm to make trip to Germany, 1–7, 1:7; returned from Germany looking well with a new bride, 7–7, 5:3

Huber, Jas.: resident of Logan County endorsing fellow German Emil Baerlocher for the position of Assessor, 4–28, 5:2

Huber, Sr. Cäcilia: one of five new novices in Pocahontas welcomed by Bishop Fitzgerald, from Rorschach in the canton of St. Gallen in the Diocese of St. Gallen, 9–9, 5:1

Huber, Theo.: resident of Logan County endorsing fellow German Emil Baerlocher for the position of Assessor, 4–28, 5:2

Hubmann, John (alternately as Hubman): president of the *Obst- und Weinzüchterverein* (Fruit Grower and Wine Producer's Association) called for a meeting in Collegeville regarding the election, 8–26, 8:2; wrote a scolding letter asking the German newspapers to keep their feud out of the effort to petition the government to allow the sale of alcohol in the state, 11–25, 3:3; notice of meeting of the Fruit Grower and Wine Producer's Association on December 12, 11–25, 4:2

Huck, J.: resident of Caulksville who along with L. Wilhelm visited farms of Jakob Elser, Jos. Bachman, and Jakob Post in Altus, 8–26, 5:4

Hülsen, Jacob: Bryant resident who visited the *Echo* offices after a broken leg left him using crutches, 8–26, 8:2

Hürlimann, Sr. Ildephonsa: one of five new novices in Pocahontas welcomed by Bishop Fitzgerald, from Walchwyl in the canton of Zug in the Diocese of Basel, 9–9, 5:1

Huffman, Frau (Mrs.): death notice for woman whose husband was at "Eagle Pass" at time of her death and was notified by telegraph; no other information given, 9–23, 5:3

Humbman, D. Fr. T.: newly elected director of the *Grütliverein* ("Forest Clearing" or Foresters' Association), 4–7, 4:5

Hummel, Joseph: director of the St. Boniface male choir in Ft. Smith, 2–11, 2:2; listed as an agent for the *Echo*, 8–5, 4:1; elected treasurer of the *St. Josephs Unterstützungs-Verein* (St. Joseph's Aid Society), 8–5, 5:3; mentioned by Jos. Limberg as a member of the Ft. Smith delegation to a statewide meeting, 9–23, 4:4

Huskamp, A.: resident of Logan County endorsing fellow German Emil Baerlocher for the position of Assessor, 4–28, 5:2

Huwiler, R. Josef, O.S.B.: priest who celebrated his first Mass at Shoal Creek, 11–25, 3:1

Ible, Leo.: resident of Logan County endorsing fellow German Emil Baerlocher for the position of Assessor, 4–28, 5:2

Ihle, Alois: resident of Logan County endorsing fellow German Emil Baerlocher for the position of Assessor, 4–28, 5:2

Imboden, Ida: bride in wedding to George Boullioun in Conway, 11–18, 5:1

Isemann, J.: farmer who thought he was purchasing 120 acres of railroad land and discovered that forty of those acres belonged to the state; alleged that state commissioner of lands C. B. Meyers treated him unfairly when he went to inquire about the situation and the taxes he had paid on the state land, which was sold to a W. Martin, 9–2, 5:2

Jäeger [*sic*], A.: resident of Little Rock who was an individual competition winner at *Turnfest* (gymnastics festival) in Hot Springs, 5–19, 6:4

Jaeger, H.: father of nine-month-old child who died, 5–19, 8:1

Jansen, P. J.: subject of letter regarding honor in case brought before Justice of the Peace J. N. Thompson; Kenney's wife was accused of lying about the character of P. J. Jansen, who had Frank Kinney arrested when he would not apologize for the statements, 4–14, 4:5

Jarret, E.: eight-year-old injured in accident with buggy, 9–2, 8:1

Jarret, W. H.: elected president of the Catholic Knights, 12–23, 8:1

Jasper, Frank: resident of Spielerville and delegate to the Third State Assembly of the German-Catholic Aid Societies of Arkansas (German title under "Bakes, M.") held in Altus, 10–28, 7:4

Johl, Sol.(oman): proprietor of a bar in Little Rock mentioned as former employer of Joseph Schmeltzer, 12–23, 8:2

Jung, Emilie: bride in wedding to Georg Krickeberg, 5–5, 8:1

Jungersfeld, Gertrud: bride in wedding to Peter Frenken in Pocahontas, 11–25, 3:1

Jungkind, Dr. John A.: founding member and treasurer of *Schützenverein* (Marksmen Club), 3–10, 2:4; father of newborn daughter (wife's name not mentioned), 6–23, 8:2; elected chairman of south central delegation for the *Turnverein*, 9–23, 5:2

Jungkind, John A. (same as Dr. J. Jungkind above?): trustee and member of building committee for *Turnverein*, 3–17, 3:1

Junker, Josef: resident of Paris, elected treasurer of the *3te General-Versammlung der Jünglings-Vereine* (Third General Meeting of the Youth Organizations), 10–7, 5:2

Justin, Fr.: officiant in wedding of George Anger and Maria Neumeier in Morrison Bluff, 2–25, 2:3

Kahn, Herman: president of an unnamed assembly organized to fight against Prohibition, 6–16, 8:2; noted that he (Mr. Kahn, presumably the same person) had returned to Little Rock with his family, 9–16, 8:3

Kallaghan, Rev. Dr.: elected "geistlicher Director" (spiritual director / chaplain) of the Catholic Knights, 12–23, 8:1

Karcher, A.: resident of Little Rock who was an individual competition winner at *Turnfest* (gymnastics festival) in Hot Springs, 5–19, 6:4

Kaufman, John: president of *Das Arkansas Echo*, 12–31–1891, 1:2; mentioned as target of attack in the *Staatszeitung* due to what they considered his paltry donation to flood victims' fund, defended by *Echo* due to his large losses in flood and because he gave other charity which he did not announce publicly, 6–2, 8:3; made a trip to Colorado for health reasons, 7–7, 5:3; remained in Colorado to take the baths, 7–29, 8:2; returned from Colorado on September 2 with much improved health and increased weight, 9–9, 8:2

Key, Herr (Mr.): father of newborn boy; mother's and child's names not given, 10–7, 5:4

Kind, A.: contributor of history of Pocahontas and Randolph County from the perspective of Catholic immigrants, 9–9, 3:1, 9–16, 3:1, and 11–11, 3:3; editorial note addressed to Kind apologized that he was being attacked by the rival *Staatszeitung* as a correspondent of the *Echo*, but noted that he was in good company, 12–30, 8:3

Kindervater, Albert: Little Rock butcher and son of Johanna Kindervater, 10–28, 8:2

Kindervater, Johanna: obituary for Little Rock resident who died at the age of 80; immigrated from Sachsen approximately a decade earlier; survived by only son, Albert Kindervater, the well-known butcher, 10–28, 8:2

evidence was presented that the group still existed, 10–28, 7:4; clarification printed that he was petitioning for two delegate seats representing the Fund for Widows and Orphans, 11–11, 5:2

Kreener, John: Fort Smith resident elected standard bearer of the *St. Josephs Unterstützungs-Verein* (St. Joseph's Aid Society), 8–5, 5:3

Kremer, A.: member of St. Scholastica and delegate to the Third State Assembly of the German-Catholic Aid Societies of Arkansas (German title under "Bakes, M.") held in Altus, 10–28, 7:4

Krickeberg, Georg: groom in wedding to Emilie Jung, 5–5, 8:1

Kuckartz, Wm.: patriarch of German family from St. Scholastica, Shoal Creek in Logan County announcing a move to Emporia, Kansas and bidding farewell to former friends and neighbors in a poem, 2–25, 2:3; publishes notice that he has sold his former farm to Arthur Miles, 6–2, 7:5

Kuhn, A.: beer producer whose wares were carried by H. Ehrenberg in Little Rock until Ehrenberg's bankruptcy, 11–25, 8:1

Kull, R.: newly elected treasurer of the *Grütliverein* ("Forest Clearing" or Foresters' Association), 4–7, 4:5

Kusener, Casp.: founding member of *Schützenverein* (Marksmen Club), 3–10, 2:4

Kutzleb, Emilie: widow of Max Kutzleb, 1–21 (physical page six numbered as page four-6)

Kutzleb, Max: death notice, member of the *Krieger- und Landwehrverein*, 1–21, 2:3; obituary, 1–28, 3:1

Lafferty, Thomas: co-chair of the committee to support flood victims along with Louis Blass, 5–26, 2:4

Lanco, A.: obituary for man described as one of the most well-known Germans in Little Rock; he was suffering from dysentery and was survived by a wife and a grown daughter; he was a member of the *Kriegerverein* (veterans' association) and they accompanied his body to the cemetery, 11–11, 8:2

Langhammer, Fr.: groom in wedding to Mary Spreck in Little Rock on February 19, 2–18, 2:5

Langhammer, Rosa: bride in wedding to H. Hansen on April 27 (announcement prior to event), 4–21, 7:2; second report of wedding, giving new couple's home address as 807 Ferry Street, 4–28, 8:1; further report of wedding reception festivities, 5–5, 8:1

Langreck, Herr (Mr.): member of *Kriegerverein* (veterans' association) who was selected as a delegate to attend national organization's conference in Kansas City, 8–26, 8:2

La Oue, Frau (Mrs.): Little Rock resident injured along with her child and Lizzie Litzke in wagon accident caused by horse being spooked by two carriages racing, 8–12, 8:2

Laux, Jake (alternately Jacob): resident of Morrilton and salesman for new liquor store in Little Rock, the Levinson-Friedheim Company; listed as agent to work especially with German customers, 7–29, 8:6; visited *Echo* offices and changed employment to being a stoker with a rail line; earned much more, 12–9, 8:1

Lehmann, Alfred: resident of Pine Bluff who was elected vice-president of the *Pine Bluff deutscher Gesang-Verein* (Pine Bluff German Singing Association), 10–14, 5:3

Lehmer, C.: owner of a large dairy in Little Rock, injured when he was investigating a well his black employee was digging and fell in; saved by his employee; noted that he was also injured when a horse went wild at the German Day celebration, 8–5, 5:1

Leimer, C. J.: resident of Little Rock, intended to move to Denver, Colorado, 8–19, 8:2

Lemmer, J.: German resident of Argenta, given twenty lashes with a whip by "white cap" vigilantes after he brutally beat his wife in a dispute regarding a black boy who hit his dog with a rock (she maintained the boy had not meant to target the animal) and refused to give him money for beer; claimed he knew many of the twenty-five men who came to mete out vigilante justice but refused to name them, 9–23, 5:2

Lenggenhager, Mr.: new immigrant in Collegeville since January, visited the *Echo* offices and intended to plant wheat and grapes for wine production, 3–31, 2:4

Lengmeyer, J.: death notice for man who died near Dixie after falling into a well; died of poor air before he could be pulled out, 10–14, 5:2

Lensing, (no first name given): party to dispute involving Hammelrath and the *Staatszeitung*; exact nature of the dispute unclear, 8–12, 8:1

Lensing, Herman: resident of Little Rock elected treasurer of the Third State Assembly of the German-Catholic Aid Societies of Arkansas (German title under "Bakes, M.") held in Altus, 10–21, 5:2; mentioned as contact for farmers and others who would like to sign the petition regarding Prohibition in Arkansas, 12–23, 5:1

Lensing, Katharina: bride in wedding to Bernhard Tenkleve at St. Scholastica on February 16, 2–25, 2:4

Lesemeister, Theresa: bride in wedding to Hubert Peters in Pocahontas, 11–25, 3:1

Lesser, Morris: salesman for new liquor store in Little Rock, the Levinson-Friedheim Company, 7–29, 8:6

Lessing, Herr (Mr.): defendant in a lawsuit brought by Philip Dietzgen, who claimed that a $50 loan to Fr. Niehaus for which Lessing was a co-signer was never paid back; Niehaus and Lessing claimed it was paid back, 9–23, 5:2

Levinson, H.: president of new liquor store in Little Rock, the Levinson-Friedheim Company, 7–29, 8:6

Levy, male child: death notice, five-year-old son of community member who was killed after street car accident, 2–18, 2:5

Lewis, Fräulein (Miss): bride in wedding to J. B. Sandefur, Dr. Calaghan officiated, 9–9, 8:1

Lienhart, Josef: agent for the *Arkansas Echo* in the Conway area, 3–17, 4:1; contributor of article on cultivation of sorghum with Mr. Heß, 4–21, 7:2

Limberg, H.: Fort Smith resident elected vice-president of the *St. Josephs Unterstützungs-Verein* (St. Joseph's Aid Society), 8–5, 5:3

Limberg, Jos.: Fort Smith resident and author of letter to editor accusing the *Staatszeitung* of publishing a libel against him, in which another German stated that Limberg said he was glad to be rid of Fr. Bonaventure during the statewide meeting of German clubs; he noted that he was not part of the delegation that day and that he praised Fr. Bonaventure as someone the entire German Catholic congregation was fond of, 9–23, 4:4

Linzel, (no first name given): founding member and vice-president of *Schützenverein* (Marksmen Club), 3–10, 2:4; character witness on behalf of Philip Dietzgen with regards to indecent postcard incident, 11–11, 8:2

Linzel, Frau (Mrs.): resident of Little Rock traveling to Chicago to visit, 7–29, 8:2

Lippke, Caroline: death notice for 14-month-old, 8–19, 8:2

Litsch, J.: resident of Logan County endorsing fellow German Emil Baerlocher for the position of Assessor, 4–28, 5:2

Litsch, M.: resident of Logan County endorsing fellow German Emil Baerlocher for the position of Assessor, 4–28, 5:2

Litzke, Lizzie: Little Rock resident injured along with Mrs. La Oue and Mrs. La Oue's child in wagon accident caused by horse being spooked by two carriages racing, 8–12, 8:2

Loetcher (alternately as Loetscher), P. P. von: visitor from Conway to *Echo* offices in Little Rock, 6–23, 5:3; marched in electoral victory parade of Democrats of Faulkner county as standard bearer, 11–18, 5:2

Lori, W.: farmer in the Little Rock area who successfully cultivated rice and offered seeds through the *Echo* office; he also built a machine to remove the hulls, which his ten-year-old son was able to use, 12–23, 5:1

Lucy, Fr.: priest assigned to Pine Bluff who put together exhibit to represent Jefferson County at the World Expo; it told the story of the black industrial school founded by Lucy in 1889 and operated by the local nuns, 11–11, 5:1

Lumpp, Geo.: resident of Logan County endorsing fellow German Emil Baerlocher for the position of Assessor, 4–28, 5:2

Maas-Kupferle, Fred L.: death notice, stepson of Nic. Kupferle, 2–4, 5:1

Mahoney, Frau (Mrs.): mentioned that her in-laws visited her in Little Rock in the previous week and were impressed by the city, 4–28, 8:2

Masur, P.: husband whose wife had been physically and mentally incapacitated for months, editors soliciting donations for the family whose address is given, 2–25, 2:2

Matthäus, P: priest who gave a sermon in English instead of his preferred German at the Bonafacius celebration in Ft. Smith due to the large number of English-speakers attending, 6–16, 7:2; intended to take a group of boys to Subiaco so they could be trained for the priesthood, 12–9, 5:2

Matthäus, Peter: participant in ceremony laying the cornerstone for the new German Catholic church in Morrilton, 5–5, 6:4

McKelvy, H. A.: listed as salesman for Cravens & Son, 5–12, 5:6–7

McQuaid, F.: participant in bishop's church consecration at Hoxie, 5–5, 7:1

Menke, Frau (Mrs.) K.: Little Rock resident who removed to Mount Nebo during the hot weather, 7–29, 8:2

Menkus, Else: death notice for wife of Justice of the Peace Menkus; she was fifty-four years old, died of stroke, and left behind four children; 11–4, 8:1

Merck, Karl: resident of Logan County endorsing fellow German Emil Baerlocher for the position of Assessor, 4–28, 5:2

Merk, Carl: groom in wedding on February 2 to Anna Boerlocher in Paris, 2–11, 2:3

Metzger, Josephine: bride in wedding to Wilhelm Rogosky in Little Rock, mentioned that she belonged to one of the oldest German families of the city, 5–5, 8:2

Meurer, C.: groom in wedding to Maria Hohenschutz in Little Rock, 10–21, 8:5; went to Judge Peay to declare himself guilty of beating Philip Dietzgen and pay the $1.50 fine; Dietzgen insisted that criminal charges be brought, but a grand jury refused to indict Meurer due to the extenuating circumstances of the *Staatszeitung* publishing inflammatory material against him, 11–18, 8:1

Meyer, Bernhart: father of Wilhelm Meyer, born during June flooding, 6–23, 7:3

Meyer, Fr.: craftsman of special plaque to be sent to the World Expo that showcased all twenty-two kinds of trees to be found in Arkansas, 3–24, 2:4

Meyer, Wilhelm: son of Bernhart Meyer, born during June flooding, 6–23, 7:3

Michel, Joe: salesman for new liquor store in Little Rock, the Levinson-Friedheim Company, 7–29, 8:6

Miles, R. D.: elected president of the Catholic Knights, 12–23, 8:1

Moll, F.: resident of Morrilton and delegate to the Third State Assembly of the German-Catholic Aid Societies of Arkansas (German title under "Bakes, M.") held in Altus, 10–28, 7:4

Mons, Julius: resident of Little Rock who was an individual competition winner at *Turnfest* (gymnastics festival) in Hot Springs, 5–19, 6:4

Morgner, Gerhard: discussed as plaintiff in complaint against County Judge Erb of damages against the (unnamed) county in the amount of $13,337.55, 7–15, 5:3

Müller, Andy: son of Dom. Müller; encountered John Kaufmann in Manitou during his recovery visit to Colorado, 9–9, 8:2

Müller, Louis: father of one of the winners of the "baby show" (pageant) in Glennwood Park, 6–23, 8:1; elected without opposition as an alderman in Little Rock to replace the outgoing Gray, 12–16, 8:1

Müller, Oscar: well-known resident of Argenta whose 12-year-old daughter died, 9–2, 8:1

Muswick, Geo: salesman for new liquor store in Little Rock, the Levinson-Friedheim Company, 7–29, 8:6

Muyres, Mathias: death notice for a German resident of Pocahontas who was born in Holland and immigrated with his wife and two children shortly before Father Weibel, 12–9, 3:4

Naegele, Jos.: member of Dixie, Arkansas, German community who wrote paragraph encouraging other Germans to join them, 3–3, 3:2

Nägele, Jos.: resident of Dixie and delegate to the Third State Assembly of the German-Catholic Aid Societies of Arkansas (German title under "Bakes, M.") held in Altus, 10–28, 7:4

Nahlen, Mr.: participant in on-going feud with *Die Staatszeitung*, alleged to have published a falsified letter under his name, 2–18, 5:3

Narra, S.: obituary for one of the most well-known citizens in Little Rock, who had suffered a stroke two years prior to his death; he emigrated from Prussia in 1831 and ran a glass and porcelain business, 12–2, 8:1

Narup, Fritz: Fort Smith resident elected to the committee for the sick of the *St. Josephs Unterstützungs-Verein* (St. Joseph's Aid Society), 8–5, 5:3

Neff, C.: former typesetter for *Die Staatszeitung*, mentioned in a post card from Philip Dietzgen to Adolf Arnold with the allegation that Neff intended to sue the *Echo* for damages, 8–5, 8:2

Neumeier, Maria: bride in wedding to George Anger in Morrison Bluff, 2–25, 2:3

Niehaus, Fr.: witness in a lawsuit brought by Philip Dietzgen against a Mr. Lessing; Dietzgen claimed that a $50 loan to Fr. Niehaus for which Lessing was a co-signer was never paid back; Niehaus and Lessing claimed it was paid back, 9–23, 5:2

Niehaus, Jos.: member of St. Scholastica and delegate to the Third State Assembly of the German-Catholic Aid Societies of Arkansas (German title under "Bakes, M.") held in Altus, 10–28, 7:4

Noiman, Cath.: bride in wedding to Bernard Ritz at St. Edward's Catholic Church in Little Rock, 11–25, 8:1

Noll, F. J.: member of St. Vincent and delegate to the Third State Assembly of the German-Catholic Aid Societies of Arkansas (German title under "Bakes, M.") held in Altus, 10–28, 7:4

Norton, (no first name given): clerk in Lescher's shoe store (*Echo* advertiser) who was greeted in English in an alley by two policemen looking for a burglar; thinking he was being attacked by robbers, he fired a gun, which missed both men by a long shot, and ran into a nearby house and locked the door; he was arrested and charged with attacking the officers with intent to kill, 12–16, 8:1

Nottenkämpfer, Johann: resident of Atkins said to be quite ill, 5–12, 7:2

Nutt, A.: author of poem "Des Wettermachers Herzeleid" (The heartbreak of the weather maker) about St. Peter growing weary of all the men on earth complaining about the weather, 6–23, 6:3

Obermeier, Mat.: resident of Logan County endorsing fellow German Emil Baerlocher for the position of Assessor, 4–28, 5:2

Oberste, F. W(illiam).: author of letter to the editor endorsing E. T. McConnel for Secretary of State, 4–21, 7:1

Olles, Peter: listed as agent for *Das Arkansas Echo*, 12–16, 4:1

Ostrich, R.: officer of "Young Men's Independent Organization," 3–17, 3:1

Otten, P.: participant in ceremony laying the cornerstone for the new German Catholic church in Morrilton, 5–5, 6:4

Ottenheimer, (no first name given): owner of carpet store damaged in fire; insured in the amount of $18,500, 12–23, 8:1

Pächter, Herr (Mr.): injured terribly in tornado at *Marienstadt*; his four-year-old son escaped unharmed, 5–19, 7:1

Peay, Jimmy: one of the winners of the "baby show" (pageant) in Glennwood Park, 6–23, 8:1

Peay, Richter (Judge): Little Rock judge to whom Carl Meurer presented himself as guilty in the beating of Philip Dietzgen, 11–18, 8:1

Penzel, C(harles). P.: one of nine men appointed to county board to discuss whether a bridge could be paid for, founder of German National Bank, 11–11, 8:1

Peterek, Ludwig: setter of *Das Arkansas Echo*, 1–7, 2:3

Peters, Hubert: groom in wedding to Therese Lesemeister in Pocahontas, 11–25, 3:1

Petersdorf, August: Little Rock resident known for his dry sense of humor naturalized, 10–14, 5:1

Pfeifer, Ph.: vice-president of Exchange National Bank, 1–28, 8:5–6

Pollock, J. S.: cashier of Exchange National Bank, 1–28, 8:5–6

Post, Jakob: farmer in Altus whose farm was visited by L. Wilhelm and J. Huck of Caulksville, 8–26, 5:4

Pratt, Nora: bride in wedding to H. F. J. Wildberger, 11–25, 8:2

Raible, John: resident of Morrison Bluff and delegate to the Third State Assembly of the German-Catholic Aid Societies of Arkansas (German title under "Bakes, M.") held in Altus, 10–28, 7:4

Raible, Wilhelm: member of St. Benedict's parish; elected secretary of newly founded Democratic Club in Spielerville, 8–12, 5:1; elected president of the *3te General-Versammlung der Jünglings-Vereine* (Third General Meeting of the Youth Organizations), 10–7, 5:2

Ranker, Carl: father of new baby boy, mother's name and child's name not listed, Friederike Schmand present as the midwife, 8–5, 8:1

Rast, Elisabeth: bride in wedding to Willi Förster, 4–29, 8:1; further mention that her father, two brothers, and a sister arrived in Little Rock to attend her wedding, 4–28, 8:2; mention of guests visiting the young couple at their home (although only groom's name is given), 5–5, 8:1

Reichert, P.: resident of Fort Smith and delegate to the Third State Assembly of the German-Catholic Aid Societies of Arkansas (German title under "Bakes, M.") held in Altus, 11–11, 5:2

Reichhardt, P.: resident of Morrison Bluff and delegate to the Third State Assembly of the German-Catholic Aid Societies of Arkansas (German title under "Bakes, M.") held in Altus, 10–28, 7:4

Reichmann, Conr.: death notice for Atkins resident who had been blind in one eye at birth and slowly lost sight in other eye; leaves behind a wife and three children, 9–2, 4:4

Reid, Frank: resident of Logan County endorsing fellow German Emil Baerlocher for the position of Assessor, 4–28, 5:2

Reider, Geo.: resident of Logan County endorsing fellow German Emil Baerlocher for the position of Assessor, 4–28, 5:2

Reiff, P.: correspondent from Atkins who discussed election results and candidates Terry and Cravens who thanked the Germans for their support, 12–2, 3:3

Reimann, Albrecht: contributor of obituary of Max Kutzleb, 1–28, 3:1

Reis, C.: death notice for "nice young German man"; Zither and Singing Club provided him with a burial and will cover the difference if the selling off of his effects does not produce enough money to cover the burial expenses, 11–11, 8:2

Reis, Paul (alternately written as Reiß): agent for *Das Arkansas Echo*, 3–24, 4:1; father of new baby boy, 5–5, 6:4; featured speaker at Assumption celebration in Altus, explained the event and gave a toast to the pope, 9–2, 5:1

Reisler, L. A.: obituary for seventy-five-year-old German man who was killed after being struck by a streetcar; he was a long-term resident of Little Rock who had recently moved in with his son; the driver had been making change and did not see Reisler, but he was arrested and put in jail, 12–23, 8:2

Remmler, J. B.: resident of Logan County endorsing fellow German Emil Baerlocher for the position of Assessor, 4–28, 5:2

Richter, Fred: German-speaking clerk of the store C.G. Lincoln, 1–28, 8:5–6

Richter, Julius: death notice for Potash Sulphur Springs resident who died suddenly at the age of 46 while taking a walk, 8–26, 8:2

Rieder, F. X.: resident of Logan County endorsing fellow German Emil Baerlocher for the position of Assessor, 4–28, 5:2

Riegler, (no first name given): resident of Little Rock whose business suffered a fire, 8–19, 8:2

Riegler, John: death notice for well-known justice of the peace originally from the Württemberg region but had lived in Little Rock for four decades; he was also the county treasurer from 1866–1874, 7–15, 5:3

Riff, H. D.: officer of "Young Men's Independent Organization," 3–17, 3:1, barbershop suffered small fire that was put out quickly, 9–9, 8:2

Ringelhaupt, Herr (Mr.): encountered John Kaufmann during his recovery in Colorado, 9–9, 8:2

Rinke, Herr (Mr.): possible witness in the case between the *Echo* and the *Staatszeitung*; typesetter Neff testified that Rinke had been with him in the typesetting room of the *Echo* (where the crime occurred) on Saturday evening, although not in the company of Mr. Dorm, 8–5, 8:2

Ritz, Bernhard: groom in wedding to Cath. Noiman at St. Edward's Catholic Church in Little Rock, 11–25, 8:1

Roesch, Fred.: trustee and member of building committee for *Turnverein*, 3–17, 3:1

Roeslein, R. G.: resident of Logan County endorsing fellow German Emil Baerlocher for the position of Assessor, 4–28, 5:2; newly elected "second secretary" of the *St. Josephs Unterstützungs-Verein* (St. Joseph's Aid Society) in Paris, 4–28, 7:2

Roessner, Fred.: trustee and member of building committee for *Turnverein*, 3–17, 3:1; character witness on behalf of Philip Dietzgen with regards to indecent postcard incident, 11–11, 8:2; recommended as new school superintendent in city council meeting, 12–9, 8:2

Rogosky, Wilhelm: groom in wedding to Josephine Metzger in Little Rock, 5–5, 8:2

Rolf, Ferd.: president of the *St. Joseph's Verein* in Morrilton, celebrating silver wedding anniversary, 3–3, 3:2

Rolf, Heinrich: son of Ferdinand Rolf and Morrilton resident who moved to Little Rock and found a position in the stave factory, 11–18, 8:1

Rolf, Theresa (née Kordsmeier): celebrating silver wedding anniversary, 3–3, 3:2

Rosen, Max: father of newborn son (wife's name not mentioned), 6–23, 8:2

Ruest, (no first name given): traveling salesman for the *Staatszeitung*, 6–30, 5:3

Rumback, H: fifteen-year-old Little Rock boy who injured himself in the face with fireworks on the Fourth of July, 7–7, 5:3

Ruschang, Frau (Mrs.): death notice for woman who was the daughter of Frau Georg; her husband died five years prior to her death, 10–7, 5:4

Rust, A.: president of the *St. Joseph's Verein*, 1–7, 2:1; mentioned in a letter by correspondent "Spottvogel" in regards to on-going dispute with Philip Dietzgen, 9–30, 4:4; wife reported as being seriously ill, 11–4, 8:1

Saddler, A.: Paris store keeper who turned over his store and assets to his creditors; W. Greenwood was named receiver, 12–23, 5:2

Sättele, Johann: deceased accountant for church endowment fund, remembered by family in announcement in which they thank the church community and particularly Fr. Burgert for help and sympathy; family writing from Döggingen, Baden, 8–12, 5:5

Sättele, Maria: family member of Johann Sättele, deceased accountant for church endowment fund, 8–12, 5:5

Sättele, Mathias: family member of Johann Sättele, deceased accountant for church endowment fund, 8–12, 5:5

Sandefuhr (alternately spelled Sandefur), J. B.: former resident of Logan County, newly moved to Little Rock to open new company with partners as secretary and treasurer of the Levinson-Friedheim Company, 7–29, 5:1; groom in wedding to Miss Lewis, Dr. Calaghan officiated, 9–9, 8:1

Sanders, Fred.: photographer in Little Rock and contributor of an article regarding the photographic process, which concludes with an advertisement for his business, 9–23, 2:4

Sanders, R. W.: death notice for a man who lived to be 46 years old (no other information given), 8–12, 8:2

Sarlo, A.: funeral notice for seventy-two-year-old buried at Catholic cemetery, 11–4, 8:1

Schaeder, A. L.: victim of burglary and theft at residence, 3–10, 2:5; elected treasurer of the Catholic Knights, 12–23, 8:1

Schaeder, Herr (Mr.): mentioned as one of the oldest German settlers in Little Rock along with Fischer, Forster, and Dreher (no first names given), 5–5, 8:1

Schäder, Joe C.: father of boy who died while swimming in the Arkansas River due to a cramp, 6–23, 8:3

Schälchlin, Salomon: death notice for farmer from Benton who was originally from Zurich, 7–15, 2:7

Schimmelpfennig, Witwe (widow): owner of a grocery on 10th and Broadway whose only son died after a long illness, 7–29, 8:1

Schulte, Theresia: celebrating silver wedding anniversary to Johann Schulte, 2–11, 2:1

Schwantz, S.: resident of Poplar Grove who was fighting with J. Parks, who shot him in the head three times; the next day, Parks was found dead with a bullet hole in his head, 11–25, 5:2

Schwenk, Herr (Mr.): brother-in-law of runaway teenage girl, whom he tried to convince to stay with his wife until her parents could retrieve her; she refused and so was taken to the city jail, 7–29, 8:2

Seifer, John: resident of Logan County endorsing fellow German Emil Baerlocher for the position of Assessor, 4–28, 5:2

Seiter, Jos.: groom in wedding to Julie Friedrich in Morrison Bluff, 10–28, 7:2

Sieveries, Mr.: participant in on-going feud with *Die Staatszeitung*, which was alleged to have published a falsified letter under his name, 2–18, 5:3

Smedes, H.: Little Rock resident and delegate to the "Third State Assembly of the German-Catholic Aid Societies of Arkansas (German title under "Bakes, M.") held in Altus, 10–28, 7:4

Sminck, Frau (Mrs.) W.A.: wife of watchmaker in Little Rock who died in Toledo, Ohio of typhoid fever; her body was returned to Little Rock for burial, 9–2, 8:1

Smith, Dr. Perrin: geologist returning to state from Germany, where he received his doctoral degree, to conduct studies before moving to California, where he accepted a professorship at Stanford, 8–12, 8:2

Smythe, Father: officiant in wedding of Max Knobel to Fräulein (Miss) Carrick in Fort Smith, 12–2, 5:1

Solf, Mrs. Otto: storekeeper and intended victim of a counterfeit check scheme, 2–18, 2:5

Solf, Otto: baker whose employee accidentally shot another employee in the head while playing with a gun in the business; shooting victim not severely injured; editor reminded everyone not to play with guns, 3–17, 2:6

Spreck, Anna Gertrud: celebrating silver wedding anniversary to Joseph Spreck, 5–12, 8:1; published thank you note for attendance at celebration and gifts, 5–12, 8:2

Spreck, Joe (Joseph): celebrating silver wedding anniversary (wife's name not listed), 5–5, 8:3; second announcement with wife's name: Anna Gertrud, 5–12, 8:1; published thank you note for attendance at celebration and gifts, 5–12, 8:2

Spreck, Mary: bride in wedding to Fr. Langhammer in Little Rock, 2–18, 2:5

Speers, W.: scrip broker at German National Bank who recognized $4000 in stolen bonds from Woodruff case when J.L. Bay attempted to sell them, allegedly at Woodruff's request, 7–15, 5:2

Spieler, Emil: elected vice president of newly founded Democratic Club in Spielerville, 8–12, 5:1; delegate to the Third State Assembly of the German-Catholic Aid Societies of Arkansas (German title under "Bakes, M.") held in Altus and part of a five-member panel that decided that F. Krebs could not be seated as a delegate on behalf of the St. Joseph's Aid Society in Little Rock that had been dissolved by the bishop, 10–28, 7:4

Spitzenberger, Sam: officer of "Young Men's Independent Organization," 3–17, 3:1

Stahrl, Prof. J.: zither virtuoso who gave concert in Little Rock to benefit the church, 5–26, 8:2

Stemick (alternately as Stemmick), Wm.: Little Rock resident and secretary of the *St. Josephs Unterstützungs-Verein* (St. Joseph's Aid Society, chapter not specified) reported on the next meeting time, 4–28, 7:2; note that he invited via postcard all clubs in the state to send delegates to the celebration for the bishop, 6–23, 8:4; secretary of the new men's organization to replace the *St. Josephs Verein*, 7–7, 3:1; took part in military exercises as sergeant in the Eagle Battery and father of newborn 12 pound baby boy (mother's and child's names not given), 8–26, 8:1; writes that members should send in dues to the SJV, 9–30, 5:1, delegate to the Third State Assembly of the German-Catholic Aid Societies of Arkansas (German title under "Bakes, M.") held in Altus, 10–28, 7:4

Stern, Frau (Mrs.): woman leaving for a summer trip for restorative health reasons, 7–22, 8:2

Stern, M.: Little Rock resident planning trip to New York to procure new merchandise for his store, 8–19, 8:2

Steuer, Rev.: priest of the Roman Catholic Diocese of Little Rock assisting in the celebration of Bishop Edward Fitzgerald's jubilee, 1–28, 1:1

Stiefvater, Dom.: resident of Ft. Smith and part of a five-member panel at the Third State Assembly of the German-Catholic Aid Societies of Arkansas (German title under "Bakes, M.") held in Altus that decided that F. Krebs could not be seated as a delegate on behalf of the St. Joseph's Aid Society in Little Rock that had been dissolved by the bishop, 10–28, 7:4

Stiel, N.: gave speech at ball of "Young Men's Independent Organization," 3–17, 3:1

Stiesberg (alternately Stießberg), Joseph [*sic*]: president of St. Boniface chapter of Catholic Knights of America, 4–14, 2:3, mentioned by Jos. Limberg as a member of the Ft. Smith delegation to a statewide meeting, 9–23, 4:4

Stiesberg, Marg.: newly elected vice president of *Brüderschaft der christlichen Mütter* (Guild ("Brotherhood") of Christian Mothers) in Fort Smith, 4–14, 3:2

Stöcker, Augustin: new priest at Subiaco Abbey, 1–14, 2:1

Storthz, (no first name given): defendant in compensation case for $50,000;

alleged that he hit Howel in the face in such a way to make him lose an eye; altercation occurred in the office of Storthz's lawyer, since he and Howel were already engaged in another legal case against each other, 9–23, 5:2

Storthz, Frau (Mrs.): divorced woman who has requested a new trial, since she maintained her husband was granted the divorce based on false information, 9–30, 5:3

Strobel, Leop(old).: member of Logan County grand jury, 1–14, 2:1

Stutzer, Fr.: priest at St. Scholastica whose patron saint's day was celebrated, 9–2, 5:2; speaker at the *3te General-Versammlung der Jünglings-Vereine* (Third General Meeting of the Youth Organizations), 10–7, 5:2

Suters, J. B.: Swiss immigrant living in Conway who lost $1000 in uninsured property to arsonists, including stall with two donkeys, pigs, a buggy, a wagon, plows and dishes, 12–2, 5:1

Tell, Bernh(ard).: new priest at Subiaco Abbey, 1–14, 2:1

Tenkleve, Bernh(ard).: groom in wedding to Katharina Lensing at St. Scholastica on February 16, 2–25, 2:4

Thalheimer, B.: Little Rock resident involved in case in which former police chief Sanders was questioned by judges regarding $25 bail that B. Thalheimer paid on behalf of a man named Meyer; Thalheimer said he never received the bail back, but records showed that he did; part of larger case of deficit at city collector's office, 11–4, 8:1

Thalheimer, Sidney: Little Rock resident who returned from a business trip to Montana during which he bought a number of horses and mares for the local market, 11–4, 8:1

Theresa, Mutter (Mother): obituary for Reverend Mother of St. Anne Academy in Fort Smith; noted that she was born in Ireland as Mary Falwell and beloved by Catholics and Protestants alike because of her acts of charity; she was seventy-six years old and served as a nun for fifty of those years, 1–28, 2:1

Thienes, P. (alternately J. P.): resident of Conway elected vice president of Third State Assembly of the German-Catholic Aid Societies of Arkansas (German title under "Bakes, M.") held in Altus, 10–21, 5:2

Thienes, Peter: obituary, teacher born in Luxembourg, 2–4, 2:3

Thieß, Herr (Mr.): mentioned as father of child being baptized, no other information provided, 4–28, 8:2

Thomas, Fred.: organizer of marching contest in West End Park announced to readers; participants paid a fee to enter and winners received a portion of the money raised as well as medals and other prizes; marching took place every evening for four hours over seven days, 8–5, 8:2

Thompson, J. N.: Justice of the Peace in Logan County in slander case of

P. J. Jansen v. Frank Kinney, 4–14, 4:5; elected president of newly founded Democratic Club in Spielerville, 8–12, 5:1

Toler, Jordan: doorkeeper of the town hall in Little Rock, died after sixteen years on the job, 6–23, 8:1

Ulrich, Fr.: gave homily for novice induction in Pocahontas, 9–9, 5:1

Uptmor (alternately as Uptmore), B. A.: Fort Smith resident elected president of the *St. Josephs Unterstützungs-Verein* (St. Joseph's Aid Society), 8–5, 5:3; mentioned by Jos. Limberg as a member of the Fort Smith delegation to a statewide meeting, 9–23, 4:4

Urbani, Carl: father to new baby girl, wife's name and child's name not given, 8–5, 8:2

Van Buren, Friedrich: Swiss farmer in Dixie who served in the papal guard, celebration of silver wedding anniversary (wife's name not mentioned), 2–25, 2:1

Vogel, Fritz: mentioned as groom in upcoming wedding, bride's name not given, 4–28, 8:2

Vogel, Theodor: mentioned as groom in upcoming wedding, bride's name not given, 4–28, 8:2

Vogler, Theodore (same person as Theodor Vogel?): groom in wedding to Lydia Behnke on May 12, 5–12, 8:2, congratulated again by *Echo* but no occasion given (pregnancy?), 6–23, 8:2

Voß, E. J.: resident of Pine Bluff who was elected treasurer of the *Pine Bluff deutscher Gesang-Verein* (Pine Bluff German Singing Association), 10–14, 5:3

Wahl, Chas. F.: newly elected treasurer of the *St. Josephs Unterstützungs-Verein* (St. Joseph's Aid Society) in Paris, 4–28, 7:2

Wahl, Martin: thanked by Mathias Klein for invitation to his 57th birthday party, 7–7, 5:4; resident of Paris and delegate to the Third State Assembly of the German-Catholic Aid Societies of Arkansas (German title under "Bakes, M.") held in Altus, 11–11, 5:2

Walbe, John: resident of Logan County endorsing fellow German Emil Baerlocher for the position of Assessor, 4–28, 5:2

Walgenbach, Witwe (widow): resident of *Marienstadt* who lost all property in a tornado, 5–19, 7:2

Walter, H.: death notice, young man married to Carry Dreher, daughter of one of the oldest German settlers in Little Rock, 5–5, 8:1

Walter: family in Little Rock whose house caught fire as part of larger arson event, 10–14, 5:1

Wehrfritz, E. C.: founding member and first president of *Schützenverein* (Marksmen Club), 3–10, 2:4; workshop narrowly avoided being burned down by fire, 5–5, 8:1; referred to as "unser Maschinenbauer" (our mechanical engineer/engine fitter) and mentioned as part of delegation inspecting a

of the Northside Park; he was allegedly murdered by Simmons, a black employee of Mr. Wildberger who was said to have doubted his trustworthiness; *Echo* reported that he was well-known and liked and that after a jury indicted Simmons for murder, Simmons turned himself in to law enforcement for fear of lynching; a lynch mob did gather, but they were unsuccessful, 11–4, 8:2

Willems, P.: priest assigned to replace P. Heitzmann at Morrilton, 11–25, 5:2

Willmann, Joe: resident of Logan County endorsing fellow German Emil Baerlocher for the position of Assessor, 4–28, 5:2

Winetzky, Captain: marched in electoral victory parade of Democrats of Faulkner county, 11–18, 5:2

Witte, Jacques: store owner in Conway whose establishment was broken into; $30 taken from the safe, 12–16, 5:1

Wittenberg, Frank: father of newborn twins, a boy and a girl (wife's and babies' names not given), 9–9, 8:1

Wohlfahrt, Anton: Alexander resident who submitted an announcement on behalf of the *Deutscher Farmer-Club* (German Farmer Club) regarding a celebration of the harvest and Columbus Day, 10–14, 5:3

Wolf, Fr.: Morrilton resident celebrating his twenty-fifth wedding anniversary, wife's name not given, 3–3, 2:2

Wolf, Johann: member of St. Benedict's parish; elected vice president of the *3te General-Versammlung der Jünglings-Vereine* (Third General Meeting of the Youth Organizations), 10–7, 5:2

Wolters, Frau (Mrs.): encountered John Kaufmann during his recovery in Colorado, 9–9, 8:2

Wolters, Fred.: trustee and member of building committee for *Turnverein*, 3–17, 3:1

Wüst, Maria: bride in wedding to Lorenz Halter in St. Vincent, 10–28, 7:1

Yeakele, R(obert).: death notice, funeral of volunteer fireman, 2–4, 5:1; *Gazette* obituary of January 28 notes he was born in America.

Zeiher, Anna: one of the original settlers of the Maria Hilf colony; celebrating her silver wedding anniversary with husband, Jakob; from Switzerland and originally immigrated to Illinois, 5–12, 7:1

Zeiher, Jakob: one of the original settlers of the Maria Hilf colony; celebrating her silver wedding anniversary with wife, Anna; from Switzerland and originally immigrated to Illinois, 5–12, 7:1

Zeiner, Ida: twelve-year-old victim of sexual assault; suspect W. Waters taken to county jail to prevent a lynching, 3–10, 2:4

Zeisler, Herr (Mr.—possibly identical with next entry): Little Rock resident whose apartment and soda water factory were destroyed in fire in which arson was suspected; furniture could be saved, but equipment lost; much of the $12,000 in damages was to his property, and he had no insurance,

10–14, 5:1; correction that house he was living in was not his property, and the owners were insured by Murrell & Mizzell, 10–21, 8:4

Zeisler, Wm.: trustee and member of building committee for *Turnverein*, 3–17, 3:1; individual competition winner at *Turnfest* (gymnastics festival) in Hot Springs, 5–19, 6:4

Zeller, Geo.: resident of Paris, stopped by *Echo* office before traveling on to Memphis for business, 3–31, 2:5; resident of Logan County endorsing fellow German Emil Baerlocher for the position of Assessor, 4–28, 5:2

# NOTES

## Preface

1. All translations in this book are my own unless otherwise noted.
2. The newspaper technically began publishing in 1891; its first issue was a one-page affair that appeared on December 29 of that year. Thus, the first full-length issue was published in 1892, and 1892 is the first full year of the paper's publication.
3. Wittke, *German-Language Press*, 205.
4. Schuette, "Germans."
5. In this regard, the *Echo* editors participated in exactly the sort of constructed identity based on a common background that historian Kathleen Conzen describes generally in her work on German immigrants. See, for example, Conzen et al., "The Invention of Ethnicity: A Perspective from the U.S.A," *Journal of American Ethnic History* 12, no. 1 (1992): 3–41.
6. Schede, "'Gone,'" 477.
7. Similarly, several researchers of the German American press were apparently unaware of the existence of the *Echo*, although they do mention other Arkansas-based German-language newspapers, of which there are no extant copies. See, for example, Wittke, *German-Language Press*, 205; Arndt and Olson, *Die deutschsprachige Presse*, 2:357.
8. Wolfe, "Background," 381.
9. Allsopp, *History*, 382.
10. Huber, *Arkansas Echo*, i (first page of non-paginated introduction to the study).
11. Wittke, *German-Language Press*, 205.

## Chapter 1

1. Faust, *German Element*, 2:366.
2. Woods, *Mission and Memory*, 121; Dougan, *Community Diaries*, 180–81.
3. Schede, "German Heritage," 482.
4. Wolfe, "Background," 381–82.
5. Blaschke places the pinnacle of the German-American press in 1892–94; Bergquist, drawing on Wittke's data, in 1892–93; and Wittke himself between 1893 and 1894. Blaschke, "Communicating," 315; Bergquist, "German-American Press," 142; Wittke, *German-Language Press*, 208.
6. *N. W. Ayer & Son's American Newspaper Annual*. Excluding Louisiana, there were twenty-eight German newspapers and five other (three Spanish or Spanish/English, two Bohemian—all in Texas) among the southern states listed. Louisiana's foreign-language press was composed of twelve French or French/English papers, three German, two Italian or Italian/English, and one Spanish. Arndt and Olson discuss how Germans in America were far more likely to publish newspapers in

their own language compared to every other immigrant group. Arndt and Olson, *Die deutschsprachige Presse*, 2:126.

7. *N. W. Ayer & Son's American Newspaper Annual.*
8. *Arkansas Gazette*, September 8, 1891, 5. Much of the material in this chapter regarding the founding of *Das Arkansas Echo* first appeared in Condray, "Newspaper War." I thank the editor of the *Arkansas Historical Quarterly*, Dr. Patrick Williams, for his republication permission.
9. *Arkansas Gazette*, May 3, 1890, 4.
10. *Das Arkansas Echo*, September 30, 4:1. All references to editions of *Das Arkansas Echo* in this manuscript refer to the inaugural year of 1892, unless otherwise noted. Traditionally, only page numbers are given in notes referencing newspaper articles, but I have chosen to include column numbers as well for the *Echo* to aid researchers who might be unfamiliar with scanning large amounts of Fraktur. In this case, the first number refers to the page and the second to the column, here page 4, column 1.
11. Kehres, "Life," 44. I am grateful to Timothy Nutt for sharing this resource with me.
12. Assenmacher, *Place*, 161.
13. Kehres, "Life," 44.
14. "A $25,000 Damage Suit," *Arkansas Gazette*, September 6, 1891, 2. Apparently, a seventh director was considered for the incorporation, as twice in the paperwork, the word "seven" is crossed out and replaced with "six," but there is no evidence regarding the person's identity. Both Kehres and Mary Meurer state that Friedrich Hohenschutz shared editorial duties during the first year, when Meurer had to be out of the office to attempt to build a subscription base. It is impossible to tell which editorials were penned by which man and whether any were a joint effort, but editorials often reflect Meurer's general worldview regarding labor rights, which Kehres also discusses. Mary Meurer noted that Hohenschutz was Carl Meurer's father-in-law. Kehres, "Life," 44–45; "Interview with Mary Meurer," 5. Although no year was recorded, Timothy Nutt, who is a past president of the Arkansas Historical Association and who alerted me to this interview, judged the interview to have occurred sometime after 1973, since Ms. Meurer referenced the annexation of Mabelvale, which took place in this year. This oral interview should be regarded with care as a reliable source, however, as it contains multiple factual errors and problematic assertions.
15. Arkansas Echo Publishing Company, "Articles," 1–2; Arkansas Echo Publishing Company, "Form," 1; Arkansas Echo Publishing Company, "Certificate," 1. While the paper ceased publication in 1932 and the paperwork lists October 5, 1932, as the date of dissolution, Probst and Meurer did not actually file until April 23, 1934. Allsopp reports that the Arkansas Echo Publishing Company underwent a reorganization in 1901 in order to name August Probst as president and manager, but this change is not reflected in paperwork filed with the Secretary of State's office. Allsopp, *History*, 382.
16. This was not an uncommon model for the German-language press going all the way back to the colonial period, as noted by Bergquist: "Often the whole paper depended upon one man who could combine the printer's skills, German verbal abilities, and enough business sense to keep the paper alive" ("German-American Press," 132).

17. A Swiss teacher, Adolph Arnold, was one of his neighbors in the settlement and would later both help found the *Echo* and be a frequent advertiser in the paper. Kehres, "Life," 43. Meurer's daughter Mary asserted that his reason for immigrating was after hearing a recruitment speech by a member of the Holy Ghost order, a Catholic denomination that settled near Conway and about which Ken Barnes and James Woods have written extensively. "Interview with Mary Meurer," 3.
18. Kehres, "Life," 43–44.
19. *Echo*, January 7, 2:3.
20. *Echo*, January 7, 2:1; March 17, 4:1; March 24, 4:1; August 5, 4:1; October 28, 4:1.
21. Beck, "Conrad Elsken"; Dillard, *Statesmen*, 136–38.
22. Durning has further investigated Philip Dietzgen's career after he left the state of Arkansas, and it would seem that he indeed had a knack for creating strife: Durning, "Philip Dietzgen."
23. "Unser Geleitsbrief" (Our letter of introduction [i.e., letter of intent]), *Echo*, January 7, 1:1: "Es möchte wiederhallen in tausenden Herzen, Allen etwas Gutes, Belehrendes, und Unterhaltendes sagen, und mitwirken im geistigen Kampfe zur Lösung der großen Probleme der Menschheit." In a medieval custom, German rulers would issue a *Geleitsbrief* to merchants traveling abroad to assure others that they were reputable. The editors are vouching for themselves.
24. Schuette, "Strangers," 72; Dougan, *Community Diaries*, 85–86.
25. "Arkansas Volksblatt (German)," *N. W. Ayer & Son's American Newspaper Annual*, 32; "*Das Arkansas Echo* (German)," *N. W. Ayer & Son's American Newspaper Annual*, 34. This made the German weeklies costlier than their English-language competitors, which typically charged $1 for annual subscriptions (Dougan, *Community Diaries*, 100).
26. The title of this paper has been cited in various ways in scholarship: "*Staats-Zeitung*" (Dougan, *Community Diaries*, 180), "*Staats Zeitung*" (Dougan, *Community Diaries*, 181; numerous contemporary *Arkansas Gazette* and *Echo* articles), and "*Staates-Zeitung*" (Woods, *Mission and Memory*, 140). The masthead of the newspaper in 1916 read "*Staats-Zeitung*." The *Echo* refers to its competitor as the "Staatszeitung," which reflects the orthography most commonly used in the German American press (with a notable exception being the *Staats-Zeitung* of New York), since "state newspaper" was a frequently used title. I will use the *Echo*'s spelling (*Staatszeitung*) throughout for consistency's sake.
27. "Arkansas Staats Zeitung (Ger.)," *N. W. Ayer & Son's American Newspaper Annual*, 34.
28. For a detailed description of this rivalry, see Condray, "Newspaper War," 327–51.
29. *Echo*, December 31, 1891, 1. The German in the last phrase of the title is a dative singular, indicating that the creators regarded the political and social spheres as necessarily linked.
30. The German term *Schmerzenskind* is an older variant of *Sorgenkind*, which refers to a child who continually causes his parents concern or makes life difficult for the family. In this sense, the use of the term *Schmerzenskind* was prophetic, since the launching of a competing German-language newspaper would create legal and practical difficulties for the stockholders during the entire inaugural year.
31. The January 7 edition was four pages, while the editors managed six pages for the next three issues. The setters struggled with consistent page numbering in the first

month, occasionally forgetting to place any number at all, or using the wrong number after they had skipped a page. The January 28 edition was the first to feature a full eight pages.

32. "Vermischtes" (Miscellaneous), *Echo*, January 21, 6 (numbered as 4):3.
33. For a discussion of these types of newspapers, see: Wittke, *German-Language Press*, 188–96.
34. Ayer's newspaper directory has no entry for a newspaper titled *Arizona Kicker* from 1892, but Kirchhoff, in a publication from 1899, referred to it as a well-known *Witzblatt* or comic (satirical) paper. Kirchhoff, *Allerhand*, 150.
35. Wittke notes that the inclusion of fiction was a common feature in the German American press and served to separate these newspapers from their English-language counterparts (*German-Language Press*, 217). The custom was likely introduced from newspapers in Germany, which published serialized novels in the nineteenth century and which still regularly offer pieces of short fiction.
36. *Echo*, February 4, 5:3.
37. "Die Notiz" (The notice), *Echo*, September 9, 8:1.
38. J. L., letter to the editor, *Echo*, February 4, 5:3.
39. The article from the *Arkansas Volksblatt* was: "Indianergebiet" (Indian country), *Echo*, April 14, 2:4. The admonition against reprinting is found in: A. Kind, "Die Geschichte von Randolph County und seinem Hautplatze Pocahontas, mit besonderer Berücksichtigung der dortigen katholischen Gemeinde und der Einwanderung der Deutschen" (The history of Randolph County and its main settlement Pocahontas with special consideration of the Catholic parish there and the immigration of the Germans), *Echo*, September 9, 3:1; "Interview with Mary Meurer," 9.
40. Bergquist, "German-American Press," 144.
41. Wittke, *German-Language Press*, 213; Bergquist, "German-American Press," 141; Dougan, *Community Diaries*, 104–5.
42. Dougan, *Community Diaries*, 106.
43. "Arbeitstheilung und Zeitungs-Geschäft" (Division of labor and the newspaper business), *Echo*, March 17, 4:1.
44. *Echo*, December 9, 8:1.
45. "Die Grippe" (The flu), *Echo*, January 28, 5:2.
46. Wittke, *German-Language Press*, 225.
47. One could argue that having family portraits made was considered a necessity rather than a luxury good. Wittke discusses how German families nationally were willing to pay to send home daguerrotypes in the 1860s (*German-Language Press*, 225). Anecdotally, my own German immigrant grandfather, a custodian and farmer with eleven children, still managed to find the money for family photographs in the 1940s.
48. *Echo*, January 28, 5:6–7. "Diese Sparkasse gewährt eine gute und sichere Anlage für die Ersparniße von Eisenbahnbeamten und für Leute aus dem Handwerker- und Arbeiter-Stande. Wir wünschen Spareinlagen von Allen und versprechen jedem Kunden eine prompte und höfliche Bedienung."
49. *Echo*, January 21, 5:7; March 10, 2:5, 5:6.
50. Dougan, *Community Diaries*, 116.
51. *Echo*, March 17, 2:6; October 14, 5:6–7; October 7, 3:4; December 2, 2:5: "Zu den

außerordentlich niedrigen Preisen unserer Waaren geben wir einen Cash Coupon für den Dollarwerth Waaren, die bei uns gekauft werden. Für 20 dieser Cash Coupon zahlen wir einen Dollar baar [*sic*]."

52. *Echo*, December 30, 8:3.
53. *Echo*, May 8, 8:2; April 14, 2:3.
54. In 1919, circulation would increase to 2,800, a time when German-speakers sought a perspective on World War I from a publication that could access news reports directly from Germany ("Das Arkansas *Echo*," *N. W. Ayer & Son's American Newspaper Annual*, 1919). This is significantly higher than the figure of 1,300, which Michael Dougan reports as the *Echo*'s circulation at its height (*Community Diaries*, 182). However, it should be noted that Ayer's used self-reported circulation figures that could easily have been exaggerated.
55. *Echo*, January 28, 4:1.
56. *Echo*, December 16, 5:1.
57. In order of their publication, these stories were "Elsie" (based on an English story and adapted into German by Clara Rheinau, appeared in twelve issues), "Am Vorabend der Hochzeit" (On the eve of the wedding, eleven issues), "Laurel Vane. Eine amerikanische Erzählung" (Laurel Vane: an American story, nine issues), "Schwer gebüßt" (Heavily attoned for, five issues), "Beryl" (three issues), "Im Banne geheimer Mächte" (Under the spell of secret powers, twelve issues), and "Im Irrenhause" (In the insane asylum, one issue—beginning of the next serialized novel that continued into 1893).
58. "Unser Geleitsbrief" (Our letter of introduction [i.e., letter of intent]), *Echo*, January 7, 1:1.
59. "Editorielles" (Editorial items), *Echo*, February 4, 4:2.
60. Wellenreuther, *Citizens*, 13.
61. Dougan, *Community Diaries*, 52.
62. Dougan, *Community Diaries*, 122.
63. *Echo*, July 15, 5:2.
64. *Echo*, October 28, 4:1; November 25, 5:1.
65. *Echo*, December 2, 5:1; December 9, 5:2; July 7, 3:1. In spite of the *Echo*'s stated disdain for the practice of free sample issues, I did come across one edition from September 2 stamped "Frei-Exemplar" (free copy) on the first page of the issues I examined, which is additionally odd because the monks at Subiaco clearly had their own subscription. Subiaco Abbey, located in Paris, Arkansas, is a Benedictine monastery that was founded by Swiss clergy; German was the main language spoken at the abbey for years, and the order possesses a complete run of the *Echo*. Several issues were generously loaned to me for this research.
66. Matthias Bauer, letter to the editor, *Echo*, August 19, 5:2.
67. "Arbeitstheilung und Zeitungs-Geschäft" (Division of labor and the newspaper business), *Echo*, March 17, 4:1: "Diese Aufgabe besteht darin, den Geschäftsleuten und Farmern, welche neben den Berufsgeschäften ihren höheren Menschen- und Bürgerpflichten in dem allgemeinen Kampf um die Existenz leider zu wenig Zeit und Muße widmen können, über alle sozialen und politischen Fragen, wo ihr Interesse und ihre Mitwirkung in Betracht kommt, zuverlässige Auskunft zu geben."
68. *Echo*, June 9, 5:1.

69. Mary Meurer intimated that the *Echo* readers were perhaps more educated than the general German-speaking population: "The *Staatszeitung* they were not high class—they were just kind of rough, you know. I mean the men were not as well educated and they were, you know, and they were a lower class of people" ("Interview with Mary Meurer," 16). The *Echo* attacked the *Staatszeitung* in an editorial on September 16 for using "halbverdauten französischen Brocken" (half-digested hunks of French) to appear more erudite (8:2).
70. "Das Große Latinum" (The large Latin curriculum) was traditionally the seven years of Latin required prior to university study. This was not due to the influence of the Catholic Church but because the first German universities used Latin as the language of instruction. Knowledge of Latin was and continues to be regarded as necessary to scholarship.
71. Michael Dougan notes that Meurer was reported to be fluent in seven languages (*Community Diaries*, 181).
72. "Ein Beispiel" (An example), *Echo*, December 16, 4:2.
73. Severus, letter to the editor, *Echo*, August 12, 5:3.
74. Urian, letter to the editor, *Echo*, August 26, 5:4. *Urian* is an appellation for the devil used in Goethe's *Faust*.
75. Philipp Stein, "Mein Freund aus Sexta. Zu Zumpt's 100. Geburtstag" (My friend from the sixth grade. On the occasion of Zumpt's 100th birthday), *Echo*, April 21, 6:1.
76. "Gefälschte Kaffeebohnen" (Counterfeit coffee beans), *Echo*, January 21, 6:4; "Das Unrecht der Trusts und Monopole" (The injustice of trusts and monopolies), *Echo*, August 19, 4:2. The latter also admonishes Adam Smith with the Latin phrase "Salus publica summa lex esto!" (The common good should be the highest law).
77. "Woher kommt der Name 'Amerika'?" (Where does the name "Amerika" come from?), *Echo*, February 4, 5:4.
78. I discuss this larger conflict regarding the association's attempt to change Prohibition laws in Condray, "Newspaper War," 327–51.
79. Spottvogel, letter to the editor, *Echo*, August 5, 5:2. In a humorous narrative tradition dating back to the sixteenth century, the citizens of a small town (*die Schildbürger*) were renowned for their wisdom and routinely pestered by neighboring rulers for advice, to the extent that their own town could no longer function. To remedy this problem, they pretended to be absurdly stupid in the hope that they would no longer be consulted. In one famous tale, they constructed a city hall without windows, which they decided was not a problem, since they could simply capture the sunlight in buckets and carry it into the building. The citizens were so good at playing simpletons that they eventually became great fools in actuality.
80. "Shakespeare als Schauspieler" (Shakespeare as actor), *Echo*, June 2, 3:3; June 9, 6:1; "Bret Harte," July 7, 2:5.
81. *Echo*, March 17, 4:2, September 23, 2:1, August 5, 2:5, October 21, 2:2, October 28, 4:4, and December 16, 3:4.
82. *Echo*, June 16, 6:4; August 12, 2:1.
83. *Echo*, April 14, 1:7.
84. *Echo*, November 4, 2:3; January 7, 1:6; March 17, 2:1; March 24, 3:3; September 2, 1:7; February 11, 3:5; August 12, 5:5; July 29, 2:3.

85. *Echo*, July 15, 3:4; June 2, 4:3; June 4, 1:4; August 26, 3:4–5; October 21, 3:3.
86. *Echo*, March 17, 2:1; December 2, 8:2; July 29, 4:1; August 5, 4:1–2.
87. *Echo*, April 21, 4:3; February 18, 4:2; May 5, 6:5; May 19, 4:4. Meurer referred to Aquinas's seminal work simply as the *Summa*, assuming his readers would be familiar with it.
88. PWS, letter to the editor, February 25, 2:3. The letter writer was from Morrison Bluff and was addressing Goldfisch, a correspondent from Sweet Home.
89. These letter writers include Mathias Bauer from Argenta, P. Reiff from Atkins, J. Hubmann of Collegeville, Jos. Limberg of Fort Smith, F. W. Oberste of Hartmann, J. N. Thompson of Morrisson Bluff, Mathias Klein of Paris, and William Kuckartz of Emporia, Kansas. Dougan found that many correspondents for community papers in the nineteenth century simply used the name of their towns as a signifier (*Community Newspapers*, 123).
90. Der hinkende Bote, letter to the editor, *Echo*, November 4, 3:3.
91. Schede, "German Heritage," 179–480.
92. C.B., letter to the editor, *Echo*, May 5, 7:2.
93. Burkett, *Stuttgart, Arkansas*, 25.
94. LeMaster, *Corner*, 210, 212.
95. Durning, "Attracting," 8; LeMaster, *Corner*, 222–23; Frauenthal, "Max Frauenthal."
96. Whitsell, "Pike-Fletcher-Terry House."
97. Civis, letter to the editor, *Echo*, September 2, 5:1.
98. For more information, see Condray, "Newspaper War," 336–38.
99. "Was wir wollen" (What we want), *Echo*, April 28, 4:1.
100. "Subiaco-Abtei" (Subiaco Abbey), *Echo*, June 2, 1:4. Mary Meurer argued that her father was friends with German Protestants and Evangelicals in a concerted attempt to unify all German speakers, reasoning that Catholics would not be able to survive in isolation ("Interview with Mary Meurer," 11).
101. "Interview with Mary Meurer," 16.
102. *Echo*, July 15, 5:3.
103. Readers most interested in the preparations that immigrants made and what immigrants endured during the journey should read Kenneth Barnes's translation of Joseph Strub's *The Guiding Star*; as well as Gerstäcker's *Tagebuch*.
104. Wolfe, "Background," 158–59.
105. In German-language scholarship, there is an impression that the ability to buy land was not a pull factor in immigration to the American South. Willi Paul Adams argued that the South could not compete with the North either in terms of the land available through the Homestead Law of 1862 or the higher wages of large industrialized regions. Adams, *Deutsche*, 13.
106. Wolfe noted that the Little Rock and Fort Smith Railway targeted Germans specifically. He gave two separate dates for the high point of immigration, first 1883 and then the later date of 1885 ("Background," 259, 260, 357). LeMaster took a longer view and titled one of her chapters: "The German Migration: 1865–1930" (*Corner*, 51).
107. "Zu den Wahlen" (About the election), *Echo*, August 26, 4:2. Wolfe discussed how 1880–81 was a particularly difficult time for the immigrant community because of drought. This resulted in many settlers leaving, so that those who

stayed must have regarded themselves as survivors and felt a kinship with their adopted state ("Background," 364, 372).

108. Lucey, "History," 215.
109. Moneyhon, *Arkansas*, 42–43.
110. Lucey, "History," 215.
111. Wolfe, "Background," 354–56.
112. "Mit vereinten Kräften" (With unified strength), *Echo*, May 26, 6:4.
113. Wolfe, "Background," 357.
114. Arndt and Olson make the opposite argument, asserting that if not for the two world wars and the resultant backlash against German language and culture, there would still be a prominent German-speaking community in the United States today. To my knowledge, they are alone in this interpretation in existing scholarship (*Die deutschsprachige Presse*, 18–19).

## Chapter 2

1. *Echo*, October 21, 1:1: "Gut Heil der Einigkeit, der Ehre und dem Einfluße des Deutschthums! . . . Einigkeit macht stark! Die Deutschen sind in diesem Lande sehr in der Minderheit—aber Einigkeit kann ihnen den Einfluß und die Achtung unter ihren Mitbürgern der anderen Nationalitäten verschaffen, welche unerläßlich sind, damit das Deutschthum den Beruf erfülle, der ihm die Vorsehung zum Nutzen der Gesamtheit des amerikanischen Volkes bestimmt hat."
2. *Echo*, November 4, 3:2: "Vor fünfzig Jahren war eine derartige Feier noch nicht zu denken, denn es fehlte den eingewanderten Deutschen an dem erforderlichen Einheitsbewußtsein. Badenser und Oldenburger, Pommern und Baiern, Mecklenburger und Württemberger wollten von einander nichts wissen, denn die Idee eines einigen Deutschlands war ihnen nahezu verloren gegangen. . . . Seit der Gründung des neuen deutschen Reichs ist das anders geworden. Das Bewußtsein, der nämlichen Völkerfamilie anzugehören, ist in den Vordergrund getreten. Und in dem Maße, in dem neu auftauchende Know-nothings deutsche Erziehung, deutsche Sitte und deutsche Gemüthlichkeit verspotteten, schlossen sich die Bedrohten immer fester aneinander." Writers in the *Echo* use the term "Know-Nothings" for both adherents of the historical political movement and contemporary critics of immigration.
3. Wittke, *German-Language Press*, 200.
4. Bergquist, "German-American Press," 144.
5. Bergquist, "German-American Press," 139, 144. Faust (*German Element*, 2:199) and Wittke (*German-Language Press*, 2) make the same argument.
6. Faust, *German Element*, 2:366.
7. Wolfe, "Background," 384.
8. *Echo*, March 31, 2:6; May 12, 6:2. The original German of this traditional closing line is, "Und wenn sie nicht gestorben sind, leben sie noch heute."
9. Mühle, "Colonist Traditions," 38–39.
10. Hoerder, "Introduction," 4.
11. "Paraguay," *Echo*, September 23, 1:6; "Deutsch-Brasilier" (German-Brasilians), *Echo*, October 21, 3:1.
12. "Die anwachsende Hochfluth" (The rising flood), *Echo*, June 2, 1:4: "Denn in

Folge der schlechten Ernten und der theuren Lebensmittelpreise haben sich viele fleißige Familienhäupter drüben entschlossen, all ihr Eigenthum zu verkaufen und mit Sack und Pack hierher zu ziehen."

13. Watkins, "Efforts," 55.
14. *Echo*, March 24, 2:4; June 2, 1:4; A. H., letter to the editor, September 30, 4:4: "Nicht wahr, hier in unseren Bergen ist's schön. Und über den harten Anfang sind wir Alle hinaus. Aber noch ist Platz für viele Ansiedler hier, und unsere Colonie bekommt langsam Zuwachs. Und wer sich unter uns niederläßt, dem wollen wir gerne mit Rath und That beistehen."
15. Wolfe, "Background," 161.
16. Wolfe, "Background," 355; Lucey, "History," 215.
17. An example of this kind of exaggeration is found in Joseph Strub's 1880 publication, *Guiding Star For the St. Joseph Colony*. German author Friedrich Gerstäcker, who wrote about his experiences in territorial Arkansas, frequently disabuses would-be settlers of unrealistic expectations in his extremely large oeuvre. Kenneth Barnes's article "Don't Go to Arkansas" shows that the state's reputation abroad was perhaps not as bad as Kind feared.
18. *Echo*, June 16, 2:5. A. Kind's series on Randolph County appeared in the following issues: August 5, 2:3; September 9, 3:1; September 16, 3:1; November 18, 2:3.
19. *Echo*, March 10, 1:7; July 15, 2:3: "Die Mehrzahl der deutschen Einwanderer werden sehr schätzenswerthe Bürger. Sie bezahlen pünktlich ihre Steuern und sind gute Muster für die amerikanischen Farmer, und es wäre zu wünschen, daß deutsche Einwanderer über unsern ganzen Staat sich vertheilen möchten, damit alle Farmer Nutzen ziehen könnten von dem Beispiel ihres bewundernwerthen Fleißes, und ihrer Sparsamkeit." This is the translation provided by the *Echo*; the original English was not printed.
20. *Echo*, August 26, 5:1: "Der deutsche Name thut's nicht allein, wir verlangen deutsche Gesinnung. Renegaten sind stets die schlimmsten Feinde ihrer früheren Genossen."
21. J. L., letter to the editor, *Echo*, June 2, 7:4.
22. Father Thomas, letter to the editor, *Echo*, February 18, 3:1; "Die Eröffnung der Sisseton. u. Wahpeton-Reservation" (The opening of the Sisseton and Wahpeton reservation), April 21, 6:4.
23. *Echo*, December 8, 8:1: "Der Hexenmeister von der Wallstraße"; "Hüben und drüben" (On both sides), December 16, 4:1: "trügerische Tricks"; December 30, 5:2.
24. "(Eingesandt.) Der Seeschrecken auf den Auswanderer-Schiffen" ([Sent in.] The horrors at sea on the emigration ships), *Echo*, October 21, 2:1: "Kurz: das Zwischendeck ist ein Schweinstall, eine Räuberhöhle, eine Mördergrube, ein verpesteter Abgrund. Wahrlich: mich nimmt nur das Wunder, daß diese schwimmende Hölle nicht regelmäßig von den Fluthen verschlungen wird."
25. A. Geyer, "Eine Warnung für Einwanderer" (A warning for immigrants), *Echo*, July 22, 3:3.
26. "Landerwerb" (Land acquisition), *Echo*, May 19, 3:5; May 26, 6:4: "Und da der Mensch ein geselliges Lebewesen ist, so gehört hierzu, daß er mit den Nachbarn auch friedlich verkehren könne. Wenn er sich nun in die Mitte brutaler und diebischer Neger begibt, so würde ihm auch eine gute Ente oder ein aufblühender Viehstand Nichts nützen"; June 23, 1:7; "Klima" (Climate); July 15,

5:4; November 25, 8:3. A discussion of the different terms German speakers in Arkansas used to refer to black Arkansans is found in chapter 5.

27. *Echo*, February 11, 3:6, 1:3.
28. *Echo*, May 12, 6:3; June 9, 2:1; September 2, 1:6; December 16, 4:4.
29. *Echo*, December 30, 3:4.
30. *Echo*, June 30, 4:3, "Ernste Erinnerungen" (Serious reminders); October 14, 3:3; "Deutsche Tage" (German days), September 8, 8:4; July 7, 4:5; October 7, 4:3; April 14, 4:4–5; June 30, 6:6; September 2, 1:6. I have translated Cleveland's statement as the *Echo* reproduced it for German speakers rather than given the original quotation in English, which appeared in Cleveland's speech accepting the Democratic nomination: "Edelmüthige Gastfreundschaft, die eine unserer hervorragendsten nationalen Eigenthümlichkeiten ist, bewegt uns, die redlichen und fleißigen Söhne aller Länder als Miteinwohner und künftige Mitbürger zu bewillkommen."
31. *Echo*, May 12, 7:3; June 30, 4:3; December 16, 4:4; June 30, 4:3; June 30, 7:2, "Der Deutschen Einfluß auf die Annahme der Unabhängigkeits-Erklärung" (The German influence on the acceptance of the Declaration of Independence); August 26, 2:4, "Der Beruf der Deutschen in Amerika" (The vocation of Germans in America), October 26, 4:2.
32. *Echo*, November 11, 1:2; "Unbegründete Furcht" (Unfounded fear), September 16, 1:6; "Lästig" (Cumbersome), September 23, 1:7; "Zurückhaltung" (Reticence), September 30, 1:7; December 30, 1:6: "Leider ist die Einwanderung aus Deutschland so gut wie abgeschnitten. Die Dampferlinien verkaufen keine Zwischendeckbillette mehr. Die wiedererwachende Cholera in Europa hat im Verein mit den nativistischen Bestrebungen, welche den Choleraschrecken benutzt hat, diese Maßregel verursacht."
33. "Die neue Anti-Chinesen Bill" (The new anti-Chinese bill), April 14, 4:4; "Vorsicht" (Caution), August 26, 1:6: "Denn wir sind der Ueberzeugung, dass die mongolische Rasse der kaukasische nicht verdrängen sollte, welche dies Land seit den Tagen des Columbus civilisiert hat. Die ungeheure Zahl der Bewohner China's bedrohte unsere Union; und wenn ein Theil der dort ansässigen vierhundert Millionen sich hierher wälzte, so war freilich Gefahr, daß ihr heidnisches Religionssystem, ihre niedrige Lebensanschauung und ihre corrupten Sitten wie eine verderbliche Fluth die aufsprossende Gesittung der Ver. Staaten bedecken würden."
34. *Echo*, June 30, 4:3: ". . . ihre geheime Gesellschaft droht Jeden zu ermorden, der ihrer Unsittlichkeit, u. dem Gelderwerb durch Lasterhöhlen in den Weg tritt."
35. Conzen et al., "Invention," 11.
36. "Einwendungen gegen die Tendenz des *Echos*" (Objections to the leaning of the *Echo*), *Echo*, February 18, 4:1: "Wir wiederholen, daß wir die gemeinsamen Interessen aller deutschen Bürger, ohne Unterschied des Bekenntnißes vertreten, um das Deutschthum durch Einigkeit zu derjenigen Geltung zu bringen, auf welche es durch seinen Antheil an der Cultur Amerika's Anspruch hat."
37. "Unbegründete Befürchtungen" (Ungrounded fears), *Echo*, October 14, 3:1.
38. "Was Volksstämmen Werth verleiht" (What confers worth to tribes), *Echo*, October 14, 8:4.
39. *Echo*, June 2, 4:1: "Indessen diesen Freveln vermag der deutsche Einfluß im Bunde mit verständigen englischen Mitbürgern noch einigermassen Einhalt zu thun."

40. This is not to say that the geographical area that would become Germany had not been witness to atrocities previously in its history; the Thirty Years War was a particularly horrific time for what are considered human rights abuses today. However, there was a common belief that this kind of barbarism was in the past. Attempting to make sense of what happened during the Third Reich was a national project that occupied leading intellectuals, artists, and every day citizens particularly in the decades following the war but which continues to this day, a process termed *Vergangenheitsbewältigung* (a difficult to translate noun that is most often rendered as "a coming to terms with the past").
41. "Was Volksstämmen Werth verleiht" (What confers worth to tribes), *Echo*, October 14, 8:4: "Ein Volksstamm, der zu irgend etwas gut sein soll, muß vor Allem an sich selbst glauben." The direct translation of *Volksstamm* is "tribe," but in American English, this word is most often associated with Native Americans. In German, it is also used to connotate a cohesive unit of people, who may or may not be defined by political or geographic borders.
42. This should not be confused with the movement referred to as "the Great Migration" of the twentieth century, but there were a significant number of black Arkansans interested in leaving the state in the aftermath of Reconstruction as part of the back-to-Africa movement, described by Ken Barnes in his excellent book on the subject (*Journey of Hope*). Many of those interested in leaving did not have the resources necessary to do so, but groups of black Arkansans were departing in enough numbers to attract the attention of both the English-speaking and German-speaking white press.
43. Arndt and Olson, *Die deutschsprachige Presse*, 16: "Was ist des Deutschen Vaterland? / So nenne mir das große Land! / So weit die deutsche Zunge klingt / Und Gott im Himmel Lieder singt, / Das soll es sein! / Das, wackrer Deutscher, nenne dein!" The full text of the poem may be found in Arndt, "Des Deutschen Vaterland."
44. *Echo*, January 21, 2:1.
45. Wolfe, "Background," 367; Watkins, "Efforts," 56.
46. Wolfe, "Background," 368.
47. "A Scoundrel's Deed," *Echo*, December 31, 1891, 1:2; January 21, 2:1; April 7, 3:4; February 11, 2:5.
48. *Echo*, October 7, 4:1: "Auch unsere deutschen Mitbürger, welche der englischen Sprache mächtig genug sind, sich dort verständlich zu machen, sollten hinkommen"; September 2, 5:1.
49. "Interview with Mary Meurer," 9; *Echo*, June 16, 7:2; June 16, 8:1: "Englisch sprechende Mitbürger"; July 5, 2:2: "Ganz besonders waren die Amerikaner zahlreich, für viele Deutsche zu zahlreich, indem die Gemüthlichkeit darunter litt"; November 25, 3:1: ". . . sprachloses Staunen und Verwundern."
50. *Echo*, June 16, 7:2; September 30, 5:3.
51. *Echo*, January 21, 2:1; "Zur Pflege deutscher Sprache und Literatur" (On the nurturing of the German language and literature), May 5, 5:4; "Gegen das Amerikanisiren" (Against Americanization), April 21, 8:3; "Bewahrung berechtigter Eigenthümlichkeit" (Protection of legitimate singularity), July 7, 3:5.
52. "Im Kampfe" (In the fight), *Echo*, May 12, 5:4: "Nur Dummköpfe, die noch unter der Linie der Neger stehen, lassen sich dasselbe wegnehmen. Denn was Sambo in der Knechtschaft hier aufgab, war doch nur ein barbarisches

Kauderwelsch, ein literarischer Stütze entbehrendes Hottentottengeschnalz. Ein Deutschamerikaner dagegen, der das Beispiel jener, unter der Peitsche sich krümmenden Sklaven nachahmt, opfert den reichsten Schatz geistiger Güter, den die Vorsehung irgend einem Volke der Erde gegeben hat." Similar racist language is found in the article "Eine ernste Mahnung" (A serious admonition), June 16, 1:5.

53. "Geschichtliche Vorbilder" (Historic examples), *Echo*, August 19, 1:6.
54. *Echo*, March 3, 6:3.
55. *Echo*, October 28, 4:2: "Nun sind aber die aus Deutschland eingewanderten freien Männer mit den aus Afrika importirten Negersklaven keineswegs auf eine Linie zu stellen. Vielmehr sind die Träger einer Cultur, die älter und kostbarer ist als die hier übliche puritanische."
56. Severus, letter to the editor, *Echo*, November 25, 3:1: ". . . Amerikanern nachzulaufen, in dem verrückten Glauben, dadurch ständen sie eine Stufe höher in der Civilisation."
57. *Echo*, July 22, 2:2; Bergquist, "German-American Press," 145; Wittke, *German-Language Press*, 2.
58. Examples are taken in order from the following *Echo* articles: April 28, 8:4; September 2, 5:2; December 23, 8:1—both *Weihnachtscandy* and *Front-Thür*, December 9, 5:2; October 14, 4:3; February 25, 5:3; May 19, 8:2; November 18, 8:2; December 30, 8:2—both *Store* and *Calabuse*, and November 25, 5:1. In rendering the translation intelligible, I have substituted the German infinitive (*buhmen*) for the English gerund (booming), though the progressive does not exist in German. In the example of *Taxe*, the word was also given a German plural formation by the German writer. *Thür* is an older spelling of the modern orthography *Tür*. While Nazi propaganda would make discussions of the Aryan race synonymous with German, I would argue that the term *die weiße Race* is clearly one that Germans adopted from their white southern neighbors, taking the English word for "race" to preserve the context in which they heard it. In the example *Behäve dich doch*, the word *doch* is a flavoring particle that gives emphasis to the command but is not translated.
59. Wittke, *German-Language Press*, 200.
60. A. Kind, "Die Geschichte von Randolph County und seinem Hauptplatze Pocahontas, mit besonderer Berücksichtigung der dortigen katholischen Gemeinde und der Einwanderung der Deutschen" (The history of Randolph County and its main settlement Pocahontas with special consideration of the Catholic parish there and the immigration of the Germans), *Echo*, September 9, 3:1.
61. Wittke, *German-Language Press*, 27.
62. *Echo*, April 21, 5:4.
63. Wittke, *German-Language Press*, 223–24; Adams, *Deutsche*, 26.
64. *Echo*, September 2, 2:5.
65. Wolfe, "Background," 356.
66. *Arkansas Gazette*, March 1, 4:5.
67. Louis E. Brister, "Image," 340.
68. Schede, "German Heritage," 484.
69. Wolfe, "Background," 371.
70. Germanist Stefan Manz argues that this network of schools played a major role in developing a German consciousness, but German American schools were not a part of the programmatic thinking that viewed groups of Germans settling abroad

as part of the larger German Reich. This became especially important in the second half of the nineteenth century, as the German middle class desired that the new German state wield the power typical of colonial empires—a power Germany could not access, as it came very late to the acquisition of colonies. The German state could not exploit the resources of sovereign states where settlers landed, as would be possible with colonies, but Germany still enjoyed a larger international presence because of broad settlement. In Arkansas, this meant pride in German culture developed organically rather than having been imposed from outside by the Prussian state, which Catholic Germans would have been loath to accept in any case. For more on the role of German schools abroad see, Manz, *Constructing*.

71. "Schlichte Pflichterfüllung" (Simple fulfillment of duty), *Echo*, December 16, 8:2; "Das natürliche Erziehungsrecht der Eltern" (The natural right of parents to educate), March 24, 4:1; "Editorielles. Die öffentlichen Schulen und die deutschen Gemeindeschulen" (Editorial. The public schools and the German parochial schools), March 17, 3:3; "Deutsche und amerikanische Jugenderziehung" (German and American methods of child rearing), November 11, 4:2. C. W. Freund, "Bischof Spalding von Peoria" (Bishop Spalding of Peoria), July 29, 2:3; January 28, 4:1.
72. "Fur das '*Echo*'. Die heutige Erziehung vom Standpunkte der Religion und Vernunft betrachtet" (three-part series; For the *Echo*. Modern education regarded from the standpoint of religion and reason), *Echo*, May 19, 5:4; May 26, 5:2; June 2, 4:2; and "Die Conferenz der amerikanischen Erzbischöfe" (The conference of American archbishops), November 25, 4:4. Interestingly, the *Echo* also published a number of sensational crime stories from German-speaking Europe, but these were never interpreted as a reflection of poor European values, whereas true-crime stories from America almost always ended with a line denigrating American values.
73. Whayne et al., *Arkansas*, 212–213; Moneyhon, *Arkansas and the New South*, 11. "Amerikanische und fremde Schulen" (American and foreign schools), *Echo*, June 23, 4:3: "Uebrigens, wer die Landschulverhältnisse hier kennt, muß zugeben, daß selbe recht armseelig [*sic*] sind. Besonders herrscht Mangel an tüchtigen Lehrern"; July 29, 8:1; August 16, 8:2; August 12, 5:1; September 16, 8:3.
74. *Echo*, February 18, 3:2, April 7, 6:1; July 7, 4:3; "Lernet von den Feinden!" (Learn from the enemies), August 12, 2:2: "Um dies schmähliche Joch abzuschütteln, haben sich Tausende tapferer lutherischer Familienväter erhoben. Ebenso viele katholische Familienväter reichen ihnen die Hand. Wenn sie treu und unbeirrt durch verruchte Hetzer, zusammen stehen, wird der Sieg sicher nicht ausbleiben"; January 14, 1:2.
75. "Ein merkwürdiges Bekenntniß" (A strange admission), July 22, 3:3. For examples of articles in which the Democratic Party is portrayed as the defender of parental educational rights, see: February 18, 3:2; March 24, 3:4; July 7, 4:3; July 22, 3:3.
76. Wittke, *German-Language Press*, 134. Albert Faust, however, notes that many colonial German settlers were actually against the production and consumption of alcohol (*German Element*, 2:147). By the nineteenth century, Germans had come to view it as a matter of personal liberty.
77. Moneyhon, *Arkansas and the New South*, 119–120; *Echo*, May 12, 6:4; February 4, 5:2.
78. *Echo*, June 2, 7:4: "Mancher Deutsche im Staate denkt vielleicht: 'Das geht mich nichts an, wo ich wohne, kann ich Wein verkaufen so viel ich will!' Ich aber frage:

'Wie lange noch?' Schon die nächste Gesetzgebung kann Dir ein solches Gesetz aufhaften. Wenn Einer hier vor 4 Jahren gesagt hätte, daß wir keinen Wein mehr verkaufen dürfen, so hätte ihn ein Jeder ausgelacht."

79. Moneyhon, *Arkansas and the New South*, 120.
80. "Die Uebel Amerika's [*sic*]" (America's evils), *Echo*, June 30, 4:2.
81. "Freiheitsfeinde und Freiheitsfreunde" (Enemies of freedom and friends of freedom), *Echo*, May 12, 7:3: "Das ist eine, halb den Türken, halb den Russen abgelauschte Platform. Denn der Koran verbietet den Gebrauch geistiger Getränke und der Czar sucht die 'fremden Sprachen' zu Gunsten des alleinglücklichmachenden Russischen aus seinem Reich zu verdrängen. Freier Männer und freier Verfassungen aber ist eine solch tyrannische Mischung gänzlich unwürdig." I have translated *Mischung* (mixture, compound) here as *Einmischung* (meddling, interference), since the former makes little sense in the context, and I believe the editors intended to write the latter.
82. Johnson, *John Barleycorn Must Die*, 12–13.
83. *Echo*, February 25, 5:1; January 21, 1:7; "Unser Licenz System" (Our licensing system), February 11, 2:4; "Die Trunksucht und die Goldkur (Aus der Köln. Zeitung.)" (Dipsomania and the gold cure, from a newspaper in Cologne) January 14, 2:4; "Prohibition," January 21, 1:6: "Ob wohl deren Bürger [in Maine] ebenso roh und unerzogen waren, wie die wilden Indianer?—"
84. Geo. A., letter to the editor, *Echo*, January 21, 5 (paginated as 3):5: "Das heißt doch der uns guarantierten persönlichen Freiheit in die Suppe spucken."
85. Strub, *Leitstern*, 13: "Die Versuche, die bereits im Weinbau gemacht wurden, ergaben das beste Resultat, und kaum möchte ein Staat in der Union noch gefunden werden, der dieselben Vortheile aufzuweisen hätte; denn das milde Klima, welches eine neunmonatliche Vegetation nachzuweisen hat, welcher wiederum ein leichter milder Winter folgt, ist sicherlich dem Weinbau am günstigen und wird demselben eine große Zukunft in Arkansas gesichert sein." Translation from the German is my own. As Kenneth Barnes notes in his analysis, Strub was prone to hyperbole in many points regarding the advantages of settling in Arkansas.
86. *Echo*, January 14, 1:2–3: "Mais, Fleisch, Heu und Brodfrüchte (aber bei Leibe keinen Wein! Anmkg. d. Red.)" *Bei Leibe* is a mild oath that does not have a direct equivalent in English. Its etymological origin is *bei Lebensstrafe*, essentially, "on risking the penalty of life-long imprisonment."
87. "Das drei Meilen Gesetz auf den Weinverkauf angewandt" (The three-mile law applied to the sale of wine), *Echo*, January 21, 1:6.
88. *Echo*, September 30, 4:4; November 18, 8:2; September 30, 4:1.
89. "Alkohol als Medizin" (Alcohol as medicine), *Echo*, February 25, 2:5; "Alkohol mit Maaß und Übermaaß" (Alcohol with moderation and excess), February 11, 3:3; "Vom Alkohol" (On alcohol), November 25, 8:2.
90. *Echo*, January 14, 2:1; August 19, 5:2; September 2, 5:1, 5:3; March 17, 3:1: "Wir wollen die unzweideutige Erklärung, daß er anerkennt, daß das Produkt der Arbeit dem Arbeiter gehöre, und daß keine Gesetzgebung in der Welt das Recht habe, ihm zu verbieten, dieses Arbeitsprodukt in irgend einer Weise zu verwerthen"; February 19, 2:1: "Eine Conferenz von fanatischen Cranks"; August 19, 8:2.
91. *Echo*, July 29, 8:1. This is perhaps the Austrian Jew Morris Gerschner, who was a second-generation immigrant and who owned a saloon on Main Street. LeMaster, *Corner*, 141.

92. *Echo*, May 12, 7:2; June 2, 4:2; November 25, 5:2; December 2, 5:2.
93. James Woods relates an anecdote about a pastor in Logan County who was arrested alongside his congregants for celebrating the day of rest with beer and card-playing (*Mission and Memory*, 127).
94. Wolfe, "Background," 168.
95. *Echo*, February 25, 2:4; Severus, letter to the editor, *Echo*, August 12, 5:2: ". . . fast in jeder Nummer auf ungerechte und gehässige Angriffe gefaßt sein kann."
96. P. W. S., letter to the editor, *Echo*, February 25, 2:3: "Unser Wasserapostel sollen rein aus dem Häuschen sein und über die bösen Dutchmans schimpfen wie die Rohrspatzen." The German phrase *schimpfen wie die Rohrspatzen* is generally translated "ranting and raving," but I have chosen to keep the playful tone of the literal translation.
97. A. G., letter to the editor, *Echo*, January 7, 1:7; "Das drei Meilen Gesetz auf den Weinverkauf angewandt" (The three-mile law is applied to the selling of wine), January 21, 1:6: "Einzelne fanatische Methodisten und Baptisten würden freilich den Alcohol aus der Natur vertilgen, wenn sie könnten. Aber die meisten ihrer Anhänger schreien nur mit. Sobald sie aber einen Tropfen Geistiges erwischen können, sind sie dabei"; Spottvogel, letter to the editor, July 15, 2:4.
98. A. G., letter to the editor, *Echo*, January 7, 1:7: "Unsere Deutschen und die liberal gesinnten Amerikaner machen eine Gegenpetition"; "Editorielles" (Editorial), September 23, 4:1: "Es ist nutzlos, unseren Mitbürgern Schimpfwörter ins Gesicht zu schleudern, sie Mucker und Fanatiker zu nennen u.s.w. Damit können wir nichts bessern, wohl aber verschlimmern." *Mucker* can have the connotation of moral coward, but the *Echo* and its correspondents used it exclusively as a synonym for Methodists and others trying to implement prohibition. "Über die Weinbaupetition" (On the viniculture petition), December 2, 4:3.
99. For examples of these reader letters, see: June 16, 8:2; November 18, 5:2; December 9, 5:2; *Arkansas Gazette*, June 16, 1:6. The attempt to secure legislation to overturn Prohibition also played a major role in the 1892 newspaper war between the *Echo* and its rival, *Die Staatszeitung*. For this aspect of the story, see Condray, "Newspaper War."
100. *Echo*, December 16, 5:3.
101. *Echo*, November 25, 4:2: "Das '*Echo*' ist durch sein entschiedenes Eintreten für die Sache der Demokratie in den einflußreichsten Kreisen der künftigen demokratischen Regierung und Legislatur bekannt und geachtet. Und da die Redaktion selbst aus Farmern besteht, welche ein warmes Interesse für den Weinbau haben, so darf das '*Echo*' sich berufen fühlen, seine Dienste zur Förderung und Verbreitung einer Weinpetition den Vereinen von Arkansas anzubieten."
102. *Echo*, December 30, 1:2; Durning, "Attracting," 6.
103. *Echo*, December 2, 4:3; December 30, 1:2; November 25, 3:3; "Prohibition," January 21, 1:6.
104. Adams, *Deutsche*, 19.
105. Adams, *Deutsche*, 19; "Stimmung in der Schulfrage" (Sentiment in the school issue), *Echo*, March 3, 2:4: "Es ist erfreulich und ermuthigend, wie man trotz der übel berühmten Uneinigkeit unter uns Deutschen, bei denen gewöhnlich dreierlei Meinung ist, wo zwei miteinander über eine Sache berathen, in der Schulfrage allerorts die schönste Einigkeit findet."

## Chapter 3

1. For further information on the disputes between the Grays and the Greens, see especially Faust, *German Element*, 1:588–89.
2. See Kenneth Barnes's discussion of rural dissatisfaction in *Who Killed John Clayton*.
3. *Echo*, June 2, 8:3: "Divide et impera, theile und herrsche, das ist die Regel durch deren schlaue Handhabung zuerst die Römer und später die Franzosen die Deutschen durch ihre Zwietracht zu regieren suchten. So macht es noch heute ein gewisser Zeitungsmensch, welcher stets darauf bedacht ist Zwietracht unter den Deutschen zu stiften. . . . Auf diese Weise hat er es bis zum Pascha gebracht." A pasha was an officer's rank in the Turkish army; when used as an insult, it means someone who has an inflated sense of self.
4. Wolfe, "Background," 355.
5. Wolfe, "Background," 375.
6. Wolfe, "Background," 365.
7. Schuette, "Strangers," 117; Wolfe, "Background," 364.
8. Dougan, *Community Diaries*, 103.
9. Kehres, "Life," 43. Mary Meurer gives the impression that her father had more extensive farming experience than Kehres does, stating that "they were [on the farm outside Little Rock] several years" ("Interview with Mary Meurer," 1–2).
10. Wittke, *German-Language Press*, 27.
11. Wellenreuther, *Citizens*, 229, 243 (quotation).
12. "Die amerikanische Wirtschaft" (The American economy), *Echo*, February 4, 5:1.
13. *Echo*, January 21, 2:3; *Arkansas Gazette*, January 17, 2:3.
14. Watkins, "Efforts," 57; Freeman, "Immigration," 213; Wolfe, "Background," 156.
15. Wolfe, "Background," 383.
16. Willard B. Gatewood, "Arkansas Negroes," 299.
17. Jonathan Wolfe discusses how important it was for railroads to obtain quick cash from land sales and then to have ongoing customers who lived along the routes. He also notes that railroad lands were open to both domestic and international migrants, although he does not mention whether blacks would have been welcome ("Background," 256–59). Given Kenneth Barnes's work regarding the treatment of black migrants settling in the same areas of Arkansas, this seems unlikely.
18. P. R., letter to the editor, *Echo*, March 24, 3:1: "Bottomland wird dieses Jahr viel liegen bleiben, keiner will es mehr pachten, trotzdem die Landbarone es zu so liberalen Bedingungen anbieten, wie noch nie."
19. *Echo*, April 28, 2:6–7: "Eisenbahn-Landereien. Farmen und Heimstätten in Arkansas. Zwei Millionen Acker zu Ackerbau, Weiden und Obstbau, Wald u. Mineral-Land. Verkauft in Stücken nach Belieben des Käufers. Mildes Klima . . . Vielfältige Produkte. Geringe Preise—Mäßige Zinsen—Leichte Zahltermine. Karten und Circulare frei."
20. "Landerwerb" (Land acquisition), *Echo*, May 19, 3:5: "Diese letztere Art des Landerwerbs hat den Vortheil, daß man seiner Nachbarn einigermaßen sicher ist, während ein Deutscher, der irgendwo Bundesland belegt, bisweilen später entdeckt, daß er von Negern oder von nativistischen Squattern umgeben ist."
21. Wolfe, "Background," 361, 358.
22. Durning, "Attracting," 5, 7. The translation is Durning's.

23. *Echo*, June 2, 7:5.
24. Wellenreuther, *Citizens*, 54.
25. Father Thomas, letter to the editor, *Echo*, February 18, 3:1.
26. Spottvogel, letter to the editor, *Echo*, October 28, 7:1.
27. "Das Mortgage-Gesetz auf die zu ziehende Ernte" ([The effects of the] Mortgage law on the upcoming harvest), *Echo*, April 21, 4:4. "Ueber das ganze Land, an jedem Kreuzwege sind Stores, ich möchte sagen Fallen, die das Lebensblut aus dem arglosen Landbearbeiter saugen"; "Ohne Zweifel werden einige Leser sich noch erinnern, welch glänzendes Geschäft im Herbste 1868 gemacht wurde, als nach der Fehlernte von 1867 kein Kaufmann im Stande war, Credit zu geben irgend einem Farmer, welche auch ohne denselben eine reiche Ernte machten."
28. "Billiges Geld für die Farmer und Schutz gegen Wucher" (Cheap money for the farmers and protection against racketeers), *Echo*, March 31, 4:3: "Der Capitalist, welcher Geld an Farmer zu 10 Prozent ausleiht, weiß selbst recht wohl, daß dieser Zins von 10 Prozent in keinem gerechten Verhältnisse zu der Arbeit und Mühe des Farmers und zu deren Ertrag steht. Er weiß, daß der Farmer dabei tiefer in Schulden kommt und sein Eigenthum verliert. Kein Farmer kann 10 Prozent aus seiner Wirthschaft erschwingen." It should be noted that Germany historically also had a similarly oppressive system of peonage farming in which *Heuerleute* (hirelings) worked for landlords for the rights to live on the land and to have some small area to grow their own crops, but they did not share in the profits of the larger harvest or have access rights to gather wood or peat for heating material or to graze their animals. This system existed largely in northwest Germany, and scholars believe it contributed to the desire to emigrate among the hireling class, although most German settlers in Arkansas were not from this region. See Kamphoefner, "German Emigration," 23; Meyer, "In-Migration," 179–80.
29. Barnes, *Who Killed John Clayton?*, 51; Moneyhon, *Arkansas and the New South*, 63–64.
30. Moneyhon discusses a lack of credit available to farmers willing to attempt diversification (*Arkansas and the New South*, 69).
31. "Die deutsche Landwirthschaft im Gegensatze zu der amerikanischen" (German agriculture in comparison to American [agriculture]), *Echo*, February 11, 4:3: "Auch die in Arkansas seit 12 oder 14 Jahren aus Deutschland und der Schweiz eingewanderten Farmer haben die in der Heimat bewährte Tüchtigkeit und Intelligenz mit hierher gebracht. Viele derselben kommen aus Weingegenden und verstehen den Weinbau, welcher hier die bestlohnende Cultur sein würde, wenn dieselbe nicht durch Prohibition unterdrückt würde. Die Farmer in Arkansas haben mit ungewöhnlichen Schwierigkeiten zu kämpfen, gegen welche schwer anzukommen ist. Manche brave deutsche Familie war hier bei harter Arbeit großen Entbehrungen ausgesetzt und kam dabei noch in Schulden. Aber trotzdem ist nicht zu zweifeln, daß auch hier die Deutschen alle Schwierigkeiten überwinden werden."
32. "Die deutsche Landwirthschaft" (German agriculture), *Echo*, February 11, 4:3: "Andererseits wollen wir auch unseren amerikanischen Farmerkollegen kein Unrecht thun. In den nördlichen Staaten gibt es schon viele in hoher Cultur stehende Farmen und die landwirthschaftliche Abtheilung der Regierung zu Washington ist eifrig und erfolgreich bemüht, den Fortschritt zu fördern."
33. *Echo*, June 16, 7:5: "Zum Ziehen einer gemischten Ernte gehört ein geschulter

Bauer, der nicht bloß in den Tag hinein lebt, sondern der seine Zeit und sein Land einzutheilen weiß. Und das kann der Durchschnitts-Amerikaner heute noch nicht."

34. "Eine Versammlung von Cottonpflanzern in Memphis, Arkansas zahlreich vertreten" (A gathering of cotton planters in Memphis, Arkansas well represented), *Echo*, January 14, 1:2; "Zur Farmer-Frage" (On the farmer issue), *Echo*, January 21, 5 (paginated as 3):3; "Diese großen Plantagen, die jetzt nur einigen Tausend Negern ein kümmerliches Leben gewähren, würden, parzellirt, in den Händen deutscher Ansiedler der Glanzpunkt des Staates werden. Solange sie aber zum Baumwollenbau verwendet werden, kann der [*sic*] Überproduktion nicht gesteuert werden"; P. W. S., letter to the editor, *Echo*, January 28, 1892, 3:4.
35. *Echo*, February 11, 1:2. For a sampling of the articles on cotton production see: P. W. S., letter to the editor, February 25, 2:3; "Das Baumwollen-Problem" (The cotton problem), March 31, 2:3; April 14, 5:2; "Ein Herr H. Benner" (A Mr. H. Benner), April 28, 5:2; June 16, 7:5.
36. "(Eingesandt.) Zur Statistik über Farmprodukte" ([Sent in.] Regarding the statistics about farm products), *Echo*, May 5, 7:3: "Mein lieber Bauernbruder! Überlasse das Spekulieren den Kapitalisten. Pflanze Korn, Baumwolle, Weizen u.s.w. Sei getrost, Kleider und Brot braucht man immer. Hast du mehr Korn als du brauchst und kannst es nicht gut verkaufen, so gib's deinen Kühen, Hühnern und Schweinen. Da bringst du dann mehr Milch, Butter, Eier, Speck und gutes Schweinefleisch. Sei versichert, die Store-Keeper werden sich schon umsehen, wo sie die Farmprodukte anbringen können."
37. J. L., letter to the editor, *Echo*, March 17, 1892, 3:2. Regarding cotton production schedules, see Moneyhon, *Arkansas and the New South*, 10.
38. Faust, *German Element*, 2:29.
39. Moneyhon, *Arkansas and the New South*, 64.
40. *Echo*, February 25, 2:4.
41. *Echo*, February 25, 1:7.
42. Dioscorides, a Greek physician and author, was popular among German doctors of the time for his work *De Materia Medica*, which included alcoholic beverages among other natural remedies.
43. Chas. (Charles) Frings, "Die Behandlung der amerikanischen Weine. I. Einleitung" (The handling of American wines. I. Introduction), *Echo*, February 11, 4:2: "Bei den amerikanischen Weinen aber gilt das Sprichwort 'time is money!' ('Zeit ist Geld!')."
44. The further installments in this series, along with the technical details, can be found in: *Echo*, February 18, 4:4; February 25, 4:2–3; March 3, 4:2–3; March 10, 4:3; March 17, 4:5.
45. *Echo*, July 15, 5:4; September 16, 5:3–5; October 14, 3:5.
46. *Echo*, March 17, 3:1; March 31, 2:4; April 14, 5:1.
47. *Echo*, May 19, 7:5.
48. *Echo*, February 25, 2:4; April 28, 7:3; March 24, 3:1; June 30, 5:4; July 7, 2:5.
49. *Echo*, February 18, 2:4; February 25, 2:4, 4:3.
50. Freeman, "Immigration to Arkansas," 210; Schede, "German Heritage," 486; Desmarais, "Interview with Henry W. Young."
51. *Echo*, October 21, 5:1; H. D., letter to the editor, November 18, 5:3; December 23, 5:3; "Ein Aparat zum Enthülsen von Reis" (An apparatus to hull rice),

December 9, 4:4. Arkansas Germans were not the only ones who discovered rice was a good crop for the South. Faust mentions rice cultivation in Mississippi as an example of German immigrants willingly abandoning traditional agricultural practices to adapt to the local climate (*German Element,* 2:55).

52. N., letter to the editor, *Echo,* June 23, 7:4; Lucius, letter to the editor, August 4, 5:2; Severus, letter to the editor, August 12, 5:2: "Und in der That, unsere deutschen Farmer hier sind sämtlich ohne Ausnahme rührige und thätige Leute, welche Trägheit nicht kennen und die Hände nie müßig in den Schoß legen. Bet' und arbeit', Gott hilft allzeit, das ist ihr Grundsatz, und der ist Geldes werth."
53. *Echo,* July 15, 2:2; August 5, 5:1.
54. *Echo,* September 16, 8:2–3; September 30, 5:1; October 7, 4:4; November 11, 5:2; October 21, 2:3; December 9, 5:1; December 16, 5:1; December 23, 5:2; October 28, 5:4; December 2, 5:2.
55. *Echo,* May 12, 5:4; May 26, 7:1; June 23, 7:5; September 23, 2:2; October 14, 7:3; October 7, 1897, 3:3.
56. P. R., letter to the editor, *Echo,* March 24, 3:1: "Viele unserer Farmer gehen mit Wucht an die Hühnerzucht. Eine hiesige Firma hat letztes Jahr für $1,000 werth Eier und Hühner von hier verschickt, und sie sagt, daß sie dieses Jahr dreimal so viel wegschicken wolle."
57. *Echo,* 8:1: "Er lebt 8 Meilen westlich von der Stadt und ist seelenvergnügt und seines Erfolges sicher."
58. *Echo,* January 28, 2:2; December 16, 5:1; December 2, 5:2.
59. *Echo,* February 11, 5:2.
60. *Echo,* February 25, 2:4; March 17, 2:2.
61. *Echo,* September 23, 4:3; October 7, 4:4.
62. Hoerder, "Introduction," 5; Faust, *German Element,* 1:134; Jackson, "Migration in Duisburg," 157.
63. Barnes, *Who Killed John Clayton?,* 48.
64. Moneyhon, *Arkansas and the New South,* 7.
65. Barnes, *Who Killed John Clayton?,* 44.
66. *Echo,* February 25, 2:4. "Wie kann der Farmer in Arkansas den durch den niedrigen Cottonpreis entstandenen Ausfall in seiner Einnahme decken?"; "Den deutschen Farmern kann es nicht schwer fallen; sie sind daran gewöhnt die Lebensmittel der Familie selbst zu produziren. Diejenigen Farmer jedoch, welche bisher nur Cotton und Mais gebaut, und die meisten Lebensmittel im Store gekauft haben, wird es schwer fallen, sich den neuen Verhältnissen anzupassen. Aber dennoch ist es nothwendig."
67. *Echo,* May 5, 7:5.
68. Durning, "Attracting," 5. Translations are Durning's.
69. *Echo,* February 18, 2:7: "Futter und Getreide sowie alle Farmerprodukte werden in Commission verkauft" and 5:5: "Höchste Preise werden für Landproducte [*sic*] bezahlt." Commission rate mentioned in the February 25 issue, 2:1.
70. *Echo,* November 25, 5:1.
71. *Echo,* February 25, 2:1; Der hinkende Bote (The limping messenger), letter to the editor, November 4, 3:3; August 12, 5:1.
72. Civis, letter to the editor, *Echo,* September 2, 5:1: "Unsere Deutschen kommen alle gut voran; und das Erfreulichste ist, sie stürzen sich nicht Hals über Kopf in

Schulden, sondern ziehen alle Nahrungsmittel selbst, 'leben zu Hause und gehen in demselben Platze in die Kost.'"

73. *Echo,* December 9, 5:1: "Die andere ist schlimme Zeiten für die Farmer, welche keine Lebensbedürfnisse, für sich selbst gezogen haben, sondern sich nur auf ihre Baumwolle verließen. Viele kleinere Geschäfte werden falliren. Vorige Woche fallirten 10. Es ist das für unsere Farmer eine ernste Lehre zuerst den Hausbedarf an Lebensmitteln, und dann erst Producte für den Markt zu ziehen"; Moneyhon, *Arkansas and the New South*, 8.
74. *Echo,* January 28, 2:1; June 23, 5:3; March 24, 6:6–7; May 5, 8:2.
75. Moneyhon, *Arkansas and the New South*, 63.
76. *Echo,* March 24, 2:3; October 7, 3:4; April 28, 7:1.
77. Durning, "Attracting," 7. Meurer also claimed in this pamphlet that Americans got the idea to begin planting strawberries from German immigrants.
78. *Echo,* February 18, 5:1; March 10, 4:4; July 29, 5:4; July 22, 2:4; August 26, 8:2–4.
79. Moneyhon, *Arkansas and the New South*, 65; Barnes, *Who Killed John Clayton?*, 40.
80. *Echo,* February 11, 3:5, 5:1; June 9, 6:5; June 16, 7:3; October 21, 5:4; October 28, 8:4; May 26, 7:3; July 22, 2:4; April 28, 7:5; March 31, 2:3; February 25, 5:1; March 31, 5:1; April 21, 7:1; May 5, 7:4; May 19, 6:5; May 26, 7:5; July 22, 5:5; July 29, 5:5; June 9, 6:4.
81. "Gemeinnütziges" (Items for the common good), *Echo,* September 9, 5:4; September 2, 5:4; October 21, 5:3; October 28, 8:4; May 12, 7:4; June 2, 8:1.
82. "Gemeinnütziges" (Items for the common good), *Echo,* June 2, 8:1; June 16, 7:4; August 12, 5:5; March 17, 5:2; May 26, 7:2; March 24, 4:6.
83. *Echo,* February 11, 5:2; March 24, 4:5; April 28, 7:5; April 21, 7:4; March 17, 5:1; March 3, 5:1; September 16, 5:4. A broad note on baking practices in German-speaking countries: German culinary tradition has many varieties of bread and rolls that incorporate yeast, although strudel dough can be made with only water, flour, oil, and salt. Quick breads such as biscuits and cornmeal muffins would not have been a foreign concept. While some German desserts feature fresh fruit, they more closely resemble what Americans consider coffee cake; the German term is *Kuchen*. Sweet pie in the American sense (as opposed to savory pie) was not traditionally known in Germany. Desserts that alternate layers of a less dense cake and a filling, as Americans understand "frosted cakes," also exist and are referred to as *Torten*, but are generally held together with fillings made of cream, marzipan, or jelly, rather than American-style frosting.
84. *Echo*, March 24, 4:5: "Eine sparsame Hausfrau, die vorher überlegt, was gekocht werden soll, frägt [*sic*] zuerst immer: Was ist bei uns an Lebensmitteln vorhanden? . . . und versucht danach aus dem Vorhandenen gefunden, nahrhafte Speisen herzustellen. In einer Haushaltung aber, wo 'Volklauf' Küchenmeister ist, pflegt die alltägliche Frage zu sein: 'Was möchten wir mal essen? Nach welcher Speise (mag sie so kostspielig und schwer zu verschaffen sein, wie sie will) hätten wir gerade jetzt verlangen?'"; Sept. 16, 5:4; May 26, 7:3; June 23, 7:5; July 7, 3:3; September 9, 5:5; September 23, 5:4; June 16, 7:4; July 29, 5:4; September 2, 5:4; March 24, 4:5.
85. *Echo*, March 31, 4:5; May 12, 6:1; June 2, 8:1; June 9, 6:5.
86. *Echo*, May 12, 7:4; July 29, 5:4.
87. *Echo*, March 3, 5:1; October 14, 3:3–4; "Der Naphtolzucker" (Naphthol sugar), January 28, 4:4; "Mittel gegen Zahnschmerz" (Method for treating tooth pain),

March 3, 4:5; March 3, 5:1: "Der Mensch lebt von dem, was er verdaut, nicht von dem, was er ißt."

88. *Echo*, February 11, 3:1. Several German American papers bore the title of *Katholischer Hausfreund*, and it is not clear which is the reprint source. It seems likely that it is the Missouri-based publication.
89. *Echo*, December 16, 5:1.
90. "Die gekreuzigten Farmer" (The crucified farmers), *Echo*, August 12, 4:2.
91. "Das Börsenspiel mit dem Schweiße des Bauern" (The stock market game with the sweat of the farmer), *Echo*, November 4, 4:1; "Schlechte Zeiten" (Bad times), March 10, 4:2: "schnellen Anwachsen des Kapitals ohne Arbeit"; November 25, 1:7; "Geld, IV" (Money, part four of a series), April 14, 4:2–3; CB, letter to the editor, May 5, 7:2.
92. "Die gekreuzigten Farmer" (The crucified farmers), *Echo*, August 12, 4:2: "Vor Jahren wollte die Farmers Allianz helfen, und jetzt will die Volks-Partei helfen. Sie kann dem Farmer nur helfen, wenn sie machen kann, daß er mehr für seine Produkte bekommt, und weniger für das, was er nöthig hat, bezahlen muß"; "Sie drehen sich selber den Strick, womit man sie aufhängt"; and "Selten wird ein Stadtkind Farmer. Ja, die Jungen in der Stadt sehen mit einer gewissen Geringschätzung auf den Farmer herab. Und selbst ein Theil unserer Presse scheint oft geneigt zu sein, dem Farmer durchschnittlich weniger Verstand zuzusprechen als den Städtern, und in wegwerfender Weise von 'Landonkeln' zu sprechen."
93. "Das Nutzen des Schutzzolls" (The benefit of the protective tariff), *Echo*, September 30, 4:1–2: "Tarif-Reform ist die einzige Rettung für die Masse der amerikanischen Farmer."
94. *Echo*, May 19, 1:1; June 2, 3:2.
95. P. W. Sch., letter to the editor, *Echo*, June 9, 7:2; June 16, 2:4: "Gespart werden muß dieses Jahr, und den hier zu Lande aufgewachsenen Amerikanern wird das viel schwerer, als unseren Landsleuten"; "Schlechte und gute Jahre" (Bad and good years), June 9, 7:2.
96. Woods, *Mission*, 65.
97. Woods, *Mission*, 67.
98. Whayne et al., *Arkansas*, 176.
99. Wolfe, "Background," 365–66.
100. Wolfe, "Background," 355.
101. Woods, *Mission*, 86, 134, 58.
102. *Arkansas Gazette*, February 4, 5–6.
103. "Zum 25 jährigen Bischofs-Jubiläum des hochw'sten [hochwürdigsten] Bischofs von Little Rock" (On the twenty-fifth bishop's-anniversary of the reverend bishop of Little Rock), *Echo*, February 4, 1:1–6: "Das Land war verwüstet vom Kriege, und die republikanische Regierung machte große Fehler."
104. Spottvogel, letter to the editor, *Echo*, February 11, 2:3: "Ihr 'katholischen Heiligen', (wörtlich aus dem Schimpfregister der Staatszeitung) die Staatszeitung wird euch Mores lehren! Sie ist ja seit 14 Tagen katholischer wie ihr geworden."
105. *Echo*, November 18, 8:1: "Für die Diozese Little Rock wäre es ein schwerer Verlust, wenn sie ihren Bischof Fitzgerald, der sehr, sehr viel für sie gethan hat, verlieren würde."
106. "Interview with Mary Meurer," 8.

107. *Echo*, January 7, 1:6: “Wer nach Paris kommt, soll es nicht unterlassen, Cravens & Sohn zu besuchen. Sie freuen sich stets, ihre Freunde zu sehen, einerlei, ob sie kaufen oder nicht.” December 23, 8:2: “Herr Je[o]seph Schmeltzer, der beliebte Bartender Sol. Johl’s und einer unserer jungen strebsamen Deutschen ging schon lange mit dem Gedanken um selbstständig zu werden. Endlich hat sich die Gelegenheit gefunden. Er will mit Anfang des neuen Jahres an Markham und Scott Str. sein Glück versuchen, und den dortigen Warehouse Saloon dem Publikum eröffnen. Wir wünschen dem jungen Familienvater Glück in seinem Unternehmen, und bürgen dem Publikum im Voraus dafür, daß die Bedienung die Zuvorkommendste und die Getränke in ‘little Joe’s saloon’ die Besten sein werden.”
108. *Echo*, April 21, 8:1: “Früher, als John Drees sie führte, war sie ein beliebter Sammelpunkt für Deutsche und Sportsleute. Dann ging sie in die Hände von G. Britton über, welcher diese Woche an Tony Heibach ausverkaufte. Tony ist als strebsamer junger Mann bekannt u. beliebt und wird die Wirthschaft völlig neu einrichten, so daß man dort in aller Gemüthsruhe sich eins trinken kann.” It is unclear from the German whether *Sportsleute* (literally, “sports people”) refers to athletes or those who enjoy spectator sports.
109. *Echo*, April 29, 4:5; December 20, 4:6.
110. *Echo*, February 11, 2:1; June 23, 8:1: “Ein Clerk der Firma, Herr C. Hohenschutz spricht deutsch und wird auf Wunsch auch brieflich in deutscher Sprache Auskunft geben.”
111. *Echo*, February 11, 1:7; March 3, 2:5.
112. *Echo*, December 31, 1:3.
113. *Echo*, June 2, 8:4; July 15, 2:3, 2:2.
114. “Die Weltausstellung zu Chicago und die Präsidentenwahl” (The World Expo in Chicago and the presidential election), *Echo*, October 14, 4:2: “Als die 400-jährige Jubelfeier der Entdeckung Amerika’s durch Christoph Columbus soll sie den Culturfortschritt der ‘neuen Welt’ in den 400 Jahren seit die weiße Race von ihr Besitz genommen hat, veranschaulichen. Durch die bewunderenswerthen Leistungen dieser Cultur, die in der Ausstellung zur Anschauung der Besucher gebracht werden wird, dieselbe sich in der That zur edelsten und schönsten Verherrlichung des Andenkens des heldenmüthigen Seefahrers und Entdeckers der neuen Welt gestalten.”
115. *Echo*, February 25, 2:2; March 3, 2:5; Lucius, letter to the editor, May 19, 7:1; June 2, 7:4; June 23, 5:3; Severus, letter to the editor, November 25, 3:1: “Mächtig erschallten die Weisen unserer schönen, unvergänglichen Volkslieder durch die stille Nacht, welche den Deutschen hier in dem fernen gefühllosen Land neu aufleben lassen und den Amerikaner in sprachloses Staunen und Verwundern versetzten.”
116. *Echo*, March 3, 2:5; April 4, 5:4; April 21, 8:2; April 28, 5:2; June 16, 7:2.
117. *Echo*, June 23, 8:3; June 23, 8:1, 8:2; August 5, 8:2.
118. *Echo*, March 3, 2:4; March 10, 2:5; May 5, 8:1: “Das Maifest vereinigt das ganze Deutschtum von Stadt und Land.—Alles, was dasselbe von drüben an Gemüthlichkeit und deutscher Sitte mitgebracht, soll hier geltend gemacht werden“; “Um die Deutschen zu ehren, werden die Geschäftshäuser hiesiger Stadt am Maifeste ihre Thüren schließen, um ihren Angestellten die Theilnahme an diesem deutschen Feste gestatten zu können.” May 5, 6:6: “Für’s gesammte Deutschthum

und seine Freunde!" Decorating parade floats according to allegorical themes was a tradition in German-speaking Europe. A major plot point of Swiss author Gottfried Keller's nineteenth-century novella *Kleider machen Leute* (Clothes make the man) involves a costumed sleigh parade with accompanying costume ball.

119. *Echo*, June 2, 8:3: "unserer englisch sprechenden Mitbürger"; "eine Anerkennung des Deutschthums durch ihre zahlreiche Betheiligung."
120. *Verein* (plural: *Vereine*) can be translated in myriad ways. It can be rendered as "association," "club," "society," or "union," and I have translated it variously depending on what connotation is best understood by English speakers. The fundamental characteristic is that a Verein is a group of laypeople who have organized themselves around the interaction with or pursuit of a specific topic, purpose, or hobby.
121. *Echo*, March 31, 3:4: "—Neue Blüthen deutscher Vereinsmeierei: In Malstatt-Burbach ein Verein von Vereinsvorsitzenden, und in Auerbach i.B. sogar ein Schwiegermutterklub!"; "Geographische Erklärung" (Geographic explanation), May 12, 3:3.
122. "Vereins-Leben" (*Verein* life), *Echo*, January 21, 5 (numbered as 3):2.
123. Wittke, *German-Language Press*, 221, 279; Adams, *Deutsche im Schmelztiegel*, 18.
124. *Echo*, June 16, 2:4: "Wo bleiben die großartigen Pläne von der Staatsversammlung. Wollen sich die einzelnen Vereine denn gar nicht darum kümmern, daß ihr Plan ausgeführt wird? Die Herren-Präsidenten fordern wir auf, die Sache einmal in die Hand zu nehmen, damit Beiträge kommen, und wir weiter arbeiten können. Die Photographien von Kirchen, Schulen und Vereinshallen bitten wir uns mit den Beschreibungen einzusenden." *Herr-Präsident* is a term of respect, literally, "Mr. President," which I have nonetheless avoided here because it sounds odd in the plural in English. It is no doubt meant to balance the somewhat negative verb *fordern*, which can mean "to demand" as well as "to call for."
125. *Echo*, May 26, 5:4: "Vereine und Logen haben alle schöne Prinzipien auf dem Papier, aber leider wird in und durch dieselben oft so viel Unheil gestiftet durch Neidhammelei, sowie durch Intriguen kleiner Gernegroße, daß mancher anständige Mensch gezwungen wird, sich zurückzuziehen." The dog-in-the-manger concept of jealousy refers to a Greek fable and indicates an individual who does not want others to be allowed to benefit from something, even if he cannot use it himself.
126. *Echo*, January 14, 2:1; January 7, 1:7; February 4, 3:5.
127. *Echo*, February 11, 2:3; May 19, 7:2–4: "Constitution des Hillsdale gegenseitigen Schutzvereins gegen Feuer."
128. *Echo*, May 12, 6:3.
129. *Echo*, June 16, 8:2; July 7, 5:4; October 14, 5:2; September 30, 5:1; February 11, 1:7; January 21, 2:3.
130. *Echo*, June 23, 8:3; March 10, 2:4; August 12, 8:2; January 7, 1:7: "Und wenn es wieder heißt, 'An die Gewehre', So kämpft ihr tapfer für Columbia's [Amerikas] Ehre." The German name of the umbrella organization is *Der deutsche Kriegerbund von Nord-Amerika.* P. T., letter to the editor, September 2, 5:2: ". . . und die Deutschen im County furchtbar blamirt und noch vollends um das Bischen politischen Einfluß gebracht würden, dessen sie sich bisher noch erfreuten"; "Einigkeit, Alle für Einen und Einer für Alle."
131. Faust, *German Element*, 2:387; Wittke, *German-Language Press*, 60.

132. Wittke, *German-Language Press*, 109; Bungert, *Festkultur*, 78–81.
133. Wolfe, "Background," 166.
134. *Echo*, February 11, 1:7; May 12, 8:2; May 19, 6:4; December 23, 8:1. In German culture, December 26 is regarded as the *zweiter Weihnachtstag* (second Christmas day) and is usually spent visiting family and friends. A ball would have given attendees the chance to catch up with many acquaintances in one location, important for Germans living in rural areas of Arkansas.
135. *Echo*, January 14, 1:7; March 17, 3:1; June 2, 8:4; September 23, 5:2; October 21, 8:5; October 28, 8:2.
136. "Die Turn Halle ist abgebrannt" (Turner hall has burned down), *Echo*, February 12, 1914, 1:3–4; "Das Deutsche Heim" (The German home), *Echo*, April 9, 1914, 1:2–3.
137. "Das Turnen u. die Turnvereine" (Exercise and the gymnastics societies), *Echo*, May 5, 4:4: "Eintracht, Einfluß und Ehre"; "Der Materialismus aber ist die Lehre, nach welcher unsere Monopolisten und Geldfürsten es für erlaubt halten ihre Mitmenschen zu unterdrücken und zu ihren Sklaven zu machen, nach welcher die Sozialisten und Radikalen den Staat zum Tyrannen Aller machen und die Anarchisten die Reichen mit Dynamit vernichten wollen. Es steht nun bei den Turnern, sich wie Herkules am Scheidewegen zu entscheiden, ob sie den Verlockungen der trügerischen Lehre des Materialismus dem Gegensatz und Todfeind des deutschen Geistes folgen, oder sich als deutsche Männer auf die Seite der Gerechtigkeit stellen wollen, welche der Arbeit ihre Ehre und gebührenden Lohn gewährt und die Unterdrückung des schwächeren Mitmenschen verbietet. Die Gerechtigkeit aber beruht einzig auf dem natürlichen Rechte, aus welchem unsere Vorväter das alt deutsche Recht schöpften und welches übereinstimmt mit den Grundwahrheiten des Christentums"; May 12, 8:2: "Wir glauben kaum, daß die Turner ein derartiges Wuthgeheul billigen. Es ist gar kein Grund dazu vorhanden."
138. *Echo*, April 14, 3:2; J. H. K., letter to the editor, June 9, 7:1; January 28, 3:2. *Maria, hilf* is a simple invocation that translates literally as "Mary, help." It is used in the name of various religious organizations.
139. Wolfe, "Background," 370. Wolfe gives this version of the state collective organization: Deutsch Römisch Katholisch Staatsverband von Arkansas, which is missing adjective endings, and translates it as "German Roman State Union of Arkansas," inadvertently omitting the "Catholic" in the title. In any case, the *Echo* published news from both the national organization and the state level organizers under the abbreviation DRKCV and did not mention the DRKSA, which might be a later version of the organization's name. The *Echo* printed the name variously as "Deutscher" and "Deutsch," without the adjective ending.
140. *Echo*, January 21, 5 (paginated as 3):5 : "Eine solche Theilnahme aber hat doppelten Zweck: 1. soll dem Kirchenfürsten die gebührende Ehre erwiesen werden, und die Vereine sollen zeigen, daß sie wissen, was dem Bischofe gebührt. 2. Die Vereine bekunden dadurch ihre Stärke, Blüthe, und Einigkeit, und zeigen daß sie ein Faktor sind, mit dem man rechnen muß." A full account of the St. Joseph Verein incident is given in Condray, "Bloody German Language Newspaper War," 327–51.
141. *Echo*, January 21, 2:3; January 28, 3:2; February 11, 1:7; April 14, 5:4; August 26, 8:2; April 7, 4:5; October 14, 5:3.

142. *Echo*, April 7, 4:5; May 12, 7:3; June 2, 3:2.
143. *Echo*, September 2, 8:1; July 29, 8:1; March 10, 2:5; March 17, 3:1; September 30, 5:2; Woods, *Mission and Memory*, 114.
144. LeMaster, *Corner*, 52–56.
145. Wolfe, "Background," 372.
146. *Echo*, January 14, 2:1. In the Anton Schmeden case discussed earlier in this chapter, the editor uses the German word *Mahnung*, which has a much stronger connotation than simple encouragement to buy an insurance policy. It is a warning that can result in dire consequences if not heeded, which would indeed have been the case for families who lost their heads of household and had no way of replacing income in the short term without a payout. February 25, 2:2: "Edle Menschenfreunde werden gebeten, sich der schwer leidenden Familie anzunehmen"; March 3, 2:6: "Der durch die Krankheit seiner Frau in üble Lage versetzte Paul Masur bittet, ihn durch Arbeitgeben zu unterstützen. Er hat seinen Expreßwagen an 2. und Louisiana Str"; September 9, 4:4: "Die Familie stammt aus Böhmen, und kam von Cincinnati um sich hier anzusiedeln. Sie ließen sich auf einer Heimstätte 6 Meilen von Argenta nieder. Das Land ist schlecht, und 4 Personen der Familie erkrankten um Typhus. Der Vater u. zwei Kinder sind noch gesund, aber völlig mittellos. Sie haben von Kornbrot gelebt, und die Mutter ist gestorben. Edle Menschen werden gebeten die an Allem nothleide[n]de Familie zu unterstützen."
147. Goldfisch, letter to the editor, *Echo*, April 7, 4:4; May 12, 6:4; G. B., letter to the editor, May 19, 7:1. G.B. and the editor both refer to the St. Joseph Colony as *Marienstadt* (City of Mary) and distinguish it from the town of Morrilton proper. For more on the St. Joseph Colony, see Metrailer, "St. Joseph Colony."
148. *Echo*, May 26, 2:4. This is perhaps the same Louis Blass discussed as a president of the B'nai Israel by Carolyn LeMaster (*Corner*, 65). It would not be unusual for these men, a Jew and a Catholic, to be working together on this campaign, since according to LeMaster, Lafferty married into the prominent Jewish family of Jett (474). Gus Blass and Jack Blass were both advertisers in the *Echo*: June 2, 8:4; May 26, 7:1; June 2, 3:1.
149. *Echo*, June 2, 8:3; J. L., letter to the editor, June 2, 7:4.
150. "Fur unsere Damen" (For our ladies), *Echo*, March 24, 5:3; April 14, 5:4; "Für die Hausfrau" (For the housewife), September 30, 3:4.
151. *Echo*, February 11, 5:2: "'Natürlich ein Junggeselle, dem das passirt!' rufen unsere verheirateten Leserinnen aus, denn welche Frau würde nicht sofort die ersten loßgelösten Stiche am Aermelfutter befestigen, wenn nur die lieben Ehemänner den Schaden gleich anzeigten."
152. Blaschke, "Communicating," 318–19.
153. Philipp Stein, "Mein Freund aus Sexta. Zu Zumpt's 100. Geburtstag" (My friend from the sixth grade. On the occasion of Zumpt's 100th birthday), *Echo*, April 21, 6:1: "Latein, meine Damen, ist nämlich nicht so einfach wie Französisch und Handarbeit"; October 7, 6:5: "Frauen brauchen oft zum Nichtsthun mehr Zeit, als Männer zur Arbeit"; December 2, 5:1; March 17, 3:2; August 5, 5:1.
154. *Echo*, August 12, 3:3.
155. "Ein Vergleich der amerikanischen u. deutschen Frauen" (A comparison of American and German women), *Echo*, December 9, 4:3: "Die Amerikanerinnen der sogenannten gebildeten Stände besitzen, in Folge ihrer verkehrten Erziehung,

durchgängig kein richtiges Verständniß für ihren weiblichen Beruf. Daher kommt ihr heftiges Streben und Verlangen nach Emanzipation d.h. nach Gleichstellung mit den Männern, nach dem Frauenstimmrecht und nach Betheiligung an den Geschäften der Männer in Politik, Gesetzgebung und Staatsverwaltung; deshalb fühlen sie sich berufen für den Prohibitionsschwindel zu agitiren und verschwenden viel Zeit an die Lektüre von Zeitungen und Romanen, oder betreiben selbst Schriftstellerei, während ihnen zur Erfüllung ihrer weiblichen Berufspflichten die nöthige Ausbildung oft gänzlich fehlt. Diese falsche Stellung der amerikanischen Frauenwelt bedeutet viel Unheil für die Familien und für die Nation. Denn die vom Schöpfer geschaffene Ordnung läßt sich nicht ungestraft umkehren. Es ist aber begreiflich, daß die von falschen Zielen mißleiteten Amerikanerinnen mit Geringschätzung auf die deutschen Frauen herabblicken, welche ihrem Beruf treu geblieben sind. Eine hochmüthige 'Lady' nannte sogar in einer Schrift die deutschen Frauen cooking animals (Kochthiere). Diesen verbildeten Amerikanerinnen zum Trotz, dürfen wir Deutsche mit gerechten Stolze auf die Berufstreue unserer Frauen blicken, welche ihr Glück darin finden als Gattinnen, Mütter u. Hausfrauen die Ihrigen glücklich zu machen und dem Vaterlande brave Töchter und wehrfähige Söhne heranzuziehen." The word *Beruf* in the first sentence can also be translated as "occupation" or "profession," which could intimate that women's roles as wives and mothers are to be pursued instead of a job in the marketplace. "Cooking animals" is provided in both English and German in the original text. The animosity between American and German women portrayed here is not reflected anywhere else in the newspaper's inaugural year.

156. For a discussion of Davidis, see Monika Goetsch, "Dir Ziehe Glück ins Haus," *Süddeutsche Zeitung*, December 15, 2017, https://www.sueddeutsche.de/leben/historie-dir-ziehe-glueck-ins-haus-1.3790093.
157. "Die Emancipation der Frauen" (The emancipation of women), *Echo*, March 17, 4:3: "Der Mann ist durch stärkere Körper und Geisteskräfte zum Herrschen geboren"; "Dazu hat der Schöpfer es mit den nöthigen Geistesanlagen ausgestattet, mit der liebevollen Sorge um den Gatten und die Kinder, für Bereitung der Speisen und der Kleidung und für die vielfachen kleinen Bedürfnisse der Familie. Ueber Allem aber liegt der guten Gattin der Erziehung der Kinder zu Religion und Gottesfurcht am Herzen."
158. "Ein Wort an junge Frauen" (A word to young women), *Echo*, September 30, 2:3: "Ihr werdet dann Euren Gatten mit dankbarem Herzen empfangen und seine aufopfernden Anstrengungen schätzen lernen, mit welchen er Euch ein gemüthliches Heim zu schaffen bemüht ist. Richtet Ihr Eure Ausgaben so ein, daß das Gemüth des Mannes nicht fortwährend von Nahrungssorgen bedrückt wird,—so wird seine treue Gehilfin das Glück des Hauses mehr als durch eitlen Glanz fördern." This article is written using the informal second person *ihr*, which is a pronoun directed toward multiple readers with whom the speaker has an informal and close relationship, and the effect is that of advice as though it were given by a family friend. May 19, 1:6; "Taktik der Frauen" (Tactic of women), November 18, 5:4.
159. "Der Beruf der Deutschen in Amerika" (The occupation of Germans in America), *Echo*, October 28, 4:2.
160. Wolfe, "Background," 373.
161. *Echo*, August 12, 3:3; Severus, letter to the editor, *Echo*, November 25, 3:1: "Wie im Allgemeinen der Fortbestand des Menschengeschlechtes durch gewisse

Factoren bedingt ist und in Ermangelung derselbe in Frage gestellt wird, so hängt auch die Zukunft reiner deutscher Ansiedelungen hier in Amerika von einigen Bestimmungen oder Bedingungen ab, ohne welche sie allmählich ihren ursprünglichen Character verlieren und in dem allgemeinen Menschengewühl der neuen Welt verschwinden und aufgehen wird. Denn wenn eine deutsche Gemeinde sich nicht angelegen sein läßt, unter einander zusammen zu halten, nicht darauf bedacht ist, ihre deutschen Gesinnungen, die guten, aus der alten Heimat mitgebrachten Eigenschaften zu bewahren und zu pflegen, kurz und gut ist ihr Augenmerk nicht dahin gerichtet, eine deutsche Jugend zu erziehen, dann ist sie zum mindestens [*sic*] in Frage gestellt u. das Saatkorn des Todes für das Deutschthum in der betreffenden Gemeinde ist gepflanzt und wird in der Folge für sie und ihre Nachkommen verderbliche Früchte zeitigen. Um dieses zu verhindern, ist es vor allen Dingen nöthig, daß die Deutschen Ehen unter ihren Landsleuten schließen und nicht viel mehr darauf ausgehen, Amerikanern nachzulaufen, in dem verrückten Glauben, dadurch ständen sie eine Stufe höher in der Civilisation." The reader should note that the phrase "pure German settlement" is not a reference, as became common parlance during the Third Reich, to someone being of "pure German blood." The writer means a pure German settlement in the sense that all of the inhabitants have a shared linguistic and cultural identity.

162. *Echo*, May 26, 5:3: "Sind die Misses auf die Ehe und auf die Männer so schlecht zu sprechen, weil sie keine haben wollen oder weil sie einfach keine bekommen können?"; March 24, 1:7: "Wenn jeder Mann und jedes Weib, die die andere Hälfte 'nicht mehr lieben', daß [*sic*] allein als genügenden Scheidungsgrund ansehen würden . . . . .wir brechen ab—die Perspektive ist zu . . . zu schrecklich"; September 23, 5:3, *Arkansas Gazette*, September 17, 6:1.

163. "Muttersegen" (Mother's blessing), *Echo*, May 26, 5:3; "Mutterliebe" (Mother's love), March 17, 3:4: "Größeres und Wichtigeres, als wir Mütter oft ahnen und glauben, ist in unsere schwachen Hände gelegt, nämlich die Heranbildung und Erziehung der Jugend, also des künftigen Menschengeschlechts." The most common translation for *schwach* is "weak." While I have chosen "lowly" to fit the context in the overall article, it is important to recognize this connotation as well.

164. "Der Penny," *Echo*, June 2, 5:2; "Vom Zahnen der Kinder" (On the teething of children), September 2, 2:1.

165. "Frauen und Frauen sind zweierlei" (Women and women are two different things), *Echo*, February 25, 3:2: "Bald machen sie als Temperenzhexen und Heulweiber sich in höchst unweiblicher Weise bemerkbar, bald spielen sie sich als Stimmrechtspriesterinnen auf, stecken unberufen die Nase in Politik und vernachlässigen Gatten und Kinder, Küche und Keller." *Weib* in general means woman, but it has a negative connotation in more recent history."Der Beruf der Deutschen in Amerika" (The calling of Germans in America), October 28, 4:2: "Die deutschen Frauen suchen und finden in ihrem weiblichen Berufe ihre höchste Ehre, sie wollen keine Einmischung in die Geschäfte der Männer, in Politik"; "Gut Heil der Einigkeit, der Ehre und dem Einfluße des Deutschthums!" (Good well-being to the unity, honor, and influence of Germandom), October 21, 1:1: "Hierin liegt das Geheimniß [*sic*] des deutschen Wesens, welches die sonst unverständliche Einigkeit der Deutschen erklärt, wo es gilt, die in diesem Lande so häufigen Frevel gegen die natürlichen Rechte, Prohibition, Frauenstimmen-Recht, Staats-Tyrannei, ungerechte Gesetze zu bekämpfen."

166. Dougan, "Arkansas Married."
167. Whayne et al., *Arkansas*, 291; Geo. A., letter to the editor, *Echo*, February 21, 5 (paginated as 3):5. Geo. A. used the German term *zu Grunde richten*, which conveys a sense of utterly wrecking something, i.e., tearing it down to the ground. July 22, 5:1; "Wochenrundschau" (Weekly roundup), January 28, 1:3; May 18, 1:5–6: "'Ich habe alle Aussicht, dann zur amerikanischen Wasser-Kaiserin gewählt zu werden'"; "elende hinterlistige Heuchlerbande"; *Arkansas Gazette*, July 1, 1:2.
168. "Ein Triumph des schönen Geschlechts auf politischem Gebiete wird aus Cheyenne in Wyoming gemeldet" (A triumph of the fair sex in the political area is reported from Cheyenne in Wyoming), *Echo*, May 19, 1:6; "Freie Gedanken" (Unfettered thoughts), May 19, 4:4: "Das Mädchen ist bei den Chinesen rechtlos, es wird nur als Ware erzogen und betrachtet. Der Mann kauft seine Frau. Damit ist sie aber auch sein volles, ganzes Eigenthum. Sie muß thun was ihr Gebieter will, und widersetzt sie sich, so kann er sie von den Polizeibehörden auspeitschen lassen. Ja er kann sie an einen Andern vermiethen, wie man ein Haus oder ein Pferd vermiethet."
169. *Echo*, July 22, 8:5; September 23, 2:4; October 7, 3:4; June 23, 8:2; *Arkansas Gazette*, March 29, 4:5.
170. Severus, letter to the editor, *Echo*, August 12, 5:2: "Wer behauptet, die Arbeit wäre eine Schande und Degradation des weiblichen Geschlechtes, der kann sich mit seinen Ansichten begraben lassen. Arbeit erniedrigt den Menschen nicht, sondern adelt ihn, und für sie sind wir alle geboren, nicht bloss das männliche Geschlecht." For dates and exact wording of these advertisements, see appendix 2.
171. *Echo*, April 14, 5:4: "Damen werden mir erlauben, sie zu informieren, daß ich vollständig ausgerüstet bin zur Anfertigung von Frühjahrs- und Sommer-Anzügen"; October 14, 5:1; LeMaster, *Corner*, 146.
172. *Echo*, June 23, 8:2: "In der Familie des H. Erber, dessen Frau das wohlbekannte City chop house führt, ist ein kleiner Junge gekommen.—Mutter und Kind sind wohl"; *Arkansas Gazette*, March 25, 4:4.
173. *Echo*, January 7, 4:6; Wellenreuther, *Citizens*, 76–77.
174. *Echo*, February 11, 5:2: "Warme Füße sind die erste Bedingung des Wohlbefindens"; July 22, 8:2.
175. Wellenreuther, *Citizens*, 288. Citations for patent medicine ads are found in appendix 2.
176. *Echo*, July 29, 8:2; December 2, 8:1: "Obwohl wir Doktoren genug haben, und zum Ueberfluß noch Patent Medizin-Männer herumziehen, die mit Tarabum und ihren Flaschen Blinde gehen und Lahmen sehen machen können, so gibt es immer noch Kurpfuscher. Ein Schwarzer H. Gray wurde am Donnerstag Morgen um $5 gestraft, weil er Medizin praktizirt hatte"; December 9, 8:1: "Eine electrische Batterie wurde angewandt, und der Blutumlauf kam wieder in Bewegung." There is no further information given regarding this method of revival.
177. Frost, "Epidemiology," 151; "Wochenrundschau" (Weekly roundup), *Echo*, January 21, 1:1; "Petersburg," January 28, 2:7; "Die Grippe" (The flu), January 28, 5:2.
178. N. Weny, "Die Grippe" (The flu), *Echo*, January 14, 2:2.
179. "Der kleine Levy" (The little Levy boy), *Echo*, February 11, 2:5; January 21, 2:3; April 28, 8:2; November 25, 5:1; November 25, 8:2; December 2, 5:2.

180. Letter to the editor, *Echo*, April 14, 3:2; April 21, 7:1; "Vergiftete Biß-Wunden" (Poisonous bite wounds), April 28, 4:3; September 16, 8:1.
181. *Echo*, January 14, 5:1: "Deshalb erziehen die Amerikaner so viele elende Sklaven ihrer Leidenschaften. . . . Nur eine bessere Erziehung ist ein sicheres Mittel nicht nur gegen Trunksucht, sondern gegen alle anderen Laster"; "Cigarrettenmißbrauch" (Abuse of cigarettes), February 25, 2:6.
182. "Einige Winke über Schlaf" (A few nods [tips] about sleep), *Echo*, February 11, 3:4; "Die Kleidung vom gesundheitlichen Standpunkt" (Clothing from a health standpoint), March 10, 6:1; "Rheumatismus, Fieber, Rippenfellentzündung, Husten, oder andere gefahrdrohende Krankheiten"; March 3, 5:1.
183. *Echo*, January 28, 4:5; February 11, 5:2; March 3, 5:1; March 17, 5:1; April 21, 7:4; May 27, 7:4; June 9, 6:5; August 19, 5:4.
184. *Echo*, January 28, 4:5; February 11, 5:2; March 3, 4:5; March 10, 5:2; March 17, 5:1; March 24, 4:7; March 31, 4:5; April 21, 7: 3–4; April 28, 7:4; May 26, 7:3–4; June 9, 6:5; June 30, 7:4; August 19, 5:5, 8:4; August 26, 8:3; September 16, 5:4; September 23, 5:4; October 21, 5:3–4; October 28, 8:4.
185. *Echo*, January 21, 6:4; February 18, 2:4; September 9, 8:2.
186. P. U., letter to the editor, *Echo*, March 10, 2:6: "Auch hier auf dem Lande kann es der Farmer mit Fleiß und Sparsamkeit noch zu Etwas bringen. Aber nicht blos in häuslicher auch in religiöser Beziehung wissen es dort die deutschen Leute leichter und besser zu machen"; Letter to the editor, March 24, 3:1; "Klein und rein" (Small and pure), March 24, 3:6: "Klein sei dein Geschäft, aber solid; klein dein Handel, aber ehrlich; klein dein Stand und Gewerbe, aber rechtschaffen; klein dein Haus, aber sauber und nicht verhypothecirt; klein dein Vermögen, aber nicht durch Schulden untergraben."

## Chapter 4

1. Huber, *Arkansas Echo*, i (unpaginated introduction).
2. Wolfe, "Background," 371. Wolfe includes this statement in the summary of his discussion of the St. Joseph Societies, but it seems intended to describe the German immigrant community generally.
3. Wolfe, "Background," 359, 361–62.
4. Whayne et al., *Arkansas*, 263; Moneyhon, *Arkansas and the New South*, 37.
5. *Echo*, July 22, 8:1.
6. *Echo*, January 14, 1:5; Manger, "John Casper Branner"; "Ein Zink Berg" (A zinc mountain), *Echo*, January 21, 2:2–4; "Der Erzreichthum von Montgommery [*sic*] County" (The ore riches of Montgomery County), *Echo*, April 7, 3:1.
7. *Echo*, April 7, 5:2; June 30, 5:3: "um die Petroleum-Quellen dort auszubeuten." The verb *ausbeuten* can also be used to mean extract in regard to natural resources, but the word itself carries a negative connotation indicative of wrongdoing. By comparison, another way to express the extraction of petroleum is to use the verb *gewinnen*, the base meaning of which is to win or gain. Given the editors' general attitudes toward the harmful excesses of American capitalism, I believe the word choice to be intentional. *Echo*, July 26, 5:1; October 14, 5:2; October 28, 5:3; November 11, 5:1; November 25, 5:1: "Logan County geht einem rapiden Auffschwung [*sic*] entgegen." Mentions of mining operations/companies can be

found here: August 26, 8:2; September 16, 8:1; October 28, 5:3; November 25, 5:1. Articles regarding coal are: January 28, 2:2: "Alle werden in Arkansas Arbeit finden und unser Kohlengeschäft in Aufschwung bringen"; July 22, 5:1; October 21, 5:1.

8. *Echo*, January 21, 1:3; March 17, 2:6; May 5, 8:2; June 23, 5:3; August 19, 5:2; December 16, 5:1; May 19, 6:4; December 23, 5:1–2; December 30, 5:2; January 21, 5 (paginated as 3):3; October 14, 5:2; October 21, 8:4; August 5, 5:1; December 2, 5:2: "Es heißt die Trust Co. machte es so überall, wo eine Oel-Mühle sei, die nicht zum Trust gehöre. Hier wird sie keinen Erfolg haben. Die Oel-Mühle hier hat Contracte mit fast allen Farmern im County für den Samen, und die Farmer wollen die hiesige Mühle im Gang halten."
9. *Echo*, January 28, 2:2; March 10, 2:5; April 21, 8:2; March 17, 3:1; June 30, 8:4; January 28, 2:2.
10. Teske, "MacArthur Park"; *Echo*, March 17, 2:6.
11. *Echo*, April 28, 8:2; May 5, 8:2; June 23, 8:2; August 26, 8:2; September 23, 5:2; October 28, 5:4; December 2, 8:2.
12. *Echo*, August 12, 8:2; August 19, 5:2; Ein alter Soldat, letter to the editor, August 26, 8:1.
13. *Echo*, May 19, 8:1; May 26, 8:2.
14. *Echo*, January 23, 2:3; February 19, 2:5; June 23, 8:2; September 23, 5:2; October 14, 5:1; January 14, 1:7; October 28, 8:2; November 4, 8:1–2; December 9, 8:2; April 21, 8:2; June 2, 3:4; November 4, 8:1; December 9, 8:2; April 28, 8:1; May 19, 8:1–2; January 14, 1:7; December 2, 8:2; December 9, 8:2.
15. *Echo*, March 31, 2:3; June 23, 5:3; December 6, 5:1; September 9, 4:4; November 25, 5:2. The *Echo* reported the Pine Bluff tax and Des Arc licensing fees as being levied against *Wirtschaften*, which can also mean restaurants, but is likely referring to pubs and saloons in this context.
16. *Echo*, January 7, 1:5: "Machen wir unsere deutschen Mitbürger auf den großen Vortheil aufmerksam, welchen diese Fluß-Correction Allen bringen wird. Hauptsächlich unseren Farmern und den Besitzern von Kohlenländereien im Arkansasthale wird die billige Wasserfracht zu Gute kommen, und viele Orte werden davon profitieren"; "Hoffen wir, daß das Werk zu Stande kommt"; January 28, 3:1; February 11,1:2, 1:7; March 24, 2:6; March 31, 2:4.
17. *Echo*, October 28,5:4; November 18, 8:2; November 25, 5:2: "Die Einwohner von Indien, China und Japan werden allmälich [*sic*] von dem vorwärtsschreitenden Geiste der westlichen Civilisation durchdrungen. Die Abgeschlossenheit, welche lange Jahre bis Annäherung europäischer Fortschritte zurückwies, giebt nach und nach dem Einflusse modernen Denkens nach. Gerechter und ehrenwerther Handel wird dem amerikanischen Verkehr die umfangreichen und werthvollen Märkte des Ostens öffnen"; "In dem werthvollen Preis sollte der kürzere Weg den Amerikanern ermöglichen, ihre europäischen Rivalen zu besiegen."
18. *Echo*, April 28, 5:3; May 19, 6:4: "Unsere Bürgerschaft wird den Deutschen diese hübsche Betheiligung hoch anrechnen"; April 21, 8:2; October 21, 8:4; December 23, 8:1; October 14, 5:2.
19. *Echo*, October 28, 7:2: "so recht in einer richtigen afrikanischen Sandwüste"; January 7, 1:5; August 12, 8:2: "Die Candidaten für das Amt des Gouverneurs sind alle drei für den Bau guter Straßen im Staate. Wird nun die nächste Legislatur über Mittel und Wege hiefür berathen oder ihre Zeit mit Unsinn vergeuden? Wir wollen sehen, und hoffen das Beste."

20. *Echo*, October 28, 8:1: "Dieser Wegebauplan mag gut sein, es kommt aber sehr auf die Ausführung an und in dieser Hinsicht haben wir mancherlei Bedenken. Besser und sicherer würde es uns scheinen, wenn zunächst der Staat mit Verwendung der Sträflinge begonnen hätte durchgehend Staatsstraßen zu bauen, an welche nach Wunsch und Bedürfnisse die Counties ihre Countystraßen anschließen und unter Gewährung von Staatsvorschüssen selbst ausbauen sollten."
21. *Echo*, July 22, 5:1; September 2, 5:3, 5:5; September 9, 4:4; August 12, 5:1; April 28, 8:2; December 23, 8:1; December 16, 5:1: "Die Bahn wird außerdem die Frachtpreise der Iron Mountain Bahn drücken, da sie eine Concurrenz-Bahn sein wird. Jedenfalls wird sie zum Aufschwunge des Staates und unserer Rosenstadt viel beitragen." Little Rock is often referred to as the "rose city" by the paper.
22. *Echo*, November 11, 8:2; Moneyhon, *Arkansas and the New South*, 27.
23. *Echo*, April 7, 5:2; October 28, 8:2; August 12, 8:1; December 30, 8:2.
24. Moneyhon, *Arkansas and the New South*, 84–85, 112.
25. *Echo*, August 5, 8:2, 8:3.
26. *Echo*, August 26, 8:2: "Die Kesselschmiede hatten eine Lohnerhöhung gefordert, weil Einzelnen von ihnen eine solche gegeben worden war. Da ihrem Begehren nicht willfahrt wurde, gingen sie an den Streik. Es wurde nun am Montag in der Versammlung die Sache erwogen, und erklärt, daß zu einem Streik kein genügender Grund vorgelegen habe, u. daß die Kesselschmiede übereilt gehandelt hätten. Alle Streiker kehrten zur Arbeit zurück."
27. *Echo*, December 23, 5:1: "Die Arbeiter dort waren unzufrieden, und versuchten die Sträflinge zu entfernen. Jedoch sie hatten keinen Erfolg. . . . Aerztliche Untersuchung der Todten stellte Arsenik-Vergiftung fest"; "Unterwegs starb noch ein Sträfling, und mehrere erkrankten. Die Fahrt war eine furchtbare, die Kranken ächzten und stöhnten von der Abfahrt bis zum Ende"; Gibson et al., *Abstract of Sanitary Reports*, 1–3; "Brought Back," *Arkansas Gazette*, December 21, 2:5.
28. *Echo*, April 14, 1:4: "Am 29. v. M. wurden in Fayette, Mo. in Gemäßheit des Vagabundengesetzes drei Neger verkauft"; ". . . die Deliquenten die ganze Zeit der ihnen auferlegten Strafe für ihre Ersteher unentgeltlich, für die bloße Nahrung arbeiten müssen."
29. *Echo*, July 22, 5:1; October 21, 5:1; September 30, 5:1; July 22, 5:1; July 29, 5:1; March 17, 2:5; December 30, 8:1; June 16, 8:2.
30. *Echo*, November 4, 8:1; July 29, 5:1; June 6, 8:2; July 29, 8:1; December 2, 5:1; March 17, 2:5; September 30, 5:2; October 21, 5:1; December 16, 8:1; September 23, 5:2.
31. *Echo*, February 25, 2:1; April 14, 5:2; April 7, 5:2; May 26, 8:1; December 23, 5:1; November 25, 5:1.
32. *Echo*, March 17, 2:7; November 25, 5:2: "Vom Thäter keine Spur"; December 30, 8:2; January 14, 1:6; January 21, 1:4; January 28, 3:1; March 10, 2:5; August 12, 8:2; October 21, 8:5; December 2, 5:2; December 16, 8:1: "Er war plötzlich angesprochen wurden, und zu Tode erschrocken, hatte aus Angst natürlich weit daneben geschossen, und lief in ein Haus und schloß die Thür. Die Polizisten folgten ihm, erlangten Einlaß und arretirten ihn."
33. *Echo*, May 5, 8:3; January 28, 3:1; November 11, 5:1; March 31, 2:3; April 28, 8:2; March 17, 2:5; September 9, 4:4; February 18, 5:3.
34. *Echo*, April 28, 8:1; July 22, 8:1; December 2, 5:1; December 30, 8:2; February 25, 1:7; October 14, 5:2.

35. *Echo*, January 21, 6 (paginated as 4):3; January 7, 1:7; March 17, 4:4: "Die Steuern müssen bis 10. April bezahlt werden. Nach dem 10. April kommt zu jedem Dollar Steuer 1/4 Dollar Strafe. Die Steuer-Umlage (Assessment machen) findet in der ersten Hälfte des Junis statt, und werden wir noch darauf aufmerksam machen"; June 2, 3:2; June 9, 2:4; June 30, 8:4; June 16, 8:2.
36. *Echo*, May 12, 8:1, December 23, 8:1–2, December 30, 8:1, July 29, 8:2.
37. *Echo*, May 5, 8:2., June 23, 8:3, and June 30, 8:4: "Die letztjährigen Dividenden waren gemeint und zwar hatten die erste Nationalbank und die Exchange Bank 2mal Dividenden erklärt, deren letzte am 1. Juni bezahlt wurden, während die Bank of Little Rock und die German Bank nur jährliche Dividenden erklärt hatten."
38. *Echo*, June 30, 8:4; November 11, 8:1; June 17, 8:2; May 19, 7:1: "Fässler und ein Amerikaner engl. Abkunft versuchten die Sache bei der Grand-Jury anhängig zu machen. Alle glaubten, daß der Sachverhalt wie oben erzählt wäre, aber mangelnder Beweise wegen mußte die Klage abgewiesen werden. (Es liegt darin eine Warnung für unsere Landsleute, erst sehen, ob die Beweise reichen, und dann klagen. Wir haben bei ehrenhaften Männern Erkundigungen über die Sache eingezogen, und würden geholfen haben, dem Manne zu seinem Recht zu verhelfen, wenn etwas zu machen wäre d.R.)."
39. *Echo*, December 23, 5:1: "Trotz der schlechten Ernte und der gedrückten Geschäfte ist die Hoffnung auf Besserung in der letzten Zeit sehr bestiegen. Neue Bahnen u. Fabriken werden im Staate gebaut, und das wird Arbeit und Verdienst geben."
40. *Echo*, March 24, 2:4; June 23, 8:1; September 9, 4:4; January 7, 1:6; October 21, 8:4; April 7, 1:3: "daß auch unser Staat würdig auf der Ausstellung vertreten ist." I would add that this quotation suggests the German settlers had internalized the infamous inferiority complex of the state's natives.
41. Lucey, "History of Immigration," 213. Eugene Weibel, quoted in *Echo*, December 16, 5:2: "Ich glaube an eine Zukunft des Staates Arkansas. Es ist nicht sowohl der Staat und das Land, welches die Leute macht, sondern umgekehrt sind es die Leute, welche den Staat machen. Gott sei Dank hat Arkansas in der deutschen Einwanderung einen gesunden lebenskräftigen Kern erhalten, der sorgfältig gepflegt zum mächtigen Baum heranwachsen wird. Ich hoffe zuversichtlich, daß das '*Echo*' einstehen wird für die Gleichberechtigung der verschiedenen Nationen in kirchlicher Hinsicht, für die Rechte der Deutschen in Staat und Kirche, und die confessionelle Schule. (Das '*Echo*' wird voll und ganz dafür eintreten.)"
42. Wellenreuther, *Citizens*, 197, 220, 240; Bergquist, "German-American Press," 134–36, 141; Adams, *Deutsche*, 29; Kamphoefner, "Forum," 10–11.
43. Wittke, *German-Language Press*, 103–104; Wolfe, "Background," 166; Barnes, *Who Killed John Clayton?*, 46. Franklin's dissatisfaction with Germans' presence in the new nation is well-documented in many sources. Readers interested in reading Franklin's own words can easily access them here: Benjamin Franklin to Peter Collinson, May 9, 1753, Teaching American History, https://teachingamericanhistory.org/library/document/letter-to-peter-collinson.
44. "Interview with Mary Meurer," 16–17.
45. "Das Arkansas Echo (German)," *N. W. Ayer*, 34. "Arkansas Staats Zeitung (Ger.),"

*N. W. Ayer*, 34. "Editorielles: Einwendungen gegen die Tendenz des Echo" (Editorial content: objections against the slant of the Echo), *Echo*, February 18, 4:1: "Wahre Freiheit und Freisinnigkeit kann nur auf dem Boden des natürlichen Rechtes, welches mit den Grundwahrheiten des Christen- und Judenthums übereinstimmt, entspringen. . . . Viele, ja fast die Mehrzahl der Menschen wurden verblendet durch die Lügen unseres modernen Materialismus, unzugänglich für das Verständniß des natürlichen Rechtes, auf welchem die Freiheit der Nationen allein beruht. Thomas Jefferson, der hochgelehrte 3. Präsident der Ver. Staaten war ein begeisterter Kenner und Verehrer des natürlichen Rechtes und dabei galt er als ein sehr liberaler Mann. Und mit Recht! Denn die Quelle wahrer Freiheit war ihm bekannt und geheiligt. Er gründete daher auf den natürlichen Menschenrechten die demokratische Partei, auf deren Prinzipien noch heute die Zuversicht der besten und einsichtsvollsten Männer der demokratischen Partei beizustimmen. Auch das Echo zählt sich zu den Anhängern dieser Prinzipien, obwohl es sich nicht für verpflichtet hält, den Mißgriffen der demokratischen Partei beizustimmen. Wir halten uns also berechtigt, die unvereinbarlichen Vorwürfe, das Echo sei zu liberal oder zu wenig liberal, gleichmäßig zurückweisen zu dürfen."

46. *Echo*, July 15, 5:3; June 23, 4:2: "Die Platform unseres Staatsconvents hechelt zuerst die republikanische Verwaltung ordentlich durch." The italics in the English translation are added. The verb *hecheln* is more often used to mean to pant like a dog or to comb through flax, but the context here would indicate it is being used in a hybridized American sense more akin to the verb "to heckle." September 16, 8:1: "Unser ganzes County Ticket ist erwählt." Emphasis mine. November 18, 5:2: "Dasselbe darf auch das '*Echo*' in Bezug seiner Arbeit für die demokratische Partei sagen."
47. Wittke, *German-Language Press*, 134; "Deutsche Tage" (German days), *Echo*, September 9, 8:2: "Unter Republikanern wie Demokraten gibt es Fanatiker, die der europäischen Einwanderung den Garaus machen wollen. Wenn nun einem solchen nativistischen Kandidaten ein verständiger und im edelsten Sinne Freigesinnter gegenübertritt, so wird der Amerikaner deutscher Abkunft dem letzteren sicher den Vorzug geben." P. J., letter to the editor, August 26, 5:2.
48. G. H., letter to the editor, *Echo*, September 2, 5:2: "Und Meyer ist wieder auf demokratischen [*sic*] Ticket. Sollen wir wieder für ihn stimmen?"; April 5, 6:3.
49. S. P., letter to the editor, *Echo*, August 19, 5:2: "Ich bin kein Politikus, möchte aber unter den hohen Staatsbeamten auch einen deutschen Mann sehen, der anerkennt, daß wir Deutsche auch Steuern zahlen, und daher zu etwas mehr berechtigt sind, als bloß zum zahlen und arbeiten. . . . Man hat den Deutschen so oft schöne Versprechungen gemacht, und nachher den einzelnen Counties infame Prohibitions-Gesetze aufgehalst, daß sie jetzt einmal einmüthig für einen guten tüchtigen Deutschen stimmen sollten, der uns Respekt verschaffen wird."
50. Civis, letter to the editor, *Echo*, August 26, 5:4; F. V., letter to the editor, September 2, 5:3: "Lassen wir uns alles dies ruhig gefallen?! Ich hoffe nicht!" Daniels, *Historical Report*, 91.
51. "Anarchistenwerk in den Wahlen" (The work of anarchists in the elections), *Echo*, September 16, 4:2: "wie er frei erklärte, als gut bezahlter, also beauftragter Wortführer der republikanischen Partei und Befürworter der Candidatur"

and "ein Ballen von mit Schund bedruckten Papier"; August 5, 8:1: "Es sind die Namen vieler als gute Bürger bekannter Männer auf dem Ticket."

52. "(Eingesandt.) Ob's geht?" ([Sent in.] Could it work?), *Echo*, March 24, 3:1: "Profit von unserm Schweiß und unserer Arbeit haben"; "Hans: 'Unsinn! Die Farmer leihen nur so viel Geld als sie schuldig sind; das Geld würde sofort in die Taschen der Capitalisten fließen, und die würden natürlich damit speculiren; so sagt das '*Echo*' und ich bin völlig damit einverstanden.'" The Farmer's Party organizers are referred to as *Groß-Mogul* in the German.

53. Barnes, *Who Killed John Clayton?*, 126; F. V., letter to the editor, *Echo*, September 2, 5:3: "Thatsache ist es, daß wir Deutsche von Arkansas uns wenig oder gar nicht um Politik kümmern. Wenigstens von einem vereinten Auftreten der Deutschen hört man sehr selten"; "Deutsche Tage" (German days), September 9, 8:2: "Der Gegensatz zwischen Demokraten und Republikanern sei zu scharf, als daß er in solcher Weise überbrückt werden könnte. Allein so sicher ist es, daß der deutsch-amerikanische Stimmgeber sich diejenigen Partei-Kandidaten wählt, die vernünftigen Anforderungen entsprechen, so darf die Rücksicht auf die Zusammengehörigkeit mit den Stammgenossen seine Erwägungen bis zu einem gewissen Grade beeinflussen"; Anderson, "German Americans," 34; *Echo,* August 26, 1:2.

54. J. L., letter to the editor, *Echo*, April 21, 7:1: "Da aber die 'Arkansas Staatszeitung' versprochen hat, Herrn Files den Kopf zu waschen, so wird wenig mehr von unserem Files übrig sein, bis diese mit ihm fertig ist." Literally, the newspaper is said to promise to wash Files' head. *Echo*, July 15, 5:2.

55. "Eine Lanze für den Schutzzoll" (A lance for the protectionist tariff), *Echo*, August 26, 4:4: "'Ganz Europa wünscht sehnlichst den Sieg der Demokratie, damit der Hochzoll ermäßigt, und die Fabrikanten Europas mit den einheimischen wieder concurriren könen [*sic*]. Geschieht das, dann wird Amerika mit europäischen Waaren überschwemmt und Hunderttausende von Arbeitern werden brotlos, oder müssen für Hungerlöhne arbeiten'"; "Da sollte einem doch eine Gänsehaut vor den bösen Demokraten überlaufen. Und die Deutschen sollen so klug sein und Alle republicanisch stimmen!! Und weiter weinte die St.-Ztg. oder wer es ihr vorschrieb, an dem oben Gesagten lasse sich nicht rütteln, es sei absolut wahr! Nun ist es freilich nicht einmal merkwürdig, daß es nicht wahr ist." To break a lance for a cause means to go to arms for it. September 16, 8:1: "Hätte die Staatszeitung wohl so gekämpft, und die deutschen Kandidaten so gelobt, wenn sie nicht gut dafür bezahlt worden wäre? Wer das '*Echo*' und die in demselben enthaltenen Correspondenzen gelesen hat, wird die Angriffe obigen Blattes zu würdigen wissen."

56. *Echo*, July 7, 5:3: "Die Vorwahlen sind am 16. Juli; dahin sollte ein jeder Bürger gehen, der von seinem Stimmenrecht Gebrauch machen will. Vor allem heißt es, die rechten Männer nominiren, sind einmal die Kandidaten nominirt, dann ist Nichts mehr zu machen. Die Vorwahlen sind die Hauptsache."

57. Whayne et al., *Arkansas*, 280; Graves, "Poll Tax"; Barnes, *Who Killed John Clayton?*, 58.

58. *Echo*, June 23, 8:2: "Geht sie mit den Republikanern, dann wird es bald mit ihr zu Ende sein, denn Arkansas will keine Negerherrschaft, und kann sie nicht ertragen. Besonders vorsichtig sollte man sein angesichts der drohenden

Erklärung in der republikanischen Platform von Minneapolis, welche das freie Votum der Farbigen im Süden schützen will, wahrscheinlich mit der im vorigen Congreß geschlagenen Force-Bill"; September 2, 4:4: "Die Erstere kommt mit der McKinley-Bill (Hochzoll-Tarif) in der einen Hand und der Force-Bill, welche Bajonett- und Neger-Herrschaft meint, in der andern. Das republikanische Reconstructions-Regiment ist noch wie ein hageres Nachtgespenst im Gedächtnisse derer, welche diese Tage durchlebten. Aber jene Schreckenszeit würde nicht zu vergleichen sein mit derjenigen, welche über Arkansas kommen würde mit Negern als Bundes-Marschalls, um die Bestimmungen der Force-Bill durchzuführen."

59. *Echo*, September 2, 4:4: "Unsere Schulen sind blühend und mit reichlichen Unterrichtsmitteln ausgestattet sowohl für Weiße als für Farbige." Obviously, given the *Echo*'s overall commitment to German-language education in lieu of sending immigrant children to local schools, it seems unlikely that the editors agreed with this particular statement in the speech.

60. "Nörgeleien in Aussicht" (grumblings on the horizon), *Echo*, September 16, 5:1: "Selbst wenn man dadurch allein der Süden betroffen würde, wenn das vorgeschlagene und von Harrison so warm empfohlene Gesetz keine andere Wirkung haben könnte, als den Süden unter die Herrschaft des Negergesindels und der 'Carpetbaggers' zu bringen, wäre dies ein nationales Unglück"; "Eingeborenen Bürgern gegenüber kann man solche Kniffe nicht anwenden, und so würde denn die erste Folge der Vorlage sein, daß die Bundesbeamten, d.h. die politischen Agenten der herrschenden Partei, überall auf die Adoptivbürger der Gegenpartei Jagd machen, ihre Papiere beanstanden, sie verhaften und auf andere Weise am Stimmen verhindern würden."

61. The *Echo* was aware of this question regarding the amendment's passage at the time. In a minor news item, it reported after the election that one lawyer, J. P. Clark, judged that the provision had passed, but the *Arkansas Democrat* asserted that it had not (September 23, 5:1).

62. Graves, "Poll Tax."

63. *Echo*, July 7, 5:3: "Wozu das anders, als damit die herrschende Partei später nachsehen kann, wie die einzelnen Bürger gestimmt haben. Und das soll bei Bewerbung um Ämter schon vorgekommen sein. Die Bestimmung, bei Stimmzettel mit Nummern zu versehen, sollte aus dem Gesetze ausgemertzt [*sic*] werden. So lange sie darin steht, ist der Stimmgeber beeinflußt u. die Wahl ist keine geheime."

64. Whayne et al., *Arkansas*, 281.

65. *Echo*, September 2, 8:1: "Jeder Wähler bekommt an seinem Stimmplatz ein Ticket, demokratisch oder republikanisch, wie er will. Er geht damit in einen der Verschläge und sieht es durch, streicht die ihm etwa nicht passenden Namen und schreibt andere dafür auf den freien Raum auf dem Ticket. Kann er selbst es nicht, so hilft ihm einer der Wahlrichter. 5 Minuten hat Jeder Zeit, nicht länger."

66. Barnes, *Journey*, 217; *Echo*, June 23, 5:2: "Es ist vorgeschlagen, diesen Herbst über ein Amendement abzustimmen, welches nur dem, der seine Steuern zahlt, das Wahlrecht gibt. Es ist nur recht und billig, daß wer nicht zum Unterhalt der Regierung beiträgt, auch kein Stimmrecht haben soll. Dann wird aber auch dem Unfug des mehrmaligen Stimmens an verschiedenen Stimmplätzen, wie es von

Schwarzen früher häufig geschehen sein soll, dadurch vorgebeugt"; Graves, "Poll Tax."

67. Civis, letter to the editor, *Echo*, September 2, 5:1: "Aber aus allen 23 Candidaten ist es nur Einem eingefallen, daß den Deutschen hierselbst ein großes Unrecht geschieht, nämlich keiner von ihnen wird zum Wahlrichter oder Gehilfen (Clerk) bestimmt, zudem daß viele Deutsche hier sind, die kein Englisch verstehen, lesen noch schreiben können, vorab die Aelteren"; September 16, 8:1: "Die Wahlen verliefen in Paris ruhig und in allen Townships war die Betheiligung gering. Einer Mehrheit des Volkes schien die neue Wahlmethode zu gefallen, während Andere nicht mit ihr einverstanden waren und Manche deshalb gar nicht stimmen wollten."

68. "The Negroes Were Indifferent," *Arkansas Gazette*, September 6, 1892, 6. I am grateful to my colleague Dr. Kenneth Barnes for sharing this article from the *Arkansas Gazette* with me. Barnes, *Who Killed John Clayton?*, 100–101, 62–63, 66–71; *Echo*, September 9, 1:1: "Die Neger hielten sich vielfach fern, es waren weder Cigarren noch Whisky da, und daher für sie nichts darin."

69. Severus, letter to the editor, *Echo*, November 25, 3:1: "Wenn auch einige Republikaner hier herum spucken und selbst die Volkspartei sich ein Nest zu bauen suchte, in welchem der neugebackene Candidat seine Eier legen sollte, so machten doch Beide wie vorauszusehen war, kläglich Fiasko u. mußten gesenkten Hauptes abziehen"; "Selbst ein alter Neger mit grauen Haaren wurde von dem allgemeinen Freudentaumel erfaßt und begeisterte sich so für die zukünftige demokratische Regierung, daß er durch die Straßen rannte und zum Aerger seiner Stammesgenossen mit lauter Stimme brüllte: Hurrah für Cleveland." The term *Stammesgenossen* is frequently translated as "tribesmen," but it can also indicate other members of a group who share characteristics such as race or religious faith. The last phrase is: "Günstling der Geldmänner."

70. *Echo*, July 15, 2:2: "So haben wir in diesem Jahre drei Parteien. Die Demokratische, die Volkspartei und die Republikaner. Wenn die beiden letzten zusammengegangen wären, so hätten sie vielleicht einigen Erfolg gehabt, so aber bedeutet es den vollen Sieg der Demokraten"; August 19, 5:2; June 16, 2:4: "Die sogenannte Peoples Party aber hat neben vielen vernünftigen Forderungen so viel absurd [*sic*] aufgestellt, daß man besser von ihr fern bleibt"; "Wir Deutsche können uns mit der republikanischen Partei und ihrem System nicht gut befreunden, besonders weil sie sich hier im Süden auf die Neger stützt"; Pierce, "Labor Movement"; Moneyhon, *Arkansas and the New South*, 80–81; *Echo*, May 12, 6:4.

71. *Echo*, August 5, 5:1: "Nun sollen die Deutschen zusammen stehen, und fordern von den demokratischen Candidaten eine Erklärung, daß sie die Deutschen nicht den Negern gleichstellen, und als das schlechtere Element betrachten. Wenn wir einig vorgehen, dann haben wir in Saline Co. die Wahlen in unseren Händen, Demokraten und die vereinigten Republikaner und Volksparteiler sind fast gleich stark, wohin wir unsere Stimmen werfen, dahin fällt der Sieg." In translating the word "nigger" into German, the paper chose to use the less inflammatory "Neger," which is more equivalent to "Negro." *Echo*, August 26, 5:1.

72. J. L., letter to the editor, *Echo*, November 18, 5:2: "Nur Schade, daß der Mann nicht vor 400 Jahren drei Wochen und drei Tagen, mit einem tüchtigen Knüppel an den Gestaden Amerikas stand, um dem Italiener-Spaniolen Columbus eines übers Ohr zu hauen. Wenn ein Schulknabe solches Blech schwatzen würde,

könnte man noch darüber lachen, aber ein Congreß-Abgeordneter sollte doch, gelinde gesagt, etwas mehr Takt zeigen." The phrase *übers Ohr hauen* also has a proverbial meaning in the sense of shortchanging or shafting someone, but I translated the phrase literally here because of the earlier reference to a cudgel.

73. Kehres, "Life," 41.
74. Kehres, "Life," 42.
75. Kehres, "Life," 43.
76. "Kapital und Arbeit" (Capital and work), *Echo*, July 15, 4:1: "Was kümmert es ihn, ob seine Arbeiter gut oder schlecht leben. . . . Und doch nimmt er ungeheure Wucherzinsen von seinem Kapital auf Kosten der Consumenten einerseits, und auf Kosten der Muskeln und Knochen der Arbeiter anderseits. Und darum die dumpfe Gährung unter den Arbeiter Massen, die revolutionäre Ausbrüche befürchten lassen. Um diese zu beschwören aber denken die Kapitalisten durchaus nicht daran, die in den Koth getretenen Menschenrechte wiederherzustellen."
77. *Echo*, March 31, 2:5: "Auch wir sehen die Mißstände und wünschen ernstliche Abhilfe. Auch wir vertheidigen den christlichen Grundsatz, daß die Arbeit das einzige Mittel ist, Werthe zu schaffen, und daß dem Arbeiter die geschaffenen Werthe gehören. Aber um die heutigen Uebelstände zu beseitigen, eine Anzahl Mitmenschen zu ermorden und zu berauben, das halten wir für ein großeres [*sic*] Unrecht als das jetzt bestehende System. "
78. "Erschütterung aller Verhältnisse durch das römische Recht" (The upheaval of all relationships through Roman law), *Echo*, July 15, 4:1: "Nicht mehr Arbeitstüchtigkeit und das Ablegen der Prüfung, sondern das Zahlen des Beitrages in die Kasse berechtigten zur Mitgliedschaft dieser Unionen. Und so schleppt jede Union eine Menge weniger fähigen Arbeiter mit, hilft ihnen zu gutem Verdienst, und schützt sie gegen das Kapital soviel sie kann. Darüber müssen natürlich die besseren Arbeiter leiden"; July 22, 4:1; "Rechte und Pflichte" (Rights and duties), August 12, 4:1.
79. "Naturrecht" (Law of nature), *Echo*, February 4, 4:1; "Das deutsche Recht am Ausgange des Mittelalters" (German law at the conclusion of the Middle Ages); March 31, 4:1; "Natürliches Menschenrecht und Naturrecht" (Natural law and law of nature), November 4, 4:3: "Und heute noch existirt dieser Communismus nicht nur in den Gehirnen von halbgebildeten Menschen, sondern in der That, und zwar da wo er paßt: unter den Thieren. Kein Wunder, daß Menschen die sich selber nur für veredeltes Vieh halten, auch die Gesetze desselben einführen wollen." "Ein merkwürdiges Etablissement" (A strange establishment), August 19, 2:3.
80. *Echo*, July 15, 1:1. Coverage of the Homestead Strike can be found here: July 7, 2:2; July 15,1:2, 1:4; July 22,1:2; July 29, 1:3, 1:7.
81. "Geld regiert die Welt" (Money governs the world), *Echo*, February 18, 3:3: "Daß du statt ein Christ / Nur ein Geldmann bist, / Stolz und Habsucht nährest, / Nur das Geld verehrest"; "Gerechtigkeit" (Justice), July 22, 4:3: "Sie [the rich] reißen den Nutzen aller Erfindungen des menschlichen Geistes, die Ausbeutung aller Naturschätze, sowie die Ausbeutung der Arbeitskraft des Volkes an sich, um nicht nur in fürstlichem Glanz und Luxus zu leben, sondern auch um durch den übermächtigen Einfluß ihrer Riesenvermögen eine Gewalt über ihre Mitbürger auszuüben, mit welcher sich die fürstliche Gewalt nicht im Entferntesten vergleichen läßt." "Schlechte Zeiten" (Bad times), *Echo*, December 16, 4:2: "gesetzlich erlaubten Manipulationen der Großkapitalisten."

82. "Hüben und drüben" (Over here and over there), *Echo*, December 16, 4:1; March 24, 2:3.
83. For a selection of articles regarding tariffs in the *Echo* of 1892, see: January 28, 1:7; May 12, 4:2; July 29, 2:4; "Drei böse T: Tarif, Trusts und Tramps" (Three evil Ts: tariffs, trusts, and tramps), August 19, 4:1; October 7, 3:5; December 9, 5:2. The editorial cartoon is found on page 3 of the October 7 edition.
84. *Echo*, April 14, 2:5; May 5, 6:4: "Wo die Arbeit gebührend geehrt und bezahlt wird, wie es in früheren Zeiten geschah, ist Alles recht. Standesunterschied muß sein und ist für Alle heilsam. Aber der jetzige Zustand spricht der Gerechtigkeit Hohn. Denn zu viele Menschen wollen ohne Arbeit ein müßiges, üppiges Leben führen und dazu noch großen Reichthum aufhäufen. Dies kann nur geschehen durch Abzüge von dem Verdienste der Arbeit."
85. Pionier (pioneer), letter to the editor, *Echo*, January 14, 2:1; J. L., letter to the editor, February 18, 2:6: "Obwohl nun seit 12 Jahren eine große Anzahl Deutscher hier wohnt, so war doch noch Keiner von ihnen Geschworener. Vor den Wahlen verspricht man uns immer: 'Das wird sich ändern, wenn ihr für den und den stimmt'. Aber es ist immer so geblieben"; anonymous, letter to the editor, February 25, 2:3.
86. *Echo*, March 3, 2:3; June 9, 8:1–2; June 16, 5:2, 8:2; June 23, 8:2; July 15, 2:3; August 19, 8:3; "Traurige Zustände" (Sad circumstances), August 26, 4:1–2; October 14, 7:5; November 11, 5:1; December 2, 4:1.
87. "Unsere Wahl-Frage" (Our election question), *Echo*, March 31, 2:4; June 2, 3:2; August 19, 8:3: "Auch darf man nicht erwarten, gute Kunststraßen umsonst zu kriegen."
88. "Der Wegebau in Arkansas" (Road building in Arkansas), *Echo*, October 7, 4:1: "Und wenn wir sogleich mit Millionen anfangen, so kommt ebenfalls nichts Ordentliches zu Stande, sondern nach vielfachen Erfahrungen würden sich Hunderte habgierige Hände ausstrecken, um ihren Beute-Antheil von den Dollars zu kriegen. Also Festina lente!—Eile mit Weile! Endlich anfangen—aber ohne Ueberstürzung!"; "Die Straßenbau-Frage" (The question of street building), *Echo*, December 2, 4:1.
89. "Abonnirt auf das Echo!" (Subscribe to the Echo!), *Echo*, August 26, 2:1: "Wir leben hier in einer Republik, in welcher es die Pflicht jedes guten Bürgers ist, an den öffentlichen Angelegenheiten soviel Antheil zu nehmen, als ihm seine Geschäfte erlauben. Sich über die durch die Wahlen zur Entscheidung kommenden Fragen zu unterrichten und zur Wahl-Urne zu gehen muß jeder Zeit haben. Denn wenn die guten Bürger ihre Pflichten für das Gemeinwohl versäumen, so haben die her- und habsüchtigen Politiker leichtes Spiel."
90. "Zu den Wahlen" (On the elections), *Echo*, August 26, 4:2.
91. Carl Eisenhardt, "Wacht am Rhein" (Vigil on the Rhine), *Echo*, July 15, 2:6: "Deutsche, wacht auf!"; "Selber hat deutsches Blut, deutsche Sitten, kommt von achtbaren deutschen Eltern, ist ein gesunder Demokrat."
92. *Echo*, March 3, 2:3; Beck, "Conrad Elsken."
93. *Echo*, September 9, 4:4; "Rauferei," September 23, 5:1.
94. *Echo*, October 28, 8:1: "ein Grund zu ernster Besorgniß vor Blutvergießen"; November 11,1:2: "Einige Arreste wurden gemacht, an der dritten Ward in der Stadt wurden mehrere Neger arretirt, die zweimal stimmen wollten, und einer der einen Wahlzettel stehlen wollte. Die U.S. Deputies hielten sich außerhalb der

Wahllokale auf der Straßen auf, und erregten keinen Anstoß"; November 18, 5:1: "In diesem Jahre ist die Wahlcampagne so ziemlich anständig geführt worden."

95. *Echo*, May 5, 6:4: "Recht so! Einigkeit macht stark." For other election coverage, see: *Echo*, September 9, 8:2; September 16, 8:1; October 14, 5:2; November 18, 5:2: "Volks- und Versöhnungsfeste," 8:1; "Die Aufgaben der Demokratie" (The duties of democracy), November 18, 4:2: "Und die neue Administration sollte sich stets gegenwärtig halten, daß die Indianer auch Menschen sind und auf die verfassungsmäßig gewährleistete Religionsfreiheit auch Anspruch haben"; December 2, 5:3.
96. *Echo*, October 21, 5:1: "'Wir haben nicht die Gewohnheit zu schwören, aber gegen die demokratische Partei möchten wir eine solche Ladung Flüche schleudern, daß sie für immer verd . . . . . . wäre.'" The *Echo* editor redacted the second half of the word "damned." October 7, 4:3: "Ein netter Candidat für die Volkspartei!"
97. Pionier, letter to the editor, *Echo*, January 14, 2:1; "Zu den Wahlen" (On the elections), August 26, 4:2: "Nun mußten wir Deutsche zwar schon mit Bitterkeit und Schaden erfahren, daß selbst die besten Grundsätze nicht immer im Stande sind, die üblen Folgen menschlicher Schwäche und Verblendung abzuwehren, denn unsere englischen Parteigenossen haben, nachdem wir ihnen den Sieg erstreiten halfen, sowohl in der Staatsverwaltung als in der Gesetzgebung manche sehr undemokratische Neigungen bekundet und uns namentlich mit tyrannischen Prohibitionsgesetzen gequält, welche den Farmern sogar den Verkauf ihres selbstgemachten Weines zum Verbrechen anrechnen."
98. *Echo*, August 19, 8:3; April 7, 4:5: "Wir als ehrliche und redliche Arbeiter, wollen es auch thun in unßerm [*sic*] Heim, werden wach bleiben, und keine Banditen erwählen, die unsern Brodkorb [*sic*] wegnehmen, oder zerstören helfen."
99. *Echo*, April 5, 6:3; April 21, 6:4: "Aber hier scheint die Annahme zu herrschen, daß die Stellung der Bürgschaft das Recht gibt, die anvertrauten Gelder in irgend einer Weise zu verwenden"; July 15, 5:2; November 18, 8:2; November 25, 8:1: "Wenn das Volk von Arkansas seine Constitution nicht dahin ändert, daß die lange Amtsführung von Männern verhindert wird, welche über einen zahlreichen Anhang verfügen und große Summen öffentlicher Gelder zu verwalten haben, so verdient es auch alle Strafen, welche aus dieser Pflichtversäumniß fließen"; December 16, 8:2.
100. *Echo*, April 5, 6:3; October 14, 5:2: "Die Aufregung ist sehr groß und es ist leicht möglich, daß Richter Lynch die Gerichtspflege in die Hand nimmt"; October 21, 5:1; July 22, 8:1; December 9, 5:2; September 2, 3:3: "Das sind die Früchte unserer herrlichen Justiz, deren enorme, aber vergebliche Unkosten aus den Taschen der Steuerzahler in diejenigen der Advokaten wandern."
101. *Echo*, March 24, 2:6; January 7, 1:6; April 21, 8:2–3; August 12, 5:1: "'Das spart Unkosten, und durch das Nichtanhäufen des Geldes in einer großen Summe wird den Einbrechern und Beamten eine Versuchung erspart'"; July 15, 2:2; November 11, 8:1; July 7, 5:3: "Die unsinnige Art, in welcher der 4. Juli gefeiert wird, kostet jährlich eine Anzahl Menschenleben, als ob die sonst so gescheiten Amerikaner sich am 4. Juli jedesmal vom gesunden Menschenverstande unabhängig erklärten."
102. For more on this line of thinking, see especially Faust, *German Element*, 2:365; Bergquist, "German-American Press," 139.

## Chapter 5

1. "Interview with Mary Meurer," 23.
2. Faust, *German Element*, 1:45.
3. Berlin and Gutman, "Natives and Immigrants," 1195.
4. Strickland, "German Immigrants," 38.
5. The slurs against fellow Germans come from Wittke, *German-Language Press*, 137; and Strickland, "German Immigrants," 45, respectively.
6. Faust also discusses the problems Germans had with the Republican Party and the Kansas-Nebraska law (*German Element*, 2:126–31); Berlin and Gutman, "Natives and Immigrants," 1195.
7. Hermann, "Memoirs," 234, 235. The translation here is that of Evans.
8. *Echo*, December 23, 8:1: "Dasselbe wurde gleich nach dem Kriege errichtet, um die freigewordenen Sklaven zu unterstützen, ist aber schon lange eingegangen"; October 21, 4:1: "Aber so gewiß als das amerikanische Volk von den hochmüthigen Pflanzern und Sklavenhaltern des Südens durch den Bürgerkrieg die Abschaffung der schwarzen Sklaverei erzwang, so gewiß wird es auch die Schaffung einer noch fluchwürdigeren weißen Sklaverei durch die, aus der Beraubung des Volkes hervorgegangenen Geldfürsten, verhindern."
9. Wittke, *German-Language Press*, 155.
10. Barnes, *Journey of Hope*, 55.
11. Data regarding the concentration of the Arkansas black population comes from Ken Barnes's excellent book on black emigration and is drawn from 1890 census records; I have used his rubric for dividing the percentage of populations (*Journey of Hope*, 36). Because there are no subscriber lists or circulation records extant for the *Echo*, I have used the data outlined in chapter 1 regarding locations of correspondents for the paper.
12. Barnes, *Who Killed John Clayton?*, 122.
13. The source for information for this paragraph and for the entries in the following paragraph is: Jacob and Wilhelm Grimm, *Deutsches Wörterbuch*. I have given brief and by no means exhaustive summaries of the Grimms' entries. Interested readers are referred to the work itself. The entry for *schwarz* is particularly fascinating, including usages as diverse as references to the Erinyes, Christian pastors, coffee preparation, weapons, and minerals.
14. A note on how frequency of language use was determined: while I read every word of every issue in the *Echo*'s inaugural year in researching this book, there is, of course, a possibility that I missed a stray usage or two in the thousands of inches of newspaper copy I examined. I kept a table to tally the various terms used to describe race and noted whether the usage was positive, negative, or neutral toward the individual described. If the same word was used to indicate an individual more than once in a single news item, letter, or editorial, it was recorded only once as a usage, i.e., the word *Neger* (Negro) might be used three to four times in a single item to indicate the same suspect in a crime.
15. *Echo*, May 26, 7:1; June 23, 1:7.
16. *Echo*, June 16, 8:1; November 11, 5:1.
17. Italics added. M. H., letter to the editor, *Echo*, April 14, 3:3: "Heute wurde das erste Neger-Paar in aller Stille getraut; möchten beide ihren Versprechen treu bleiben und den Kern für eine, wenn auch kleine, schwarz-katholische Gemeinde

bilden. Nach den bereits gemachten Erfahrungen darf man keine zu kühnen Erwartungen hegen. Es ist eine gar lange, schwere Arbeit, die Mohren weiß zu waschen, zumal ihre Prediger sie weis machen, wir seien eigentlich die Schwarzen, sie hätten nur äußerlich die dunkle Farbe." The phrase *in aller Stille* might also indicate that the couple was wedded secretly.

18. *Echo*, May 19, 8:2; Griffith, "Henry James."
19. *Echo*, January 28, 5:3; February 11, 2:5; May 26, 2:4; March 3, 2:2; March 10, 6:2; April 28, 8:3.
20. *Echo*, February 18, 2:5; March 10, 2:5; March 10, 1:7; November 25, 5:2.
21. "Indianergebiet" (Indian country), *Echo*, April 14, 2–4.
22. "Hottentottenpotentatentantentintenattentat" (Hottentot potentate aunt ink assassination), *Echo*, April 14, 2–4.
23. Barnes, *Who Killed John Clayton?*, 128.
24. This is a very brief synopsis of the fascinating history of Afro-Germans or Black Germans, a field that was largely unexplored until the 1980s. Readers of English interested in this topic are referred to the volume that founded this field (Opitz et al., *Showing*) as well as to the works of Tina Campt, Sara Friedrichsmeyer, and Sara Lennox, among others.
25. Dougan, *Community Diaries*, 121.
26. Carl Moneyhon, "Post-Reconstruction."
27. Barnes, *Who Killed John Clayton?*, 128; Carl Moneyhon, "Post-Reconstruction."
28. Office of the Historian, United States House of Representatives, "Bruce, Blanche Kelso," https://history.house.gov/People/Detail/10029; "Zur Negerfrage" (On the question of the Negroes), *Echo*, March 10, 6:2: "Die Schwarzen in Amerika seien Afrikaner nur mehr der Farbe nach; ihr ganzes Wesen, Trachten und Denken sei amerikanisch, und es sei nicht mehr Grund für sie vorhanden, das Land ihrer Geburt zu verlassen und nach Afrika zu wandern, weil ihre Urväter dort lebten, als für irgend einen Frisch- oder Deutsch-Amerikaner nach Europa zurückzugehen, weil seine Ahnen dort gewohnt [haben]. Wären die Fortschritte der Farbigen des Südens seit der Emancipation weniger zufriedenstellend, so wäre vielleicht für die Begünstigung der Auswanderung ein Vorwand vorhanden; aber es säßen jetzt eine und eine Drittel-Million farbiger Schüler in den öffentlichen Schulen, 37,000 in Privatschulen, 8000 in Kirchenschulen, was zusammen 1,370,000 Schüler mache. Es gäbe ferner siebzig höhere Erziehungsanstalten für Farbige, über 7,000 Farbige bilden sich zu Lehrern heran, Hunderte studiren Theologie, Medizin und die Rechte; trotz der Nachtheile, mit denen sie zu kämpfen hatten, hätten es die Farbigen allein im Staate Virginien auf einen Besitz von $15,000,000 gebracht, und in Louisiana, Mississippi u. Süd-Carolina würden sie noch bessere Ergebnisse aufzuweisen gehabt haben, hätte der Census auf den Besitz der Farbigen besondere Rücksicht genommen. Der Neger werde sich mit der Zeit schon machen; man lasse ihn nur in Ruhe und gebe ihm die nöthige Gelegenheit." I have translated Bruce's statement directly from the German, as German speakers would have experienced it, rather than using an original transcript of his words. Turner was able to arrange for emigration for around five hundred Americans to Liberia in 1895 and 1896.
29. "A Question of Race Inferiority," *Arkansas Gazette*, April 27, 4:3; *Arkansas Gazette*, April 29, 4:2.

30. "Die Neger" (The Negroes), *Echo*, May 12, 3:4: "Der Neger ist ein Schmerzenskind unseres Gemeinwesens. Daß man die armen Schwarzen aus Afrika hierher schleppte, um sie in den Sklaververdienst zu pressen, war ein Unrecht, mit dessen Folgen wir zu rechnen haben und das uns die Verpflichtung aufregt, für diese Kinder des dunklen Erdtheils zu thun, was wir zu thun vermögen. Bislang hat man sich freilich fast nur um den Neger bekümmert, weil seine Stimme bei Wahlen der des Weißen gleichgeachtet wird, weil eben jede Stimme zählt. Das Hereinziehen des Negers in diese Sorte Politik muß ihn moralisch nur noch tiefer drücken. Auch die christliche Mission hat bisher für den Schwarzen nur wenig gethan, obwohl hier und da vielversprechende Anfänge gemacht sind. Diese stille Arbeit der christlichen Mission ist es, von der man am ehesten guten Erfolg erwarten darf. Denn was sonst an Weißen in den durch Schwarze am dichtesten bevölkerten Districten wohnt, treibt zumeist Halsabschneidegeschäfte mit Mordgages [mortgages] und Schuldverschreibungen, die dem von Natur leichtsinnig wirthschaftenden Neger eine erdrückende Bürde sind und ihn auch moralisch versumpfen."
31. "Die Neger" (The Negroes), *Echo*, May 12, 3:4: "weil dieselbe [die farbige Bevölkerung] im fremden Lande gleich einem versetzten Baum unmöglich so gedeihen kann wie auf heimathlichen Boden"; "der Schmutz, in dem die Neger sich gefallen."
32. "Die Neger" (The Negroes), *Echo*, May 12, 3:4: The quotation marks around "reverend" were likely due to doctrinal rather than racial differences. German-speaking Catholics disdained the American Protestant practice of allowing anyone to designate himself a minister outside of a church sanctioned process.
33. "Weiße und Schwarze" (Whites and blacks), *Echo*, July 15, 4:4: "Zuletzt wollen wir noch einen kurzen Blick auf die Farbe unserer Bevölkerung werfen und zwar verstehen wir hierbei unter 'Farbigen' alle Nicht-Weißen, mögen sie nun von afrikanischer Herkunft oder auch Chinesen und Japanesen bez. Indianer sein"; "Aussterben der Indianer." Another possible translation for *Aussterben* is "extinction," but it is unclear from the context whether the author means that Native Americans would one day no longer exist entirely or whether the birth replacement rate was no longer keeping pace with the mortality rate.
34. "Was Volksstämmen Werth verleiht" (What gives ethnic groups value), *Echo*, October 14, 8:4.
35. Barnes, *Who Killed John Clayton*, 24–29; Griffith, "Atkins Race War"; Griffith, "Hampton Race War." Similar fears of a race war would later be used in the German colony of German Southwest Africa (Namibia) from 1904 to 1908 to commit genocide against the Herero people; the claim of blacks attacking whites without provocation was a common trope in the homeland as well. See Hammerstein, "'Who Owns Hereroland?'"
36. *Arkansas Gazette*, May 15, 1:3.
37. *Arkansas Gazette*, September 20, 1:1.
38. *Arkansas Gazette*, September 22, 6:2.
39. *Echo*, November 11, 5:1: "In Paragould sind die Neger von den Bürgern aufgefordert worden, die Stadt zu verlassen"; June 23, 5:3: "Der Rassenhaß steigert sich, und kann noch schlimme Früchte tragen"; July 15, 1:4: ". . . um 12 Uhr erschien plötzlich ein bewaffneter Haufen von 75 Negern und eröffnete Feuer auf die um

das Gefängniß stehenden Männer." Randy Finley mentions the Lonoke County eviction attempt in "Lynching State," 65.

40. Frank Mehring and Willard Gatewood both discuss the propensity of white newspapers not to report on black citizens unless it was to mention them as criminal suspects. Mehring, "'Nazi Jim Crow,'" 152; Gatewood, "Arkansas Negroes," 293; *Echo*, December 9, 8:1: "Fisher war Kellner im Richelieu Hotel, also nicht in Noth, sondern beging einen frechen Straßenraub"; *Echo*, March 10, 2:5: ". . . die Diebe seien Niggerbuben."
41. *Echo*, June 9, 8:1: "Da jedoch keine directen Schuldbeweise gegen die eingekerkerten Neger vorlagen, so gingen die Leute wieder auseinander."
42. *Arkansas Gazette*, June 2, 1892, 2:3, "Edith Gordon Discharged," *Arkansas Gazette*, June 11, 1892, 8:3.
43. *Echo*, March 17,3:1; December 2, 5:3; December 2, 8:1; November 18, 5:1; August 5, 5:1; November 18, 5:1: "Der Neger ging auch an die Außenseite der Schiene, ob er nun glaubte der Zug werde auch sein Theil ausweichen, oder ob er ihn aus dem Geleise werfen wollte, ist nicht bekannt."
44. *Echo*, July 7, 5:3; April 7, 5:1; August 19, 8:1; March 31, 2:3; April 7, 3:2; August 19, 8:1: "einem armen hart arbeitenden Neger."
45. *Echo*, February 11, 2:5; May 19, 6:3; February 25, 2:1; March 3, 2:5; M. H., letter to the editor, April 14, 3:3: "Viele sind berufen, Wenige auserwählt, gilt ganz besonders von den Schwarzen"; April 14, 3:6: "'Die Knaben zeigen einen stärkeren Hang zum Stehlen und Lügen, für Gesang und Turnen bekunden sie das größte Interesse.'"
46. Barnes, *Who Killed John Clayton?*, 129; *Echo*, May 26, 1:5: "In der Legislatur von Arkansas vertreiben sie sich die Langweile auf verschiedene Weise"; July 29, 8:2: "In der Volkspartei-Convention waren 8 Farbige, während die republikanische zu drei Vierteln aus Negern bestand. Die Ideen dieser Leute kennzeichnete Einer von ihnen der farbige Schuhmacher Bradford; er sagte, er habe keine Zeit gehabt, richtig sprechen zu lernen, da er vor dem Kriege geboren sei, und die Demokraten ihm nie Gelegenheit gegeben hätten, eine Erziehung zu erhalten; sie hätten ihn stets am Arbeiten gehalten bis auf diesen Tag. Ich bin ein schwarzer Republikaner, und wir schwarze Republikaner müssen diesmal alle Vorurtheile bei Seite legen und gewinnen; geben wir den Weißen diesmal den Vortritt, und wir kommen das nächste Mal. Ich bin für das Eingehen in eine Confusion (statt Fusion) mit einer andern Partei. Ich bin immer in Confusion gewesen. Wir schwarze Burschen müssen still sitzen, und unser Geheimniß bewahren. Laßt den Nigger dismal [*sic*] stillstehen und dieser Pferdehandel-Wählerei zusehen. In 2 Jahren von jetzt setzen wir dann den schwarzen Mann herein."
47. *Echo*, December 2, 8:1.
48. A. Kind, "Die Geschichte von Randolph County " (The history of Randolph County), *Echo*, September 9, 3:1; September 16, 3:1; November 11, 3:3: "Aber so grauenhaft der Volksmund die Umtriebe dieser maskirten Reiter auch ausmalen mag und durchaus mit Berechtigung über deren späteres Unwesen empört war, so muß doch festgehalten werden, daß dieser Bund nicht entstand, um ein willkürliches Spiel mit den Schwachen zu treiben, sondern einzig u. allein um seine Mitbürger zu beschützen u. vor unrechten Bedrückungen von Seiten des vereinigten Staaten-Militär's zu bewahren. Deshalb finden wir, daß im Anfange die

'Kuklux Klan' sich aus Männern der besten Familien rekrutirte und ehrenwerthen Character aufzuweisen hatten." The type is clearly "F. u. G.," but I believe this to be an error, since a lower case "u" would make sense neither in German nor English spelling conventions. Further, Michael Dougan writes that German American Jacob Frolich Jr., who was prominent in the English-speaking press in Arkansas at the time, had been a confederate soldier and was reputed to be a Klan member as well. Thus, it was not unheard of for a German immigrant to have joined the Klan.

49. A. Kind, "Die Geschichte von Randolph County" (The history of Randolph County), *Echo*, November 11, 3:3: "Jedermann that oder konnte thun, was er wollte, kein Gesetz fand Anerkennung oder wurde befolgt, weil der Staat die Gewalt nicht in Händen hatte, um seiner Autorität Geltung zu verschaffen"; December 30, 8:3.

50. J. L., letter to the editor, *Echo*, February 4, 4:3: "Da möchte man wahrhaftig fragen: 'Wer ist der Dieb? Der Staat oder diese?"; T., letter to the editor, May 12, 7:2: "Ist es ein Wunder, wenn man täglich vom Richter Lynch in den Zeitungen liest bei einer solchen Justiz?!"

51. *Echo*, August 19, 5:1 is an example of lynching being expected after a black man accused of a sexual crime against a white woman; May 26, 2:3: "Die erbitterten Bürger aber hängten ihn am ersten passenden Baum"; July 7, 5:2: "einen der Ihrigen [*sic*]." The last case is likely that of Robert Donnelly and is discussed in Griffith, "'At the Hands.'"

52. *Echo*, March 17, 1:1: "Es muß ein furchtbar rohes Element hier im Süden aufwachsen, welches an solchen Gräuelthaten Geschmack findet. Wenn ein Mörder den Tod verdient hat, so hat doch eine Anzahl Menschen nicht das Recht, ihn zu bestrafen"; Finley, "Lynching State," 67; *Echo*, March 31, 2:5: "Echt amerikanisch"; "geröstet."

53. "Gerechtigkeit und Lynchjustiz" (justice and lynch law), *Echo*, May 19, 5:4: "Wir mißbilligen die Lynchjustiz ebensosehr, wie sie jeder Recht und Ordnung liebende Mensch mißbilligen muß. . . . Mit Redensarten läßt sich nichts bessern; sie dienen nur als heuchlerische Ausflüchte, um der Besserung und Abstellung von Uebelständen auszuweichen"; "Aber dieses heuchlerische Treiben mag wohl das Gewissen dieser Herren einschläfern, aber es löscht nicht den Schandfleck aus, welcher uns in den Augen aller civilisirten Nationen entehrt."

54. *Echo*, June 9, 4:2: "Die brutalen Gewaltthaten von Negern gegen weiße Frauen, welche in letzter Zeit geradezu epidemisch werden, haben in den Süd-Staaten eine Stimmung erzeugt, welche für die Schwarzen nichts Gutes weissagt. Irgend ein zufälliges Ereigniß mag den bisher unterdrückten Funken zu lichter Lohe entfachen und dann mag es ein entsetzliches Blutbad geben. Die Ehre unserer Frauen muß geschützt werden, koste es was es wolle, und keine scheinheiligen Klagen nördlicher Philantropen, die nichts von der Sachlage verstehen, können etwas daran ändern."

55. "Gewaltthaten" (Violent acts), *Echo*, July 22, 3:4: "Denn so lange farbige Scheusale Verbrechen begehen und die ordentliche Gerichte es an der nöthigen Schneidigkeit fehlen lassen, werden sich die bedrohten Weißen immer zusammenrotten und 'das Gesetz in die eigene Hand nehmen.'" The practice of using euphemisms in the *Arkansas Gazette* is described in Finley, "Lynching State," 69.

56. Griffith, "Lynching of the Biscoe Family."
57. *Echo*, February 18, 2:3–4: "Ein Farbiger, Biscoe, hatte eine kleine Farm, welche er seit 10 Jahren fleißig bearbeitete"; "[sie] ermordeten den Farmer, seine schwangere Frau, die einen Säugling an der Brust hatte, und den ca. 14 Jahre alten Knaben"; "(Warum ihn also wegen Beleidigung verhaften wollen?)"; "Das ist kein Lynchgericht, sondern ein schändlicher Raubmord, und die Mörder nebst ihren Helfershelfern verdienen sämtlich, gehängt zu werden"; *Arkansas Gazette*, February 9, 6:3 and February 12, 6:1.
58. LeMasters, "Edward Coy"; *Echo*, February 25, 1:7; *Echo*, March 3, 1:6: "Schandthat und Bestrafung des Negers Coy."
59. "Coy's Carcass," *Arkansas Gazette*, February 23, 2:4.
60. *Echo*, March 17, 1:1; *Echo*, June 9, 2:5.
61. Griffith, "Henry James"; *Echo*, May 19, 8:2: "Einer der Führer sagte: Wir sollen den schändlichen Nigger hier schlafen lassen, während das von ihm mißbrauchte Kind im Sterben liegt? Die Männer waren überhaupt furchtbar entschlossen, den Verbrecher aufzuhängen, möge kommen was wolle. Die Wuth blitzte ihnen aus den Augen"; "Er hatte die Sachlage gleich überschaut und gesehen, daß irgendein Eingriff zu furchtbarem Blutvergießen führen müßte."
62. Griffith, "Eugene Baker"; *Echo*, August 5, 5:1: "zu seiner Sicherheit"; "Mit vorgehaltenen Revolvern zwangen sie den Wärter den Schlüssel herauszugeben, drangen ins Gefängniß, schleppten Becker heraus, banden ihn an einen Baumast, und schoßen ihn auf bestialische Manier todt [*sic*]."
63. Griffith, "G. P. F. Lightfoot"; *Echo*, December 16, 5:1.
64. Griffith, "Robert Donnelly"; *Echo*, July 7, 5:2: "die wüthenden Neger."
65. Finley, "Lynching State," 79, 81; and Jones, "'Doubtless Guilty,'" 29.
66. Condray, "Kerl."
67. Barnes, *Journey*, 13, 35, 38, 43; Watkins, "Efforts," 37–38, 49; Whayne et al., *Arkansas*, 259; *Echo*, October 14, 8:4: "So wird ein deutscher Bauer schwer vorankommen, wenn er sich mitten zwischen Negern niederläßt. Das Rassegefühl ist bei diesen Leuten so stark, daß sie einen aus Deutschland eingewanderten 'Fremdling' mit Mißtrauen ansehen. Und in dem Leben jedes Neulings kommen Umstände vor, die den Beistand der Nachbarn nothwedig machen. Wenn derselbe nun in feindseliger Kälte verweigert wird, so bringt dies über die verlassene Familie nicht selten Verderben."
68. Barnes, *Journey*, 29; *Echo*, March 3, 2:2: "auf Plantagen im südlichen Theile des Staates"; "Viele andere Neger im Staate sollen dieselbe Absicht haben"; March 10, 1:7.
69. News items that noted the departure of black Arkansans included: *Echo*, March 3, 2:2; March 10, 1–7; April 7, 3–2; April 14, 2–3; June 2, 3:2; May 12, 7:2: "Die Einwanderung nach Oklahoma unter den Schwarzen ist ganz großartig. Täglich ziehen sie gruppenweise hier durch und fast alle ohne jegliche Mittel. Sie kommen fast alle von Mississippi und Tennessee."
70. *Arkansas Gazette*, December 3, 4:3. Barnes discusses the Morrilton departure and reporting in white newspapers (*Journey*, 1, 93).
71. *Echo*, April 14, 2–4: "wo in ihrer Phantasie Milch und Honig fließt, Oklahoma, dem gelobten Lande"; "weder Geld noch etwas zum Kauen"; "da ihm das der einzige Weg dünkte, die unglückliche Schar loszuwerden"; "Plunder, welchen

die Neger mit sich schleppten"; "Die Indianer lachen sich über den Streich ins Fäustchen. Laß die dort jetzt sehen, was sie weiter mit den Negern anfangen. Wir sind sie los." To my knowledge, this is the only extant material remaining from *Das Arkansas Volksblatt*. "Dey's Gwine Da," *Arkansas Gazette*, March 15, 1:2.

72. *Echo*, April 21, 6:4: "Sie sind in üblen Umständen, Viele von ihnen haben nicht die nöthigen Kleider. Damit sie weiter reisen können, werden Gelder bei ihren Stammesgenossen gesammelt."
73. Barnes, *Who Killed John Clayton?*, 45; Woods, *Mission*, 185–87; November 11, 5–1: "Die Knaben lernen da Handwerke und die Mädchen nähen, stricken und flicken neben gründlichen Unterricht. Sie sagen, jedes County sollte eine solche Schule haben, um unsere Neger zu braven, nützlichen Menschen zu erziehen."
74. *Echo*, June 9, 2:5: "In Pine Bluff sind die meisten Neger wieder an der Arbeit, und erhalten Samen und die nöthige Nahrung. Doch gibt es noch eine Menge, welche nicht arbeiten wollen, sondern Unterstützung vom 'Gubment' erwarten"; May 26, 2:4–5, 7:1; June 2 ,3:1, 8:3; December 2, 8:2: "Nach der '*Gazette*' sind 2000 beschäftigungslose Neger in der Stadt. Selbe sind durch Arbeitsmangel auf dem Lande in die Stadt getrieben worden. Ihre Aussichten, hier die Lebensnothdurft für den Winter zu verdienen ist schlecht."
75. Strickland, "German Immigrants," 37.
76. *Echo*, January 14, 1:3; January 21, 2:4; Gabler, "Lovely's Purchase," 33–34.
77. *Echo*, February 11, 3:1: "Unsere Vertreter sollten daher mit aller Macht die Rechte unseres Staates auf dieses Land geltend machen, damit es als Theil des Staates Arkansas unter dem Heimstätte-Gesetz baldigst eröffnet werden"; June 23, 8:1; November 4, 8:4; November 11, 8:4; April 24, 6:4.
78. *Echo*, February 4, 3:1; "Die Neger" (The Negroes), May 12, 3:4: "Die Regierung hat den Rothhäuten nicht nur Zahlung geleistet für die von ihnen der Besiedelung freigegebenen Landdistrikte, wodurch der Indianer Geld in die Hand bekam, für das er keine vernünftige Verwendung kannte, sondern sie hat auch die Rothhaut gefüttert und füttert sie heute noch und macht sie dadurch zu einem Tagedieb und Faulenzer ersten Ranges"; November 25, 8:1.
79. Wellenreuther, *Citizens*, 213; November 25, 2:1; January 28, 4:5: "'Du, segg mol, Chrischan, wo hest dat: 'Buffalo Bills Wild West?' 'Dat sünd twee Indianers, Buffalo und Bills, de sind fröher wild west, nu sünd se abers tahm'"; July 29, 5:1.
80. "Indianerlob" (Praise for Indians), *Echo*, May 26, 1:6; June 2, 2:4; "Die sechs Nationen" (The six nations), September 16, 1:6.
81. July 22, 5:1; September 2, 8:1; October 22, 4:4; December 16, 2:1; August 2, 2:5; September 30, 5:5.
82. February 11, 1:2; July 16, 5:2, 8:3; December 2, 5:2; "Zwei Stiefelputzer" (Two shoe polishers), May 12, 6:2; Civis, letter to the editor, *Echo*, August 26, 5:4.
83. LeMaster, *Corner*, 73, 98, 104–105, 113, 117–18, 119, 123, 131, 137, 492. It is possible that there were German-speaking Jewish merchants represented in LeMaster's book with ties to the *Echo* who are not accounted for here. I have only included individuals whom she notes specifically as emigrating from Austria or Germany. *Echo*, June 16, 8:2; November 11, 8:2.
84. *Arkansas Gazette*, June 2, 3:7, September 22, 2:1, October 1, 2:1, December 18, 6:6.
85. LeMaster, *Corner*, 73; November 18, 3:1, December 23, 1:7: "Die Folgen des Anti-Semitismus des Raufboldes de Mores stricken ihn auf das Krankenbett."

86. *Echo*, October 14, 4:1: "Es besteht nur der Unterschied, daß die Juden vernunftige Leute sind, welche begreifen, daß auf der gegenseitigen Achtung dessen, was den Andersgläubigen heilig ist, das freundliche, schöne Verhältniß beruht, welches unter gesitteten Menschen ein Bedürfniß ist. Deshalb feiern die Juden ungestört ihren Sabbath und achten auch den christlichen Sonntag"; "Für das '*Echo*.' Die heutige Erziehung vom Standpunkte der Religion und Vernunft betrachtet" (For the *Echo*. Modern education regarded from the perspective of religion and reason), *Echo*, May 19, 5:3; July 7, 5:3; July 29, 2:5. Frick's attacker was Alexander Berkman. *Echo*, July 22, 2:1. For more on the Buschoff acquittal, see "Xanten." *Echo*, August 12, 1:2; "Der Wunder-Rabbi" (The miracle rabbi), December 23, 3:2: "An erfinderischem Geiste zum Handelsschwindel und Speculationsspiel übertrifft er thatsächlich alle Anderen. Und dies imponirt seinen 'Unterthanen' so außerordentlich. Sie erblicken darin eine höhere göttliche Eingebung."
87. *Echo*, May 12, 7:3; March 31, 2:6; June 9, 5:4.
88. "Moltke's Weltanschauung" (Moltke's worldview), *Echo*, April 28, 6:4; "Freie Gedanken" (Free thoughts), May 12, 4:3: "Ueberhaupt sollte nicht jedes fromme Gebet, möge es nun an Buddha, an Allah oder Jehove gerichtet sein, an denselben Gott gelangen, außer dem es keinen gibt? Hört doch die Mutter die Bitte des Kindes, in welcher Sprache es auch ihren Namen lallt"; July 7, 1:7: ". . . Schätze zu gewinnen, mit welchen der Kampf christlicher Cultur gegen den kulturfeindlichen Islam siegriech entscheiden werden könnte."
89. Vinikas, "Thirteen Dead," 120.
90. Woods, *Mission and Memory*, 188.

## Conclusion

1. Wittke, *German-Language Press*, 197.
2. Wolfe, "Background," 357; Wittke, *German-Language Press*, 224.
3. Dan Durning, "Attracting the German Immigrant," 2–8. For discussions of Germany's rise to power and its impact on American immigration, see Faust, *German Element*; Wittke, *German-Language Press*; Adams, *Deutsche*; and Barfuss, "Foreign Workers."
4. Woods, *Mission and Memory*, 127; Wellenreuther, *Citizens*, 113–114.
5. Pryor, foreword, 5.
6. Dougan, *Community Diaries*, 96, 117; Wittke, *German-Language Press*, 4–5.
7. *Echo*, December 30, 1:1–7: "Vivat Arkansas, ich glaube an das Land u. seine Zukunft"; "Möge Arkansas im kommenden Jahre wachsen und gedeihen, und Alle unsere Leser mit Segen überschütten. Mögen die lang erhofften besseren und glücklicheren Zeiten mit dem neuen Jahre anfangen und dauern. . . . Unser Herrgott selbst kann uns im Paradiese nicht glücklich und zufrieden machen, wenn wir nicht glücklich und zufrieden sein wollen. Wir müssen also auch das unsrige thun, um das vorgestreckte Ziel zu erreichen. So können wir, trotz der schlechten Zeiten, das neue Jahr mit frohen Hoffnungen beginnen. Von allen Seiten werden Anstrengungen gemacht, die Hilfsquellen unseres schönen Staaten zu entwickeln. . . . Das *Echo* will Alles thun, was in seinen Kräften steht, um seinen Landsleuten zu helfen und sie zu belehren und die Schwierigkeiten, die sich ihnen entgegenstellen besiegen zu helfen."

# BIBLIOGRAPHY


Adams, Willi Paul. *Deutsche im Schmelztiegel der USA: Erfahrungen im größten Einwanderungsland der Europäer*. Berlin: Senatsverwaltung für Gesundheit und Soziales—Ausländerbeauftragte, 1991.

Allsopp, Frederick. *History of the Arkansas Press for the First Hundred Years and More.* Little Rock: Parke-Harper, 1922.

Anderson, Kristen L. "German Americans, African Americans, and the Republican Party in St. Louis, 1865–1872." *Journal of American Ethnic History* 28, no. 1 (Fall 2008): 34–51.

Arkansas Echo Publishing Company. "Articles of Agreement and Incorporation." Little Rock, AR: Secretary of State of Arkansas, 1892.

———. "Certificate of Dissolution of a Corporation." Little Rock, AR: Secretary of State of Arkansas, 1892.

———. "Form for Use of a Domestic Corporation." Little Rock, AR: Secretary of State of Arkansas, 1892.

"Arkansas Staats Zeitung (Ger.)," *N. W. Ayer & Son's American Newspaper Annual and Directory.* Philadelphia: N. W. Ayer & Son, 1892.

*Arkansas Union List of Newspapers*. Fayetteville: University of Arkansas Libraries, 1993.

Arndt, Ernst Moritz. "Des Deutschen Vaterland." Deutsche Geschichte in Dokumenten und Bildern: German Historical Institute, April 1, 2020. http://germanhistorydocs.ghi-dc.org.

Arndt, Karl, and May Olson. *Die deutschsprachige Presse der Amerikas: 1732–1968, Geschichte und Bibliographie*. Vol. 2. Pullach near Munich: Verlag Dokumentation, 1973.

Assenmacher, Hugh, O.S.B. *A Place Called Subiaco: A History of the Benedictine Monks in Arkansas*. Little Rock: Rose Publishing, 1977.

Bade, Klaus. "Conclusion: Migration Past and Present—The German Experience." In Hoerder and Nagler, *People*, 399–412.

Barfuss, Karl Marten. "Foreign Workers in and around Bremen, 1884–1918." In Hoerder and Nagler, *People*, 201–24.

Barnes, Kenneth C. *Anti-Catholicism in Arkansas: How Politicians, the Press, the Klan, and Religious Leaders Imagined an Enemy, 1910–1960*. Fayetteville: University of Arkansas Press, 2016.

———. "'Don't Go to Arkansas': How the Prussian Government Tried to Curb Emigration to the Arkansas River Valley in 1881 and 1882." *Faulkner Facts and Fiddlings* 44 (2001/2002): 9–13.

———. *Journey of Hope: The Back-to-Africa Movement in Arkansas in the Late 1800s.* Chapel Hill: University of North Carolina Press, 2004.

———. *Who Killed John Clayton? Political Violence and the Emergence of the New South, 1861–1893*. Durham, NC: Duke University Press, 1998.

Beck, Joseph C. "Conrad Elsken." *Encyclopedia of Arkansas*, October 22, 2013. https://encyclopediaofarkansas.net.

Bergquist, James M. "The German-American Press." In *The Ethnic Press in the United*

*States: A Historical Analysis and Handbook*, edited by Sally M. Miller, 131–59. New York: Greenwood Press, 1987.

Berlin, Ira, and Herbert Gutman. "Natives and Immigrants, Free Men and Slaves: Urban Workingmen in the Antebellum American South." *American Historical Review* 88, no. 5 (1983): 1175–1200.

Blaschke, Monika. "Communicating the Old and the New: German Immigrant Women and Their Press in Comparative Perspective around 1900." In Hoerder and Nagler, *People*, 313–27.

Branam, Chris M. "Election Law of 1891." *Encyclopedia of Arkansas*, September 11, 2018. https://encyclopediaofarkansas.net.

Brendel, Shirley J, ed. *Arkansas Newspapers: A Directory of Newspapers Available in Arkansas Libraries.* Fayetteville: University of Arkansas Press, 1987.

Brister, Louis E. "The Image of Arkansas in the Early German Emigrant Guidebook: Notes on Immigration." *Arkansas Historical Quarterly* 36, no. 4 (Winter 1977): 338–45.

Bungert, Heike. *Festkultur und Gedächtnis: Die Konstruktion einer deutsch-amerikanischen Ethnizität, 1848–1914*. Band 32: Studien zur historischen Migrationsforschung. Osnabrück: Ferdinand Schöningh, 2016.

Burkett, Bennie Frownfelter. *Stuttgart, Arkansas: One Hundred Years on the Grand Prairie.* Stuttgart, AR: Standard Printing, 1980.

Condray, Kathleen. "The Bloody German Language Newspaper War of 1892." *Arkansas Historical Quarterly* 74 (Winter 2015): 327–51.

———. "The Kerl in the Wild West: Friedrich Gerstäcker's *Die Regulatoren in Arkansas* (1846) and Friedrich Schiller's *Die Räuber* (1781)." *Arkansas Historical Quarterly* 73 (Spring 2014): 69–77.

Conzen, Kathleen Neils. "Mainstreams and Side Channels: The Localization of Immigrant Cultures." *Journal of American Ethnic History* 11, no. 1 (1991): 5–20.

Conzen, Kathleen Neils, David A. Gerber, Ewa Morawska, George E. Pozzetta, and Rudolph J. Vecoli. "The Invention of Ethnicity: A Perspective from the U.S.A." *Journal of American Ethnic History* 12, no. 1 (1992): 3–41.

Daniels, Charlie. *Historical Report of the Secretary of State.* Fayetteville: University of Arkansas Press, 2008. https://www.scribd.com/document/13324614.

"Das Arkansas Echo (German)," *N. W. Ayer & Son's American Newspaper Annual and Directory.* Philadelphia: N. W. Ayer & Son, 1892.

Desmarais, Ralph H. "Interview with Henry W. Young." Butler Center for Arkansas Studies: Central Arkansas Library System, April 3, 2020. https://cdm15728.contentdm.oclc.org.

Dillard, Tom. *Statesmen, Scoundrels, and Eccentrics: A Gallery of Amazing Arkansans.* Fayetteville: University of Arkansas Press, 2010.

Dillard, Tom, Michael B. Dougan, and Timothy G. Nutt. *Arkansas History: An Annotated Bibliography*. Westport, CT: Greenwood Press, 1995.

Dougan, Michael B. "Arkansas Married Woman's Property Law." *Encyclopedia of Arkansas*, November 18, 2011. https://encyclopediaofarkansas.net.

———. *Community Diaries: Arkansas Newspapering, 1819–2002*. Little Rock: August House, 2003.

Durning, Dan. "Attracting the German Immigrant: A German Immigrant Describes Arkansas' Advantages to His Countrymen." *Pulaski County Historical Review* 28 (Spring 1980): 2–8.

———. "'The "Trouble" Is in Existence': Philip Dietzgen of the *Arkansas Staats Zeitung* Wages War on the Arkansas *Echo*." *Eclectic (at Best)*, July 31, 2016. https://www.eclecticatbest.com/2016/07.

Faust, Albert Bernhardt. *The German Element in the United States, with Special Reference to Its Political, Moral, Social, and Educational Influence.* 2 vols. Boston: Houghton Mifflin, 1909.

Finley, Randy. "A Lynching State: Arkansas in the 1890s." In Lancaster, *Bullets*, 61–85.

Frauenthal, Jeannie. "Max Frauenthal." *Encyclopedia of Arkansas*, February 1, 2011. https://encyclopediaofarkansas.net.

Freeman, Felton D. "Immigration to Arkansas." *Arkansas Historical Quarterly* 7 (Autumn, 1948): 210–220.

Frost, W. H. "The Epidemiology of Influenza (1919)." Commentary by Thomas Daniel, *Public Health Reports: Historical Collection, 1878–2005* 21, no. 1 (2006): 148–159.

Gabler, Ina. "Lovely's Purchase and Lovely County." *Arkansas Historical Quarterly* 19 (Spring 1960): 31–39.

Gatewood, Willard B. "Arkansas Negroes in the 1890s: Documents." *Arkansas Historical Quarterly* 33, no. 4 (Winter 1974): 293–325.

Gerstäcker, Friedrich. *Tagebuch einer Amerikareise: 1837–1843.* Braunschweig: Friedrich Gerstäcker Gesellschaft, 2005.

Gibson, L. P., H. D. Wyman, L. L. Geddings, Cyrus Edson Williams, H. S. Hussey, and J.A. Dunwoody. *Abstract of Sanitary Reports* 8, no. 1 (Marine Hospital Bureau, Washington, DC, January 6, 1893): 1–8.

Goetsch, Monika. "Dir Ziehe Glück ins Haus." *Süddeutsche Zeitung*, December 15, 2017. https://www.sueddeutsche.de/leben/historie-dir-ziehe-glueck-ins-haus-1.3790093.

Graves, John William. "African Americans." *Encyclopedia of Arkansas*, December 3, 2018. https://encyclopediaofarkansas.net.

———. "Poll Tax." *Encyclopedia of Arkansas*, July 10, 2012. https://encyclopediaofarkansas.net.

———. "Separate Coach Law of 1891." *Encyclopedia of Arkansas*, November 17, 2017. https://encyclopediaofarkansas.net.

Greene, Larry A., and Anke Ortlepp, eds. *Germans and African Americans: Two Centuries of Exchange.* Jackson: University Press of Mississippi, 2011.

Griffith, Nancy Snell. "'At the Hands of a Person or Persons Unknown': The Nature of Lynch Mobs in Arkansas." In Lancaster, *Bullets*, 35–59.

———. "Atkins Race War of 1897." *Encyclopedia of Arkansas*, January 3, 2013. https://encyclopediaofarkansas.net.

———. "Eugene Baker (Lynching of)." *Encyclopedia of Arkansas*, November 25, 2014. https://encyclopediaofarkansas.net.

———. "G. P. F. Lightfoot (Lynching of)." *Encyclopedia of Arkansas*, February 11, 2016. https://encyclopediaofarkansas.net.

———. "Hampton Race War of 1892." *Encyclopedia of Arkansas*, May 6, 2012. https://encyclopediaofarkansas.net.

———. "Henry James (Lynching of)." *Encyclopedia of Arkansas*, April 3, 2018. https://encyclopediaofarkansas.net.

———. "Lynching of the Biscoe Family." *Encyclopedia of Arkansas*, August 23, 2012. https://encyclopediaofarkansas.net.

———. "Paragould Race Riot." *Encyclopedia of Arkansas*, May 17, 2016. https://encyclopediaofarkansas.net.

———. "Robert Donnelly (Lynching of)." *Encyclopedia of Arkansas*, December 16, 2014. https://encyclopediaofarkansas.net.

Grimm, Jacob, and Wilhelm Grimm. *Deutsches Wörterbuch*. Kompetenzzentrum für elektronische Erschließungs- und Publikationsverfahren in den Geisteswissenschaften. http://dwb.uni-trier.de/de/.

Hammerstein, Katharina von. "'Who Owns Hereroland?': Diverse Women's Perspectives on Violence in the German-Herero Colonial War." In *Women Writing War: From German Colonialism through World War I*, edited by Katharina von Hammerstein, Barbara Kosta, and Julie Shoults, 27–56. Berlin: De Gruyter, 2018.

Handley, Lawrence R. "Settlement across Northern Arkansas as Influenced by the Missouri & North Arkansas Railroad." *Arkansas Historical Quarterly* 33, no. 4 (Winter 1974): 274–92.

Henderson, Catherine. "German National Bank." *Encyclopedia of Arkansas*, April 21, 2010. https://encyclopediaofarkansas.net.

Hermann, Karl Friedrich. "Memoirs, Letters, and Diary Entries of German Settlers in Northwest Arkansas, 1853–1863." Translated by Clarence Evans. *Arkansas Historical Quarterly* 6, no. 3 (Autumn 1947): 225–49.

Herndon, Dallas. *Centennial History of Arkansas*. Chicago: S. J. Clarke Publishing Company, 1922.

Hoerder, Dirk, and Jörg Nagler, eds. *People in Transit: German Migrations in Comparative Perspective, 1820–1930*. Cambridge: Cambridge University Press, 1995.

Hoerder, Dirk. "Introduction." In Hoerder and Nagler, *People*, 1–16.

———. "Research on the German Migrations, 1820s to 1930s: A Report on the State of German Scholarship." In Hoerder and Nagler, *People*, 413–21.

Huber, Sr. Herbert. *Arkansas Echo 1892–1906: An Arkansas German Language Newspaper*. Little Rock: Diocese of Little Rock, 1989.

"Interview with Mary Meurer." No interviewer, n.d. Archives of the University of Central Arkansas.

Jackson, James. "Migration in Duisburg, 1821–1914." In Hoerder and Nagler, *People*, 147–75.

Johnson, Ben F., III. *John Barleycorn Must Die: The War Against Drink in Arkansas*. Fayetteville: University of Arkansas Press, 2005.

Jones, Kelly Houston. "'Doubtless Guilty': Lynching and Slaves in Antebellum Arkansas." In Lancaster, *Bullets*, 17–34.

Kamphoefner, Walter. "Comments and Context." *Journal of American Ethnic History* 28, no. 1 (Fall 2008): 70–76.

———. "Forum: German Americans and Their Relations with African Americans during the Mid-Nineteenth Century. Introduction." *Journal of American Ethnic History* 28, no. 1 (Fall 2008): 10–12.

———. "German Emigration Research, North, South, and East: Findings, Methods, and Open Questions." In Hoerder and Nagler, *People*, 19–33.

Keil, Hartmut. Preface to Hoerder and Nagler, *People*, ix-xi.

Kehres, Gregory. "The Life of a Charter Member of the Catholic Union of Arkansas." *Souvenir Program: 105th National Convention [of] the Catholic Central Verein of America and Forty-Fourth National Convention [of] the National Catholic Women's Union*, 40–49. Little Rock: Paragon Printing, 1960.

Kelz, Robert. "Expanding *Exilforschung*: *Die Freie Deutsche Bühne* (Free German Stage) and the *Deutsches Theater in Argentinien* (German Theater in Argentina) in Buenos Aires, Argentina, 1938–1945." In *Culture as Text, Text as Culture*, edited by Elodie LaFitte, Christina Wall, and Mary Cobb Wittrock, 199–222. Newcastle Upon Tyne: Cambridge Scholars, 2010.

Kirchhoff, Theodor. *Allerhand heiteres aus Californien*. Leipzig: Eduard Avenarius, 1899.

Lancaster, Guy, ed. *Bullets and Fire: Lynching and Authority in Arkansas, 1840–1950*. Fayetteville: University of Arkansas Press, 2018.

Lancaster, Guy. "Wineries." *Encyclopedia of Arkansas*, March 16, 2017. https://encyclopediaofarkansas.net.

LeMaster, Carolyn Gray. *A Corner of the Tapestry: A History of the Jewish Experience in Arkansas, 1820s–1990s*. Fayetteville: University of Arkansas Press, 1994.

LeMasters, Larry. "Edward Coy (Lynching of)." *Encyclopedia of Arkansas*, July 2, 2016. https://encyclopediaofarkansas.net.

Lessing, Gotthold Ephraim. *Nathan der Weise*. Stuttgart: Reclam, 1995.

Lintelman, Joy K. "Making Service Serve Themselves: Immigrant Women and Domestic Service in North America, 1850–1920." In Hoerder and Nagler, *People*, 249–65.

Lucey, John M. "History of Immigration to Arkansas." *Publications of the Arkansas Historical Association* 3 (1911): 201–19.

Mageean, Deirdre M. "Acculturation of Immigrant Women in Chicago at the Turn of the Twentieth Century." In Hoerder and Nagler, *People*, 295–309.

Manger, Walter. "John Casper Branner." *Encyclopedia of Arkansas*, October 22, 2015. https://encyclopediaofarkansas.net.

Manz, Stefan. *Constructing a German Diaspora: The "Greater German Empire," 1871–1914*. New York: Routledge, 2014.

Mehring, Frank. "'Nazi Jim Crow': Hans Jürgen Massaquoi's Democratic Vistas on the Black Atlantic and Afro-Germans in *Ebony*." In Greene and Ortlepp, *Germans*, 141–65.

Metrailer, Jamie. "St. Joseph Colony." *Encyclopedia of Arkansas*, June 22, 2016. https://encyclopediaofarkansas.net.

Meyer, Susanne. "In-Migration and Out-Migration in an Area of Heavy Industry: The Case of Georgsmarienhütte, 1856–1870." In Hoerder and Nagler, *People*, 177–99.

Miller, C.J. "Lovely County." *Encyclopedia of Arkansas*, May 27, 2008. https://encyclopediaofarkansas.net.

Moneyhon, Carl H. *Arkansas and the New South: 1874–1929*. Fayetteville: University of Arkansas Press, 1997.

———. "Brooks-Baxter War." *Encyclopedia of Arkansas*, June 1, 2018. https://encyclopediaofarkansas.net.

———. "Post-Reconstruction through the Gilded Age, 1875 through 1900." *Encyclopedia of Arkansas*, March 3, 2015. https://encyclopediaofarkansas.net.

Mühle, Rainer. "Colonist Traditions and Nineteenth-Century Emigration from East Elbian Prussia." In Hoerder and Nagler, *People*, 35–55.

Office of the Historian, United States House of Representatives. "Bruce, Blanche Kelso." April 3, 2020. https://history.house.gov/People/Detail/10029.

Opitz, May, Katharina Oguntoye, and Dagmar Schultz, eds. *Showing Our Colors: Afro-German Women Speak Out*. Amherst: University of Massachusetts Press, 1992.

Pierce, Michael. "Labor Movement." *Encyclopedia of Arkansas*, May 30, 2018. https://encyclopediaofarkansas.net.

Pryor, David H. Foreword to *Community Diaries: Arkansas Newspapering, 1819–2002*, by Michael B. Dougan, 5–6. Little Rock: August House, 2003.

Quack, Sibylle. "Changing Gender Roles and Emigration: The Example of German Jewish Women and Their Emigration to the United States, 1933–1945." In Hoerder and Nagler, *People*, 379–97.

Reich, Uwe. "Emigration from Regierungsbezirk Frankfurt/Oder, 1815–1893." In Hoerder and Nagler, *People*, 79–99.

Rössler, Horst. "Traveling Workers and the German Labor Movement." In Hoerder and Nagler, *People*, 127–45.

Schede, Simone. "'Gone, but not forgotten'—But Almost: The German Heritage of Arkansas." *Amerikastudien / American Studies* 44, no. 4 (1999): 477–96.

Schuette, Shirley Sticht. "Germans." *Encyclopedia of Arkansas*, May 13, 2015. https://encyclopediaofarkansas.net.

———. "Strangers to the Land: The German Presence in Nineteenth-Century Arkansas." MA thesis, University of Arkansas at Little Rock, 2005.

Sinke, Suzanne. "The International Marriage Market: Theoretical and Historical Perspectives." In Hoerder and Nagler, *People*, 227–48.

Strickland, Jeffery. "German Immigrants and African Americans in Charleston, South Carolina, 1850–1880." In Greene and Ortlepp, *Germans*, 37–49.

———. "How the Germans Became White Southerners: German Immigrants and African Americans in Charleston, South Carolina, 1860–1880." *Journal of American Ethnic History* 28, no. 1 (Fall 2008): 52–69.

Strub, Joseph. *Leitstern zur St. Joseph's Colonie (unter Leitung der Väter vom hl. Geist) im Westen des Staates Arkansas.* Morrilton: n.p., 1880. Republished and translated by Kenneth Barnes as *The Guiding Star for the St. Joseph Colony: A Guide Book for Catholic Emigrants to the Arkansas River Valley*. Conway: Faulkner County Historical Society, 1997.

Taylor, Larry. "Plumerville Conflict of 1886–1892." *Encyclopedia of Arkansas*, September 30, 2014. https://encyclopediaofarkansas.net.

Teske, Steven. "MacArthur Park." *Encyclopedia of Arkansas*, July 3, 2018. https://encyclopediaofarkansas.net.

Turner, Alvin O. "Cherokee Outlet Opening." *The Encyclopedia of Oklahoma History and Culture*, accessed March 2, 2020. https://www.okhistory.org/publications/encyclopediaonline.

Vinikas, Vincent. "Thirteen Dead at Saint Charles: Arkansas's Most Lethal Lynching and the Abrogation of Equal Protection." In Lancaster, *Bullets*, 103–29.

Watkins, Beverly. "Efforts to Encourage Immigration to Arkansas, 1865–1874." *Arkansas Historical Quarterly* 38, no. 1 (Spring 1979): 32–62.

Wehner, Silke. "German Domestic Servants in America, 1850–1914: A New Look at German Immigrant Women's Experiences." In Hoerder and Nagler, *People*, 267–93.

Wellenreuther, Hermann. *Citizens in a Strange Land: A Study of German-American Broadsides and Their Meaning for Germans in North America, 1730–1830*. Max Kade Research Institute Series: Germans Beyond Europe. University Park: Penn State University Press, 2013.

West, Elliott. Foreword to *Arkansas and the New South: 1874–1929*, by Carl H. Moneyhon, ix–x. Fayetteville: University of Arkansas Press, 1997.

Whayne, Jeannie, Thomas A. DeBlack, George Sabo, and Morris Arnold. *Arkansas: A Narrative History*. 2nd ed. Fayetteville: University of Arkansas Press, 2013.

Whitsell, Charles, Jr. "Pike-Fletcher-Terry House." *Encyclopedia of Arkansas*, August 6, 2018. https://encyclopediaofarkansas.net.

Williams, Patrick G. "Politics and Government." *Encyclopedia of Arkansas*, July 10, 2018. https://encyclopediaofarkansas.net.

Wittke, Carl. *The German-Language Press in America*. Lexington: University of Kentucky Press, 1957.

Woods, James. *Mission and Memory: A History of the Catholic Church in Arkansas*. Little Rock: August House, 1993.

Wolfe, Jonathan. "Background of German Immigration." *Arkansas Historical Quarterly* 25, no. 2 (Summer 1966): 151–82.

———. "Background of German Immigration." *Arkansas Historical Quarterly* 25, no. 3 (Autumn 1966): 248–78.

———. "Background of German Immigration." *Arkansas Historical Quarterly* 25, no. 4 (Winter 1966): 354–85.

"Xanten." *Jewish Virtual Library*. American-Israeli Cooperative Enterprise, March 2, 2020. https://www.jewishvirtuallibrary.org/xanten.

# INDEX

When correspondents' last names are identified only by initials, they are listed first initial first, *e.g.*, "P. R. (Atkins correspondent), 156"

KATHLEEN CONDRAY is associate professor of German at the University of Arkansas. The author of *Women Writers of the Journal "Jugend" from 1919–1940,* Condray has published numerous articles on migration and national identity. She is the recipient of two Fulbright awards, an NEH grant, and several national teaching awards.